INTRODUCTION TO THE LAW OF CARRIAGE OF GOODS

BY

DAVID A. GLASS, LL.M.(LOND.)
Lecturer, Cardiff Law School

AND

CHRIS CASHMORE, LL.B.
Chief Examiner in Law to the
Chartered Institute of Transport
Senior Lecturer in Law,
City of London Polytechnic

LONDON
SWEET & MAXWELL
1989

Published by
Sweet & Maxwell Ltd. of
South Quay Plaza,
183 Marsh Wall, London E14 9FT
Laserset by
LBJ Enterprises Limited
Chilcompton, Somerset
Printed in Scotland by Thomson Litho

British Library Cataloguing in Publication Data

Glass, David A.
An introduction to the law of carriage of goods.
1. England Freight transport Law
I. Title II. Cashmore, Chris
344.203'932

ISBN 0–421–39700–4

AUSTRALIA AND NEW ZEALAND
The Law Book Company Ltd.
Sydney : Melbourne : Perth

CANADA AND U.S.A.
The Carswell Company Ltd.
Agincourt, Ontario

INDIA
N.M. Tripathi Private Ltd.
Bombay
and
Eastern Law House Private Ltd.
Calcutta and Delhi
M.P.P. House
Bangalore

ISRAEL
Steimatzky's Agency Ltd.
Jerusalem : Tel Aviv : Haifa

PAKISTAN
Pakistan Law House
Karachi

In memory of
Hiro Keswani

PREFACE

The writers have for long noticed the absence of an introductory but academically sound work on the law of carriage and also of any adequate modern text on the law of inland carriage. This book therefore attempts to lay out in simple readable form the basic principles of the law relating to carriage of goods by all modes of transport. A brief summary of the law relating to carriage of passengers will also be found in most chapters. The writers appreciate that many readers will not have easy access to law libraries and therefore in the Appendices will be found most of the essential statutes affecting the law of carriage of goods together with many sets of standard contractual conditions used in the industry.

While this work is aimed partly at professional students from a non-legal background the writers would like to think that it might be of value as an introductory work to undergraduate and post-graduate law students studying the subject for the first time and as a handy reference book to practitioners. We therefore try, where possible, to footnote adequate authority for the points we make and do not hesitate, where space permits, to briefly outline areas where the law is unclear or unsatisfactory. Likewise we do not hesitate to put forward, with due humility, our views on such vexed matters as the law relating to the parties to a contract of carriage at common law and deviation even where these views may differ from more established texts. In addition we do not hesitate to quote Commonwealth, European and American cases where they are particularly illustrative of important points of law or where United Kingdom case law is lacking.

While the writers assume full responsibility for the views expressed and any mistakes and misapprehensions under which they labour they have been saved from many blunders by the following gentlemen who kindly gave them the benefit of their specialist knowledge in different fields:

Maurice England, Senior Lecturer in the Law of Transport Insurance, City of London Polytechnic.

Robert Hunter, Solicitor, Allen and Overy.

The late Captain Hiro Keswani, Shipping Arbitrator and Barrister whose tragic and premature death in September 1988 is keenly felt by the authors.

Amir Majid, Lecturer in Air Law, City of London Polytechnic.

Vivian Slight, sometime Legal Advisor to British Caledonian.

We also thank Professor Norman Palmer of the University of Essex for his kind permission to borrow some ideas from his leading work, *Bailment,* and also for the general inspiration and assistance he has given to at least one of the authors.

The authors accept joint and several responsibility for this work. Nevertheless most of the preparation of Chapters Two, Three, Four and Seven fell to David Glass and of Chapters One, Five and Six to Chris Cashmore. The authors were much stimulated by their mutually constructive criticism of one another's work! They would also like to express their thanks to the editorial staff of Sweet & Maxwell.

The law is as stated up to February 1989

D. Glass, Cardiff.
C. Cashmore, London.

CONTENTS

TABLE OF CASES

TABLE OF STATUTES AND STATUTORY INSTRUMENTS

CONVENTIONS*

**Not otherwise set out in statutes/statutory instruments.*

TABLE OF STANDARD TRADING CONDITIONS

ACKNOWLEDGMENTS

The authors and publishers are grateful to the following bodies for granting permission to reproduce in the Appendices Standard Trading Conditions in which they hold copyright.

The Baltic and International Maritime Council
British Rail
The Institute of Freight Forwarders
The Road Haulage Association

Acknowledgment is also due to the Controller of Her Majesty's Stationary Office for permission to reproduce statutory materials.

Chapter One

INLAND CARRIAGE

INTRODUCTION

Contents **1.01**

This Chapter contains an outline of the duties and liabilities of carriers of goods (including passengers' luggage) by land and their customers at common law. A comparison of the position under the Road Haulage Association's 1982 Conditions and British Rail's Conditions of Carriage of General Merchandise 1986 is also included as is a very brief comparison of the liability of carriers of passengers. Copies of the R.H.A. and British Rail Conditions will be found in Appendices 1.A. and 1.B. respectively and they should be referred to whenever they are discussed. The most important provisions of the Sale of Goods Act 1979 that concern carriers of goods will be found in Appendix 1.C.

Terminology **1.02**

A person who makes the arrangements with the carrier to have goods carried is called the "consignor" and the person to whom they are to be delivered is called the "consignee." Sometimes the consignor and the consignee will be the same person, as where, for example, a person has his furniture carried by a furniture remover to his new home. More often, however, the consignor and consignee may be different people, as where A sells goods to B and has them delivered to B via C, a carrier.

Contract and bailment **1.03**

A contract for the carriage of goods by land is an example of a bailment for reward. A bailment comes into existence "whenever one person is knowingly and willingly in possession of goods which belong to another."[1] In order for there to be a bailment a person must be *in possession* of the goods. Thus where A gives possession of his (A's) goods to C, a carrier, to be redelivered to A at the place of destination, A is the bailor and C is the bailee. On the other hand, if C merely gives A permission to place goods on his property but C never actually takes control of them this is merely a "licence" not a bailment[2] and C is under no duty to care for them.

Although a bailment is usually for reward (*i.e.* the owner of goods will pay the bailee/carrier) and thus is accompanied by a contract, liability in bailment is a separate form of liability quite distinct from contract and tort.[3] In addition to a bailment for reward it is also

[1] Palmer, *Bailment* (1st ed., 1978), p. 2.

[2] *Ibid.* pp. 195-213.

[3] *The Kapetan Marcos (No. 2)* [1987] 2 Lloyd's Rep. 321. Winfield, *The Province of the Law of Torts,* (1931) pp. 99-100.

possible to have a "gratuitous bailment," *i.e.* one without reward, for example where a carrier carries goods free of charge or, in a different context, where A lends B a book. The duties of a carrier/bailee are to carry safely and deliver the goods intact.[4] A breach of these duties is called a "breach of bailment."[5] A bailee however has a duty to take reasonable care of the goods and is only liable for loss or damage caused by his negligence or deliberate wrongdoing[6] (or that of his servants acting in the course or scope of their employment).

There are, however, two types of carrier by land, private carriers and common carriers.[7] Private carriers are liable as bailees for reward on the basis discussed above. Common carriers are also almost always bailees but, in addition, by "custom of the realm" they are strictly liable for loss or damage. In other words they are liable for loss or damage to consigned goods even if they are not negligent but they do have certain specific defences to this strict liability.[8]

Parties to a Contract of Carriage

1.04 Owners and bailees

One of the basic principles of English law is the doctrine of privity of contract. Only the parties to the contract can sue or be sued on the contract.[9] Who then are the parties to a contract of carriage? Where A contracts with C, a carrier, to have his (A's) goods redelivered to himself at the place of destination no difficulty will normally arise as to who are the parties to the contract of carriage. Even if A is not the owner of the goods, *e.g.* because he is hiring them, he can sue (and be sued) on the contract. In addition A can, in such a situation, recover substantial, *i.e.* full, damages from the carrier. This is true as long as he has possession of the goods or the right to possess them.[10] Normally to have such rights he must himself be a bailee of the goods. So where, for example, a road carrier had some goods belonging to his customers carried by rail to be delivered to himself it was held that he was entitled to recover the full value of the goods from the rail carrier when that carrier lost them.[11] It does not matter in this context whether the consignor/bailee is liable to his customers under his contract with them or not; he can still recover full damages from the carrier.[12] Obviously in such a case the consignor cannot pocket the damages he recovers from the carrier but must hold the proceeds for the benefit of the owners of the goods.[13]

[4] *Travers* v. *Cooper* [1915] 1 K.B. 73, 88.
[5] N. Palmer uses this term in his leading textbook, *Bailment* (2nd ed., 1989).
[6] *Morris* v. *Martin* [1966] 1 Q.B. 716.
[7] See 1.21-136.
[8] See 1.28.
[9] *Scruttons* v. *Midland Silicones* [1962] A.C. 446.
[10] *Maddocks* v. *Meers* (1822) L.J.(O.S.) 216.
[11] *Crouch* v. *London & North Western Railway (No. 1)* (1849) 2 Car. & K. 789.
[12] Compare *Great Northern Railway* v. *L.E.P. Transport* [1922] 2 K.B. 742.
[13] Compare *The Winkfield* [1902] P. 42; *Great Northern Railway* v. *L.E.P. Transport* [1922] 2 K.B. 742, especially Scrutton L.J. at p. 765.

"Three party" contracts. Owner is normally contracting party 1.05

Where the consignor and the consignee are different people the position is more complicated. For convenience this is described as a "three party contract." The most common illustration is where A sells goods to B and it is agreed either expressly or impliedly between them that the seller should send the goods to the buyer via a land carrier. If the goods are lost or damaged who is the principal party to the contact of carriage and thus the correct person to sue the carrier, the seller or the buyer? At first sight one might have thought that the seller who actually did business with the carrier, agreed the conditions of carriage and possibly even paid the freight (*i.e.* carriage charges) was the correct person to sue, but basically this is wrong. The position is in fact that "The person whose property the goods are is prima facie the party with whom the contract is made. . . . "[14] In other words it is presumed that the contract is made between the carrier and the owner of the goods and it does not matter who actually has paid or agreed to pay the freight.[15] "Owner" in this context includes a bailee in possession or with immediate right to possess, *e.g.* a person who had hired goods for a year but did not own them.[16] Whether the presumption is that the contracting party is the owner of the goods at the time they are delivered to the carrier or rather the owner at the time of the breach of contract (*i.e.* when the carrier loses or damages them) is unclear.[17] However, this point is not very important in practice in carriage of goods by land within the United Kingdom, as opposed to sea, as it is rather unlikely that the ownership of the goods will change during transit.[18]

Consignment notes 1.06

A land consignment note in the United Kingdom is not, unlike a bill of lading in carriage by sea[19] and land consignment notes in other countries,[20] a document of title. Possession of such a note is not therefore evidence of ownership or thus of any right to sue in contract,[21] tort or of any right to take delivery of the goods.[22] Of course, however, the consignment note may be evidence of the contract between the carrier and the owner of the goods.

[14] *Mullinson* v. *Carver* (1843) L.T.(O.S.) 59. See also *Dickenson* v. *Lano* (1860) 2 F. & F. 188.

[15] *King* v. *Meredith* (1811) 2 Camp. 639.

[16] *Crouch* v. *London & North Western Railway (No. 1)* (1849) 2 C. Car. & K. 790 (bailee-carrier with right to immediate possession).

[17] *Coombs* v. *Bristol & Exeter Ry. (No. 2)* (1858) 3 H. & N. 510 and *Tronson* v. *Dent* (1853) Moo.P.C. 419 suggest that it is the owner at the time of the breach of contract. *Sargent* v. *Morris* (1830) 3 B. & Ald. 277 and *Howard* v. *Shepherd* (1850) 9 C.B. 297 suggest that it is the owner at the time of the delivery of the goods to the carrier.

[18] In carriage by sea the problem of the change of ownership of the goods arising from their sale during transit led to the passing of the Bills of Lading Act 1855. See 5.12.

[19] See 5.11.

[20] *e.g.* India where a railway receipt has been held to be a document of title giving the possessor the right to sue the carrier. *Dolatram* v. *Bombay, Baroda and Central Ry.* [1914] Ind.L.R.(Bomb.Ser.) 652. A similar position exists in the U.S.A. where the land document is "an order 'bill of lading.' "

[21] *London and South Western Railway* v. *Bishop* (1898) 22 S.J. 255.

[22] Unlike a document sent by a carrier to a consignee saying that the goods have arrived at their destination. See 1.70.

Notice clause 5 of the R.H.A. Conditions reproduced in Appendix 1.A. Such clauses are discussed in the context of carriage by sea in 5.09. It may be that this clause amounts to an exemption clause for the purposes of the Unfair Contract Terms Act 1977, in which case it is subject to the "reasonableness test."[23] In other words the carrier cannot rely on the clause if the court considers it unreasonable.

1.07 **Passing of property, ascertained goods**

In order to understand who is the owner of the goods, and therefore presumably the principal party to the contract, it is necessary to study the provisions of the Sale of Goods Act 1979, especially section 18 (see Appendix 1.C). Under Rule 1 of section 18 where there is a sale of specific goods, (*e.g.* A sells to B a specific secondhand machine that B has perhaps inspected) then the ownership/property passes to B immediately even though B has not paid for the goods nor taken delivery. In that case the seller/consignor ceases to be the owner and becomes a bailee of the goods that now belong to the buyer who is his bailor (section 20(3) of the Sale of Goods Act 1979, see Appendix 1.C).

However, Rule 1 may not apply when the seller has agreed to send the specific goods to the buyer via a carrier. Rule 1 says that for property in specific goods to pass they must be in "a deliverable state." "Deliverable state" is defined in section 61(5) as "such a state that the buyer would under the contract be bound to take delivery of them." Where the goods are to be sent via a carrier this must mean that the buyer's agent, the carrier must "be bound to take delivery of them." We suggest that the carrier is bound to take delivery of them when he comes to receive them from the seller's premises under the contract of carriage on behalf of the buyer. Therefore the property cannot pass until that moment.

Further, the carrier would not be bound to take delivery of the goods if it is the seller's duty to load them on to vehicles.[24] In that event the property would not pass until the goods were loaded on to the vehicles. So the law relating to unascertained goods is much the same as it is in relation to unascertained goods. See 1.08, below.

1.08 **Unascertained goods**

What is the position if the goods are unascertained, *e.g.* B contracts to buy "an X.Y.Z. computer," to be sent to him via a carrier, from a dealer without identifying any particular X.Y.Z. computer. Under section 18, rule 5(1) (see Appendix 1.C), where there is an agreement to sell unascertained goods then the property passes when the goods are appropriated[25] to the contract and under Rule 5(2) a delivery to a

[23] See 1.45.

[24] *Anderson* v. *Morrice* (1875) L.R. 10 C.P. 609, 618, Blackburn, J. The cases of *Young* v. *Hobson* (1949) 65 T.L.R. 365 and *Underwood* v. *Burgh Castle Cement* [1922] 1 K.B. 343 are not against this view because this point was not argued. See also *Coombs* v. *Bristol & Exeter Ry. (No. 2)* (1858) 27 L.J.Ex. 401, 403. ". . . on the sale of an *ascertained* chattel . . ., The delivery of the goods to a carrier vests the property in the verdee . . .," *Per* Brett J.

[25] "To constitute an appropriation of the goods to the contract, the parties must have had, or be reasonably supposed to have had, an intention to attach the contract irrevocably to those goods, so that those goods and no others are the subject of the sale and become the property of the buyer." Pearson J. in *Federspiel & Co.* v. *Twigg & Co.* [1957] 1 Lloyd's Rep. 240.

carrier normally amounts to an appropriation to the contract.[26] So we can conclude that usually where A sells goods to B and has them delivered to B via a carrier then at the latest the property in the goods passes to buyer/consignee at the time they are delivered to the carrier. At that point the buyer becomes liable to pay the seller the price and if the goods have been lost or damaged in transit the buyer can sue the carrier for breach of contract.[27] This leads logically to the strange result that if the goods are damaged in transit and the consignee rejects them and refuses to pay the seller (both of which he has no right to do)[28] then the consignor/seller cannot sue the carrier.[29] His remedy is to sue the buyer for the price and the consignee/buyer in turn can sue the carrier for the damage to the goods.

Of course one could have the exceptional case where, for example, goods are sold on a "sale or return" basis, sold subject to a "*Romalpa* Clause"[30] or where the contract of sale is null and void.[31] In those cases the consignor would remain the owner and he would be the correct person to sue in contract.

Risk and ownership 1.09

Unless otherwise agreed the ownership/property and the risk of loss or damage pass together by virtue of section 20(1) of the Sale of Goods Act 1979, (see Appendix 1.C.). However one can have a situation where the ownership remains in the seller but the goods are at the buyer's risk. Say, for example, A agrees to sell goods to B to be delivered to B via C, a carrier, and it is agreed between A and B that during transit the goods will still belong to A but the risks of transit will fall on B (*i.e.* B will still have to pay for them if they are damaged in transit). In that case the property remains in A and he is the correct person to sue the carrier in contract and the question of risk is irrelevant.[32] Thus in the *Sanix Ace*[33] a charterer of a ship who owned the cargo agreed to sell parts of the cargo to various buyers. The ownership of the different parts did not pass under section 18 of the Sale of Goods Act 1979, because it is impossible to pass the ownership of unascertained goods (see section 16 of the Act). Nevertheless under the contract of sale the goods were at the risk of the buyers and they had to pay even if the goods never arrived. During the voyage

[26] s.32(1) of the Sale of Goods Act 1979. See also *Wardars Co.* v. *Norwood & Co.* [1968] 2 Q.B. 663.

[27] "The property passes to [the buyer] by the delivery to the carrier and he is the proper person to sue the carrier if the goods are lost." Parke B. in *Swain* v. *Shepherd* (1832) 1 M. & Rob. 223.

[28] *Halcrow* v. *Le Mesurier* (1884) 10 Q.L.R. 239 (Canada), a case that is unfortunately only reported in French! The buyer can of course reject the goods if, for example, they do not correspond to their description. See *Hanlon* v. *Armitage* (1827) 5 B. & Ald. 857.

[29] Because he was not the owner at the time of the delivery of the goods to the carrier or at the time of the breach of contract. This point has been overlooked in several cases, *e.g. Horne* v. *Midland Railway* (1873) L.R. 8 C.P. 131.

[30] *i.e.* a clause in the contract of sale stating that the seller will remain the owner of the goods until the buyer pays for them in full. *Aluminium Industrie Vassen B.V.* v. *Romalpa Aluminium* [1976] 1 W.L.R. 676.

[31] *Egan* v. *Great Northern Railway* (1879) 14 I.L.T. 28 (Ireland). See 1.69.

[32] *Paul* v. *National Steamships* [1937] 59 Lloyd's Rep. 28.

[33] *The Sanix Ace* [1987] 1 Lloyd's Rep. 465.

the cargo spontaneously combusted due to a breach of contract by the carrier and was virtually all destroyed. The court held the carrier liable to pay the seller/charterer the full value of the cargo as damages even though the seller had in fact been paid the purchase price by the buyers. In these circumstances of course the charterer had to pay the damages over to the buyers.

1.10 **Consignor as agent**

Normally, however, as explained above, the consignee is the owner during transit and he is the correct person to sue on the contract. "Under such circumstances the ordinary inference is that the contract of carriage is between the carrier and the consignee, the consignor being the agent for the consignee to make it."[34] The seller/consignor cannot sue on the contract even if he has paid the freight.[35] As an agent the consignor must make a reasonable contract of carriage on behalf of the consignee by virtue of section 32(2) of the Sale of Goods Act 1979, (see Appendix 1.C.). For example he must not send delicate goods at "owner's risk."[36]

If the contract is for the sale of unascertained goods (or the property has not already passed to the buyer for some other reason) and the seller has made an unreasonable contract of carriage then the buyer can refuse to treat the delivery to the carrier as a delivery to himself and is not liable to pay the price to the seller.[37] The ownership would presumably stay in the consignor and he should be the person to sue the carrier for any loss or damage in transit. If the consignee decides to accept the goods it is not clear whether he can sue the carrier if they have been damaged in transit. In strict legal theory the answer should be that he cannot sue because the goods were not the buyer/consignee's property at the time they were damaged. The contract cannot be:

> "Ambulatory, . . . to hold that (the carrier) is not liable to the consignee unless the latter does some act shewing an intention to treat the contract (of sale) as valid but that he may be made liable by the act of the consignee . . . would be most inconvenient. But the liability of the carrier cannot be altered by anything that which takes place after the loss; it must be certain at the time of the loss."[38]

[34] Mellor J. in *Cork Distilleries* v. *Great Southern and Western Railway* (1874) L.R. 7 H.L. 269. Although the consignor/seller is only the agent as regards the main contract of carriage, there is nothing to stop him making a separate collateral contract with the carrier concerning, for example the delivery of goods and recovering damages for economic loss in the event of the breach of that contract even though he is not the owner of the goods. Thus in *Jacobs* v. *Nelson* (1811) 3 Taunt. 432 the plaintiff recovered damages against a carrier who failed to collect "Cash on delivery" as payment for the goods from the buyer as instructed. See also 1.76.

[35] *Dawes* v. *Peck* [1799] 8 T.R. 330.

[36] *Young* v. *Hobson* (1949) 65 T.L.R. 365.

[37] *Young* v. *Hobson*. See n.36 above, *B.C. Fruit Market* v. *National Fruit Co.* (1921) 59 D.L.R. 87 (Canada).

[38] *Coombs* v. *Bristol & Exeter Railway (No. 2)* (1858) 3 H. & N. 510, *per* Pollock C.B. Presumably therefore, where the seller is the owner at the time of the loss he and only he can sue in contract or tort. See also Lord Kenyon in *Dawes* v. *Peck* [1799] 8 T.R. 330 to the same effect.

Where there is a sale of specific goods to be delivered by a carrier we argued in 1.07 that property will pass normally when the carrier is ready to take delivery under the contract of carriage. The law on this topic is very unclear and the Sale of Goods Act is ambiguous, but we suggest that if the contract of carriage is an unreasonable one then the property and risk in specific goods do not pass at the moment of sale, nor when the contract of carriage is made nor when the goods are delivered to the carrier.[39] Therefore the property does not pass from seller to the buyer until the buyer accepts the goods at the place of destination. The result is again that it is the seller, as owner, who should sue the carrier in the event of loss or damage.

Bailees returning goods to bailors 1.11

Of course where A gives goods to C, a carrier, to be delivered to a third party (B) this may not be the result of A having sold or agreed to sell the goods to B. There may be many other relationships other than a sale that might lead A to send goods to B. For example A may be a bailee returning goods to his bailor. Say that A has hired goods from B and A is now returning them to B via C, a carrier. If C, the carrier, loses or damages them, who is the correct person to sue C? Although there are cases to the contrary[40] it seems that the correct view is that it is B, the bailor/consignee, who should sue because he probably is the owner and certainly has the right to the possession of the goods once they are delivered to the carrier. By analogy with the position discussed above in 1.07 where a seller/bailee sends goods to his buyer/bailor it seems that the hirer/bailee loses his right to the possession of the goods at the moment when he delivers them to the carrier. Once he loses his right to possession of the goods he has no interest left in them and should not be allowed normally to sue. This is illustrated by *Scott Maritime Pulp* v. *B.F. Goodrich (Canada) Limited*[41] in which the plaintiff sent a machine to be repaired. The repairers returned it via the defendant carriers who damaged it. It was held that the repairers were the plaintiff's agents and the plaintiffs, as principals to the contract of carriage, could sue the carriers. Therefore where goods are sent by a bailee to his bailor the presumption should be that the bailor is the party to the contract of carriage. Of course if it was agreed that the right to possession of the goods would remain in the consignor/bailee during transit then it might be a different matter.[42]

Whom should the carrier pay? 1.12

Where A sends goods to B via C, a carrier, then of course the carrier may have no idea who owns the goods or who has the right to

[39] Delivery to the carrier under an unreasonable contract would not amount to a good delivery to the buyer.

[40] *Freeman* v. *Birch* [1843] 3 Q.B. 492n. *Gwyatt* v. *Hayes* (1871) 2 A.J.R. 107 (Australia).

[41] (1977) 72 D.L.R. 680 (Canada). *Re Tappenbeck* [1876] 2 Ch.D. 278 and *R* v. *Kay* (1857) Dears & B. 231 also support our view.

[42] This is the only basis upon which *Freeman* v. *Birch*, see n. 40 above, can be supported.

possess them. What then is the position if he loses or damages the goods and admits liability? Who should he pay, A or B? It seems that the carrier is entitled to presume that the goods have been delivered to him as the result of a contract of sale and that B, the consignee, is the owner and thus is the principal contracting party to whom he is liable.[43] In the event of loss or damage the carrier (unless there are circumstances to make him suspect that the consignee is not in fact the owner) does not pay the consignee at his peril. On the other hand he does pay the consignor at his peril and may end up paying out twice if he does.[44] If he is not sure who to pay, as where, for example, both the consignor and the consignee are making claims on him then he should "interplead." In other words he should go to the court and let them decide to whom he is liable.

1.13 Non-owner/seller cannot recover substantial damages as principal

The above presumption that the owner of the goods is the contracting party can of course be rebutted. It may be that, for example, the consignor/seller can prove that he has made a "special contract," *i.e.* a contract which he has in fact entered into as principal and not merely as agent for the consignee.[45] If this is so and the consignor sues upon the contract then normally he cannot recover the full value of the goods but merely nominal damages (*e.g.* £10) because at the time of the breach of contract (*i.e.* the time the goods were lost or damaged) they did not belong to him so he has suffered no loss.[46] However in this situation the consignee/owner can sue the carrier either in tort or for breach of bailment. The danger here to the carrier is that, if the consignee sues in tort or bailment, the carrier may not be able to rely on any exemption or limitation clauses in the contract.[47] This is because the consignee in these circumstances is not a party to the contract and therefore is arguably not bound by its terms. Presumably the same principles ought normally to apply in reverse in those rare cases where a consignee non-owner contracted as principal.[48]

1.14 Exceptional cases

There appear to be two exceptions to the rule that a non-owner cannot recover substantial (*i.e.* full) damages if he contracts as principal and sues on the contract of carriage. These are:

(1) "In a commercial contract concerning goods where it is in the contemplation of the parties that the proprietary interests in the goods may be transferred from one owner to another after the contract has been entered into and before the breach causes the loss or damage to the goods, an original party to the contract, if such be

[43] *Coombs* v. *Bristol & Exeter Railway (No. 1)* (1858) 3 H. & N. 1, *Dyer* v. *Great Northern Railway* (1892) 53 N.E. 714 (U.S.A.).
[44] See n. 43 above.
[45] *Dunlop* v. *Lambert* (1838-9) 6 Cl. & F. 600.
[46] *The Albazero* [1977] A.C. 774.
[47] See 1.77-187.
[48] Such as occurred in *Mead* v. *South Eastern Railway* (1870) 18 W.R. 735. See 1.14.

the intention of them both, is to be treated in law as having entered into the contract for the benefit of all persons who have or may acquire an interest in the goods before they are lost or damaged and is entitled to recover by way of damages for breach of contract the actual loss sustained by those for whose benefit the contract was entered into." *Per* Lord Diplock in the *Albazero*.[49]

This would presumably be illustrated by the following example. Say A gave goods to C, a carrier by land, to be carried to C's depot in London and A explained to C that he (A) would probably be selling the goods while they were in transit. Say that the goods were damaged in transit after A had in fact sold them to B. In that case A could sue C and get substantial damages on behalf of B to whom he must, of course, pay over those damages.[50]

(2) It seems that if a consignee (or equally consignor[51]) who is not an owner contracts as principal then he can recover substantial damages if he can prove reasonably forseeable economic loss if he sues on the contract of carriage. This seems to follow from the case of *Mead* v. *South Eastern Railway*.[52] In this case the plaintiff, a miller in Kent, agreed to buy corn from one Buckmaster in Norfolk. The contract of sale between them was not evidenced in writing as was at that time required by the now repealed Statute of Frauds. Therefore the plaintiff did not become the owner of the corn. Buckmaster sent the corn to London via the Great Eastern Railway and then the plaintiff in turn contracted as principal with the South Eastern Railway to have the corn delivered to him in Kent. The corn arrived damaged and the plaintiff sued and apparently recovered substantial damages. Although the report of the case is silent on the point it seems reasonable to assume that the plaintiff had accepted the damaged corn and had in fact paid Buckmaster the agreed price for it. It follows therefore that although he was not the owner at the time of the loss he had in fact suffered real and possibly foreseeable financial damage as the result of the defendants' breach of contract and rightly succeeded in his action for substantial damages.[53]

The danger of double liability 1.15

There is however a difficulty that arises with these two cases that allow a non owner in some special circumstances to sue in contract for substantial damages. Say that the non owner sues and gets damages in contract but goes bankrupt before he can pay the money to the owner. What is to stop the actual owner suing in tort or for breach of

[49] See n. 46 above.

[50] Of course if A never told C of the intended sale during transit then this principle would not come into operation.

[51] The fact that a consignor/non-owner can recover damages for economic loss under a separate collateral contract with the carrier was recognised by the House of Lords in *Cork Distilleries* v. *Great Southern and Western Railway* (1874) L.R. 7 H.L. 269. If he can recover such damages under a collateral contract then he can recover them where he is a party to the main contract of carriage.

[52] (1870) 18 W.R. 735.

[53] It is not necessary for a person to be the owner of goods to recover substantial damages in contract as opposed to tort. Thus in a contract for the sale of goods a person who has contracted to buy goods can recover damages for non-delivery even though the property in the goods has never passed to him.

bailment and in fact recovering damages again for the same loss? The result would be that the carrier has to pay out twice![54]

1.16 **The position under the standard conditions of carriage**

The British Rail Conditions (see Appendix 1.B.) define the other party to the contract under the word "Trader" in the introduction to the Conditions. The definition does not seem to assist us when it comes to deciding to whom British Rail are liable under the contract. The Road Haulage Association 1982, Conditions (see Appendix 1.A.) define in clause 1 the word "Trader" as "the customer who contracts for the services of the carrier." This could mean the consignor who physically makes the contract or it could mean the consignee/owner who is normally the contracting party at common law. The more likely interpretation is the latter (*i.e.* the consignee) as it is in accordance with the common law and common sense. If a non-owner consignor was the contracting party then, as explained above, he could not normally recover substantial damages from the carrier.[55] Nevertheless the word "Trader" is used very loosely in the Conditions and it sometimes seems to mean "consignor" rather than consignee. For example[56] clause 8(1) makes freight "payable by the Trader without prejudice to the Carrier's right to proceed against the consignee." If, as suggested above, "Trader" means the consignee this Clause is incomprehensible!

LIABILITY IN BAILMENT AND TORT

1.17 **Actions by the non-contracting owner of the goods**

As explained in 1.13 the presumption that the contract of carriage is made by the owner of the goods and the carrier can be rebutted. If the owner[57] of the goods carried is not a principal party to the contract then he can sue the carrier in tort[58] or in bailment[59] for negligent loss or damage to the goods. Thus in *Martin* v. *Great Indian Peninsular Railway*[60] the Government of India entered into a contract with the defendants to have all Indian Army Officers' luggage carried by rail free of charge to the officers. The defendants negligently allowed the plaintiff's luggage to be destroyed by fire and they were held liable to him for "a breach of duty" irrespective of the fact that there was no privity of contract between them and the plaintiff.

When a bailee/carrier is sued in these circumstances it is best to sue him in bailment rather than in tort. In other words one should allege a

[54] s.7 of the Torts (Interference with Goods) Act 1977 prevents two persons recovering damages in tort for the same loss but it does not prevent one person recovering damages in tort and another person recovering damages in contract.

[55] See 1.13.

[56] See also clause 12(3) discussed at 1.99.

[57] "Owner" in this context includes a person with an immediate right to possession. See *Transcontainer* v. *Custodian Security* [1988] 1 Lloyd's Rep. 128.

[58] *Lee Cooper* v. *Jeakins* [1967] 2 Q.B. 1.

[59] *Johnson Mathey* v. *Constantine Terminals* [1976] 2 Lloyd's Rep. 215.

[60] (1867) L.R. 3 Ex. 9.

breach of the duty of a bailee to carry safely and deliver intact. This is because in an action for breach of bailment if the owner of the goods can prove loss of, or damage to[61] the goods during transit then the burden of disproving negligence falls on the bailee/carrier. Thus in *Port Swettenham Authority* v. *Wu*[62] W placed his goods in P's warehouse. When he went to collect them they had disappeared and P could give no explanation as to what had happened to them. The court held that the onus was upon P to prove on the balance of probabilities that the loss was not caused by their negligence. As they were unable to do this they were held liable. This principle is similar to, but not the same as, the doctrine of *res ipsa loquitur* ("the thing speaks for itself") in the tort of negligence (see 1.117).

Liability of a bailee for thefts by his servants 1.18

The liability of an employer for the acts of his servants is called "vicarious liability." A bailee, such as a carrier, is vicariously liable in the event of the theft of the consigned goods by one of his servants if the goods have been entrusted to the servant for safe keeping. If the bailee delegates the safe keeping of the goods to a servant and that servant steals them then the bailee is liable.[63] Say, for example, two parcels of goods are given to a carrier. The first parcel is stolen by the lorry driver who is supposed to be delivering the goods. The carrier would be vicariously liable for this theft as the parcel had been entrusted to the lorry driver. The second parcel is stolen from the carrier's loading bay by a secretary. The carrier is not vicariously liable for this theft because the parcel was never entrusted to the secretary to look after. Of course, in such an instance, the carrier may be primarily liable for his own negligence if, for example, his security precautions are inadequate but he would not be vicariously liable for the theft by the secretary.

Actions against sub-contractors 1.19

The remedy of suing the carrier in bailment or negligence can also be a useful remedy where the carrier subcontracts the goods to another carrier. If A gives his goods to C, a carrier, and C (with A's express or implied permission) in turn, acting in his own right and not as A's agent, subcontracts the goods to D, another carrier who loses them then A can sue D in tort or bailment. In this case it is possible that D will not be able to rely on either his own or C's Conditions of Carriage to exempt or limit his liability to A because there is no privity of contract between himself and A.[64] In the above example A is the bailor; C is the primary bailee and D is called a sub-bailee. A sub-bailee owes exactly the same duties to the bailor as does the primary bailee. It is also possible that C will never actually have possession of the goods himself, for example he may sub-contract all the carriage to D without the goods ever going

[61] *Travers* v. *Cooper* [1915] 1 K.B. 73.
[62] [1979] A.C. 580.
[63] *Morris* v. *Martin* [1966] 1 Q.B. 716.
[64] See 1.77-1.88.

through his (C's) hands.[65] This is called "quasi bailment." Again the duty owed by D, the quasi-bailee, to the owner of the goods, A, is exactly the same as if he were a full/primary bailee of A's goods. In other words it is just the same as if A had delivered the goods directly to D without ever contracting with C. Subcontracting is discussed further in 1.77-1.87.

1.20 **Actions in tort by non-owners**

We have discussed above the situation where the OWNER of the goods sues the carrier in tort or bailment. However the carrier may also be sued in the tort of negligence by someone who is not the owner of the goods. For example he might be sued by someone whom he knows has agreed to buy the goods but who is not yet the owner of them. If such a non-owner sues in tort for economic loss then he cannot succeed however forseeable the loss to him may be.[66] The proper person to sue the carrier is the owner/consignor,[67] and his remedy is normally in contract.[68] Alternatively the owner can assign (*i.e.* transfer) his right to sue the carrier to the buyer[69] but cannot be forced to do so.

Common Carriers

1.21 **Introduction**

Not all carriers are ordinary bailees. Some carriers of goods by land are common carriers. "By custom of the realm"[70] they are under a heavier liability for loss or damage to the consigned goods than that of a bailee for reward who is only liable for negligent loss or damage. Being a common carrier, like a common inn-keeper, is thus one of the "status professions" or "common callings." The common law imposes heavy liabilities upon such persons. The law does however give a common carrier the privilege of a special lien for unpaid freight.[71] He also has the benefit of the Carriers Act 1830, as regards undeclared valuables.[72]

1.22 **Definition**

A common carrier is one who holds himself out as being prepared to carry for reward[73] for all and sundry without reserving the right to refuse the goods tendered.[74] In *Belfast Ropework Co.* v. *Bushell*[75] the

[65] As in *Metaalhandel* v. *Ardfields Transport* [1987] 2 S.T.L.R. 319. Discussed in 2.05.

[66] *The Aliakmon* [1986] A.C. 785; *Mitsui & Co. Ltd.* v. *Flot & Morante* [1988] 1 W.L.R. 1145.

[67] *Margarine Union* v. *Cambay Prince* [1969] 1 Q.B. 219.

[68] As in *Crouch* v. *London & North Western Railway (No. 1)* (1849) 2 C. Car. & K. 790. See also 1.05.

[69] This was recognised in *The Aliakmon* [1986] 2 W.L.R. 902.

[70] *i.e.* by the common law of England. *Rich* v. *Kneeland* (1613) Hobart 17, Cro.Jac. 330.

[71] See 1.111.

[72] See 1.32.

[73] He must carry for reward. *Tyly* v. *Morrice* (1699) Carth. 485.

[74] *James* v. *Commonwealth* (1939) 62 C.L.R. 339, 367-369 (Australia). *Hyland* v. *Mullaby & Byrne* (1923) V.L.R. 193 (Australia).

[75] [1918] 1 K.B. 210.

defendant was a common carrier of certain types of goods between Liverpool and Manchester. Occasionally on return journeys to Liverpool he would at his discretion carry return loads if it was convenient to him and the price was right. It was held that as regards the return journey he was not a common carrier. However if a manager of a haulage company admits that his firm carries for any customer provided he can pay then this will normally make the company common carriers.[76] Charging standard freight rates to customers (as do many parcel companies) is strong evidence of being a common carrier but it is not a prerequisite of being one.[77] Nor is it necessary that he should operate between fixed termini.[78] The test as to whether a carrier is a common carrier is objective not subjective.[79] In other words the test is whether the carrier has behaved as a common carrier not whether he intends to be a common carrier.

Actions in tort for refusal to carry 1.23

A common carrier may, of course, limit the scope of his profession to certain classes of merchandise or to certain geographical areas.[80] For example he could be a common carrier only of coal and coke within a radius of 100 miles of his depot in London. If so he could not be required to carry, for example, fruit from London to Glasgow.[81] However if he refuses to carry goods within his profession he can be sued in tort for unreasonable refusal to carry.[82] Thus in *Crouch* v. *London and North Western Railway*[83] a railway company refused to carry packed parcels for a road carrier who was using the railway company's services to undercut their freight rates. They were held liable to pay damages in tort to the road carrier. There are defences to this liability however. A common carrier is not, for example, liable if his lorry is full,[84] if the goods are tendered at an unreasonable hour[85] or if reasonable freight rates are not paid in advance.[86] It seems that charging unreasonable freight rates may be a constructive refusal to carry.[87]

The decline of common carriers in the United Kingdom 1.24

There has been a tendency in the United Kingdom, as opposed to other Commonwealth countries,[88] in recent times to hold that most land carriers are not common carriers.[89] Nevertheless common car-

[76] *Eastman Chemical International* v. *N.M.T. Trading* [1972] 2 Lloyd's Rep. 25.
[77] *Great Western Railway* v. *Sutton* (1869) L.R. 4 H.L. 226, 237.
[78] *Belfast Ropework Co.* v. *Bushell* [1918] 1 K.B. 210.
[79] *Siohn* v. *Hagland Transport* [1976] 2 Lloyd's Rep. 428.
[80] *Johnson* v. *Midland Railway* (1849) 4 Ex. 367, 373.
[81] *Johnson* v. *Midland Railway*. See n. 80 above.
[82] *Jackson* v. *Rogers* (1683) 2 Show. 327. Judgment of the infamous Jeffreys C.J.
[83] *Crouch* v. *London and North Western Railway (No. 2)* (1854) 14 C.B. 255.
[84] *Jackson* v. *Rogers*. See n. 82 above.
[85] *Lane* v. *Cotton* (1701) 12 Mod. 472, 481.
[86] *Wyld* v. *Pickford* (1841) 8 M. & W. 443.
[87] *Garton* v. *Bristol & Exeter Railway* (1861) 1 B. & S. 112.
[88] There are innumerable modern cases in other Commonwealth countries where carriers have been held to be common carriers.
[89] *e.g. Webster* v. *Dickson* [1969] 1 Lloyd's Rep. 89.

riers are not extinct[90] and an understanding of the law relating to common carriers (especially in relation to the "excepted perils") is essential in order to understand modern conditions of carriage in which many private carriers by contract undertake a liability similar to that of common carriers at common law.[91]

1.25 Who are common carriers today?

1. British Rail and other rail carriers are not common carriers by virtue of section 43 of the Transport Act 1962; before that Act there was no doubt that they were.[92]
2. Carriers of passengers' luggage by bus are almost certainly common carriers.[93] This is so even though the passenger may accompany his luggage in which case there is an implied term in the contract that he should take proper care of his luggage.[94]
3. Parcel carriers are very often common carriers because they hold themselves out to carry for all and sundry.[95]
4. Furniture removers can be common carriers if they do not reserve to themselves the right to refuse to carry.[96]
5. Freight forwarders apparently can be common carriers.[97]
6. Carriers of hanging garments for the "rag trade" can be common carriers.[98]
7. The fact that a carrier has a public carrier's licence that requires him to carry for customers without discrimination does not automatically make him a common carrier.[99]

1.26 Denial of common carrier status

Many modern conditions of carriage state that the carrier is not a common carrier. The R.H.A. 1982, Conditions[1] do precisely this in their introduction. Although such a statement in a carrier's conditions may be evidence that he is not a common carrier it is not conclusive of his status.[2] The status of common carrier is one imposed by law and one cannot divest oneself of such a status merely by saying so.

[90] *Siohn* v. *Hagland Transport* [1976] 2 Lloyd's Rep. 428. Note however that the Post Office are not common carriers. They are virtually under no liability for loss or damage. See the Post Office Act 1969, ss. 29-30.

[91] See 1.54-1.65.

[92] For example the plaintiffs admitted they were common carriers in *Great Northern Railway* v. *L.E.P. Transport* [1922] 2 K.B. 742.

[93] A carrier of passengers by sea has been held to be a common carrier of their luggage. *Bennett* v. *Peninsular Steamboat Co.* (1848) 6 C.B. 773.

[94] *Great Western Railway* v. *Bunch* (1883) 13 App.Cas. 31, 48. See 1.119.

[95] The defendants in *Hunt and Winterbotham* v. *B.R.S. Parcels* [1962] 1 Q.B. 617 admitted that they were common carriers.

[96] *Watkins* v. *Cottell* [1916] 1 K.B. 10 is often quoted as authority for the proposition that furniture removers are not common carriers. However *Geering* v. *Stewart Transport* [1967] N.Z.L.R. 802 (New Zealand) shows that this is not so. In *Geering* the defendant/furniture removers were held to be common carriers.

[97] *New Zealand Express* v. *Minahan* (1916) 35 N.Z.L.R. 816 (New Zealand).

[98] *Siohn* v. *Hagland Transport* [1976] 2 Lloyd's Rep. 482.

[99] *Cadbury Schweppes Hudson* v. *Secutitas (N.Z.)* (1985). (Unreported). (New Zealand High Court).

[1] See Appendix 1.A.

[2] Gorton. *The Concept of the Common Carrier in Anglo American Law,* (1971) p. 89.

Whether a person is a common carrier or not depends on the way he runs his business not on how he describes himself. "A transporter who behaves like a common carrier cannot remove himself from that category by stating in fact that he is not a common carrier. The conduct of his business must be consistent with his description of himself."[3]

The common carrier's strict liability for loss and damage 1.27

A common carrier is strictly liable for loss or damage to the goods[4] (*but not for delay or apparently misdelivery—see 1.37 and 1.68*) unless he can prove one of the four common carrier's excepted perils. Thus in *Siohn* v. *Hagland Transport*[5] a common carrier was robbed by thieves despite the fact that he had taken all reasonable care. It was held that he was liable even though he had not been negligent.

The excepted perils 1.28

Although a common carrier is strictly liable for loss or damage his liability is not absolute. The common carrier has four defences or "excepted perils." The burden of bringing himself within the excepted perils falls on the carrier[6] and he cannot rely on them if his negligence has caused or aggravated the loss or damage. If he proves that the likely cause of the loss or damage is an excepted peril then the burden of proving negligence is placed back on the plaintiff.[7] The excepted perils are:

(1) Act of God. An "Act of God" is an act of nature that cannnot be guarded against by any reasonable care.[8] Examples are flood,[9] a sudden unexpected storm,[10] lightning,[11] earthquake and the worst rainfall in living memory.[12] An Act of God must involve no human intervention but it can occur to a human being, for example if he has an unexpected heart attack.[13] Ordinary bad weather conditions do not amount to an Act of God.

(2) Act of the Queen's enemies. This is a very narrow defence and is limited to acts of the armed forces of a foreign power with which this

[3] *Dar es Salaam Motor Transport* v. *Mehta* [1970] H.C.D. 179, 180 (Tanzania).

[4] Some textbooks and old cases suggest that the common carrier's strict liability is based on tort rather than contract. Whatever the truth of this it is clear from the House of Lords decision in *Bristol and Exeter Railway* v. *Collins* (1859) 7 H.L.C. 194 that the common carrier's strict liability only extends to those with whom he has a contract. We suggest that *Eastman Chemicals* v. *N.M.T. Trading* [1972] 2 Lloyd's Rep. 25 to the contrary was decided *per incuriam, i.e.* through carelessness.

[5] See n. 98 above.

[6] *Gill* v. *Midland, Scottish and London Railway* (1873) L.R. 8 Q.B. 186, 196.

[7] *The Glendaroch* [1894] P. 226.

[8] *Nugent* v. *Smith* (1876). Compare the views of Brett J. at first instance at (1876) 1 C.P.D. 19 with those of James L.J. on appeal at (1876) 1 C.P.D. 423.

[9] *Makins* v. *London & North Eastern Railway* [1943] K.B. 467.

[10] *Nugent* v. *Smith* (1876) 1 C.P.D. 423.

[11] *Forward* v. *Pittard* (1785) 1 T.R. 27.

[12] *Nichols* v. *Marsland* (1876) 2 Ex.D. 1.

[13] *Ryans* v. *Young* [1938] 1 All E.R. 522.

country is at war,[14] even though war has not been declared. An example would be bomb damage caused by enemy aircraft in time of war. Note that riots, the acts of terrorists, robberies and even probably armed uprisings against the Crown are not within the defence.[15]

(3) Inherent vice in the goods. This means "unfitness for the treatment the contract of carriage authorised or required"[16] and extends to the containers within which the goods are placed.[17] If the goods are unfit to stand the journey because they are perishable or have a tendency to rot, leak or evaporate then the common carrier is not liable. The tendency of animals to injure themselves in transit can be inherent vice but the burden of proof in such cases is the subject of debate.[18] An illustration of inherent vice is the case of *Hudson* v. *Baxendale*[19] in which a cask of gin leaked in transit and it was held that the defendant was not liable because of inherent vice. Improper packing may be an example of this peril although it is sometimes included under the fourth defence of "fault or fraud." If a carrier accepts goods that he *knows* are improperly packed then the law is unclear as to whether he can still rely on the defence.[20]

(4) Fault or fraud on the part of the consignor or consignee. As stated above this may include improper packing. It would also cover the case where goods are lost or misdelivered because they are misleadingly addressed.[21] A carrier will not be liable if the consignor fraudulently misleads him as to the nature of the goods. Thus in *Bradley* v. *Waterhouse*[22] a consignor hid a bag of gold coins in a consignment of tea and misled the carrier as to the nature and value of the consignment. The court held that the carrier was not liable because the customer had bought the loss of the gold upon himself by his fraudulent behaviour. In a "three party"[23] contract where the consignee is the principal party to the contract of carriage he will be bound by the fault or fraud of his agent, the consignor.[24]

1.29 **Common carriers and the interpretation of exclusion clauses**

The common carrier's strict liability can, subject to the "reasonableness test" in the Unfair Contract Terms Act 1977, be exempted (see, 1.45). It has been argued that a common carrier who exempts his strict liability is not a common carrier but section 5 of the Carriers Act 1830,

[14] *Case of the Marshal of the Marshalsea* (1455) Y.B. 33 Hen VI, 1. pl. 3.

[15] See the criticism by Leslie, *Law of Transport by Railway* (2nd ed., 1928, p. 35) of the case of *Secretary of State for War* v. *Midland and Great Western Railway* [1923] 2 Ir.R. 102.

[16] *Lister* v. *Lancashire and Yorkshire Railway* [1903] 1 K.B. 879, especially the judgment of Channell J.; *Albacora* v. *Westcott & Lawrence* [1966] 2 Lloyd's Rep. 53, 59.

[17] See *Lister* v. *Lancashire and Yorkshire Railway* [1903] 1 K.B. 878.

[18] See 1.88.

[19] *Hudson* v. *Baxendale* (1857) 2 H. & N. 575.

[20] See 1.92.

[21] See *Stewart* v. *Gordon* (1852) 14 Sess.Cas. (2nd Ser.) 434.

[22] (1828) 3 C. & P. 318.

[23] See 1.05.

[24] See the shipping case of *Berkley* v. *Watling* (1837) 7 A. & E. 382 (consignee/principal bound by consignor/agent's fraud on carrier).

makes it clear that a carrier who excludes his common law liability may remain a common carrier.[25] However a clause, for example, saying "we exempt liability for fire damage" in a common carrier's conditions would leave him liable for fires caused by his negligence.[26] This is due to the *contra proferentem* rule[27] to the effect that any ambiguity in an exemption clause will be interpreted against the person relying on it.

The Carriers Act 1830, introduction 1.30

A common carrier by land has the protection of the Carriers Act 1830, as regards undeclared valuables worth over £10. *The Act does not apply to private carriers or to common carriers by other modes of transport.* The "valuables" listed by the Act are out of date and for example include "writings" (*e.g.* books?) and do not include platinum which had not been discovered in 1830. In addition the sum of £10 has not been revised since the date of the Act and there is no doubt that it is in need of repeal or amendment and can lead to substantial injustice.

Carriers Act 1830, declarations and notices 1.31

The Act requires that valuables worth more than £10 and breakables must be declared to the carrier.[28] If he displays a clear and public notice to that effect he is entitled to a surcharge for carrying valuables.[29] He is only liable for such undeclared valuables upon proof of theft, embezzlement or forgery by his servant.[30] The onus of proving same falls upon the plaintiff.[31] The Act forbids common carriers from excluding liability for loss or damage by means of a public notice[32] but there is nothing to stop them excluding liability by means of a "special contract."[33] This has been interpreted, in effect, as meaning that the carrier can exclude liability by any means other than a public notice, for example by means of a clause in a leaflet handed to consignors.[34] There is no duty to bring the provisions of the Act to the notice of customers.[35] The Act does not apply to delay[36] in the delivery of valuables as opposed to their loss or damage and, it seems, not to a loss after transit has ceased.[37] It is often stated that a carrier who has unjustifiably deviated from the agreed route can still rely on the Act but in fact this point is undecided.[38]

[25] See also Leslie, *The Law of Transport by Railway* (2nd ed., 1928), p. 186.

[26] See *Martin* v. *Great Indian Peninsular Railway* (1867) L.R. 3 Ex. 9.

[27] See 1.44.

[28] Carriers Act 1830, s.1.

[29] Carriers Act 1830, s.2.

[30] Carriers Act 1830, ss.1 and 8 as amended by the Criminal Law Act 1967, s.10(1) and Schedule 2, para. 4.

[31] *M'Queen* v. *Great Western Railway* (1875) L.R. 10 Q.B. 569.

[32] Carriers Act 1830, s.4.

[33] Carriers Act 1830, s.6.

[34] *Walker* v. *York & North West Railway* (1853) 2 E. & B. 750.

[35] *Caswell* v. *Cheshire Lines Committee* [1907] 2 K.B. 499.

[36] *Hearn* v. *London and South Western Railway* (1855) 10 Ex. 793.

[37] Compare *Mc'Kinnon* v. *Arcadian Lines* [1978] 81 D.L.R. 480 (Canada), a case decided under the Canadian equivalent of the Carriers Act 1830.

[38] *Morritt* v. *North Eastern Railway* (1876) 1 Q.B.D. 302 does not decide this point because the court held that the carrier had not deviated. However one judge in the case favoured the view that a deviating carrier can still rely on the Act.

1.32 The injustice of the Act

The Act is the main advantage of being a common carrier and by successfully pleading that he is a common carrier and relying on the Act a carrier could cause substantial injustice to a customer.[39] Say for example a student takes this textbook in his briefcase on to a scheduled bus and his briefcase is lost or destroyed by the gross negligence or deliberate wrongdoing of the bus company's employees then, unless the student has taken the unlikely precaution of declaring the nature and contents of his briefcase to the bus conductor, the carrier would not be liable for any of the contents!

Private Carriers

1.33 Private carriers only liable for negligence

Any carrier who is not a common carrier is a private carrier. A private carrier is only liable as a bailee for reward (see 1.03 and 1.17-1.19 above) and is thus only liable for loss or damage if negligent or guilty of a conversion, etc. (unless by contract he undertakes a heavier duty). Thus in *Cadbury Schweppes Hudson Ltd.* v. *Securitas (N.Z.) Ltd.*[40] it was held to be negligent only to supply one security guard when delivering a valuable cash consignment and in *Cowper* v. *J.G. Goldner Pty. Ltd.*[41] it was held to be negligent to fail to inspect regularly a valuable racehorse during transit. It is interesting to note, however, that many private carriers (*e.g.* British Rail) do not carry subject to their common law liability for negligence but often undertake a stricter liability (see 1.60-1.65 below).

1.34 The bailee's duty to protect the owner's interests

Even if the bailee has taken reasonable care of the goods while they are in his possession that does not always mean he will escape liability. If the goods are, for example, stolen without his negligence he must notify the police and/or the owner as soon as possible. If he fails do so he may be held liable.[42]

1.35 Roadworthiness and railworthiness

Unlike carriage by sea at common law[43] there is no absolute duty of roadworthiness or railworthiness in carriage by land.[44] Thus a private carrier does not guarantee that his vehicle is safe for the journey. The exact nature of the duty is unclear although it is based on negligence. However it may be that his duty is to supply a vehicle as safe as reasonable care can make it. Presumably he would therefore be liable for any faults arising from negligence in the manufacture or in the servicing of the vehicle even though he could not have detected the

[39] As in *Caswell* v. *Cheshire Lines Committee*, see n. 35 above.
[40] (1985), New Zealand High Court (unreported).
[41] (1986) 40 S.A.S.R. 457 (Australia).
[42] *Coldman* v. *Hill* [1919] 1 K.B. 443.
[43] *The Glenfruin* (1885) 10 P.D. 103. See 5.18.
[44] *John Carter* v. *Hanson Haulage* [1965] 1 Q.B. 495.

defect himself through the use of reasonable care. This question of roadworthiness and railworthiness is less important for common carriers because at common law such a carrier cannot escape liabilty for defects in his vehicles however unforeseeable those defects may be. It might however be important if a common carrier tried to rely upon one of the excepted perils. He could not do so if the peril was aggravated by his negligent use of an unroadworthy vehicle. The same would apply if the common carrier by contract only undertook liability for negligence as opposed to strict liability.

Public carriers? 1.36

It has been argued that there is a third class of carriers by land, namely "public carriers."[45] They allegedly cannot be sued for refusal to carry but are strictly liable for loss or damage. This view however, seems to be based on a misunderstanding of the case of *Liver Alkali* v. *Johnson*[46] which is in fact a case on carriage of goods by water and not land. It is suggested that there is no such third class of carriers of goods by land.

Liability for Delay at Common Law

All carriers only liable for delays caused by their negligence 1.37

Both private carriers and common carriers are only liable at common law for delay in delivering the goods if the delay is caused by their negligence.[47] Thus a carrier is not liable if a delay is caused by persons over whom he has no control. So in *Taylor* v. *Great Northern Railway*[48] goods were delayed by the acts of another railway company which had running rights over the defendants' lines. The goods were delivered late despite all the efforts of the defendants to deliver promptly. The court held that the carrier was not liable. Equally a carrier is not liable where the delay is caused by the consignor's ambiguous addressing of the consignment[49] or by weather conditions[50] outside his control. If the goods have not been delivered within a reasonable time this is prima facie evidence of a delay caused by negligence.[51] In other words it is sufficient evidence to place the burden on the carrier to prove on the balance of probabilities that the delay was caused through no fault of his. If the consignor tells the carrier that the goods must arrive by a certain date and the carrier makes no objection then that is evidence that failure to deliver by the named date amounts to negligence.[52]

[45] See Leslie, *The Law of Transport by Railway*, (2nd ed., 1928), pp. 9-13.
[46] (1872) L.R. 7 Ex. 267, (1874) L.R. 9 Ex. 338.
[47] *Raphael* v. *Pickford* (1843) 5 Man. & G. 551.
[48] (1866) L.R. 1 C.P. 385.
[49] *Caledonian Railway* v. *Hunter* (1858) 20 Sess.Cas. (2nd Ser.) 1097.
[50] *Briddon* v. *Great Northern Railway* (1858) 28 L.J.Ex. 51.
[51] *Raphael* v. *Pickford*, see n. 47 above.
[52] *Horne* v. *Midland Railway* (1873) L.R. 8 C.P. 131.

1.38 Guaranteed delivery times

Some carriers, such as parcel companies, in their conditions of carriage guarantee delivery within, for example, 24 hours. Of course if the carrier has guaranteed delivery within such a time limit then he is strictly liable for failure to deliver as agreed whether caused by his negligence or not unless he has an exemption clause to that effect in his conditions of carriage.

DAMAGES FOR LOSS, DAMAGE AND DELAY AT COMMON LAW

1.39 Introduction

Most carriers by land attempt to limit or exempt liability for loss, damage or delay.[53] If they fail to do so or if they are unable to rely on such exclusion clauses then they are liable in damages to the owner of the goods in accordance with the following principles. The basic principle is that the carrier is liable if the damage to the owner is "reasonably foreseeable" within the Rule in *Hadley* v. *Baxendale*.[54]

1.40 Damages for non-delivery of and damage to goods

If the goods are not delivered because the carrier has lost them or has delivered them to the wrong person then the normal basis on which damages are awarded is as follows. The owner can recover from the carrier the market value of the goods at the time and place at which they should have been delivered[55] and not the value at the time they were delivered to the carrier or lost. If the customer has not paid the freight then this amount must be deducted from the value of the goods when assessing damages.[56] The fact that the owner has agreed to resell the goods at less than the market price is irrelevant.[57] If there is no market in the goods at the time and place of delivery then it seems that the damages will be the value of the goods at the time of delivery to the carrier plus freight charges and a reasonable sum as lost profit to the consignee.[58] If the goods are damaged in transit then damages are assessed by computing the difference between the market value they would have had if they arrived undamaged and their actual market value as damaged goods.[59]

[53] See 1.54-1.65 for a discussion of the British Rail and R.H.A. Conditions of Carriage.
[54] (1854) 9 Ex. 341.
[55] *Rice* v. *Baxendale* (1861) 7 H. & N. 96.
[56] *Rodocanachi* v. *Milburn* (1887) 18 Q.B.D. 67.
[57] *Ibid.*
[58] *O'Hanlan* v. *Great Western Railway* (1865) 6 B. & S. 484.
[59] *Slater* v. *Hoyle* [1920] 2 K.B. 11.

Damages for delay 1.41

If the goods are delivered late in breach of contract and have wasted or deteriorated as a result then damages are assessed on the same basis as if they had been damaged.[60] If the goods are delivered late undamaged then the normal basis upon which damages are awarded is the difference between the market value on the day the goods should have arrived and their value on the day they were actually delivered.[61]

Damages for consequential loss 1.42

If the goods are lost, damaged or delayed then normally, if there is a ready market in the goods at the place of destination, the owner cannot recover any damages for consequential loss (*e.g.* loss of profits on resale).[62] This is because his remedy is to buy equivalent goods in the market and use them to perform any contract of resale. However it seems that the consignee can recover the expenses incurred in searching for replacement goods.[63] If however there is no ready market in the goods at the place of delivery there are various types of consequential loss that might be recoverable. These are:

(1) Loss of profits on use of the goods. If the consignee of goods has been deprived of the use of them then he can usually only recover as damages a sum equivalent to interest on the value of the goods.[64] For example if goods worth £1,000 are delivered six months late then he can recover six months' reasonable interest on £1,000. It is difficult to recover more because the loss of profits is not normally within the contemplation of the carrier as the reasonably foreseeable consequence of his breach of contract. A carrier is not normally expected to know the details of the consignee's business activities (whereas a seller of goods is much more likely to have such knowledge of his buyer's intentions).[65] Thus in *Gee* v. *Lancashire and Yorkshire Railway*[66] the plaintiff's mill was idle as the result of the carrier's delay in delivering cotton. The loss of profits was held to be irrecoverable because the carrier had not been told of any particular inconvenience that would follow from delay and he was not to know that the mill owner did not have other cotton in stock. However in exceptional cases loss of profits on use of the goods can be recovered if the carrier has, for example, knowledge of precisely why the goods are needed and what will happen to the consignee's business if they are lost or delayed.[67]

[60] *Hawes* v. *South Eastern Railway* (1884) 54 L.J.Q.B 174.

[61] *Collard* v. *South Eastern Railway* (1861) 7 H. & N. 79; *Czarnikow* v. *Koufos* [1969] 1 A.C. 350.

[62] See *Williams* v. *Agius* [1914] A.C. 510, a sale of goods case.

[63] See *Heskell* v. *Continental Express* [1950] 1 All E.R. 1033.

[64] *British Columbia Sawmills* v. *Nettleship* (1868) L.R. 3 C.P. 499.

[65] See the *dicta, i.e.* comments, of Asquith L.J. in *Victoria Laundry* v. *Newman Industries* [1949] 2 K.B. 528, 536-537.

[66] (1860) 6 H. & N. 211.

[67] *Montivideo Gas Company* v. *Clan Line* (1921) 37 T.L.R. 544 and 866 (Court of Appeal).

(2) Replacement goods. If the consignee is forced[68] to buy the nearest equivalent goods that he can find at a higher price then this sum is recoverable as damages.[69]

(3) Loss of profit on a sale. If the consignee loses a profit on resale of the goods as a result of loss, damage or delay then this loss is not usually recoverable as damages for the same reasons as loss of profits on use of goods is not recoverable (see, (1) above). However in exceptional cases loss of profits on resale is foreseeable and recoverable. Thus in *Simpson* v. *London and North Western Railway*[70] the plaintiff was a dealer in cattle foods and regularly exhibited samples of his stock at agricultural shows. He delivered parcels of his samples to the defendants' agent at the Bedford showground to be delivered to the Newcastle showground "on Monday certain." The samples failed to arrive and the plaintiff recovered the resulting profits lost on selling cattle food at the show on the basis that this loss must have been "within the contemplation of the parties."[71]

(4) Compensation to a sub-buyer. If the carrier does not deliver goods as agreed and the consignee has agreed to resell the goods to a sub-buyer the consignee may well be held liable in damages to the sub-buyer for breach of his contract of sale. These damages and any legal costs incurred cannot normally be recovered from the carrier because, as explained above, the carrier is not expected to have knowledge of the consignee's business commitments.[72]

(5) Searching for the goods. It seems that expenses involved in searching for lost or delayed goods are recoverable from the carrier.[73]

(6) Futile expenditure. If a consignee lays out money in anticipation of receiving the goods then these expenses can only be recovered as an alternative to a claim for loss of profits (which, as explained above, are not usually recoverable in any event). However, claims for wasted expediture such as wages paid out by the consignee to his employees,[74] or hotel expenses incurred while waiting for the goods[75] do not seem easy to recover.

Exclusion Clauses

1.43 Incorporation of exclusion clauses

A carrier may wish to exempt his common law liabilities. For example he may wish to exempt the liability for damages for breach of

[68] "Forced" in this context means that the buyer has acted reasonably in buying alternative goods, *Le Blanche* v. *London and North Western Railway* (1876) 1 C.P.D. 286.
[69] *Millen* v. *Brasch* (1882) 10 Q.B.D. 142.
[70] [1876] 1 Q.B.D. 274.
[71] Cockburn C.J. at p. 277.
[72] See n. 65 above.
[73] *Heskell* v. *Continental Express*, see n. 63 above.
[74] *Le Peinteur* v. *South Eastern Railway* (1860) 2 L.T. 170.
[75] *Candy* v. *Midland Railway* (1878) 38 L.T. 226; *Woodger* v. *Lancashire and Yorkshire Railway* (1861) 9 C.B.(N.S.) 632. Compare *Black* v. *Baxendale* (1847) 1 Ex. 410.

contract discussed above in 1.39-1.42. For example he may wish to carry upon terms that he is not liable for any consequential loss, such as loss of profit on resale. Alternatively he may wish to limit his liability. For example he may want to impose a maximum liability for loss or damage of £2,000 per metric tonne. Exemption and limitation clauses are collectively known as "exclusion clauses." The Road Haulage Association and British Rail exclusion clauses are discussed in 1.54-1.67 below. If the carrier wishes to rely on any exclusion clause in his conditions of carriage he must give reasonable notice of the conditions to the customer.[76] The notice must normally be given before, or at the time of, the making of the contract[77] but can also be incorporated as a result of a course of dealing between the parties.[78] The notice must be given upon a "contractual document," *i.e.* a document upon which a reasonable person would expect to find the terms of a contract and not, for example, upon a mere receipt.[79] An exclusion clause in conditions of carriage will not avail a carrier if he breaks a collateral contract, *i.e.* a separate contract ancillary to the main contract of carriage. Thus in *Gallagher* v. *B.R.S.*[80] a limitation clause in a contract for the carriage of a valuable consignment of tobacco was held not to apply when the defendants broke an oral promise to take special security precautions. In addition a carrier cannot rely on his conditions if he has misled the other party as to their effect[81] or where he has unjustifiably deviated (see, 1.46-1.53 below).

Interpretation of exclusion clauses 1.44

A clause must be worded as an exemption clause to have any effect.[82] If it is merely a "statement in the nature of a warning to customers" it will not exempt liability. For example if a carrier displayed a notice saying "We do not guarantee the safety of customers' goods" that is merely a restatement of his existing common law liability, not an exemption clause, and the carrier's liability would remain unaltered. As the result of the *contra proferentem* rule any ambiguity in an exclusion clause will be interpreted against a carrier.[83] For example a clause exempting liability for "loss of goods in transit" would not exempt a carrier if the goods were damaged[84] in transit. For another illustration in the context of common carriers see, 1.29 above.

The Unfair Contract Terms Act 1977 1.45

A detailed consideration of this very important piece of legislation is outside the scope of this work. However section 2 of the Act makes

[76] *Van Toll* v. *South Eastern Railway* (1862) 12 C.B.(N.S.) 75.
[77] *Fosbroke-Hobbs* v. *Airwork Ltd.* [1937] 1 All E.R. 108.
[78] *B.R.S.* v. *Crutchley* [1968] 1 All E.R. 811.
[79] *D.J. Hill & Co.* v. *Walter H. Wright* [1971] V.R. 749 (Australia).
[80] [1974] 2 Lloyd's Rep. 440.
[81] *Curtis* v. *Chemical Cleaning & Dyeing* [1951] 1 K.B. 805.
[82] *Hollier* v. *Rambler Motors* [1972] 2 Q.B. 71.
[83] *Thomas National Transport* v. *May & Baker* (1960) 115 C.L.R. 353 (Australia).
[84] Compare *Gordon* v. *Great Western Railway* (1881) 8 Q.B.D. 44.

attempts to exempt or limit liability for negligence subject to the "reasonableness test"[85] which is discussed below. "Negligence" in this context includes both the tort of that name and a breach of a contractual duty to use reasonable care. So a clause that purports to exempt the implied contractual duty of a carrier to deliver goods within a reasonable time would be within the ambit of the Act. Similarly section 3 makes any attempt to exempt or limit other contractual liability subject to the same test if the contract is made with a consumer or if the contract is made on "written standard terms of business" (*e.g.* standard conditions of carriage). If an exclusion clause fails the "reasonableness test" then the carrier cannot rely on it. Various guidelines[86] are given in the Act as to when an exclusion clause is reasonable. For example when considering whether a carrier could limit his liability to £800 per ton the courts would take into account his financial resources and whether he could easily insure his liability. When considering exclusion clauses generally they take into account such factors as the bargaining strength of the parties and whether the customer knew of the exclusion clause.

Whether the customer "received an inducement" to agree to the exclusion clause is a factor of particular importance in relation to contracts of carriage. For example if a customer has received a reduction in freight rates in return for agreeing to a reduced liability on the part of the carrier this may make the contract "reasonable" (see, 1.55). One can rarely generalise as to whether an exemption clause is or is not reasonable because it all depends on the nature of the goods and the circumstances of the parties. For example a limit of £800 per ton may be reasonable in a contract to carry iron ore but would be very unreasonable in a contract made by a security company to carry gold bars.

Deviation

1.46 Deviation and fundamental breach

Until recently there was in the law of contract a rule known as the doctrine of "fundamental breach."[87] The result of this rule was that an exclusion clause in a contract would not be interpreted as covering the situation where the person relying on the clause had failed to fulfil their fundamental duties under the contract.[88] For example in a contract to supply a car the seller could not rely on an exclusion clause if he provided a vehicle that was totally unroadworthy.[89] The fundamental breach rule, however, has in effect been abolished by two

[85] s.11 of and Sched. 2 to the 1977 Act.

[86] See n. 85 above.

[87] There was much debate as to whether it was a doctrine of law or a rule of construction, see N. Palmer, *Bailment* (2nd. ed., 1989).

[88] As to the relationship between deviation and fundamental breach see *Bailment*, (above) and C. Mills in *Lloyd's Maritime Law Quarterly* [1983] 587 where the writer comes to a different conclusion to that drawn by us below.

[89] *Karsales (Harrow)* v. *Wallis* [1956] 1 W.L.R. 939.

recent House of Lords decisions.[90] The difficulty in the context of contracts of carriage of goods and other bailments is to decide if these recent cases have also abolished what is arguably a separate doctrine of law (or maybe a rule of construction), namely the doctrine of deviation. This point is a very difficult one that cannot be debated in depth in an introductory textbook. However, the view taken here is that the doctrine of deviation is a doctrine of bailment (whether the bailment be gratuitous or contractual) and is therefore independent from the rule of fundamental breach and survives the "abolition" of that purely contractual doctrine. It is suggested that the House of Lords decisions referred to above do not overrule the House's previous decision in *London and North Western Railway* v. *Neilson*[91] to the effect that the doctrine of deviation applies to contracts for the carriage of goods by land. Thus an exclusion clause in a bailment agreement will not normally be interpreted as covering a situation where the bailee has himself repudiated the terms of the bailment by an unjustified deviation from those agreed terms.

Deviations by route **1.47**

Presuming therefore that deviation survives as a rule of construction in all bailment agreements the law as regards deviation in carriage by land is as follows. Firstly the carrier must not unjustifiably deviate from the agreed or normal route.[92] However if a driver loses his way that is not an unjustified deviation.[93] Presumably by analogy with the law relating to carriage by sea[94] some departures from the agreed route, for example, to save life, to avoid danger or to further the journey are justified, but not one to save property. Where goods belonging to different consignees are loaded on to one lorry then delivering to one customer before another in the reasonable course of the carrier's business is justified and is therefore not a repudiation.[95]

Other deviations **1.48**

Likewise the carrier must not deviate from the agreed mode of carriage.[96] Thus if the contract is to carry goods by passenger train but the goods are carried on a goods train this is an unjustified deviation and repudiation by the carrier.[97] Other possible deviations are delivery to a person whom the carrier has no reasonable grounds to believe has any right to receive the goods,[98] unauthorised subcontracting[99] and leaving the goods to their fate,[1] but not a mere act of negligence.[2]

[90] *Photo Production* v. *Securicor Transport* [1980] A.C. 827 and *George Mitchell* v. *Finney Locke Seeds* [1983] 2 A.C. 803.

[91] [1922] A.C. 263.

[92] *Mallet* v. *Great Eastern Railway* [1889] 1 Q.B. 309.

[93] Compare *Rio Tinto* v. *Seed* (1926) 24 Lloyd's Rep. 316.

[94] See 5.23.

[95] *Mayfair Photographic Supplies* v. *Baxter Hoare* [1972] I Lloyd's Rep. 410.

[96] *Sleat* v. *Flagg* (1822) 5 B. & A. 342.

[97] *Gunyon* v. *South East and Chatham Railway* [1915] 2 K.B. 370.

[98] *Mc'Kinnon* v. *Acadian Lines* (1978) 81 D.L.R. 484 (Canada); *Alexander* v. *Railway Executive* [1951] 2 K.B. 882.

[99] *Garnham, Harris & Elton* v. *Alfred W. Ellis Transport* [1967] 1 W.L.R. 940.

[1] *Lee Cooper* v. *Jeakins* [1965] 3 W.L.R. 753.

[2] *Kenyon & Son & Craven* v. *Baxter Hoare* [1971] 1 W.L.R. 519.

1.49 **Liberty to deviate clauses**

Clause 12(1) of the British Rail Conditions is an example of what is known as a "liberty to deviate" clause. Such a clause will almost certainly be interpreted restrictively against the carrier as is the case in carriage by sea.[3] Thus if goods are to be carried from London to Exeter by rail and are in fact mistakenly carried via Edinburgh it is suggested that carriage via Edinburgh is not a "route" at all in the circumstances and the carrier will be unable to rely on such a clause.

1.50 **Deviating carrier loses benefit of exclusion clauses**

The first consequence of an unjustified deviation is that the bailee/carrier loses the benefit of any terms of the bailment in his favour, *e.g.* any exclusion clauses. Thus in *London and North Western Railway* v. *Neilson*[4] the railway agreed to carry "at owner's risk" a quantity of theatrical properties from Llandudno to Bolton and a van was appropriated to this purpose and labelled "through to Bolton." Due to a blunder or misapprehension by the carrier's servants when the train arrived at Manchester the properties were unloaded from the van. Some were put in the left luggage office and the rest were sent in accordance with their old labels to Bath, Scarborough, Newcastle, etc. The Court of Appeal and the House of Lords held that when the goods were unloaded at Manchester this was an unjustified deviation and that the "owner's risk" contract did not protect the defendants "while they are doing something wholly different from that which they had contracted to do."[5]

1.51 **Deviating bailee liable as wrongful possessor**

The second consequence of an unjustified deviation is that the carrier/bailee becomes liable as a wrongful possessor. In other words his only defence is if he can prove that the loss or damage would have occurred even if he had not deviated.[6] Some textbooks[7] state that a carrier who deviates is under the liability of a common carrier but it is suggested that this is wrong or at best only applies to carriage by sea. Thus in the ancient but important case of *Coggs* v. *Barnard*[8] Lord Holt gave the following interesting example of deviation in a gratuitous bailment. He put the case of a man who lends a friend a horse for a month to go on a journey to the West. Instead the friend rides to the North and keeps the horse for over a month. If the horse is injured while on the journey to the North or after the month has expired then the bailee is liable irrespective of negligence because if the horse had been on the correct journey the accident might never have happened. It follows that a deviating "bailee" can only escape liability if he proves that the risk was "independant of his acts."[9] Thus if a private carrier deviated by using the wrong mode of carriage (*e.g.* an ordinary

[3] See 5.24.
[4] [1922] 1 K.B. 192 (Court of Appeal), [1922] A.C. 263 (House of Lords).
[5] [1922] 1 K.B. 192, 202.
[6] *Lilley* v. *Doubleday* [1881] L.R. 7 Q.B.D. 510, 511.
[7] *e.g.* Carver and Colinvaux, *Carriage by Sea* (13th ed., 1982), para. 1196.
[8] (1703) 2 Ld.Raym. 909, 938.
[9] *Lilley* v. *Doubleday* [1881] 7 Q.B.D. 510, 511.

lorry instead of a refrigerated one as agreed) and the goods were destroyed by rioters he would not be liable if he could prove the rioters would have destroyed the goods even if he had used the correct lorry. This is true even though destruction in a riot is not one of the common carrier's excepted perils.

Burden of proving a deviation 1.52

Some cases[10] suggest that the mere loss of (or even damage to) the bailed goods, and certainly a refusal to give any explanation as what has happened to them, are evidence of a fundamental breach and therefore, by analogy, evidence of a deviation/repudiation of the bailment. However these cases do not take into account the House of Lords decision of *H.C. Smith* v. *Great Western Railway*[11] in which the defendants lost the plaintiff's goods and refused to give him any explanation as to what had happened to them. The plaintiff argued that the defendants' behaviour amounted to a repudiation of the contract depriving the carrier of his exemption clauses. Lord Buckmaster, however, said that if the plaintiff "desires to show that the contract was repudiated, it is incumbent upon him to bring evidence to establish the repudiation, and it is certainly not incumbent upon the defendants to go into the box to prove that they did not repudiate it."[12] The plaintiff's allegation of a repudiation thus failed. Therefore it is suggested that the burden of proving a deviation/repudiation always falls upon the plaintiff even though this burden may be a heavy one as only the bailee/carrier is likely to know what has happened to the goods if they have disappeared.

The deviating carrier's right to freight 1.53

It seems that if there has been an unjustified deviation then the carrier, because he has repudiated the bailment, is not entitled to the agreed freight. However if the goods have actually been delivered then he is entitled to a *"quantum meruit," i.e.* reasonable compensation for the work that he has done.[13] Of course what a court might decide is reasonable compensation in the circumstances might not be the same amount as the contractually agreed freight.

Liability under the Road Haulage Association's Conditions 1982

Status of conditions of carriage 1.54

The Road Haulage Association's Conditions of Carriage are the most widely used in the industry.[14] They are reproduced in Appendix 1.A. The R.H.A. and British Rail Conditions like all terms of a contract have, of course, no statutory force unlike Acts of Parliament. In addition, as explained above, the carrier cannot rely on them in

[10] *e.g. Levison* v. *Patent Steam Cleaning Company* [1978] Q.B. 69.
[11] [1922] A.C. 178.
[12] At p. 188
[13] *Weiss* v. *Northern Traffic* (1919) 1 Lloyd's Rep. 241.
[14] The Freight Transport Association have produced a most valuable guide to the R.H.A. 1982 Conditions of Carriage.

various circumstances, *e.g.* where he has unjustifiably deviated (see 1.50). Also many of their provisions can be challenged under the "reasonableness test" in the Unfair Contract Terms Act 1977, (see, 1.45). There must, of course, be reasonable notice[28] of the Conditions, and exclusion clauses will be interpreted *"contra proferentem,"* *i.e.* against the carrier if they are ambiguous (see, 1.43-1.44).

1.55 **No liability for loss and damage under clause 9(1)**

There are three schemes of liability under the R.H.A. 1982 Conditions. The first, under clause 9(1), is to the effect that if the "Trader" so agrees in writing the carrier is not liable at all for anything! By analogy with cases under the now repealed Railway and Canal Traffic Act 1854, it is suggested that this provision is almost certainly bound to fail the "reasonableness test" in the Unfair Contract Terms Act 1977, and be declared ineffective. The 1854 Act, similarly required all contracts of carriage by railway to be in writing and "just and reasonable." There are only two circumstances where clause 9(1) would perhaps be considered "reasonable." The first is where the customer had unwisely insisted on carriage subject to clause 9(1) himself because he had his own "goods in transit" insurance policy.[15] The second would be where the customer was offered the "fair alternative" of carriage under clause 9(1) or under 9(2) and is offered an "inducement" to agree to 9(1) in the form of a reduction in freight rates. So in the leading House of Lords decision on the 1854 Act of *Peek* v. *South Staffordshire Railway*[16] Blackburn J. said

> "a condition exempting the carriers wholely from liability for the neglect and default of their servants is prima facie unreasonable. I do not go as far as to say that it is necessarily in every case unreasonable and void . . . if (a carrier) offers in the alternative to carry on terms that he shall have no liability at all and holds forth as an inducement a reduction of the price below that which would be reasonable remuneration for carrying at owner's risk, . . . I think that a condition thus offered may be reasonable enough."

1.56 **Liability for negligent loss or damage under clause 9(2)(i)**

This clause deals with liability for loss, damage or misdelivery in relation to animals and a list of "valuables" not dissimilar to those in the Carriers Act 1830. Note that the carrier is only liable if three requirements are satisfied. The first two requiring the written agreement of the carrier and a written agreement to reimburse any extra costs to him are exemption clauses for the purposes of the Unfair Contract Terms Act 1977.[17] They might well fail the "reasonableness test." In any event a carrier who did not enforce these requirements as to writing in practice would be deemed to have waived compliance with them and would be "estopped" (*i.e.* prevented) from relying on them.[18] Say that a carrier agreed orally to carry animals and did not

[15] As in the dubious decision of *Coupar Transport* v. *Smith's (Acton)* [1959] 1 Lloyd's Rep. 369.

[16] (1862-1863) 10 H. & C. 472, 511.

[17] See 1.56.

[18] See *Barrett Brothers Taxis* v. *Davies* [1966] 1 W.L.R. 1334.

require the customer to sign anything, the carrier could not avoid liability by relying on clause 9(2)(i)(a) or (b). The third requirement is that the carrier must be negligent.

Strict liabilty under clause 9(2)(ii) **1.57**

Under this scheme the carrier undertakes strict liability similar to that of a common carrier with an extended list of excepted perils. The perils are almost identical to those in clause 5A of the British Rail Conditions (see, 1.60-1.65 below). Although the conditions are silent on the point it is submitted by analogy with the position of common carriers and carriers by sea[19] that the burden of bringing himself within the perils falls on the carrier. In addition the Conditions do not deal with the position where the negligence is the cause of the loss as opposed to negligence which fails to minimise the loss. On similar reasoning, however, it seems that the carrier cannot rely on the perils if his negligence is the cause of the loss/damage[20] (*e.g.* he has negligently driven his lorry into a riotous area).

The perils themselves are discussed in detail below at 1.62 in the context of the British Rail Conditions. A close examination of the perils will however reveal some minor differences in the wording of perils (d) and (j) between the two sets of Conditions. These differences are only of minimal importance.

It is rather difficult to interpret clause 17 of the R.H.A. Conditions in the light of clause 9. Presumably, however, clause 9 deals with loss or damage and clause 17 with total non-performance. It may amount to an exemption cause for the purposes of the Unfair Contract Terms Act 1977, and be subject to the "reasonableness test"[21] if, for example, a carrier were unable to deliver goods because of a strike and tried to rely on clause 17 as an excuse for not making alternative arrangements for delivery for the benefit of his customer.

Liability for delay **1.58**

There is in the R.H.A. Conditions rather surprisingly no provision expressly dealing with delay except clause 11(2)(a). This deals with the limit of liability for delay if the carrier makes a declaration of "special interest" if an agreed time limit for delivery has been exceeded. It does not deal with the grounds of liability as opposed to the limit of liability where there is such a declaration. Presumably therefore the carrier's liability for delay must be the same as discussed in 1.37 above, *i.e.* the carrier is only liable for delays caused by his negligence. Clause 9 is not relevant here because it only covers loss, damage and misdelivery and not delay. What would be the position if the customer has made no declaration of "special interest?" clause 11(2) limits liability for "consequential loss or damage, however arising" to the carriage charges. No doubt the draftsman of the Conditions intended the words "however arising" to include claims for delay although it is doubtful whether it is well enough worded to achieve this. If liability for delay, where there is no declaration of

[19] See 1.28 and 5.41.
[20] *Gill* v. *Midland, Scottish and London Railway* (1873) L.R. 8 Q.B. 186, 196.
[21] See 1.45.

interest, is not covered by clause 11 then the common law applies and, if negligent, the carrier is liable without any financial limit on the principles discussed in 1.39-1.42 above. Let us presume however that clause 11(2) does cover consequential loss arising from delay then does it also cover deterioration to the goods arising from delay in delivery? Deterioration is certainly not "consequential loss." Could a deterioration caused by delay amount to "damage" for the purposes of clause 11(1)(a)?[22]

1.59 **Limits of liability**

The limit of liability under clause 11(1) for loss, misdelivery or damage is £800 per ton. At first sight this appears a very low limit of liability and it certainly has not changed since the R.H.A. 1961 Conditions. It might seem likely to fail the "reasonableness test" in the Unfair Contract Terms Act 1977,[23] especially where "valuables" were carried under clause 9(2)(i). However clause 11(1)(b)(iii) allows for the limit of liability to be increased where there is a declaration of value and the payment of a surcharge. This makes the clause much more reasonable and it is in fact based on Article 24 of The Convention on the Contract for the International Carriage of Goods by Road. "C.M.R. Convention" implemented into English law by the Carriage of Goods by Road Act 1965.[24] It is hardly likely that a contractual clause based on a provision in an Act of Parliament would be declared unreasonable. The only dubious part of this sub-clause is the requirement for seven days written notice to the carrier. This might be considered unreasonable. The limit of liability for delay (if any) where there has been no declaration of special interest under clause 11(2)(a) has been discussed in 1.58.

British Rail Conditions of Carriage

1.60 **Carriage at owner's risk, clause 5B**

British Rail, as the result of section 43 of the Transport Act 1962, are no longer common carriers. Their Conditions are no longer subject to control by any tribunal and operate purely on the same contractual basis as do the R.H.A. Conditions discussed in 1.54-1.59. For historical reasons, however, the British Rail Conditions of Carriage evolved as a result of the previous status of railways as common carriers and the now repealed Railway and Canal Traffic Act 1854. This Act led the railways to offer customers the choice of having their goods carried at "Owner's Risk" or "Company's Risk" (now Board's Risk) at different freight rates. These two schemes of liability still appear purely as a matter of contract in the current British Rail Conditions. A copy of the Conditions appears in Appendix 1.B.

[22] In *Allday* v. *Great Western Railway* (1864) 5 B. & S. 903 a deterioration in the condition of animals due to a delay was held to be an "injury" for the purposes of the now repealed Railway and Canal Traffic Act 1854.

[23] See 1.45.

[24] See 3.66.

If goods are carried at owner's risk under clause 5B then the Board is only liable for partial loss, damage, misdelivery or delay upon proof of "wilful misconduct." Even at owner's risk total loss of the goods or loss of a separate package are covered by clause 5A (*i.e.* Board's Risk, see, 1.62 below). This point should be born in mind when examining some of the older cases as, at that time, all loss or damage was covered by clause 5B when goods were carried at owner's risk. *It is important to note in the context of domestic carriage by land that "wilful misconduct" is not a doctrine of law applying to all contracts of carriage by land.* It is a purely contractual provision that has no application to other contracts of carriage.

Wilful misconduct means an act of deliberate or reckless wrongdoing without care for the consequences.[25] Negligence even of the grossest nature is not sufficient.[26] Examples of wilful misconduct include:

(1) Knowingly failing to measure a large load in accordance with a railway company's own regulations with the result that it is damaged by hitting a bridge.[27]
(2) The "blacking" of the plaintiff's goods by railway company employees in furtherance of a trade dispute.[28]
(3) A theft by employees of goods entrusted to them by the carrier.[29]
(4) Delivery of goods to a person called Jarvis when they were consigned to a Mr. Jeeves.[30]

The test of wilful misconduct is subjective not objective. The fact that any reasonable person would realise that the misconduct was likely to cause loss or damage is not enough.[31] The individual responsible for the loss or damage must personally appreciate the wrongful nature of his acts. It is not even sufficient to prove that some other railway employee appreciated that a mode of carriage was dangerous or unsuitable. Thus in *Forder* v. *Great Western Railway*[32] the plaintiff complained that a consignment of sheepskins had been damaged by being placed on a bedding of wood chips and he was assured by the station master at Winchester that it would not happen again. Nevertheless exactly the same thing happened to a subsequent consignment. The court held that the plaintiff's action in respect of the second consignment failed as he could not prove that the actual persons who loaded his sheepskins knew that wood chips were likely to damage them.

In one recent case[33] concerning the Institute of Freight Forwarders Conditions the court had to consider the meaning of the similar

[25] *Graham* v. *Belfast & Northern Counties Railway* [1901] 2 Ir.R. 13.
[26] *Lewis* v. *Great Western Railway* [1877] 3 Q.B. 195; *Hartstoke Fruiterers* v. *London, Midland and Scottish Railway* [1942] 2 All E.R. 488.
[27] *Bastable* v. *North British Railway* [1912] S.C. 555.
[28] *Young* v. *British Transport Commission* [1955] 2 Q.B. 177.
[29] *Rustenberg* v. *South African Airways* [1979] 1 Lloyd's Rep. 19.
[30] *Hoare* v. *Great Western Railway* (1877) 37 L.T. 186.
[31] See *Horabin* v. *B.O.A.C.* [1952] 2 Lloyd's Rep. 450, 487.
[32] [1905] 2 K.B. 532.
[33] *Swiss Bank Corporation* v. *Brinks Mat* [1986] Q.B. 853.

provision "wilful default." There is no doubt that this expression means exactly the same as wilful misconduct.[34] The court held that "wilful default" meant such default in the course and scope of a servant's employment. The result was that the carriers were not liable for a theft that was caused by one of their employees giving details about valuable consignments to a gang of thieves. This was "wilful default" but was not default in the scope of his employment because the goods stolen were not actually entrusted to the dishonest servant.[35] This decision is dubious because there seem to be other cases[36] where railways carrying at owner's risk have been held liable for the acts of servants who do not seem to have been acting in the course of their employment.

1.61 The burden of proving wilful misconduct under clause 5B

The person who alleges wilful misconduct must prove it. Thus the mere fact that goods have disappeared or have been damaged in transit is not evidence of wilful misconduct. This is so even where the railway refuse to reply to queries as to what has happened to the goods or make any attempt to explain the loss.[37] If however on the balance of probabilities theft by an unknown railway employee is proved that is sufficient. Thus in *H.C. Smith* v. *Midland Railway*[38] a parcel was opened during a journey, part of its contents stolen and then it was skilfully resealed to hide the theft. The court concluded that a theft by a railway employee was most likely because only an employee was likely to have the opportunity or time to commit such a theft. Thus on the balance of probabilities wilful misconduct was proved. Note that it was not proved that the goods were entrusted to the dishonest employee.

1.62 Clause 5B and the Unfair Contract Terms Act 1977

Clause 5B is quite likely to fail the "reasonableness test" in the 1977 Act,[39] unless the customer is offered a reduction in freight rates in return for agreeing to carriage at "owner's risk" under 5B and is also offered "the fair alternative" of carriage at Board's Risk subject to clause 5A.[40]

1.63 Loss or damage at board's risk, clause 5A

Under clause 5A British Rail undertake strict liability for loss, damage or misdelivery similar to that of a common carrier subject to a list of extended perils. In addition British Rail remain liable where they have not taken all reasonable care of the goods under clause

[34] *H.C. Smith* v. *Midland Railway* (1914) L.J.K.B. 868.

[35] See 1.18.

[36] *H.C. Smith* v. *Midland Railway* (1914) L.J.K.B. 868; *Young* v. *British Transport Commission* [1955] 2 Q.B. 177.

[37] *H.C. Smith* v. *Great Western Railway* [1922] 1 A.C. 178.

[38] *H.C. Smith* v. *Midland Railway*, see n. 36 above.

[39] See 1.45; *Waldron-Kelly* v. *British Rail* [1981] C.L.Y. 303 and *Wight* v. *British Rail* [1983] C.L.Y. 424.

[40] This was the approach of the courts to the now repealed Railway and Canal Traffic Act 1854 which required contracts to be both in writing and "just and reasonable." See *Peek* v. *North Staffordshire Railway* (1862-1863) 10 H.L.C. 473.

5A(1)(i). They exempt all liability if the trader has been fraudulent (clause 5A(1)(ii)). The burden of proving that the loss or damage was caused by the excepted peril falls on the carrier. British Rail are thus in clause 5A actually undertaking a heavier liability than that imposed upon them at common law as private carriers.[41] Therefore it seems that these perils are not exemption clauses and should not on the whole be interpreted against them. It is suggested that the *contra proferentem* rule[42] has no application in this context. The perils are:

(a) Act of God. This peril was discussed in the context of common carriers in 1.25 above.

(b) War, etc. "War" perhaps includes wars between two foreign countries. Invasion perhaps includes a "peaceful occupation" of British territory. The last words concerning seizure by local authorities, etc., presumably from the context, only cover seizure in time of war or public emergency. This defence is wider than the common law defence of Acts of the Queen's enemies but probably still does not include most terrorist activities.

(c) Seizure by legal process. This possibly covers such things as seizure by the police in the belief that the goods are stolen or by a court bailiff.

(d) Act or omission of the trader. Most such omissions would fall under perils (f) and (g) anyhow but failure to give proper instructions as to special care required for valuables would be covered by this peril.

(e) Inherent vice, etc. This longwinded exception adds little to the common carrier's excepted peril of "inherent vice" discussed in 1.28 above.

(f) Insufficient or improper packing. This is really a form of inherent vice or "act or omission of the trader." If the Board accept badly packed goods under protest they are probably not estopped, *i.e.* prevented, from pleading the defence.[43]

(g) Insufficient labelling, etc. This peril seems superfluous in the light of peril (d).

(h) Riot, etc. "Strikes," etc., probably include the acts of British Rail's own employees.[44] Do the words "from whatever cause" include a strike caused by British Rail's own negligence? Probably not as that interpretation would arguably clash with British Rail's duty under clause 5A(1)(i) to use "all reasonable . . . care. . . . "

(i) Consignee not accepting delivery within a reasonable time. This seems superfluous in the light of peril (d).

[41] See 1.33-1.35.
[42] See 1.44.
[43] See 1.92.
[44] See *Young* v. *British Transport Commission* [1955] 2 Q.B. 177.

1.64 **Liability for delay under clause 5A**

Under clause 5A(ii) British Rail are liable for any delay in delivering the goods that is caused by their negligence on the same basis as they are at common law. See, 1.37 above.

1.65 **Limits of liability**

As with all attempts to exempt or limit liability for loss, damage or delay, the British Rail exclusion clauses are subject to the "reasonableness test" in the Unfair Contract Terms Act 1977.[45] By virtue of clause 6(1) all forms of liability are limited to a maximum of £2,000 per metric tonne and to a minimum of £20. This is of course higher than the limit in the R.H.A. Conditions discussed in 1.59 above. However the British Rail Conditions, unlike those of the R.H.A., do not give the "Trader" the opportunity to increase these limits by means of a declaration of value and payment of a surcharge. This makes them, in a suitable case, more susceptible to challenge under the 1977 Act. In addition British Rail attempt in clause 6(2) to exempt all liability for consequential loss. It is not entirely clear if this provision covers consequential loss arising from delay as opposed to such loss arising from the loss of, damage to, or misdelivery of the goods.

TRANSIT AND DELIVERY

1.66 **Commencement of transit**

A carrier's liability as carrier only lasts during transit. Thus if he is a common carrier he is only strictly liable for loss or damage during transit and not once transit has ceased. Transit at common law commences when goods are delivered to the carrier and accepted by him for the purpose of carriage. This includes an acceptance by the carrier's servants or agents acting within their apparent authority. So it has been held that a porter at a railway station wearing the railway company's uniform has apparent authority to accept passengers' luggage.[46] Transit does not mean "moving" so goods can be in transit while they are in the carrier's depot[47] or on a parked lorry.[48]

1.67 **End of transit**

Transit ceases when the goods are delivered or where there is a good tender of delivery. Tender of delivery would occur, for example, if the carrier arrived at the consignee's address during normal business hours but through no fault of his was unable to effect delivery. It seems that it is presumed to be the carrier's duty to deliver to the consignee's residence or place of business,[49] but basically this is a question of interpreting the contract. If the contract is one under which the goods are to be kept "till called for" then transit ceases a

[45] See 1.45.
[46] *Sloane* v. *London and South Western Railway* (1919) 35 T.L.R. 276.
[47] *Sadler* v. *Meredith* [1963] 2 Lloyd's Rep. 293.
[48] Compare *Tomlinson* v. *Hepburn* [1966] A.C. 457.
[49] *Hyde* v. *Trent Navigation* (1793) 5 T.R. 429.

reasonable time after they have reached their destination.[50] If the carrier knows the consignee's address is he under a duty to tell him that the goods have arrived? The law on this point is not entirely clear[51] but it seems that the answer is "yes." In any event it is in the carrier's interest to do so. This is because, if the consignee knows the goods have arrived, what will be a reasonable time to collect them will perhaps be shorter than if he does not know. The shorter the period of transit, the shorter is the period of the carrier's liability as carrier.[52] Transit for the purpose of the standard Conditions is defined in clause 6 of the R.H.A. and clause 10 of the British Rail Conditions.[53] Note particularly clause 10(2) of the British Rail Conditions concerning "suspension of transit."

What is a good delivery? 1.68

Once the goods are delivered or where there is a good tender of delivery[54] the carrier has performed his obligations under the contract and transit ceases. In this context a delivery in the normal and reasonable course of the carrier's business is a good delivery.[55] If the delivery is not in the normal and reasonable course of the carrier's business then he will be liable to the owner of the goods. Thus in *Carlos* v. *City and Suburban Parcels Delivery*[56] the defendants attempted to deliver a parcel at the plaintiff's house but nobody was there to receive it. They therefore placed the parcel on the corner of the verandah. When the plaintiff returned home some of the contents were missing. The court held that this was not a delivery in the normal and reasonable course of the carrier's business and the defendants were therefore liable for a negligent misdelivery.

Delivery to a fraudulent consignee, title to sue 1.69

If the consignee has defrauded the consignor and the carrier delivers to the fraudulent consignee, has the consignor any remedy against the carrier, for example by suing him for the tort of conversion? The cases on this point are mainly old, cannot be reconciled and many appear to be wrongly decided or decided in favour of the correct person for the wrong reasons![57] It is suggested that the law is

[50] *Chapman* v. *Great Western Railway* (1880) L.R. 5 Q.B.D. 278.

[51] *Golden* v. *Manning* (1773) 3 Wils. 429 and *Mitchell* v. *Lancashire and Yorkshire Railway* (1875) L.R. 10 Q.B. 256 suggest that there is such a duty. However there is no such duty in carriage by sea. *Houlder* v. *General Steam Navigation* (1862) 3 F. & F. 170.

[52] This is very important if the carrier is subject to strict liability for loss or damage as opposed to liability only for negligence. Such liability would arise if he were a common carrier or if he undertook a similar strict liability by contract, as do British Rail in clause 5A of their Conditions. See 1.63.

[53] See Appendices 1.A and 1.B.

[54] See *Heugh* v. *London and North Western Railway* (1870) L.R. 5 Ex. 51.

[55] Compare the bailment case of *Beckar* v. *Lavender* (1946) 62 T.L.R. 504.

[56] (1921) 15 Q.J.P. 107 (Australia).

[57] With the exception of *Egan* v. *Great Northern Railway* (1879) 14 I.L.T. 28, discussed below, all the cases are open to criticism. They are *Duff* v. *Budd* (1823) 3 B. & B. 177; *Stephenson* v. *Hart* (1828) 4 Bing. 476; *Mc'Kean* v. *Mc'Ivor* (1870) L.R. 6 Ex.; *Heugh* v. *London and North Western Railway* (1879) L.R. 5 Ex. 51; *Hoare* v. *Great Western Railway* (1877) 37 L.T. 186. For a full discussion of these cases see Chapter 15 of the Second Edition of *Bailment* (1989) by N. Palmer.

(or ought to be!) as follows. Firstly, the consignor must prove he is the owner of the goods. As explained in 1.13, above, a consignor cannot usually sue a carrier in tort or in contract because he is not usually the owner of the consigned goods. The property in the goods has passed to the buyer and the seller cannot sue in contract, tort or bailment. Even if the consignee has obtained the goods by fraud the same principles apply. A contract of sale obtained by misrepresentation is *voidable* not *void*. If B obtains goods from A by pretending to be honest and creditworthy or by ordering them in the name of a fictitious person then the buyer, B, gets a *voidable* title to the goods. In other words they belong to B until A finds out he has been defrauded and repudiates the contract with B. So merely because A has been defrauded, that gives him no right to sue the carrier. A only has title to the goods and therefore the right to sue the carrier if the contract of sale between himself and B is null and void for a unilateral mistake of identity.

In order for the sale to be void A must prove that he intended to deal with a definite existing person other than B. A mistake as to the attributes (*e.g.* solvency, honesty or even the name) of the buyer is not enough. If the consignor can prove that he intended to deal with some identifiable definite person other than the fraudulent buyer, then, as owner of the goods, he can sue the carrier but he must also prove a misdelivery (see, 1.68 and 1.70). Thus in *Egan* v. *Great Northern Railway*[58] Boylan fraudulently ordered goods in the name of his neighbour, O'Reilly from the plaintiff Egan. Egan sent them *via* the defendants addressed to O'Reilly to be collected from Gormanstown station. Boylan, however, dishonestly managed to obtain possession of them there. The court held that Egan intended to contract with O'Reilly and O'Reilly only and not with Boylan and therefore Egan remained the owner of the goods and could sue the railway company for a misdelivery to Boylan rather than O'Reilly as agreed.

1.70 Delivery to a fraudulent consignee, misdelivery by carrier

Even if the plaintiff has title to sue he must also prove a misdelivery by the carrier, in other words a delivery other than one in the normal and reasonable course of the carrier's business.[59] The difficulty for the consignor/owner here is that, as explained in 1.08-1.11 above, the carrier is entitled to presume that the named consignee is the owner of the goods and therefore it is suggested the carrier is employed "for the purpose of obeying his directions respecting them."[60] Also, as explained at 1.75-1.76 below, the consignee has, perhaps, the right, as presumed owner of the goods, to change the place of destination. Therefore merely because a fraudulent consignee, in order to facilitate his fraud on the consignor, asks the carrier to change the place of delivery and the carrier obeys that instruction, that alone it is

[58] (1879) 14 I.L.T. 28, compare *Chicago Railway* v. *Flanders* 56 Fed.R. (2d) 114 (1932) (U.S.A.) which strongly supports the views expressed in the text above.

[59] See 1.68.

[60] *Scothorn* v. *South Staffordshire Railway* (1853) 8 Ex. 341.

submitted is no evidence of a breach of duty by the carrier.[61] In addition it has even been held that where the consignee is NOT the owner the carrier should still obey his instructions because "the contract is to deliver the goods to the consignee at the place named by the consignor unless the consignee directs them to be delivered at a different place."[62] It is suggested therefore that in these circumstances the carrier should only be liable to the consignor for delivering to the named consignee and/or in accordance with his instructions if both[63] the following factors are present. Firstly the circumstances must be such that it should be obvious to the carrier that the consignee is not the true owner.[64] The carrier is entitled to presume that the consignee is the owner and is entitled to delivery.[65] Secondly the circumstances must be such as suggest to a prudent carrier that the consignee is defrauding the consignor. Even if the consignee does not appear to be the owner, the contract is still to deliver to him.[66] It would not be a delivery in the normal and reasonable course of the carrier's business, however, if the carrier had every reason to believe that the consignee was not the owner and was also defrauding the consignor.[67] If the consignee does not appear to be the owner and does appear dishonest then the carrier should make investigations as to title[68] before delivering. If he does not then he may be liable to the defrauded owner/consignor.

Although a consignment note is not a document of title,[69] it may be that, where goods are "to be called for" by the consignee, the carrier may send him a document saying the goods have arrived. In this case the document may be one authorising delivery to its holder as a result of section 1 of the Factors Act 1889, and section 61 of the Sale of Goods Act 1979.[70] It would follow that the carrier would not be liable if the document came into the hands of a thief and the carrier delivered the goods to him.[71]

[61] This is one of the many reasons why the well known case of *Stephenson* v. *Hart* (1828) 4 Bing. 476 is probably wrongly decided, but see n. 67 below.

[62] *London and North West Railway* v. *Bartlett* (1863) 7 H. & N. 400.

[63] As in *Egan* v. *Great Northern Railway* (1879) 14 I.L.T. 28 discussed at 1.69 above.

[64] With the exception of *Hoare* v. *Great Western Railway* (1877) 37 L.T. 186 (where goods were sent to one Jeeves but were delivered instead to a man called Jarvis) it is difficult to say that any of the cases noted in n. 57 above entirely satisfy this requirement.

[65] *Cork Distilleries* v. *Great Southern and Western Railway* (1874) L.R. 7 H.L. 269, discussed at 1.69.

[66] As where a carrier is asked to deliver goods to someone who is hiring rather than buying them or has agreed to buy them but does not yet own them, as in *London and North West Railway* v. *Bartlett* (1861) 7 H. & N. 400.

[67] It is just arguable that *Stephenson* v. *Hart* (1828) 4 Bing. 476 can be defended on this grounds as regards the misdelivery point as the circumstances were perhaps suspicious. Nevertheless the case cannot be supported because the plaintiff was not the owner of the goods and had no right to sue. See the excellent dissenting judgement of Gasalee J.

[68] It is not a conversion to refuse to deliver while you investigate title to the goods. *Lee* v. *Bayes* (1856) 18 C.B. 599; *Clayton* v. *Le Roy* [1911] 2 K.B. 1039.

[69] See 1.10.

[70] See *Official Assignee of Madras* v. *Mercantile Bank of India* [1935] A.C. 53.

[71] See *Heugh* v. *London and North Western Railway* (1870) L.R. 5 Ex. 51.

1.71 **Liability after transit at common law**

Once transit, either at common law, as defined above, or in the Conditions, has ceased or been suspended then the carrier has no right to return the goods immediately to the consignor but rather must keep them in a reasonable place for the convenience of the owner.[72] If the carrier loses or damages the goods after transit then if, like British Rail (clause 11), he has incorporated his Warehousing Conditions into the Conditions of carriage then they will obviously govern his liability.[73] Similarly if by the express or implied agreement of the owner the carrier is charging warehousing fees then his liability is that of a bailee for reward.[74] The difficult point arises if the carrier is not charging for warehousing. The carrier has, perhaps, only agreed to be a bailee of the goods during the period of transit, not indefinitely. However, at least for a reasonable time once transit has ceased he must, as a person who was at least originally a bailee for reward, take reasonable care of the goods.[75] In other words he is liable as a bailee. In *Mc'Kinnon* v. *Acadian Lines*[76] the defendants were held liable for a negligent misdelivery of the plaintiff's luggage to a thief after transit has ceased. The court held that the carriers were liable as warehousemen, *i.e.* bailees for reward.

1.72 **Liability after transit, R.H.A. and British Rail Conditions**

Clause 11 of the British Rail Conditions incorporates their Warehousing Conditions for most goods where transit has ceased or been suspended. However they exempt all liability for goods for which they have given notice they have no accommodation (clause 11(1)(b)). The R.H.A. in clause 9(3) of their Conditions purport to exempt all liability for loss or damage after transit has ceased but, as explained above, a carrier is liable for negligence as a bailee for reward once transit has ceased so one could presumably challenge this provision under the "reasonableness test" in the Unfair Contract Terms Act 1977.[77]

Interruption of Transit and Change of Destination

1.73 **Stoppage in transit, when exercisable**

Even though usually the ownership of goods passes to the buyer upon delivery to the carrier[78] the law grants an unpaid seller the anomalous right of stoppage in transit. This right is codified in sections 44-46 of the Sale of Goods Act 1979, and the sections are reproduced in Appendix 1.C. In order for an unpaid seller to stop

[72] *Crouch* v. *Great Western Railway* (1874) L.R. 9 Ex. 86.

[73] If he does not exempt liability he will become liable for negligent loss or damage as a bailee for reward. See 1.03, 1.17 and 1.33

[74] See *Mitchell* v. *Lancashire and Yorkshire Railway* (1875) L.R. 10 Q.B. 256.

[75] See *Heugh* v. *London and North Western Railway* (1870) L.R. 5 Ex. 51.

[76] (1978) 81 D.L.R. 484 (Canada).

[77] See 1.45.

[78] See 1.05-1.07.

goods in transit three conditions must be satisfied. Firstly the seller must be unpaid. Secondly the buyer must be insolvent, in other words he must have "ceased to pay his debts in the ordinary course of business, or he cannot pay his debts as they become due" (section 61(4) of the Sale of Goods Act 1979). Thirdly the goods must still be in transit. Transit has been discussed generally at 1.66-1.67 and is defined for the purpose of stoppage in transit in section 45(1). If the buyer interrupts transit and obtains possession of the goods then the right of stoppage in transit is lost[79] (section 45(2)). Likewise if the buyer changes the destination then the right of stoppage is lost.

> "If the goods are not in the hands of the carrier by reason either of the terms of the contract or of the directions of the purchaser to the vendor, but are *in transitu* afterwards in consequence of fresh directions given by the purchaser for a *new transit* then such transit is not part of the original transit and the right to stop is lost. So also if the purchaser gives orders that the goods shall be sent to a particular place, there to be kept till he gives fresh orders as to their destination to a new carrier, the original transit is at an end when they have reached that place."[80] (emphasis added).

Where the goods have arrived at the destination and the carrier acknowledges to the buyer that he is holding them on behalf of the buyer then the right to stop in transit is lost (section 45(3)). The right is also lost if the carrier wrongfully refuses to deliver the goods to the buyer (section 45(6)) but is not lost if the buyer rejects the goods (section 45(6)).

Stoppage in transit, how exercised 1.74

Section 46 deals with the method of exercising stoppage in transit. To be effective, notice must reach the person in possession of the goods before transit ends. The seller can give fresh directions to the carrier but must pay any expenses involved. He must also satisfy any common law lien[81] that the carrier may have for unpaid freight. A general lien clause[82] in the carrier's conditions will only bind the seller if he is either a party to the contract of carriage, which is unlikely, see 1.10, or if he has notice of the clause.

Change of destination, the position in "two party" contracts 1.75

Apart from the statutory right of stoppage in transit discussed above does the consignor or alternatively the consignee have the right to interrupt transit and demand the goods from the carrier or alternatively require the carrier to take the goods to a destination other than that originally agreed? If the consignor contracts to have goods delivered to himself at the place of destination then he can recover the goods from the carrier at any stage of the journey or by mutual agreement have them delivered elsewhere. Thus in *Scothorn*

[79] See *Foster* v. *Frampton* (1826) 6 B. & C. 107; *Reddall* v. *Union Castle Mail Steamship Company* (1915) 84 L.J.K.B. 360.
[80] *Bethell* v. *Clark* (1888) 20 Q.B.D. 615, 617, *per* Brett L.J.
[81] See 1.110-1.111.
[82] See 1.114.

v. *South Staffordshire Railway*[83] the plaintiff contracted to have his goods carried to the East India Dock in London. During transit it was agreed that the goods should instead be delivered at no extra charge at the Bell Wharf. Instead they were delivered as originally agreed and lost. Baron Martin said that the owner of goods "is entitled to receive them back at any period of the transit when they can be got at" and the carriers were held liable for not delivering as per the revised agreement. So where the consignor/consignee are the same person he can demand the goods back during the journey. Whether he can demand that they be delivered to somewhere other than the original destination as of right as opposed to by agreement with the carrier is unclear.[84] If the owner exercises this right of taking possession during transit then he is not entitled to a return of any of the freight charges.[85]

1.76 **Change of destination, the position in "three party" contracts**

If the consignor and consignee are two different persons then the position is rather more difficult. If the consignee is the owner of the goods then he has the right to obtain possession of the goods during transit. Thus in *Cork Distilleries* v. *Great Southern and Western Railway*[86] the plaintiffs consigned a cask of "bonded" whisky to be delivered to the buyers at a bonded customs warehouse. The buyers/owners of the whisky obtained it from the railway company during transit and the plaintiffs forfeited the bond (*i.e.* they had to pay the excise duty on the whisky) and sued the carriers for the loss. The House of Lords held they were not liable as the buyers were entitled to delivery "at any . . . place at which they . . . preferred to receive the goods."[87] The court said there was nothing to stop the plaintiffs from making a separate contract[88] with the carriers to deliver at a named place only[89] but that they had not done so.

Even if the consignor is the owner during the transit then still the consignee has the right to obtain delivery (and possibly alter the destination) during transit. This is because, even if the consignee is not the owner of the goods, the carrier is entitled to presume that he is[90] and because the contract is to deliver in accordance with the consignee's instructions whether he is the owner or not.[91] Presumably before a carrier redelivers to a consignor, other than one exercising a right of stoppage in transit,[92] he should make extensive enquiries

[83] (1853) 8 Ex. 341.

[84] See 1.76 below.

[85] *Troy* v. *Eastern Company* (1921) 37 T.L.R. 837.

[86] (1874) L.R. 7 H.L. 269.

[87] Lord Cairns, p. 278.

[88] Lord Cairns, pp. 279-280.

[89] If they had done so then, even though they were not owners of the goods and not principal parties to the contract of carriage, there would have been a separate collateral contract between themselves and the carriers under which they could have recovered damages for reasonably foreseeable economic loss. Compare *Mead* v. *South Eastern Railway* (1870) 18 W.R. 735 discussed at 1.14.

[90] See 1.12.

[91] *London and North Western Railway* v. *Bartlett* (1861) 7 H. & N. 400.

[92] See 1.73-1.74.

before giving the goods to him because he is entitled to presume that the consignee is owner rather than the consignor. They redeliver to a consignor at their peril.[93]

It is unclear whether a consignee/owner has the right to demand that the goods be delivered to a destination other than that originally named other than by agreement with the carrier though some statements in cases appear to support the view that he can.[94] For example Brett L.J. seems to recognise this right in the passage quoted from *Bethell* v. *Clark*[95] at 1.73, above. Presumably, on the principles discussed above, the consignor/non-owner on the other hand has no such right. Perhaps the owner has the right to alter the destination if the new destination is convenient for the carrier and the owner is prepared to pay any extra charges involved.[96]

SUBCONTRACTING

Liability of the first carrier 1.77

Of course there is no automatic right to subcontract the carriage of goods. In fact unauthorised subcontracting may amount to the tort of conversion or an unjustified deviation.[97] However almost all modern Conditions of Carriage grant the carrier the right to subcontract all or part of the carriage to a subcontractor.[98] One difficult question arising here is discussed in 2.03-2.06 in the context of freight forwarders. It is the question as to whether the first carrier remains liable for any breach of his contract by his subcontractor. Although the R.H.A. Conditions are not explicit on this point there is little doubt that carriers using the R.H.A. Conditions remain liable for breaches by their subcontractors.[99] The same comments apply to British Rail except where they subcontract the goods to carriers by water as opposed to other modes of carriage. Where they subcontract to carriers by water then British Rail, under clause 12(2) of their Conditions, act merely as agents[1] and exempt all liability for loss or damage to goods.

Liability of the subcontractor and "Himalaya" clauses 1.78

Say that A contracts to have his goods carried by C and C subcontracts all or part of the carriage to D. If the subcontractor, D, damages or loses the goods through his negligence then as a

[93] Just as they pay him damages at their peril. The consignee is presumed to be the owner of the goods and is presumed to have the right of control over them. See 1.12.

[94] *e.g.* Pollock C.B. in *London and North Western Railway* v. *Bartlett* (1861) 7 H. & N. 400, 407-408.

[95] (1888) 20 Q.B.D. 615.

[96] This view would be particularly tenable if the carrier was a common carrier and the new destination was one to which he had held himself out as being prepared to carry to. See *Anthony & Jones & Co.* v. *New York Central, etc., Ry.* 119 N.E. 90 (1918) (U.S.A.) and also 1.23.

[97] *Garnham, Harris & Elton* v. *Alfred W. Ellis Transport* [1967] 1 W.L.R. 940.

[98] See clause 2(1) of the British Rail Conditions (Appendix 1.B) and clause 2(2) of the R.H.A. Conditions (Appendix 1.A).

[99] This seems implicit in clause 2 of the Conditions which are reproduced in Appendix 1.A.

[1] They must, as agents, select the subcontractors with due care and skill. *Gillette Industries* v. *Martin* [1966] 1 Lloyd's Rep. 570.

sub-bailee[2] he is liable either for a breach of duty as a bailee or for the tort of negligence to the owner of the goods, A. The danger in this situation is that A, instead of suing the first carrier (C), will sue the subcontracor (D) in tort or bailment and D will be unable to rely on either his own or C's conditions of carriage to exclude liability.[3] He will, at first sight, be unable to rely on them because of the doctrine of privity of contract. As the result of this doctrine only the parties to the contract can rely on any exclusion clauses in the contract. There is privity of contract between the owner of the goods (A) and the first carrier (C) and, in turn, between C and the subcontractor (D), but there is no privity between A and D. D may limit his liability under his conditions of carriage to, for example, £800 per ton but if he is carrying goods worth £10,000 per ton he and his insurers will be held fully liable for that amount to A if A sues him in tort or bailment.

Unsurprisingly many legal arguments have been put forward to try to get round this unfortunate result. Many of them depend on the inclusion in the conditions of the first carrier (C) of a "Himalaya" clause. Examples of such clauses are clause 2(3) of the R.H.A. Conditions and clause 2(2) of the British Rail Conditions.[4] In effect these clauses attempt to introduce separate collateral contracts between A, the owner of the goods and all the servants, agents and subcontractors of C, the first carrier. By virtue of such alleged privity of contract it is argued that D, the subcontractor, can limit or exempt liability by virtue of C's conditions of carriage. Whether such clauses or other legal arguments can overcome the doctrine of privity of contract and allow D to rely on either his own or C's conditions of carriage is discussed in 1.79-1.85, below.

1.79 **The vicarious immunity argument**

Is it possible that one person in his own contract can exempt the liability of a person who is not a party to that contract? In other words, in our context, can the first carrier (C) exempt the liability of the subcontractor (D) by a clause to that effect in his contract with A, the owner of the goods? The cases of *Scrutton* v. *Midland Silicones*[5] and *Cosgrove* v. *Horsfall*[6] in effect say "no." Although there are cases that may support a contrary view[7] it is suggested that the authority of the above cases is so overwhelming that there can be little real doubt in the matter.

[2] See 1.19 and *Bailment* by N. Palmer (2nd ed., 1989).

[3] *Victoria Fur* v. *Roadline* [1981] 1 Lloyd's Rep. 570.

[4] The authors gratefully acknowledge the kind permission of Professor N. Palmer to use the same approach to this subject as that taken in his leading work, *Bailment* (above, n. 2), to which readers are referred for a more comprehensive and learned coverage.

[5] [1962] A.C. 445.

[6] (1945) 62 T.L.R. 140.

[7] *e.g.* the difficult case of *Elder Dempster* v. *Paterson Zochonis* [1924] A.C. 522 from which it is almost impossible to extract a rational *ratio decidendi* (*i.e.* reason for the decision) that is consistent with other cases.

The unilateral contract argument 1.80

A unilateral contract is one where there is a promise made in return for an Act; for example, I promise you £100 if you use a Carbolic Smokeball and catch influenza.[8] The obligation is said to be unilateral or one-sided because you do not promise to use the ball or catch influenza. The unilateral contract argument only really arises where there is a contract that includes a "Himalaya" Clause. The argument is to the effect that when A makes his contract with C the inclusion of a Himalaya Clause in that contract amounts to an offer made by A to D, the subcontractor. The offer is to the effect that "If you (D) handle my goods I (A) will give you the benefit of the exclusion clauses in C's contract." Various difficulties arise in this context. One basic principle of contract law is that a person cannot accept an offer he does not know about or has forgotten about.[9] It follows that in our example D cannot accept A's "offer" unless at the time he handled the goods he knew of the Himalaya Clause in C's conditions of carriage.[10] Secondly the contract does not come into existence until D accepts the offer by handling A's goods. Until D does handle them presumably A could phone him up and say "I withdraw the offer."[11] Thirdly if one reads Himalaya Clauses they are not worded as offers. An offer is "an expression of willingness to contract on certain terms made with the intention that it shall become binding as soon as it is accepted."[12] Himalaya Clauses are worded at the best more like "declarations of intent" rather than offers and it is difficult to see how a term in a contract between A and C can be interpreted as a promise to D. If the Himalaya Clauses said "I hereby offer to the servants, agents and subcontractors of C the benefit of all the exclusion clauses in C's contract and this offer is accepted when they handle my goods" then the argument would be much more convincing. Despite these difficulties it seems to have been decided in two Privy Council cases[13] that the unilateral contract argument has succeeded. Nevertheless it is suggested that the majority judges in the first of these cases[14] were too much influenced by commercial considerations rather than the correct legal principles and that the view of the minority judges is to be preferred.[15]

The bilateral contract argument 1.81

A bilateral contract is, unlike the unilateral contract discussed above, one where both parties undertake liabilities. In our context A

[8] As in the famous case of *Carlill* v. *Carbolic Smokeball Company* [1893] 1 Q.B. 256.

[9] *R.* v. *Clarke* (1927) 40 C.L.R. 227 (Australia).

[10] In *New Zealand Shipping Company* v. *Satterthwaite* [1975] A.C. 154 the stevedores (*i.e.* the equivalent of the subcontractors in our example) did know of the carrier's conditions because the stevedores were a subsidiary company of the carriers.

[11] An offer can be withdrawn at any time prior to acceptance. *Routledge* v. *Grant* (1828) 4 Bing. 653.

[12] Treitel, *The Law of Contract* (7th ed. 1987), p. 7.

[13] *New Zealand Shipping Company* v. *Satterthwaite* [1975] A.C. 154; *The New York Star* [1981] 1 W.L.R. 138.

[14] *New Zealand Shipping Company* v. *Satterthwaite* [1975] A.C. 154.

[15] See in particular the lucid and convincing judgment of Lord Simon at p. 173. Note that Privy Council cases are not "binding" on English courts, *i.e.* they do not have to follow such decisions.

promises D the benefit of the exclusions in C's contracts and in return D promises to carry A's goods. This argument again can only effectively be raised where there is a Himalaya Clause in C's conditions. Unlike the alleged unilateral contract this contract comes into existence at the moment that A makes his contract with C and not when D takes over the goods from C. In *Scrutton* v. *Midland Silicones*[16] Lord Reid said that for this argument to prevail FOUR TESTS would have to be satisfied.[17] They were:

(1) Consideration. Every simple contract[18] requires consideration. English law enforces bargains not gratuitous promises. It is obvious in our illustration that A, the owner of the goods, would provide consideration. He promises D, the subcontractor, the benefit of the exclusion clauses in the conditions of carriage of C, the first carrier. The difficulty is to discover what consideration D provides in return for A's promise. This is particularly true if, at the time A makes his contract with C, C has not entered into any agreement with D that D will carry A's goods for C. In other words at the time of the contract between A and C, C has not already agreed with D to subcontract the goods to him. In such circumstances it is suggested that there is no consideration and thus no binding contract between A and D imposing C's exclusion clauses on A. If D has however already promised C that he will handle A's goods before A has contracted with C then there may be a consideration. D's consideration in return for A's promise of the benefit of the exclusion clause may be the performance of his pre-existing contract with C. The performance of an existing contractual obligation is not normally a good consideration.[19] If however the promise is made not by the original contracting party, but rather by a third party, then rather illogically the performance of an existing obligation is a good consideration.[20] So, in our example, if D has agreed to act for C, at the time of A's contract with C, the performance of D's existing contractual obligation to C is, at first sight, good consideration for A's promise of the benefit of the exemption clause. However the difficulty remains that D's promise is made to C, not to A. For there to be a valid bilateral contract the parties must exchange promises (*i.e.* consideration) with one another. In our example A makes a promise to D (*i.e.* to give D the benefit of the exclusion clause) through the agency of C. D, however, never makes a promise to A either himself or via C. It seems, therefore, that in strict legal theory this first test can hardly ever be satisfied. Perhaps, however, one could just argue that C makes the promise on

[16] [1962] A.C. 445.

[17] These tests caused great confusion in *New Zealand Shipping Company* v. *Satterthwaite* [1975] A.C. 154 because the majority judges attempted to apply them to the unilateral contract argument (discussed at 1.80, above) whereas it is submitted Lord Reid clearly intended them to apply to the bilateral contract argument.

[18] *i.e.* one not made under seal. A contract made under seal does not require consideration.

[19] *Stilk* v. *Myrick* (1809) 2 Camp. 317; *The Proodos* [1981] 3 All E.R. 189.

[20] *Shadwell* v. *Shadwell* (1860) 9 C.B.(N.S.) 159.

D's behalf and that D can subsequently ratify it[21] but C never seems to make such a promise to A in the standard Himalaya Clauses.

(2) Authority. A person cannot enter into a contract on behalf of another without that person's authority. Unless C had obtained D's permission to contract on his behalf then, at first sight, there would be no contract between A and D. Perhaps, however, this difficulty can perhaps be overcome if D subsequently ratifies or confirms C's unauthorised contract made on his behalf.[22] Needless to say D would be very pleased to ratify C's contract (if the law permits him to do so) because if he did not he would be unable to take advantage of C's exclusion clauses.

(3) Agency. In order to contract on D's behalf C must show that he is intending to act as D's agent. The British Rail Himalaya Clause refers to them making a contract "on behalf of," and the R.H.A. even more specifically "as agent for," their respective servants, agents and subcontractors. There is no doubt that in these Conditions of Carriage this requirement is satisfied.

(4) Subcontractors specifically covered. The fourth of Lord Reid's tests was that the subcontractor must be specifically covered by the clause. Unlike some conditions in use in the road haulage industry it is quite clear that in the R.H.A. and British Rail Conditions subcontractors are covered by the respective Himalaya Clauses. This test, in their case, again would obviously be satisfied.

The consent argument 1.82

A person who consents to what would otherwise be the deliberate commission of a tort against him[23] or equally consents to the risk of harm[24] cannot sue in tort. Could it be argued in our context that if the owner of goods (A) contracts with C on terms that C and his subcontractor, D, are not to be liable for negligence and A subsequently sues D, the subcontractor, in tort that D could plead *volenti* or consent as a defence? This alleged doctrine is in effect an attempt to resuscitate the "privity of contract" heresy that was effectively stamped out in the famous case of *Donoghue* v. *Stevenson*.[25] Before that case it was argued that if X had a contract with Y his only duty in relation to the performance of that contract was to Y. Thus if X sold tainted ginger beer to Y and the beer poisoned Z, the heresy maintained that X's only liability was to Y under the contract of sale with Y and there was no liability on the part of X to Z. That heresy was supressed in *Donoghue* v. *Stevenson*[26] and X was held liable in tort

[21] See "Test 2" below.

[22] An undisclosed principal cannot ratify. *Keighley Maxted & Co.* v. *Durant* [1901] A.C. 240. Whether a principal whose existence is revealed but who is not immediately identifiable, *e.g.* an unnamed subcontractor, can ratify is unclear. See *Watson* v. *Swann* (1862) 11 B.B. 756, 771, *per* Willes J.

[23] *e.g. Bravery* v. *Bravery* [1954] 1 W.L.R. 1169.

[24] *e.g. Simms* v. *Leigh Rugby Football Club* [1969] 2 All E.R. 923.

[25] [1932] A.C. 562.

[26] See n. 25 above.

to Z. The contract with Y was irrelevant. If the existence of a contract with Y is irrelevant as regards X's liability to Z so should be the contents of any such contract, even if they were known to Z. Could the manufacturer of the ginger beer in *Donoghue* v. *Stephenson*[27] have avoided liability to the plaintiff who drank the beer if in his contract with the cafe owner to sell him the beer there had been a clause to the effect that he would not be liable to anybody who drank the beer? Surely the answer would be "no."

1.83 **The reduced duty of care argument**

Is it possible that an exclusion clause in the contract of carriage between the first carrier (C) and the subcontractor (D) could cut down D's duty of care to A the owner of the goods? In the tort of negligence the standard of care is that required of a reasonable man. If D in his contract with C has exempted that duty towards A, the owner of the goods, and A sues D for negligence is D's duty to A reduced, or even excluded entirely, because of his (D's) contract to that effect with C? There are some statements in cases[28] and even one decision[29] which support this view. However this approach has been emphatically rejected by Lord Brandon when giving the judgment of the House of Lords in *The Aliakmon*[30] and it seems unsatisfactory. Suppose that in *Donoghue* v. *Stevenson*[31] the plaintiff's friend, when he or she bought the ginger beer for the plaintiff, had agreed with the cafe owner to an exemption clause excluding all liability on the part of the manufacturer of the ginger beer to the ultimate consumer. Would that exemption clause have stopped the plaintiff from successfully suing the manufacturer? It is suggested that the answer is "no."

1.84 **The bailment on terms argument**

If A, the owner of goods, sues D, the subcontractor for breach of bailment is he bound by the terms of that bailment? In other words is A bound by the terms of the contract subject to which C, the first carrier, bailed the goods to D? There is no necessity for there to be a Himalaya Clause in C's contract for this argument to be put forward. The argument is to the effect that if A relies on the fact that his goods have been bailed with his permission to D he cannot sue on that bailment without being bound by the terms upon which the goods have been bailed, *i.e.* any exclusion clauses in the contract between C and D. Of course this argument may even work in A's favour. If D was for example a common carrier with no exemption clauses in his contract of carriage then the terms of C's bailment to D would make him (D) strictly liable to A irrespective of negligence.[32] The leading case that supports the doctrine of bailment on terms is *Johnson Mathey* v. *Constantine Terminals*.[33] In this case J.M. bailed a consignment of

[27] See n. 25 above.

[28] *e.g.* by Lord Roskill in *Junior Books* v. *Veitchi* [1983] A.C. 520, 546.

[29] *Southern Water Authority* v. *Carey* [1985] 2 All E.R. 1077.

[30] [1986] A.C. 785.

[31] [1932] A.C. 562.

[32] This actually happened in *Eastman Chemicals International* v. *N.M.T. Trading* [1972] 2 Lloyd's Rep. 25 but the judgment is so unsatisfactory in many respects that little credence can be given to the decision.

[33] [1976] 2 Lloyd's Rep. 215.

silver to N who in turn sub-bailed the silver to C.T. The actual contract with C.T. had been made by I, a freight forwarder. J.M. sued C.T. and it was held that although there was no privity of contract between J.M. and C.T. nevertheless C.T. could rely on the exclusion clauses in their contract with I because J.M. was bound by the terms of the bailment to C.T. There are other cases that appear inconsistent with this decision[34] but they can mostly be explained on the grounds that bailment on terms was not specifically argued. Nevertheless most subsequent decisions[35] appear to show that, in order for A to be bound by the terms of C's bailment to D, A must know of the terms upon which the goods are to be sub-bailed. Thus in *The Kapetan Marcos (No. 2)*[36] the owner of goods lost at sea, who had no contract with the sea carrier, sued the carrier in bailment but was bound by the Hague Visby Rules[37] because he had authorised the sub-bailment and *knew* the goods would be carried subject to the Rules.

We suggest that the mere fact that A knows his goods may be bailed by C to D does not make A bound by the terms of C's bailment to D if A sues D. Nor does the mere fact that A knows that hauliers generally put exclusion clauses in their conditions of carriage. It is suggested that in order for A to be bound by the terms of C's bailment to D, A must know that, for example, D uses the R.H.A. 1982, Conditions of Carriage and that A's goods will be carried by D subject to those conditions.[38]

The trust argument 1.85

Is it possible that the contract between A, the owner of goods and C, the first carrier, might amount to a trust in favour of D? The Himalaya Clause in the R.H.A. Conditions (*i.e.* clause 2(3)) refers to the carrier acting as "trustee for" his subcontractors. The courts are on the whole against interpreting contracts of this type as a trust.[39] In addition only property can be the subject matter of a trust and an exclusion clause is hardly property.[40]

Protection for subcontractors by the use of indemnity clauses 1.86

One way in which subcontractors attempt to protect themselves against liability in tort or bailment in excess of their liability under their conditions of carriage is by the use of indemnity clauses. An example of such a clause is clause 12(2) of the R.H.A. Conditions.[41]

[34] *e.g. Victoria Fur* v. *Roadline* [1981] 1 Lloyd's Rep. 570; *Moukatoff* v. *B.O.A.C.* [1967] 1 Lloyd's Rep. 396; *Lee Cooper* v. *Jeakins* [1967] 2 Q.B. 1; *Philip Morris* v. *Transport Commission* [1975] Tas.S.R. 128 (Australia).

[35] *Chellaram* v. *Butler's Warehousing* [1978] 2 Lloyd's Rep. 412; *The Kapetan Marcos (No. 2)* [1987] 2 Lloyd's Rep. 321. However *Singer Co.* v. *Tees and Hartlepool Port Authority* [1988] 2 Lloyd's Rep. 164, does not appear to support this view.

[36] [1987] 2 Lloyd's Rep. 321.

[37] See Chap. 5.

[38] This seems to follow from *Chellaram* v. *Butler's Warehousing* [1978] 2 Lloyd's Rep. 412 but not from *Singer Co.* v. *Tees and Hartlepool Health Authority*, see n. 35 above.

[39] *e.g. Dunlop* v. *Selfridge* [1915] A.C. 847.

[40] Thus *Southern Water Authority* v. *Carey* above, n. 29, shows that one cannot have a trust of an exclusion clause.

[41] See Appendix 1.A.

British Rail do not have such a provision in their Conditions presumably because they do not themselves act as subcontractors as opposed to appointing subcontractors to carry goods for them. The intention of these indemnity clauses is that if D, the subcontractor, is sued by A, the owner of the goods, and is held liable to pay A the actual value of the goods, then D can recover an indemnity from C, the carrier with whom D contracted for the carriage of those goods. Say that the goods worth £10,000 per ton are lost by D and he is held liable in bailment to pay that amount to A. We are of course assuming here that D has been unable to rely on his conditions of carriage because of the doctrine of privity of contract and that none of the arguments outlined in the preceding paragraphs has been successful. Assume also that D's maximum liability under his conditions is £800 (*e.g.* under clause 11 of the R.H.A. Conditions). D can now sue C, by virtue of clause 12(2), and, if successful, recover by way of indemnity the difference between his maximum contractual liability (£800) and the sum for which he has been held liable to A (*i.e.* £10,000). Thus D will recover from C the sum of £9,200 per ton.

1.87 **Interpretation of indemnity clauses**

Indemnity clauses are interpreted *contra proferentem*[42] as are exclusion clauses (see 1.29 and 1.47). Thus if a carrier wishes to include liability for negligence in an exclusion or indemnity clause then usually he must expressly refer to negligence.[43] For example he might in his conditions claim an indemnity "against all demands including those arising from our neglect or default." In *Gillespie Bros.* v. *Roy Bowles Transport*[44] it was held that the words "all claims and demands whatsoever" in the equivalent clause of the R.H.A. 1967 Conditions were an express reference to negligence. Thus the first carrier had to indemnify the subcontractor for the consequences of the subcontractor's own negligence. Since then there have been two House of Lords decisions[45] to the effect that the use of the word "whatever" or something similar in an indemnity clause is not an express reference to negligence but is merely a "word of emphasis." *Gillespie* has not actually been overruled[46] but the effectiveness of clause 12(2) must now be doubtful where a carrier attempts to obtain an indemnity on account of his own negligence from the other contracting party. Let us assume, however, that the clause is effective. Let us also assume that in our situation, in addition to there being an indemnity clause in the contract between C, the first carrier, and the subcontractor D, there is also such a clause in the separate contract between C and A, the owner of the goods. A now sues D in bailment or in tort for

[42] *Gillespie Bros* v. *Roy Bowles Transport* [1973] 1 Q.B. 400.

[43] Compare *Spriggs* v. *Sotheby Parke Bernet* [1986] 1 Lloyd's Rep. 487.

[44] [1973] 1 Q.B. 41.

[45] *Smith* v. *South Wales Switchgear* [1978] 1 W.L.R. 165; *Smith* v. *U.M.B. Chrysler Scotland* [1978] S.C. 1.

[46] Lord Fraser in *Smith* v. *South Wales Switchgear*, above, at p. 26 said that he agreed with the decision in *Gillespie* v. *Roy Bowles Transport* on its facts, *i.e.* it was correctly decided even if on the wrong grounds.

£10,000 per ton, being the value of the goods lost by D. D is held liable to pay that amount to A. There is a clause in D's conditions of carriage limiting his liability to £800 but he cannot rely on it because there is no privity of contract between him (D) and A. D sues C under clause 12(2) of the R.H.A. Conditions and recovers £9,200. C's conditions of carriage also limit liability to £800. C's contract with A also includes an indemnity clause (such as clause 12(2) of the R.H.A. Conditions). Can C now in turn recover an indemnity of £8,400 (*i.e.* £9,200 minus £800 which is C's maximum liability in his conditions) by virtue of clause 12(2) from A? If C could do this then the doctrine of privity of contract would be completely circumvented and A's action in bailment or tort against D would have been almost completely frustrated. All the £10,000 he had recovered from D, less £1,600, would have to be repaid to C.

Precisely such a point came up in *Davis* v. *Gilyott and Scott*[47] but the attempt by the first carrier to obtain an indemnity from the owner of the goods failed. A clause very similar to clause 12(2) was interpreted "as relating to costs and demands made against the first defendants in respect of their own conduct in relation to the goods" and a claim for an indemnity brought by a subcontractor did not come within this definition. No doubt a skilled draftsman could produce a clause to achieve this effect but clause 12(2), as it stands, is not one.

Carriage of Animals

Common carriers of animals 1.88

Some writers[48] are of the opinion that where animals are carried by a common carrier and arrive at their destination dead or injured this is prima facie evidence of the common carrier's excepted peril of inherent vice.[49] In other words it is presumed that the animal has injured itself through its own restlessness and that the common carrier is not liable unless the owner of the animal can prove negligence on the part of the carrier. However in *Prior* v. *London and South Western Railway*[50] the plaintiff's horse was sent via the defendants' railway and was found to be dead on delivery. The court held that the arrival of an animal dead or in an injured condition was prima facie evidence of negligence, *i.e.* sufficient to place the burden of disproving negligence on the carrier. A common carrier cannot rely on an excepted peril if his negligence is the primary cause of the loss or damage.[51] The defendants were therefore held liable. Pollock B. said "the company would have to discharge themselves at all events. It may be that the horse's death was not owing to any negligence but it was for the company as common carriers to discharge themselves."

[47] [1975] 2 Lloyd's Rep. 422.
[48] *e.g.* Leslie, *The Law of Transport by Railway* (2nd ed., 1928) pp. 220-222.
[49] See 1.27.
[50] (1885) 2 T.L.R. 89.
[51] See 1.27.

This case has subsequently been followed in Canada.[52] It is submitted therefore that the arrival of an animal dead or in injured condition is not prima facie evidence of inherent vice. Presumably, however, if the carrier can show that he has used the normal reasonable methods of carrying animals and that the injuries are consistent with the animal having injured or killed itself through its own restlessness then he has proved that inherent vice is a real convincing possibility. In that case it seems that the burden would then be placed back on to the owner to prove negligence.[53]

1.89 **Private carriers of animals**

There is a remarkable shortage of cases on the liability of private carriers and other bailees for reward of animals. It is suggested that the true position is illustrated by the Australian case of *Cowper & Cowper* v. *J.G. Goldner Pty. Ltd.*[54] in which a horse became ill in transit and subsequently died and the court held that the burden of disproving negligence fell on the carrier. As he could not disprove negligence he was held liable.[55] Of course it is not necessary for a private carrier/bailee for reward to prove precisely how the loss or damage occurred. Provided he can show a convincing way in which the loss or damage may have occurred without his negligence then the burden of proving negligence falls back on the plaintiff.[56] Presumably, therefore, if a private carrier of animals can prove that the injured animal was especially restless and therefore more likely to injure itself, then the burden of proving negligence would fall back on the owner of the animal.

1.90 **Carriage of animals under the R.H.A. Conditions**

Clause 9(2)(i) of the R.H.A. Conditions which deals with the carriage of animals has been dealt with generally at 1.56. Assuming that the statement in the introduction to the Conditions that the carrier is not a common carrier is effective,[57] the carrier is only a private carrier. Therefore probably the best view is that clause 9(2)(i) does no more than state the common law as regards the liability of private carriers and the burden of proof is unchanged. It follows therefore that the position of a carrier of animals using the R.H.A. Conditions is exactly the same as that of a private carrier of animals as discussed in 1.89. In other words the carrier must disprove negligence if the animal arrives either dead or injured.

1.91 **Carriage of animals under the British Rail Livestock Conditions**

British Rail do not carry animals under the General Conditions of Carriage that are reproduced in Appendix 1.B but rather under their

[52] *Carter* v. *Ferguson* (1943) 2 D.L.R. 647 (Canada). See also *Vaughan* v. *Wabash Railway Company* 188 S.W. 2d. 352 (1945) (U.S.A.) to the same effect.

[53] This seems to follow from *Kendall* v. *London and South Western Railway* (1872) L.R. 7 Ex. 373. See also *Ballard* v. *North British Railway* [1923] S.C.(H.L.) 43 as to the burden of disproving negligence generally.

[54] (1986) 40 S.A.S.R. 457 (Australia).

[55] The burden of proof falls on the bailee to disprove negligence. See 1.17

[56] *Ballard* v. *North British Railway* [1923] S.C.(H.L.) 43.

[57] See 1.26.

separate Conditions of Carriage of Livestock. Under clause 5 of these Livestock Conditions British Rail are liable for loss, misdelivery or delay in the carriage of animals unless they can disprove negligence. So the burden of proof is placed on British Rail. In the case of injury to an animal on the other hand the burden of proving negligence is firmly placed upon its owner. Thus in the unreported Court of Appeal case of *Langton* v. *British Transport Commission*[58] a mare arrived at the destination injured. It was held that the burden of proof under the Livestock Conditions fell on the plaintiff to prove negligence. The injury to the animal was not evidence of negligence under the Conditions and the defendants (now called British Rail) were not liable. Whether death of an animal amounts to a "loss" or rather to "damage" for the purposes of clause 5 of these Conditions is unclear (but see, 6.54). If animals are carried at owner's risk[59] under clause 6 of the Livestock Conditions then British Rail are only liable for injury, loss, misdelivery or delay in relation to animals upon proof of "wilful misconduct"[60] by the owner.

IMPROPERLY PACKED GOODS

Defective packing, common carriers, B.R. and R.H.A. Conditions 1.92

If improperly packed goods are carried subject to clause 9(2)(i)[61] of the R.H.A. Conditions then the carrier would presumably be in the same position as a private carrier of improperly packed goods at common law.[62] Where such goods are carried under clause 5A of the British Rail Conditions it is on the same basis as other goods. However British Rail can rely on the excepted perils discussed below more easily than they could in the case of properly packed goods. Where improperly packed goods are carried by British Rail at "owner's risk"[63] under clause 5B then the owner must prove "wilful misconduct"[64] on their part.

Apparently a common carrier is entitled to refuse to carry improperly packed goods.[65] At common law if the goods are improperly packed this may be evidence of the common carrier's excepted peril of inherent vice[66] or alternatively of consignor's or consignee's own fault or fraud.[67] Likewise where goods are carried subject to clause 5A of the British Rail Conditions[68] or clause 9(2)(ii)[69] of the R.H.A. Conditions the carrier could plead perils (d), (e) and especially (f), *i.e.* improper packing. The state of the goods and their packing when delivered to the carrier will be evidence of what

[58] Noted at [1956] C.L.Y. 7211.
[59] As to "owner's risk" contracts see 1.61-1.62.
[60] As to the meaning of "wilful misconduct" see 1.61-1.62.
[61] As to clause 9(2)(1) generally see 1.55.
[62] See 1.92.
[63] See n. 59 above.
[64] See n. 60 above.
[65] *Munster* v. *South Eastern Railway* (1858) 4 C.B.(N.S.) 676, 701.
[66] See 1.28.
[67] See 1.28.
[68] See 1.63.
[69] See 1.57.

treatment the carrier should give them.[70] If safety measures can easily be taken and the carrier fails to do so he will be guilty of negligence and will be unable to rely on the perils. Furthermore if the improper packing becomes apparent during the journey the carrier cannot always ignore it and leave the goods to their fate.[71] Again he must do what is reasonable in relation to the goods. If the defective packing is apparent to the carrier when he accepts the goods and the carrier objects then the position is not entirely clear. The weight of authority[72] seems to favour the view that the carrier can still rely on the excepted perils provided he has given the goods the same normal reasonable care that he would to other goods of that class.[73] If the carrier knows that the goods are improperly packed and he does not object then it seems that the carrier cannot rely on the perils.[74]

1.93 **Defective packing, private carriers**

Where improperly packed goods are carried subject to clause 9(2)I(i) of the R.H.A. Conditions[75] or are carried by a private carrier subject to his normal common law liability for negligence[76] the position is unclear. In fact there seem to be no cases in which the point has ever arisen. On general principles and by analogy with the position of common carriers and private carriers of animals[77] the carrier must disprove negligence. Provided he can prove that he has taken reasonable care of the goods then he should not be liable. If he can prove that defective packing is a convincing possible cause of the damage then the burden of proving negligence is placed back on the customer.[78]

Whether the carrier is a private or a common carrier and whether he is liable for damage to improperly packed goods or not he has the right to repack them and charge the owner a reasonable sum accordingly.[79]

Consignor's Warranty of Fitness and Dangerous Goods

1.94 **Consignor's warranty of fitness, introduction**

It is possible that if dangerous goods are consigned to a carrier they may damage his property or even kill or injure him. It is also possible that dangerous goods may damage or destroy goods belonging to other customers of the carrier or may kill or injure the carrier's

[70] *Stuart* v. *Crawley* (1818) 2 Stark. 323.

[71] *Beck* v. *Evans* (1812) 16 East 244.

[72] *Gould* v. *South East and Chatham Railway* [1920] 2 K.B. 186; *Barbour* v. *South Eastern Railway* (1876) 34 L.T. 67. Compare *Stuart* v. *Crawley* (1818) 2 Stark. 323 and *Richardson* v. *North Eastern Railway* (1872) L.R. 7 C.P. 75.

[73] See *Gould* v. *South East and Chatham Railway* [1920] 2 K.B. 186.

[74] See Lord Atkinson at p. 340 of *London and North Western Railway* v. *Hudson* [1920] A.C. 324.

[75] See Appendix 1.A.

[76] See 1.33-1.35.

[77] See 1.88-1.89.

[78] Compare *Ballard* v. *North British Railway* [1923] S.C.(H.L.) 43.

[79] *Littleton Collieries* v. *London and North Western Railway* (1916) 16 Ry. & Can.Tr.Cas. 169.

employees. To deal with this problem the common law has developed the "consignor's warranty of fitness." This is to the effect that the consignor warrants that the goods are fit to be carried in the condition in which they are delivered to the carrier. The warranty extends to both common and private carriers.[80] Whether the warranty is a form of liability in tort or contract has never been precisely decided. Whatever its nature the warranty can be excluded by contract between the consignor and the carrier.[81] Presumably such a contract would not exclude the warranty as regards actions brought directly by the owners of other goods[82] or by the carrier's servants because they would not be parties to the contract that excluded the warranty *vis-á-vis* the carrier.

Consignor's warranty, liability to the carrier 1.95

As regards actions brought by the carrier against the consignor there is no doubt that the warranty is absolute in nature. The absence of negligence or knowledge of the danger on the part of the consignor is no defence to the consignor of the dangerous goods. Thus in *Bamfield* v. *Goole and Sheffield Transport Co.*[83] the defendants were a firm of freight forwarders who without any negligence on their part consigned a cargo of ferro-silicon to a carrier by barge. The ferro-silicon came into contact with water during the journey and gave off poisonous fumes which killed the carrier. It was held that the defendants were liable to the carrier's estate. Although the warranty is absolute in nature there are circumstances where no warranty of fitness comes into existence. Thus there is no warranty at common law where the dangerous nature of the goods has been revealed to the carrier or where it is self-evident.[84]

Consignor's warranty, liability to owners of other goods 1.96

Dangerous goods belonging to the carrier may damage those belonging to other customers of the carrier. Where this happens the carrier can sue on their behalf irrespective of his liability to those customers. Thus in *Great Northern Railway* v. *L.E.P. Transport*[85] the defendant freight forwarders delivered a quantity of acid to the defendants, the container leaked and the acid damaged felt hats belonging to another customer. The railway company compensated the owner of the felt hats and sued the forwarders for an indemnity. The carriers/bailees recovered substantial damages from the consignor/forwarder irrespective of whether they, the carriers, were liable to the owner of the felt hats under the contract of carriage with him. Any damages recovered by a carrier/bailee in these circumstances must be paid over to the owner of the goods.[86] Whether the owner of goods damaged in these circumstances can force the carrier/bailee in possession to sue on his behalf never seems to have

[80] *Burley* v. *Stepney Borough Council* [1947] 1 All E.R. 507.
[81] *Burley* v. *Stepney Borough Council*, see n. 80 above.
[82] See 1.97.
[83] [1910] 2 K.B. 94.
[84] *Acatos* v. *Burns* (1878) 3 Ex.D. 282.
[85] [1922] 2 K.B. 742.
[86] *Ibid.*

been decided.[87] If the carrier refused to sue in these circumstances could the owner of the damaged goods sue the consignor in his own right under the strict warranty of fitness irrespective of whether the consignor has been negligent? It appears to be the law that the carrier's servants can sue the consignor directly[88] irrespective of negligence or privity of contract between them and the consignor so presumably the owners of damaged goods can do likewise.

1.97 **Consignor's warranty, liability to the carrier's servants**

It has been held that the strict warranty of fitness can be enforced by the carrier's employees so as to recover damages for their own injuries caused by dangerous goods irrespective of negligence on the part of the consignor or privity of contract between the servant and the consignor. Thus in *Bamfield* v. *Goole and Sheffield Transport Co.*[89] the carrier's widow was also his employee working with him on the barge and she was herself also injured by the poisonous fumes. She not only recovered damages for the death of her husband, in her capacity as executrix of her late husband's estate, from the consignor but also recovered damages for her own injuries in her separate capacity as the servant of her late husband.

1.98 **Dangerous goods, British Rail conditions**

"Dangerous Goods" for the purposes of the British Rail Conditions[90] are defined in the introductory definition section. The liability of the Board as regards dangerous goods is dealt with in turn in clause 20. As will be seen, there are, in clause 20, provisions as regards packing and declaring the nature of dangerous goods. In addition, if the goods are damaged, lost or delayed then the customer must prove that this arose other than through his own failure to comply with clause 20. The main provision, however, is clause 20(2)(e). It states that where the provisions of clause 20 are not complied with the "Trader" must indemnify the Board against all loss or damage and all claims brought against the Board. At first sight this basically does little more than restate the common law discussed above. However the difficulty arises with the use of the word "Trader." This word is defined in clause 1 as "any person sending or receiving goods." Does this mean that the contractual warranty in clause 20(2)(e) falls on the consignee as well as the consignor? In any event, such a clause amounts to an indemnity clause for the purpose of the Unfair Contract Terms Act 1977, and therefore subject to the "reasonableness test," only if the consignee/other contracting party is a "consumer" as opposed to a business customer.[91] So if a business customer/consignee was sued by British Rail under clause 20(2)(e) he could not invoke the 1977 Act. Presumably if the consignee is held liable under clause 20(2)(e) for some act of negligence on the part of

[87] Lord Diplock in *The Albazero* [1977] A.C. 774 doubted if the bailee could be forced to sue.
[88] See 1.96.
[89] See n. 83 above.
[90] See Appendix 1.B.
[91] Unfair Contract Terms Act 1977, s.4(1).

the consignor then he could sue the consignor for an indemnity for negligence[92] in the performance of his duty as agent.

Dangerous goods, R.H.A. conditions 1.99

"Dangerous Goods" for the purpose of the R.H.A. Conditions are defined in clause 1 and the provision as regards packing and declaration of their nature is clause 3. There is no provision in the Conditions as to what is the position if clause 3 is not complied with and the goods are thus damaged, lost or delayed. Presumably if dangerous goods were being carried subject to clause 9(2)(ii)[93] non-compliance with clause 3 would come under one or more of perils (d) to (g) inclusive. The provision equivalent to British Rail clause 20(2)(e) discussed above, *i.e.* the indemnity clause as regards dangerous goods, is clause 12(3). It will be noted that the clause is slightly wider than the common law consignor's warranty of fitness. clause 12(3), unlike the common law warranty, extends even to goods whose dangerous nature has been declared. This is rather harsh but again cannot usually be challenged under the "reasonableness test."[94] The main difficulty in clause 12(3), however, again arises in the use of the word "Trader." It has been argued above at 1.16 that, as defined by clause 1 of the R.H.A. Conditions, "Trader" means consignee, *i.e.* the person with whom the carrier has contracted. If this is correct then a carrier under the R.H.A. Conditions can sue the consignor under the common law consignor's warranty of fitness (but not under clause 12(3)?) and can also sue the consignee under clause 12(3). Presumably again, however, the consignee would have some remedy against his negligent[95] agent, the consignor, for an indemnity.[96]

THE CARRIER'S RIGHT TO SELL THE CONSIGNED GOODS

Agency of necessity 1.100

If the goods start to deteriorate during transit or the carrier is unable to deliver the goods then can he sell them? The answer is normally that he cannot and any such sale would amount to the tort of conversion. There is only one situation in which the common law allows the bailee to sell the bailed goods. This is where there is an agency of necessity. In order for this right to be exercised three tests must be satisfied:

[92] But not presumably if the consignor had not been negligent as in *Bamfield* v. *Goole & Sheffield Transport Company* [1910] 2 K.B. 94 and *Great Northern Railway* v. *L.E.P. Transport* [1922] 2 K.B. 742.

[93] See 1.57.

[94] Unless the customer is a "consumer" as opposed to a business customer. See the Unfair Contract Terms Act 1977, s.4(1).

[95] If he was negligent.

[96] As with the R.H.A. Conditions discussed above this clause could be challenged under the "reasonableness test." s.4(1) of the Unfair Contract Terms Act 1977 concerning "unreasonable indemnity clauses" only protects "consumers" and not business customers.

(1) There must be an existing bailment by agreement. In other words the bailee/carrier must be in possession of the goods with the consent of the bailor/customer. This test is obviously satisfied in the case of a carrier.

(2) There must be a real emergency. Thus the goods must be perishable or of a similar nature. Mere inconvenience to the carrier is insufficient.[97]

(3) It must be commercially impossible to obtain the owner's instructions. This test can also be satisfied if the bailor knows of the emergency and fails to give the bailee/carrier instructions.[98] An inability to contact the owner is less likely in modern commercial conditions with improved methods of communication.

These principles are illustrated by the leading case of *Springer* v. *Great Western Railway*[99] A consignment of tomatoes being carried from Jersey to Covent Garden market in London was delayed by bad weather and by a rail strike for which, by virtue of their conditions of carriage, the defendants were not liable. At Weymouth it seems that the plaintiff's tomatoes were in fairly sound condition but the defendants sold them without making any effort to contact him. The plaintiff sued for the tort of conversion and the defendants pleaded agency of necessity. The court held that the defence failed because "there was time to communicate with the plaintiff and it was commercially possible to do so and to ask him what he wished to do with the tomatoes."[1]

If the carrier exercises his right as an agent of necessity to sell the consigned goods he must, of course, obtain the best possible price and also pay over all the proceeds of sale less bona fide expenses to the customer. In suitable cases a carrier may have an agency of necessity to warehouse the goods etc. rather than to sell them. Thus in *Great Northern Railway* v. *Swaffield*[2] nobody turned up at the station to collect a horse that had been carried there by the plaintiffs. There was nowhere at the station where the horse could safely be kept so the plaintiffs contracted to have it kept in the local livery stable. The court held that the plaintiffs were entitled to be compensated by the owner of the horse for the livery charges incurred by them.[3]

In addition to the common law agency of necessity the carrier may also have a statutory right to sell the consigned goods under the Torts (Interference With Goods) Act 1977. The rights of sale granted by the Act only come into effect once the terms of the bailment (*i.e.* in our context the transit) have ceased.[4] Notice must be given to the owner where possible[5] and the rights granted by the Act do not prevail over

[97] *Sachs* v. *Micklos* [1948] 2 K.B. 23.
[98] *China Pacific* v. *Food Corporation of India* [1982] A.C. 939.
[99] [1921] 1 K.B. 257.
[1] Scrutton L.J. at p. 268.
[2] (1874) L.R. 9 Ex. 132.
[3] The court took the view that even though transit had ceased the carriers still owed a duty of care towards the goods. See 1.71.
[4] Torts (Interference With Goods) Act 1977, s.12.
[5] Sched. 1, pt. 1, para. 1.

rights of sale given by contractual terms[6] such as those in the R.H.A. and British Rail Conditions discussed below.

Carrier's right to sell, British Rail conditions 1.101

Under clause 9 of the British Rail Conditions[7] the carrier is given certain contractual rights to sell the consigned goods "after transit or where transit is suspended." Transit and suspension of transit are defined in clause 10 of the Conditions which should be read closely. Under the current Conditions it is submitted that British Rail have no right to sell the goods if the necessity to sell has arisen from their own breach of contract.[8] If they are unable to deliver due to a breach of contract on their part, or on the part of their servants for whom they are liable, then it seems transit has not ceased or been suspended. It follows that unless they sold as agents of necessity they would be liable in conversion if they sold the goods as a result of their own breach of contract.

British Rail may only exercise their rights of sale under clause 9 once they have made all reasonable efforts to notify the consignor or consignee and have given them a reasonable time to collect or otherwise dispose of the goods.[9]

Carrier's right to sell, R.H.A. conditions 1.102

The carrier's right to sell under the R.H.A. Conditions is governed by clause 7. This clause is headed "Undelivered or Unclaimed Goods." In fact, however, it grants the carrier the right to sell the goods where he is "unable for any reason to deliver" them and not just where they are undelivered or unclaimed. In *Young* v. *British Transport Commission*[10] a similarly worded clause was interpreted as allowing the carrier to sell where the cause of his inability to deliver was his own breach of contract. In addition the sale of the goods discharged the carrier from liability to the owner for the prior breach of contract that gave rise to the necessity to sell. If that interpretation also applies to clause 7 then the clause most certainly could be challenged under the "reasonableness test"[11] in the Unfair Contract Terms Act 1977. Clause 7 also refers to the carrier being discharged from liability if he sells the goods "without prejudice to any claim" the customer may have against him. It was held in *Young* that identical words referred to any loss, damage, etc., that arose prior to the events that gave rise to the necessity to sell them. It did not give the customer the right to claim damages, for example, for the breach of contract that actually gave rise to the necessity to sell the goods. This aspect of clause 7 is equally open to challenge under the 1977 Act.

6 Torts (Interference With Goods) Act 1977, s.12(8).

7 See Appendix 1.B.

8 Whereas they did have such a right under the Conditions considered in *Young* v. *British Transport Commission* [1955] 2 Q.B. 177. It is submitted that *Chitty on Contracts* (25th ed., 1983), at para. 2850, is wrong in this respect and does not take into account the changes in the wording in the Conditions.

9 This seems an eminently reasonable provision that is likely to pass the "reasonableness test" in the Unfair Contract Terms Act 1977. See 1.45.

10 [1955] 2 Q.B. 177.

11 See 1.45.

An obligation, similar to that in the British Rail Conditions, on the part of the carrier not to exercise his rights of sale unless he has made reasonable efforts to contact the consignor (or failing him, the consignee) is imposed by clause 7(b).[12]

Time Limits for Claims

1.103 **Time limits, general principles**

An action for breach of contract, breach of bailment or in tort is subject to the Limitation Act 1980. Under this Act any such action must be brought within six years of the alleged wrong. Needless to say this could cause considerable injustice to a carrier. Therefore all carriers insert in their conditions various time limits. Usually customers must advise the carrier of a claim within, for example, seven days of delivery and make a claim against him within, for example, 14 days. "Advice" within seven days in this context means that the customer must inform the carrier that the goods have been, for example, damaged. "Claim" means that the carrier must submit a detailed claim for compensation, for example he must claim £250 compensation for goods damaged in transit. Such time limits are subject to the "reasonableness test" in the Unfair Contract Terms Act 1977.[13] It is unlikely that the time limits will pass the test if the carrier has been orally advised of the damage or advised on one of his own documents, such as a receipt for the goods signed by the consignee, even though most carriers' conditions require the advice and claim to be in writing and not on one of their own documents. Alternatively a carrier who does not in practice rely on the time limits may be held to be estopped (*i.e.* prevented) from relying on them.[14] A carrier who unjustifiably deviated could not rely on the time limits.[15]

1.104 **Time limits, R.H.A. conditions**

Time limits under the R.H.A. Conditions[16] are dealt with in clause 13. It will be seen that damage and partial loss must be advised within three days and a written claim must be made within seven days from the end of transit.[17] Under clause 16 time periods of seven days and less do not include days at weekends and public holidays. For total loss, loss of a separate package, etc., or misdelivery the periods are 28 and 42 days respectively from the commencement of transit.[18] If it is

[12] As the consignee is normally the owner at common law (see 1.04-1.12) it would be more logical to notify him before the consignor. The fact that notice has to be given in this context to the consignor rather than the consignee gives some slight credence to the idea that the word "Trader" in the R.H.A. Conditions means "consignor." See 1.16.

[13] See 1.45.

[14] Compare *Barrett Brothers Taxis* v. *Davies* [1966] 1 W.L.R. 1334.

[15] See 1.46-1.53 and *Garnham, Harris & Elton* v. *Alfred W. Ellis Transport* [1967] 1 W.L.R. 940.

[16] See Appendix 1.A.

[17] Transit for the purposes of the Conditions is defined in clause 6. As to transit at common law see 1.66-1.72.

[18] See n. 17 above.

not reasonably possible for the customer to advise or claim against the carrier within these time limits he must claim within a reasonable time.[19] It will be noted that there are no time limits for the advice of, or claims for, delay. In other words the time limit for bringing them is six years under the Limitation Act 1980!

Time limits, British Rail conditions 1.105

The clause dealing with time limits in the British Rail Conditions is clause 7. It will be seen again, this time under clause 14, that periods of seven days or less exclude weekends and public holidays. The periods for partial loss, damage, misdelivery and delay are three and seven days respectively from the end of transit.[20] The inclusion of "misdelivery" here as opposed to appearing in the 28/42 day period with total loss as it does in the R.H.A. Conditions is most unreasonable. If goods sent by A to B are misdelivered, *i.e.* delivered to the wrong person, how is the consignee (B) ever going to know about this within three days or claim from the carrier within seven days, especially if he is not expecting the goods and does not know their nature or value? This objection to clause 7 is not too serious, however, because, again, if the carrier cannot reasonably comply with the time limits in clause 7 then they are extended to a "reasonable time." For total loss or loss of a separate package the periods are again 28 and 42 days from the commencement of transit. Notice that the words "whole of the consignment" in clause 7(2) include an empty container when that is all that is being carried.[21]

FREIGHT

Freight, by whom payable at common law? 1.106

In a "two party" contract where the consignor and consignee are the same person no difficulty arises as to who is liable to pay the freight (*i.e.* carriage charges). In a "three party" contract, where the consignor and consignee are different persons, then, as was pointed out in 1.04-1.16, the consignee is normally the principal party to the contract of carriage. The consignor merely contracts as agent on his behalf. If the consignee/owner is presumed to be, the correct person to sue the carrier for loss or damage on the contract then logically he should, prima facie, be the correct person to be sued on the contract by the carrier for unpaid freight. The consignor, as agent, should not be prima facie liable to pay the freight. There is no principal of law that an agent is normally liable to pay his principal's debts.[22] This was

[19] This clause is likely to pass the "reasonableness test" in the Unfair Contract Terms Act 1977. See 1.45.

[20] Transit for the purposes of the Conditions is defined in clause 10. As to transit at common law, see 1.66-1.72.

[21] *Acme Transport* v. *Betts* [1981] 1 Lloyd's L.R. 131.

[22] "Where a party contracts as agent for a principal the contract is the contract of the principal and not that of the agent; and prima facie, at common law, . . . the only person who can be sued is the principal." *Per* Wright J., *Montgomerie* v. *U.K. Mutual S.S. Association* [1891] 1 Q.B. 370, 371.

view of the eminent judge Blackburn J. in *Dickenson* v. *Lano.*[23] A stronger case in favour of the view expressed above is *Great Eastern Railway* v. *Nix*[24] where N sold goods to H and sent them via the plaintiff railway company with instructions that H would pay the freight. The carriers delivered the goods without obtaining the freight from H and later sued N, the consignor/seller, for the freight instead. The court held that the defendant was not liable to pay the freight as "the contract with the carrier is, therefore, made by the seller as agent for the purchaser." It is suggested that in principle the result should have been the same even if the defendant had not given instructions that H would pay. It is therefore submitted that unless the conditions of carriage make the consignor liable to pay the freight or there has been a course of dealings between the parties (*i.e.* regular business transactions under which the consignor has paid freight) then the consignor as a mere agent is not liable. The liability of the consignor to pay freight by virtue of the conditions of carriage or a course of dealings arises as a separate collateral contract between himself and the carrier quite separate from the main contract of carriage which is between the owner/consignee and the carrier.[25] Just because the consignor has promised to pay the freight does not mean that he can also sue the carrier for loss or damage.[26]

The case of *Great Western Railway* v. *Bagge,*[27] shipping cases and cases from other jurisdictions which make the consignor liable to pay freight[28] can be explained on various grounds. Firstly they can be explained on the grounds that at the time of the delivery of the goods to the carrier the consignor was still the owner or bailee of the goods and had contracted as principal. Alternatively they were decided on a misunderstanding of the case of *Dunlop* v. *Lambert.*[29] This case was at one time wrongly considered as authority by some for the proposition that a consignor could always sue on the contract for substantial damages. If he could sue, then it followed logically that he could be sued. The House of Lords have since explained in *The Albazero*[30] that *Dunlop* v. *Lambert*[31] was never authority for that proposition.

If the consignee is the owner of the goods then he is therefore liable to pay the freight as principal. If he is not the owner then he is not prima facie liable, *i.e.* presumed to be the correct person, to pay the freight. It is also possible, however, on appropriate facts to imply a contract between the consignee and the carrier to pay the freight even

[23] (1860) 2 F. & F. 188. *Drew* v. *Bird* (1828) 1 Mod. & M. 156 seems to show that this also was the view of Lord Tenterden (the author of the famous book *Abbott on Shipping*).

[24] (1895) 39 S.J. 709.

[25] See 1.04-1.06. This liability to be sued for freight arises under a separate collateral contract. Likewise he may have the right to sue under a separate collateral contract. See 1.76.

[26] This heresy was rejected as long ago as 1799 in *Dawes* v. *Peck* (1799) 8 T.R. 330.

[27] (1885) 15 Q.B.D. 625.

[28] *e.g. Fox* v. *Nott* (1861) 6 H. & N. 637 (shipping); *C.N.R.* v. *Butler Manufacturing* [1984] 3 W.W.R. 655 (Canada).

[29] (1838-1839) 6 Cl. & Fin. 600.

[30] [1977] A.C. 774.

[31] See n. 29 above.

where the consignee is not the owner.[32] In return for the carrier giving up his lien[33] on the goods for unpaid freight by delivering the goods to the consignee, the consignee impliedly promises to pay the freight. Presumably if the carrier has no common law lien it would be much more difficult to imply such a contract.[34]

Freight, when payable at common law 1.107

Most of the cases on when freight is payable relate to carriage by sea and the most important are noted in 5.52. A common carrier can refuse to carry goods unless freight is paid in advance.[35] If he charges an unreasonable rate then the excess can be recovered from him.[36]

It was held in *R.H. and D. International* v. *I.A.S. Air Services*[37] that a rule in carriage by sea known as the rule in the *Aries Tanker*[38] applies to carriage by land under the C.M.R. Convention.[39] This rule is to the effect that a customer cannot defend an action brought by the carrier for unpaid freight by claiming that the goods were damaged or delayed in transit. The customer has to bring separate legal proceedings to recover damages for such delay or damage. This decision is unfair, contrary to the normal principles of contract law[40] and has been criticised.[41] It is suggested that, even if the decision is correct, it has no application to carriage by land where C.M.R. does not apply.

Freight, British Rail conditions 1.108

Clause 8(1) of the British Rail Conditions[42] makes the freight payable by the consignor without affecting British Rail's right to sue the consignee or any other person. This is an example of the situation discussed in 1.106 above where the consignor/agent makes himself liable to pay the freight on a separate collateral contract with the carrier. Clause 8(2) contractually incorporates the rule in *The Aries Tanker*[43] discussed above. This unjust provision may amount to an exemption clause for the purpose of the Unfair Contract Terms Act 1977,[44] but it seems unlikely that a court would hold a principle of

[32] *White* v. *Furness Withy* [1895] A.C. 40, although on the facts there was no such implied contract. Compare *Atomic Transfer* v. *Alta Horse Meat Traders* (1961) 32 D.L.R. 398 (Canada) where such a contract was implied.

[33] As to liens generally see 1.110-1.113.

[34] A private carrier probably has no common law lien (see 1.110). Thus it would be difficult to imply such a contract in the case of a private carrier who delivers goods to a person who is not the owner. This criticism can be levelled at the case of *World Transport* v. *Tealing* [1936] 2 All E.R. 573 where it seems the carrier was probably a private carrier and therefore arguably had no common law lien.

[35] *Wyld* v. *Pickford* (1841) 8 M. & W. 443.

[36] *Greene* v. *St. John & Maine Railway* (1882) 22 N.B.R. 252 (Canada).

[37] [1984] 1 W.L.R. 573.

[38] [1973] 1 W.L.R. 185.

[39] See Chap. 3.

[40] See *Morgan* v. *Johnson & Co.* [1949] 1 K.B. 107.

[41] [1985] J.B.L. 68. C. Cashmore. In addition the shipping rule evolved because "freight is the mother of wages" and that principle certainly has no application in the modern world of transport.

[42] See Appendix 1.B.

[43] See n. 38 above.

[44] Presumably it is covered by s.3(2)(b)(i) of the Unfair Contract Terms Act 1977 as an attempt "to render a contractual performance substantially different from that which is reasonably expected."

shipping law, upheld by the House of Lords, unreasonable when applied to carriage by land.

1.109 **Freight, R.H.A. conditions**

Clause 8(1) of the R.H.A. Conditions makes the freight payable by the "Trader" without affecting the carrier's right to sue the consignee or anybody else. The difficulty with this provision is that, as discussed at 1.16, the word "Trader," as defined in clause 1, probably means consignee. This makes clause 8(1) incomprehensible. It is possible that the word "Trader" might be interpreted by the courts as meaning sometimes "consignor," sometimes "consignee" and sometimes "both consignor and consignee" depending upon where the word appears in the Conditions. This would be most unsatisfactory but there is no doubt that the intention of the draftsman in clause 8(1) is to make the consignor liable to pay the freight. Whether the courts would interpret the word "Trader" to mean consignor in this context and make him liable to pay the freight is pure speculation.

Clause 8(3) makes the freight subject to interest charges if it is not paid within an agreed time limit. Presumably if there is no agreed time limit in which the freight is to be paid then clause 8(3) would not apply and no interest would be payable.

The Carrier's Lien

1.110 **Do private carriers have a common law lien?**

A lien means the right to hold on to somebody else's property as security for a debt. It never seems to have been decided whether a private carrier has a lien on the goods for unpaid freight charges. The case of *Electric Supply Stores* v. *Gaywood*[45] is sometimes quoted as authority for the proposition that a private carrier has no lien. However, all that case decided was that a private carrier could not exercise a lien against the owner of the goods who was not a party to the contract of carriage. The case is silent as to whether he would have had a lien on the goods against the person who actually contracted with him. Comments, *i.e. obiter dicta,* in *United States Steel Products* v. *Great Western Railway*[46] seem to suggest that all carriers of goods have a common law lien for unpaid freight but not too much weight should be attached to these comments because the case concerned not the common law but rather the interpretation of the contractual conditions of a common carrier. Such carriers undoubtedly do have a lien.[47] All carriers by sea apparently have a lien[48] and such carriers are hardly ever common carriers.[49] Arguably, however, carriers by water are by custom of the realm under the liability of common carriers.[50] If so it could be argued that they also have the privileges of a common carrier, *e.g.* a common carrier's lien.

[45] (1909) 100 L.T. 855.
[46] [1916] A.C. 189.
[47] See 1.111.
[48] See Carver, *Carriage by Sea* (13th ed., 1982), para. 1325.
[49] But see 5.06.
[50] This arguably is the *ratio decidendi* (*i.e.* reason for the decision) of the difficult case of *Liver Alkali* v. *Johnson* (1872) L.R. 7 Ex. 267, (1874) L.R. 9 Ex. 338.

As pointed out in 1.34-1.36 a private carrier is a bailee for reward. Bailees for reward do not have a common law lien on the goods unless they improve the goods.[51] Thus, for example, a repairer of goods has a lien for his unpaid charges.[52] Therefore it is submitted that a private carrier does not have a common law lien on the goods, as opposed to perhaps a contractual lien granted by his conditions of carriage, because he does not improve them. This point was specifically left open in the case *Hirst* v. *Page*.[53] The exercise of a non-existent "lien" by a carrier against his customer amounts to the tort of conversion.[54]

The common carrier's lien 1.111

There is no doubt however that a common carrier has a lien for unpaid freight.[55] This lien can even be exercised against the true owner of the goods who is not a party to the contract of carriage.[56] This lien is known as a particular lien because it cannot be exercised in respect of debts other than the outstanding freight on the particular consignment of goods over which the lien is exercised. Thus if the customer owes the carrier £1,000 but the freight owing on the goods over which the lien is exercised is only £50 then if the customer tenders £50 the lien is discharged. If the common carrier refused to release the goods to the customer upon tender of the £50 then he would commit the tort of conversion.[57] Even if there is a common law lien it gives no right to sell the goods[58] to satisfy the debt. Likewise, although a carrier who has a lien can charge for maintaining the goods (*e.g.* feeding animals) he has no right to charge warehousing on them.[59] A lien can only be exercised once the carrier is ready to deliver the goods and not, for example, as soon as he receives them.[60]

Liens, British Rail conditions 1.112

British Rail are private carriers[61] and therefore at common law probably have no lien on the goods for unpaid freight.[62] Clause 15 of the British Rail Conditions,[63] however, grants them a contractual lien. It will be noted that this lien is a general lien. In other words it grants, in addition to a lien on the goods for the freight in respect of those goods, a lien "for any money or charges . . . for any services . . . in relation to the custody or carriage of goods." Thus in the illustration given in 1.111 British Rail could exercise their contractual lien for all freight charges owing to them and not just for those in respect of the

[51] Presumably a private carrier who repacked improperly packed goods would have a lien for the charges of repacking them but not for unpaid freight.

[52] *Chase* v. *Watmore* (1816) 5 M. & S. 180; *Tappenden* v. *Artus* [1964] 2 Q.B. 185.

[53] (1891) T.L.R. 537.

[54] *Close* v. *Beatty* (1878) 28 U.C.C.P. 470 (Canada).

[55] *Skinner* v. *Upshaw* (1702) 2 Ld.Raym. 752.

[56] *Exeter Carrier's Case* (undated) 2 Ld.Raym. 867.

[57] See n. 54 above.

[58] *Mulliner* v. *Florence* (1878) L.R. 3 Q.B.D. 484.

[59] *Somes* v. *British Empire Shipping* (1860) 8 H.L.C. 338.

[60] *Wiltshire Iron Co.* v. *Great Western Railway* L.R. 6 Q.B. 776.

[61] Transport Act 1962, s.43.

[62] See 1.110 above.

[63] See Appendix 1.B.

goods over which the lien is exercised. Note that the last words of clause 15 state that the lien does not affect the unpaid seller's right of stoppage in transit.[64] This is a very generous provision because at common law a seller who exercises his right of stoppage in transit cannot demand the redelivery of the goods to him unless he discharges the carrier's lien.[65] Under these conditions on the other hand he can recover the goods from the carrier without paying off the carrier's lien. It should be noted that the word "owners" in clause 15(b) does not mean literally the owners in the legal sense. This point arose in the case of *United Steel Products* v. *Great Western Railway*[66] in relation to a clause that was very similar to clause 15 but which did not contain the provision that the lien did not affect the carrier's right of stoppage in transit. In this case U.S. sold goods to X on credit, gave them to G.W.R. to deliver to X and paid G.W.R. the freight. During transit U.S. exercised their right of stoppage in transit over the goods (see, 1.73-1.74) and demanded that G.W.R. redeliver them to them. G.W.R. refused to do this because X also owed them money. They claimed that X was the "owner" of the goods by virtue of the sale of them by U.S. to X and that they (G.W.R.) were exercising their lien in respect of the debts of the "owner," *i.e.* X. The House of Lords held that the word "owners" should not be taken literally as meaning X, the legal owner. It meant instead "the persons entitled to delivery of the goods," *i.e.* U.S. As U.S. owed the G.W.R. nothing it was held that the carriers could not exercise their lien against the consignors/sellers, U.S.

Notice that British Rail also have, unlike a common carrier at common law,[67] by virtue of clause 15, a right to sell the goods to satisfy the lien. It seems, however, that the clause only permits British Rail to exercise their right of sale once they have given notice to the "owner." Whether the word "owner" in this context means "person entitled to delivery" as it did earlier in the clause[68] or whether it should here be taken literally as meaning "legal owner" is unclear. As British Rail may have no idea who is the legal owner it is suggested that justice requires that it should again mean "person entitled to delivery."

1.113 Liens, R.H.A. conditions

Assuming that the statement in the introduction to the R.H.A. Conditions to the effect that the carrier is not a common carrier is effective, then probably the carrier, as a private carrier, has no common law lien.[69] However clause 14 grants the carrier a general lien over the goods against "the owner" for "any monies due from the Trader or such owner." As so often in the R.H.A. Conditions this use of the ambiguous word "Trader" gives rise to difficulty especially

[64] As to stoppage in transit see 1.73-1.74.
[65] See 1.74.
[66] [1916] A.C. 189.
[67] See 1.111.
[68] See *United States Steel Products* v. *Great Western Railway* [1916] 1 A.C. 189, discussed earlier in this paragraph.
[69] See 1.110.

when coupled with the words "or such owner." Various interpretations could be given to the unsatisfactory wording in both the first and second line of the clause. Presumably however, by analogy with the British Rail Conditions discussed above, the words "owner" in the first line and "Trader or such owner" in the second against most likely mean "persons entitled to delivery."

It will be noted that clause 14 of the R.H.A. Conditions is less generous than its equivalent in the British Rail Conditions. It is exercisable in respect of all debts and not just those in respect of transport services. It presumably does prejudice the unpaid seller's right of stoppage in transit and finally the right to sell the goods to satisfy the lien can be exercised without even notifying the owner. This last power, in particular, is very onerous and certainly makes clause 14 a likely candidate to fail the "reasonableness test" in the Unfair Contract Terms Act 1977.[70]

Contractual liens, exercise against non-contracting parties 1.114

Could a carrier of goods exercise a contractual lien against the owner of goods who was not a party to the contract of carriage? Some clauses used by carriers and warehousemen, etc., are apt to cover non-contracting owners and make the lien exercisable against them for the debts of non-owning contracting parties. At first sight the lien could not be exercised against a non-contracting party because of the doctrine of privity of contract.[71] However the law about contractual liens and non-contracting parties appears to be based upon the same principles as "bailment on terms" as discussed in 1.84. In other words the owner non-contracting party is only bound by the carrier's general lien clause if he knew about and consented to it.[72]

Carriage of Passengers

Passengers, basic principles of liability 1.115

A detailed consideration of the law relating to the carriage of passengers is outside the scope of this work. As with carriers of goods, carriers of passengers can be either common or private carriers. A common carrier of passengers can be sued in tort for unjustified refusal to carry.[73] However both common and private carriers of passengers are only liable for death and injury caused by their *negligence.* As is the case in carriage of goods there is no absolute warranty of rail or roadworthiness though the standard of care required is a very high one.[74] Any attempt by a carrier of passengers to exempt or limit liability for negligently killing or injuring his passengers is null and void (and not subject to the "reasonableness

[70] See 1.45.

[71] See 1.78.

[72] See *Chellaram* v. *Butler's Warehousing* [1978] 2 Lloyd's Rep. 412.

[73] See the shipping case of *Bennett* v. *Peninsular & Oriental Steamboat Company* (1848) 6 C.B. 775.

[74] *Readhead* v. *Midland Railway* (1869) L.R. 4 Q.B. 379; *Barkway* v. *South Wales Transport* [1950] 1 All E.R. 392, 403-4.

test") under section 2 of the Unfair Contract Terms Act 1977.[75] In other words the carrier can *never* rely on such a clause to avoid liability.

1.116 **Passengers, vicarious liability of carriers**

Carriers of passengers are vicariously liable for the negligent acts of their servants acting in the course or scope of their employment.[76] An act is in the course and scope of the servant's employment if the servant is doing in a wrong way that which he is employed to do in a correct way.[77] Thus a bus company is not normally liable if a bus conductor drives the bus and has an accident as driving buses is completely outside the scope of the conductor's employment.[78] The fact that a servant has been instructed not to perform an act does not automatically take the act out of the course and scope of his employment.[79] A carrier is not normally liable for the negligent acts of independant contractors,[80] as opposed to his servants, unless he has authorised their acts[81] or negligently selected an incompetent independant contractor.[82]

1.117 **Passengers, burden of proof of negligence**

Unlike the position where goods are goods damaged or lost in transit[83] the burden of proving negligence in the case of death of or injury to passengers falls on the passenger.[84] However if the plaintiff can bring the doctrine of *res ipsa loquitur, i.e.* "the thing speaks for itself," into play then the burden is upon the carrier to disprove negligence. The doctrine comes into effect if the plaintiff can prove:

(1) The thing causing the accident (*e.g.* the railway system) was under the exclusive control of the carrier or his servants.
(2) The accident was of a type that does not normally happen if reasonable care is used.
(3) The exact cause of the accident is unexplained.[85]

Examples of situations in which the doctrine of *res ipsa loquitur* has been held to come into effect are collisions between two trains[86] and a train becoming unrailed.[87] The doctrine does not automatically apply to a collision between two moving road vehicles as the accident is just

[75] The Act has the same effect even if the passenger is carried free of charge and there is therefore no contract between him and the carrier.
[76] *Ricketts* v. *Thomas Tilling* [1915] 1 K.B. 644.
[77] See Salmond and Heuston on *The Law of Torts* (19th ed., 1987).
[78] *Beard* v. *London General Omnibus Company* [1900] 2 Q.B. 530.
[79] *Limpus* v. *London General Omnibus Company* (1862) 1 H. & C. 526.
[80] *Reedie* v. *London and North Western Railway* (1849) 4 Ex. 244. Compare *Phillips* v. *Brittania Hygiene Laundry* [1923] 1 K.B. 347.
[81] See *Jolliffe* v. *Willmett* (1970) 174 S.J. 619.
[82] See *Robinson* v. *Beaconsfield R.D.H.* [1911] 2 Ch. 188.
[83] See 1.17.
[84] *Readhead* v. *Midland Railway* (1867) L.R. 2 Q.B. 412, (1869) L.R. 4 Q.B. 379.
[85] *Barkway* v. *South Wales Transport* [1950] A.C. 185 shows that if the exact cause of the accident is explained then the doctrine of *res ipsa loquitur* has no application and the court must judge from the facts whether there is sufficient evidence of negligence.
[86] *Skinner* v. *Lonson, Brighton and South Coast Railway* (1850) 5 Ex. 787.
[87] *Flanery* v. *Waterford & Limerick Railway* (1877) Ir.R. 11 C.L. 30.

as likely to be the fault of the other driver as it is of the driver of a bus.[88] If the doctrine of *res ipsa loquitur* applies then that does not mean that the carrier is liable. It is still open to him to escape liability by proving that the accident was not caused by his negligence[89] but the burden of disproving negligence falls on him.

Carriage of Passenger's Luggage

Meaning of "luggage" at common law 1.118

At common law a passenger is allowed to take a reasonable amount of luggage with him on his journey without extra charge. Not everything comes under the common law definition of luggage and thus can be taken on board a vehicle as of right. At common law luggage comprises goods in the nature of a package[90] that are for the personal use or convenience of the passenger with reference to the purpose of his journey.[91] Thus at common law household items,[92] a rocking horse[93] and articles required for a profession, trade or business[94] are not passengers' luggage. The fare that the passenger pays to be carried includes an unstated sum for the carriage of his luggage so his luggage is not carried free of charge by the carrier but under a contract as a bailee for reward or as a common carrier.[95] If goods taken on board a vehicle are not "luggage" as defined above then the carrier has never agreed to carry them and is not liable for loss or damage to them even if he is negligent.[96]

Common carriers of luggage 1.119

Neither British Rail nor London Regional Transport are common carriers of passenger's luggage by rail.[97] London Regional Transport and other carriers by bus are, however, probably common carriers of passengers' luggage and therefore not liable for undeclared valuables under section 1 of the Carriers Act 1830.[98] If a carrier by bus' conditions of carriage stated that he would carry luggage up to, for example, 50lbs in weight then he would be a common carrier of luggage up to that weight limit. A common carrier of passengers and their luggage can be sued for unreasonable refusal to carry.[99] A common carrier is strictly liable,[1] subject to the four excepted perils,[2]

[88] See Scrutton L.J. in *Mc'Gowan* v. *Stott* (1923) 99 L.J.K.B. 357n.

[89] *Readhead* v. *Midland Railway* (1869) L.R. 4 Q.B. 379.

[90] Therefore a bicycle is not luggage at common law; *Britten* v. *Great Western Railway* [1899] 1 Q.B. 243.

[91] *Macrow* v. *Great Western Railway* (1871) L.R. 6 Q.B. 612.

[92] *Ibid.*

[93] *Hudston* v. *Midland Railway* [1869] L.R. 4 Q.B. 366.

[94] *Gilbey* v. *Great Northern Railway* (1920) 36 T.L.R. 562.

[95] *Cohen* v. *South Eastern Railway* (1873) 2 Ex.D. 235, 238.

[96] *Belfast & Ballymena Railway* v. *Keys* (1861) 9 H.L.C. 556.

[97] Transport Act 1962, s.43.

[98] See 1.31.

[99] See the shipping case of *Bennett* v. *Peninsular & Oriental Steamboat Company* (1848) 6 C.B. 775.

[1] See 1.27.

[2] See 1.28.

for any loss or damage to luggage that he takes into his possession, *e.g.* that he puts in the boot of his coach. The fact that the passenger may accompany his luggage and remain in control of it does not stop the carrier being a common carrier of luggage.[3] However, where the passenger accompanies his luggage there is an implied term of the contract that he will take reasonable care of it.[4] He need not keep too close an eye on it[5] but he must not be negligent.[6]

1.120 **Private carriers of luggage**

Private carriers of passengers' luggage are liable for negligent loss or damage as bailees for reward if the luggage is unaccompanied.[7] Thus in *Houghland* v. *R. Low Ltd.*[8] the plaintiff's luggage disappeared from the boot of a coach. It was held that the burden of disproving negligence fell on the carrier and as he could not disprove it he was held liable. Presumably if the passenger keeps possession of the luggage himself then there is no bailment to the carrier because he never has care and control of the luggage, *i.e.* he never obtains possession of it. However if the goods were damaged or destroyed by the carrier's servants[9] or wrongfully handed by a bus conductor to the wrong person while the owner was not looking there might be liability in the torts of negligence or conversion respectively.[10] The burden of proof would remain on the passenger because there would be no bailment.[11]

1.121 **Luggage, transit at common law**

Transit of unaccompanied luggage commences at common law when the luggage is received by the carrier or one of his servants acting in the course or scope of his apparent authority[12] a reasonable time before the journey.[13] It ends when the passenger has had a reasonable opportunity to collect it at the end of the journey.[14] Once transit has ceased then it seems that the carrier is liable as a warehouseman.[15]

[3] *Lovett* v. *Hobbs* (1680) 2 Show. 127.
[4] *Richards* v. *London, Brighton and South Coast Railway* (1849) 7 C.B. 839.
[5] *Vosper* v. *Great Western Railway* [1928] 1 K.B. 340.
[6] *Talley* v. *Great Western Railway* (1870) L.R. 6 C.P. 44.
[7] See 1.33-1.35.
[8] [1962] 1 Q.B. 694. The Court of Appeal obviously disapproved of the County Court judge's finding that the carrier was a gratuitous bailee as opposed to a bailee for reward but they did not find it necessary to overrule it.
[9] See *Fairline Shipping* v. *Adamson* [1975] 1 Q.B. 180 (negligent damage by an occupier who was not a bailee).
[10] It is not necessary to be in possession of goods in order to be liable for conversion, see *Hiort* v. *Bott* (1874) L.R. 9 Ex. 86.
[11] See 1.03.
[12] *Soanes* v. *London and South West Railway* (1919) 35 T.L.R. 267.
[13] *Great Western Railway* v. *Bunch* (1883) 13 A.C. 31.
[14] *Patscheider* v. *Great Western Railway* (1878) 3 Ex.D. 153.
[15] *Firth* v. *North Eastern* (1886) 36 W.R. 467; *McKinnon* v. *Acadian Lines* (1978) 81 D.L.R. 848 (Canada).

Luggage, British Rail Conditions 1.122

The liability of British Rail, who are of course private carriers,[16] for passengers' luggage is covered by the British Rail Conditions of Carriage for Passengers and their Luggage (June 1986) and not by the General Conditions that are reproduced in Appendix 1.A. The maximum liability for loss, damage or delay in the carriage of luggage is £500 per person.[17] "Luggage" under the Conditions does not mean the same as it does at common law.[18] It is defined as "articles (including motorcycles and similar vehicles, bicycles, perambulators and animals) which passengers may keep with them on the train without inconvenience to other passengers or which can be readily accommodated in the guard's or luggage van." In the case of accompanied luggage the burden is on the passenger to prove neglect or default on the part of British Rail or its staff. In the case of luggage placed in the guard's or luggage van then the burden is on British Rail to disprove negligence.[19] British Rail exempt liability for:

(a) improper packing or labelling,
(b) the goods being of a fragile nature,
(c) loss or damage arising from the passenger's own negligence,
(d) the passenger's failure to accompany his luggage,
(e) the passenger's failure to comply with the Conditions,
(f) any loss arising outside British Rail trains or premises,
(g) consequential loss or damage.

Transit ceases when the journey is finished and the luggage has been removed from the compartment or unloaded from the guard's or luggage van on to the platform and the plaintiff has had a reasonable opportunity to claim it.[20] British Rail disclaim liability as carriers or warehousemen once transit has ceased unless the luggage is left in left luggage lockers or in left luggage offices.[21] However it could be argued that they may be liable as gratuitous (*i.e.* unpaid) bailees for negligent loss or damage at common law.

[16] Transport Act 1962, s.43.

[17] clause 45(b)(i). Because of the quasi-monopolistic position of British Rail and the relevance of the bargaining strength of the parties to the "reasonableness test" in the Unfair Contract Terms Act 1977 this limit may be declared unreasonable by the courts. See 1.45.

[18] See 1.92.

[19] clause 45.

[20] clause 49(a).

[21] clause 49(b).

Chapter Two

FREIGHT FORWARDING

INTRODUCTION

2.01 **Contents**

In this Chapter we outline the legal position of freight forwarders.[1] Traditionally the forwarder was regarded simply as an agent who makes arrangements necessary for the transport of goods on behalf of his customer. Over the years, however, the developing complexity of the transport industry has meant that forwarders have undertaken increasing responsibilities and have become more and more involved in the provision of transport itself. Freight forwarders are important links in the chain of transport and their liabilities need to be fully considered.

We begin with a brief discussion of types of forwarding operations and go on to discuss the problem of classifying such operations. Then we discuss the duties and rights of forwarders. In common with other transport operators forwarders will normally contract on terms contained in standard trading conditions. The chief among these are those of the Institute of Freight Forwarders which are available for use by members of the Institute. The latest set of conditions are those of 1984 which are reproduced in Appendix 2. These conditions will be examined where appropriate. It is important to remember that such conditions can only apply if they are incorporated into the contract between the forwarder and his customer,[2] otherwise the common law will apply.

2.02 **Types of forwarding operations**

It has been said[3] that the forwarder acts as an intermediary between the consignor or consignee and the carriers, warehouse-keepers, customs authorities or other persons in the transport chain with whom his customer would otherwise have to deal. Thus his principal role traditionally has been to make contracts with such persons on behalf of his customer. In addition forwarders will often advise on routes, provide export and import information, and prepare and handle the documentation necessary to enable the goods to reach their destination.[4]

For many years forwarders have engaged in the grouping of consignments from several consignors into a single load to take advantage of bulk rates or discounts offered by carriers.[5] They often

[1] The leading text is Hill, (1972) *Freight Forwarders*.

[2] See 1.43. The nature of freight forwarding often makes this a matter of some difficulty, see *Von Traubenberg* v. *Davies Turner* [1951] 2 Lloyd's Rep. 462. Compare *Circle Freight International* v. *Medeast Gulf Exports* [1988] 2 LLoyd's Rep. 427.

[3] By Hill at p. 4.

[4] Much practical information on forwarding can be found in the National Economic Development Office report on *The Freight Forwarder* published in 1970.

[5] Called "groupage." It is called "consolidation" where carriage by air is involved.

contract with the carrier in their own name, receiving the relevant transport document from him and then, in turn, issuing their own document, such as a "house bill of lading"[6] to the customer as a receipt. Such a "groupage" service, provided by a forwarder, may well be used by an importer as a convenient method of obtaining delivery from a variety of exporters. Groupage arrangements have received much impetus in recent years with the advent of containerisation.[7] Forwarders also frequently provide services such as the packing of goods ready for export, warehousing, and the collection and delivery of the goods to and from a port or airport, etc. Some forwarders even provide scheduled carriage services and, where they do so, are indistinguishable from carriers such as are considered in Chapter One. However, where such carriage is by sea or air it is rare for forwarders actually to own the ship or aircraft used to carry the goods.[8]

PRINCIPAL OR AGENT

The forwarder as principal or agent 2.03

The variety and complexity of forwarding operations can make it difficult to classify them for legal purposes. It is not possible to treat forwarding as a distinct activity subject to its own special rules. Each operation that a forwarder undertakes must be examined to determine which legal rules apply to it. Thus where, for instance, the forwarder simply handles transport arrangements for a customer, and makes contracts with carriers, etc. on the customer's behalf, or fills in the relevant transport documentation, he will be considered to be acting as an agent.[9] In such a case he will be subject to the common law rules of agency unless these are affected by his trading conditions. For example he must select the carrier with reasonable care.[10]

Where however the forwarder provides a service such as the packing, warehousing or carrying of goods he will not be acting as an agent but will be directly responsible for the performance of that service. Thus, for instance, if he carries the goods in his own road vehicle and the goods are lost or damaged whilst in his charge he will be liable to his customer in the same way as any other carrier by road. The position is the same if the forwarder subcontracts the performance of the service to a third party. He will remain responsible for the correct performance of the service by that third party.[11]

[6] It is not a true bill of lading (as to which see 5.07) since the forwarder normally accepts responsibility only as an agent. Compare, however, the exceptional case of *Troy* v. *Eastern Company* (1921) 37 T.L.R. 837. Note also the important F.B.L. used where forwarders provide combined transport, see 7.13.

[7] See generally Chap. 7.

[8] Although they may provide carriage services by means of chartering from the owners of such means of transport. In a trade sense they often operate, in effect, as retailers of wholesale transport services.

[9] See 2.07-2.10 below. See, however, 2.04, especially n. 22.

[10] See 2.07.

[11] See 2.05 below. See also 1.77.

Difficulties arise, however, because it can often be difficult to tell whether a forwarder has, in fact, agreed to perform the particular service or simply to arrange for its performance as an agent on behalf of a customer. The problem has arisen frequently in the courts where there has been carriage of the goods by a third party under instructions given by a forwarder. The courts, in such cases, have to decide whether the third party is a subcontractor of the forwarder or has been brought into a direct contractual relationship with the customer by the forwarder acting as his agent.[12] The factors used by the courts to determine this question are discussed further in 2.04.

2.04 **The forwarder as principal or agent in carriage cases**

The legal difficulty described in 2.03 can be illustrated by contrasting two cases. In *Lee Cooper* v. *Jeakins*,[13] goods were shipped to London. The plaintiff goods owner instructed a forwarder to clear the goods through customs and to forward them to Dublin. The forwarder employed the defendant to collect and carry the goods to a warehouse and in the course of doing so the goods were stolen due to the negligence of the defendant's servant. The defendant looked to the forwarder, with whom he had a standing arrangement to supply vehicles and drivers, rather than the goods owner for payment of his charges. The court held that the forwarder was subcontracting the carriage of the goods to the defendant and not acting as agent for the plaintiff goods owner. This meant that there was no privity of contract between the plaintiff and the defendant who was therefore held to be unable to rely on his standard trading conditions to limit liability.[14]

On the other hand in *Hair and Skin Trading* v. *Norman Airfreight Carriers*,[15] the plaintiff requested a forwarder to arrange storage in bond for goods which had arrived at Heathrow Airport from China. The forwarder was a member of an association which had a standing arrangement with the defendant carrier to collect goods cleared through customs. Through the negligence of the defendant carrier's driver the goods were stolen. The judge held that in this case the forwarder was acting as agent on behalf of the customer. This meant that the defendant carrier was able to rely on the standard trading conditions contained in the contract made through the forwarder.[16]

Various factors can be identified as relevant to the question whether the forwarder has contracted to perform the carriage as principal[17]:

[12] Compare the continental "contract of commission" whereby the forwarder has a special legal status and is considered to be an agent so far as his customer is considered but acts as a principal towards third parties employed to perform the required services. See generally Hill, p. 50.

[13] [1967] 2 Q.B. 1.

[14] He was also held to be unable to rely on the conditions in the forwarder's contract with the plaintiff. See further, however, 1.78.

[15] [1974] 1 Lloyd's Rep. 443.

[16] The forwarder's knowledge of such standard trading conditions at the time the contract is made with the carrier will normally be effective to bind the forwarder's customer to them. Compare, however, *Victoria Fur Traders* v. *Roadline* [1981] 1 Lloyd's Rep. 570.

[17] The matter will be beyond doubt if the forwarder physically performs it himself.

(1) The terms of the contract. If it is expressly stated in the contract that the forwarder agrees to act only as an agent[18] there will be little doubt about the matter. However, contracts are rarely so clear. Standard trading conditions normally acknowledge that a forwarder may act either as agent or principal,[19] but they do not determine in which capacity he is acting in a particular case.[20]

(2) The language used at the time of contracting. Was the forwarder asked to "arrange carriage" or simply to "carry"?

(3) The method of charging adopted by the forwarder. Did he charge an all-in rate for the transport, thus appearing to act like a principal,[21] or simply contract for a commission on top of the actual cost of transport?

(4) The extent to which the customer is informed of the arrangements made on his behalf.[22]

(5) The usual course of business of the forwarder. Has the forwarder acted previously as an agent or as principal?[23]

(6) Finally it is also relevant to know the extent to which the forwarder has invested in capital equipment such as road vehicles, etc. He is more likely to be considered to be operating a carriage service as principal if he in fact runs a fleet of vehicles.[24] This is of considerable importance in carriage by sea or air where a forwarder is not likely to be regarded as a carrier if he neither owns nor charters a ship or aircraft.[25]

The issue of whether the forwarder is acting as principal or agent is relevant both to the liability of the forwarder himself and of any third-party carrier. The liability of the forwarder is likely to be governed, in any case, by standard trading terms if these are incorporated into the contract.[26] However, where international carriage is involved a forwarder may find himself subject to mandatory rules which override his trading conditions if he is held to have contracted as a carrier rather than as an agent.[27]

[18] As in *Victoria Fur Traders* v. *Roadline*, see n. 16 above.

[19] See clause 16(A) of the I.F.F. Standard Trading Conditions 1984.

[20] Although the recognition of the possibility of the forwarder acting as a principal by standard trading conditions was treated as an important factor in *Elektronska Industrija* v. *Transped* [1986] 1 Lloyd's Rep. 49.

[21] See *Colley* v. *Brewer's Wharf and Transport* (1921) 9 Ll. L. Rep. 5. Compare, however, clause 16(B) of the I.F.F. Conditions 1984.

[22] An important factor in *Tetroc* v. *Cross Con* [1981] 1 Lloyd's Rep. 192. See further 3.17. See also clause 16(D) of the I.F.F. Conditions.

[23] See *Marston Excelsior* v. *Arbuckle Smith* 115 S.J. 654.

[24] Whether as owner or under a hiring arrangement.

[25] See *The Maheno* [1977] 1 Lloyd's Rep. 81. An important factor in that case was that the actual shipowner would not have recognised the transport document issued by the forwarder as entitling the holder of it to obtain delivery of the goods so that it could not operate in the normal way as a bill of lading. See 5.11 and 7.10 n. 67.

[26] Subject to the Unfair Contract Terms Act 1977, see 1.45.

[27] *e.g.* under the C.M.R. Convention, see 3.17.

2.05 **The forwarder contracting as a principal**

Where the forwarder agrees personally as principal to pack, store, or carry goods he will be directly responsible for the proper performance of these operations. If he subcontracts their performance he will remain responsible for their proper performance by the subcontractor. Thus in *Metaalhandel* v. *Ardfields Transport Ltd.*,[28] Ardfields agreed to store goods belonging to the plaintiff. They subcontracted this storage to another company and through the negligence of that company the goods were stolen. The judge held that Ardfields never became bailees of the goods because they never had physical possession of them. Nevertheless he held them to be "quasi-bailees" and responsible for the goods just as much as if they were true bailees.[29]

In *Metaalhandel*[30] the defendants were also held to be liable under section 13 of the Supply of Goods and Services Act 1982 which implies, into contracts for a service, a term that the service will be carried out with reasonable care and skill. In this case the defendants were in breach of that term by failing to take steps to see that the subcontractors had secure premises and a suitable system for protecting the goods. This standard of care will apply as a minimum (subject to any trading conditions) to any service which a forwarder performs whether as a principal or as an agent. How it is applied will depend on the circumstances and the extent of the forwarder's duties under the contract. It is the same as the duty of care that would otherwise normally be implied under the common law.[31] Where, however, the forwarder agrees to carry goods, as for instance under a collection and delivery service, the position is more complex.

As discussed in Chapter One the common law makes a distinction, in respect of the carriage of goods, between a common carrier and a private carrier.[32] It is possible for a forwarder to be held to have undertaken the more onerous liability of a common carrier if he held himself out as prepared to carry for anyone in the ordinary course of his business.[33] See 2.06 below, however, for reference to standard trading conditions which purport to deal with this point.

2.06 **The forwarder as a principal, standard trading conditions**

Where a forwarder contracts subject to Institute of Freight Forwarders Standard Trading Conditions 1984,[34] he is entitled under clause 16(A), in the absence of special agreement between himself and the customer, to provide services such as the carriage of the goods either in the capacity of agent or of principal. Clauses 34-35 deal specifically with the situation where a forwarder acts as a principal. Clause 34 purports to provide that the forwarder does not act as a common carrier. Whether or not a clause such as this is effective to achieve this is discussed in 1.26.

[28] [1988] 1 Lloyd's Rep. 197.

[29] See 1.19.

[30] See n. 28 above.

[31] See *Pringle of Scotland* v. *Continental Express* [1962] 2 Lloyd's Rep. 80 at p. 87.

[32] See 1.03.

[33] *Hellaby* v. *Weaver* (1851) 17 L.T. (o.s.) 271; *N.Z.E.C.* v. *Minahan* [1916] N.Z.L.R. 816 (New Zealand). Compare Hill, p. 19.

[34] See Appendix 2.

Clause 34 goes on to give the forwarder a reasonable liberty as to the means, route, and procedure to be followed in the handling, storage and transportation of goods. Clause 35 provides that the forwarder undertakes to perform these agreed services or to procure performance of them. This would seem to imply that it gives a right to the forwarder to subcontract for these services although this is not expressly stated.[35] Clause 35 also states that the forwarder accepts liability for loss or damage to goods between the time they are taken in charge, either by himself or his servants or agents, and the time when the forwarder can call on the customer to take delivery. This contrasts with previous editions of such trading conditions which restricted the liability of the forwarder to the period when he was in actual custody of the goods.[36] The liability in clause 35 is, however, subject to various limits and exclusions which are discussed further in 2.11.

THE FORWARDER AS AN AGENT

The forwarder's responsibilities as agent at common law 2.07

Where a forwarder is engaged to act as an agent he has an obligation to carry out the instructions of his principal with reasonable skill and care.[37] What is implied by the instructions and the degree of discretion open to the forwarder is a matter of interpretation of the instructions in the circumstances of the case and the usual course of dealing with the customer. A good illustration of this is the case of *World Transport Agency* v. *Royte*.[38] In this case a forwarder was held not liable for failure to clear his customer's goods through customs despite the fact that if he had done so he could have saved his customer an increase in customs duty. This decision was reached because the usual course of dealing with the customer was for the forwarder to clear goods only on receiving instructions from the customer to do so and because the forwarder thought it reasonably likely that the goods would have been sold to a third party who would himself have cleared them.

Where his instructions are ambiguous the forwarder will not be liable if he takes a reasonable interpretation of them.[39] He cannot, however, depart from clear instructions unless, perhaps, there is an emergency and he is unable to contact his principal. He may, however, be expected to go back to his customer and to seek clarification or further instructions. Thus in *Von Traubenberg* v. *Davies Turner*[40] the defendant was instructed to forward a suitcase containing silver heirlooms from London to Liverpool. On loss of the suitcase the customer received only limited compensation from the railway because the defendant had failed to make the declaration necessary

[35] The right to subcontract is also implied in clause 11. See, however, *Garnham Harris & Elton* v. *Alfred W. Ellis Transport* [1967] 1 W.L.R. 940. See 1.48 and 1.77.

[36] As did clause 13(1) of the 1970 edition of the I.F.F. Standard Trading Conditions, see Hill, p. 298. See also, *e.g. Gillette Industries* v. *Martin*, n. 43 below, and *Troy* v. *Eastern Company*, n. 6 above.

[37] Both at common law and under s.13 of The Supply of Goods and Services Act 1982.

[38] [1957] 1 Lloyd's Rep. 381.

[39] *Ireland* v. *Livingston* (1872) L.R. 5 H.L. 395.

[40] [1951] 2 Lloyd's Rep. 462.

under the Carriers Act 1830.[41] The forwarder was held to have been negligent in failing to get appropriate instructions from the customer or discovering whether the goods were insured. Where the forwarder is dealing with ordinary commercial goods, however, he is under no duty to obtain insurance or to inquire whether the goods are insured.[42]

Where the forwarder's instructions are to arrange for the carriage of the goods, or some other service in respect of them, his duty is to take care to engage apparently competent persons to do the task.[43] Provided he has exercised due care he is not responsible should such persons fail to perform the task or if their negligent performance leads to the loss, damage or delay of the goods.[44] Likewise he is not liable if loss etc., should occur whilst the goods are in the hands of a third party, such as customs authorities, into whose hands the goods must pass.[45] Furthermore the forwarder is under no obligation to supervise the actions of persons engaged to perform services for the customer.[46] However, if the forwarder becomes aware that problems have arisen concerning goods in transit or that they have been lost or damaged he must inform his customer[47] or be held liable if his failure results in the customer being unable to protect his interest, *e.g.* by failing to make a claim against the carrier within a contractual time limit. The same rule will apply if the forwarder fails to make investigations if facts have come to his attention which should have indicated to him that there was a problem concerning the goods.[48]

2.08 **The forwarder's responsibilities under standard trading conditions**

Clause 4 of the I.F.F. Standard Trading Conditions 1984 sets out the responsibilities of a freight forwarder using these conditions. The forwarder[49] is required to perform his duties with a reasonable degree of care, diligence, skill and judgment. This is in accord with the common law duty of care, in stark contrast to the 1981 edition of the Conditions, which only imposed responsibility if the forwarder had been guilty of wilful neglect or default.[50] The forwarder is also required to carry out his services in a reasonable time and to take reasonable steps to perform the customer's instructions. However, clause 4(D) also gives the forwarder a discretion to depart from the customer's instructions should he reasonably consider that there is good reason to do so in the customer's interest.[51] Under clause 5 if events occur which make it impossible for the company to fulfil its duties it must take reasonable steps to inform the customer and seek further instructions.

[41] See 1.30-1.32.
[42] *W.L.R. Traders Ltd.* v. *B. & N. Shipping Agency Ltd.* [1955] 1 Lloyd's Rep. 554.
[43] For an example see *Gillette Industries* v. *Martin* [1966] 1 Lloyd's Rep. 57.
[44] *Marston Excelsior* v. *Arbuckle Smith* [1971] 2 Lloyd's Rep. 306.
[45] *Jones* v. *European & General Express* (1920) 4 Ll.L. Rep. 127.
[46] *Marston Excelsior* n. 44 above.
[47] *G. Peereboom* v. *World Transport Agency* (1921) 6 Ll.L.Rep. 170.
[48] *George Pulman* v. *Crowe* (1920) 3 Ll.L.Rep. 100.
[49] Referred to as "The Company" in the Conditions.
[50] See 1.60. See also *Circle Freight International,* above n. 2.
[51] Compare clause 3 of the 1981 edition of the Conditions which left it to the forwarder's opinion whether there was such good reason. See also clause 4(E) of the 1984 Conditions in Appendix 2.

Other clauses are also relevant to the performance of the forwarder's tasks. Clause 21 purports to relieve the forwarder of any duty to insure the goods unless expressly instructed to do so. Clause 22 purports to relieve him of any obligation to declare the nature or value of goods or special interest in delivery for the purpose of any statute, (*e.g.* the Carriers Act),[52] convention or contract. Clause 32, which is one of a set of clauses (clauses 29-32) dealing specifically with the situation where the forwarder acts as a forwarding agent, is similar to clause 22. It, likewise purports to relieve the forwarder from the responsibility of choosing a freight rate which would produce a recovery more favourable for the customer. It also relieves him from liability should the contract made on behalf of the customer with the carrier, warehouseman or other person contain exclusions or limits of liability (subject to express instructions). In so far as these clauses purport to relieve the forwarder from obligations which would otherwise apply,[53] they are subject to the possibility of challenge under the "reasonableness test" in the Unfair Contract Terms Act 1977.[54]

When acting as an agent the forwarder is given a wide authority[55] in respect of the contracts he makes on the customer's behalf as regards, *e.g.* route, means of transport or carrier selected. Clause 31 also gives the forwarder authority to subcontract the performance of its obligations. This is important because usually an agent cannot delegate his authority unless this is clearly authorised by the principal.[56] This clause also purports to give such subcontractors the benefit of the forwarder's Conditions.[57]

Note, finally, that clauses 26-28 require express agreement in writing with a forwarder using these conditions before certain goods can be accepted for forwarding. These are dangerous goods, goods likely to harbour vermin, and other goods listed in clause 28(A) which are valuable, or are difficult to carry, such as livestock.

Whose instructions must the forwarder obey? 2.09

In the first instance a forwarder will be under a duty to follow the instructions of his principal.[58] Finding the relevant principal can be a problem. A forwarder may well find himself arranging a complex transport of goods from the point of despatch to destination (perhaps involving several carriers), clearing the goods through customs, warehousing them, delivering them to the consignee as well as handling all the necessary documentation. In such a situation a forwarder may begin as the agent of the consignor-seller and at a later point become the agent of the consignee-buyer.[59]

[52] See 1.30-1.32.

[53] See 2.07 and especially the *Von Traubenberg* case, n. 40 above.

[54] See 1.45.

[55] By clause 30.

[56] See generally Markesinis and Munday, *An Outline of the Law of Agency* (2nd ed., 1986).

[57] It is an "Himalaya Clause," see 1.78.

[58] However, only where he has contractually bound himself to perform will a forwarder be legally obliged to carry out an order given by a principal.

[59] He may even be considered to be the agent of a series of principals in respect of a particular transaction, see *Brown, McFarlane* v. *Shaw Lovell* (1921) 7 Ll.L. Rep. 36.

Even when this occurs he may only be the agent of the consignee for a particular purpose, *e.g.* clearing the goods through customs whilst remaining the agent of the consignor for the purpose of delivery to the consignee.[60] The precise circumstances must be examined carefully since not only will the answer to the question, whom is he acting for affect the rights and liability of the forwarder but may well also determine whether a right of stoppage in transit can be validly exercised.[61] Thus if a forwarder comes into possession of goods and is held at that point to be the agent of the consignee-buyer, even if at an earlier stage he was acting for the consignor-seller, the seller's right to stop the goods in transit will be defeated.[62]

As discussed in 1.05-1.09 a carrier by land is presumed to have contracted with a consignee by reason of the latter's ownership in the goods. It is common however, for the courts to find that by giving instructions to a forwarder the consignor will have entered into a contract with him on his own behalf unless it was clear to the forwarder that the consignor was contracting as agent for the consignee.[63] Even if the forwarder is considered to be the agent of one party he must be wary of the fact that the goods may in fact belong to another. An agent is not entitled to obey an instruction if by doing so he commits a tort (such as conversion) against another.[64] He may therefore be liable in conversion if he withholds goods from the true owner[65] or delivers them to a person whom he knows not to be the true owner.[66] Furthermore, a forwarder must be especially careful when handling documents of title.[67] In these various circumstances it is an advantage for forwarders to ensure that their standard trading terms are incorporated into the contract with their principal. Clause 7 of the I.F.F. Conditions is an example of a clause which is intended to protect a forwarder in these situations.

Note finally that forwarders often receive instructions from other forwarders. Thus a receiving agent in the country of import may well receive his instructions from the sending agent in the country of export. In such a case the receiving agent will be acting as a sub-agent and will probably only have privity of contract with the sending agent and not the latter's principal whoever that may be. This can have important implications in respect of the receiving agent's rights and liabilities.[68]

[60] See *Lund* v. *A.O.T.* [1955] 1 Lloyd's Rep. 142. Such an arrangement can give rise to conflicts of duty which often arise because of the fact that forwarders frequently act for more than one party. See further Hill, p. 44.

[61] For the right of stoppage in transit see 1.73.

[62] See *Jobson* v. *Eppenheim* (1905) 21 T.L.R. 468, and *Johann Plischke* v. *Allison Bros.* (1936) 55 Ll.L. Rep. 262.

[63] See *Universal Shipping and Forwarding Co. Ltd.* v. *Commercial and Industrial Co. Ltd.* (1919) 1 Ll.L. Rep. 635, and *E.W. Taylor* v. *Bell* [1968] 2 Lloyd's Rep. 63.

[64] *Per* Devlin J. in *Angelo Casteletti* v. *Transmaritime* [1953] 2 Lloyd's Rep. 440 at p. 447.

[65] In the absence of a right to retain the goods such as a right of lien, see 2.14 below.

[66] See generally Hill, Chap. 6.

[67] See *Kolbin & Sons* v. *United Shipping Company Ltd.* (1931) 40 LL.L Rep. 241, and *Brown, McFarlane,* n. 59 above.

[68] See *Angelo Casteletti* v. *Transmaritime* n. 64 above.

The forwarder and third parties 2.10

Where a forwarder contracts with his customer as a principal rather than as an agent then he will also contract as a principal with persons whom he engages to perform those parts of his contract which he does not perform personally. Where he acts as an agent however, it is normally the case as is usual in the law of agency, that he will not be under any personal liability towards those persons with whom he makes arrangements on behalf of his customer. Thus he cannot normally be required to pay, *e.g.* a carrier's charges if his customer does not pay.

Such a personal liability, however, may be imposed by statute or regulation, *e.g.* a duty to pay port charges. Forwarders may also be under a personal liability by reason of a custom of a particular trade or industry. Thus in carriage by air, airfreight agents are personally liable for freight to the carrier by air under a custom incorporated into I.A.T.A.[69] resolutions.[70] Personal liability for dead freight[71] is also undertaken by forwarders when booking freight space on the London freight market under a custom of the market.[72] Where such personal liability is undertaken by the forwarder in accordance with law or custom, the forwarder has the right to an indemnity from his customer.[73] If however a forwarder chooses to incur a liability to a third party[74] which the law or custom does not otherwise impose on him he will need to ensure that his contract provides him with an indemnity.[75]

Note also that when a forwarder delivers goods to a carrier he will be subject to the "consignor's warranty of fitness" discussed in 1.94. Thus the common law imposes a personal liability on him regardless of his actual knowledge of the fitness of the goods for carriage.[76] The I.F.F. Conditions contain clauses designed to protect the forwarder[77] by requiring the customer to give him proper information and to ensure that the goods are properly packed.[78] Special arrangements are required in respect of dangerous goods.[79]

DEFENCES AND EXCLUSION OF LIABILITY

Defences and exclusions of liability under standard trading conditions 2.11

The I.F.F. Conditions 1984 contain provisions which exempt and limit the liability of a forwarder whether acting as principal or agent

[69] International Air Transport Association.
[70] *Perishables Transport* v. *N. Spyropoulos* [1964] 2 Lloyd's Rep. 379.
[71] See 5.56.
[72] *Anglo Overseas Transport Ltd.* v. *Titan Industrial Corp. Ltd.* [1959] 2 Lloyd's Rep. 152.
[73] See 2.13 below.
[74] Which he may do simply by acting in his own name without revealing the name of his principal.
[75] See clause 9(B) of the I.F.F. Conditions 1984.
[76] *Brass* v. *Maitland* (1856) 6 E. & B. 470.
[77] Under the common law, when acting as an agent, he can only sue his customer for negligence. See Hill, p. 134.
[78] Clauses 12-13. [79] Clauses 26-27. See 2.08 above.

on behalf of the customer. Clause 36 sets out the defences available to the forwarder and places the burden on him to prove them. These include the familiar defences of "act or omission of the customer"[80] and "inherent vice,"[81] etc., but also the general defence of: "any cause or event which the Company was unable to avoid and the consequences whereof the Company was unable to prevent by the exercise of reasonable diligence." This ties in with the overall duty of the forwarder stated in clause 4[82] so that, in essence, the forwarder is liable for the failure to exercise reasonable care. However, the burden is on him to prove that loss, etc., occurred despite the exercise by him of such care, if he seeks to escape from liability.

Note also that clause 28(A) excludes the liability of the forwarder, should the customer deliver goods listed in this clause to him without prior agreement in writing unless the forwarder is proved to have waived his right to rely on this exclusion, *e.g.* by knowingly accepting such goods for carriage.

Clause 37(A) imposes limits on the liability of the forwarder. In the case of claims for loss or damage to goods the limit is 2 S.D.R.'s[83] (*i.e.* approx. £1.70) per kilo,[84] not exceeding the value of the goods. In respect of all other claims[85] the limit is either 2 S.D.R.'s per kilo up to the value of the goods involved in the transaction, or 75,000 S.D.R.'s (approx. £40,000) in respect of any one transaction, whichever is the least. In the case of loss or damage as a result of failure to deliver or to arrange delivery within a reasonable time, or to adhere to agreed arrival or departure dates, clause 37(B) imposes a limit of twice the amount of the company's charges in respect of the relevant transaction.[86] These various limits can be increased, if the customer wishes on payment of an additional charge[87] and this possibility will be an important factor in determining whether these limits satisfy the "reasonableness test" in the Unfair Contract Terms Act 1977.[88]

Clause 15 requires the customer to make a claim in writing and without delay and excludes the liability of the company if a delay causes prejudice to it. Furthermore clause 17 requires claims to be brought in any event, and written notice to be given within nine months from the date of the event or occurrence giving rise to the claim.

Note that all of these various exclusions and limits are subject to the possibility of their being displaced by compulsory rules which might apply to the particular service performed by the forwarder. Thus, if a forwarder provides international road carriage as a principal for his customer he will be subject to the C.M.R. Convention,[89] and unable to rely on the I.F.F. conditions in so far as they derogate from the Convention.[90] The I.F.F. conditions recognise this by referring to such

[80] See 1.28.

[81] See 1.28.

[82] See 2.08 above.

[83] These are explained in 3.60.

[84] This is about twice the limit applied by the R.H.A. Conditions, see 1.59.

[85] Such as, presumably, failing to clear goods through customs in time resulting in expense to the customer.

[86] Liability for consequential loss is otherwise excluded by clause 37(C). See further, however, clause 37(D), n. 87 below.

[87] Clause 37(D). See also clause 37(E).

[88] See the discussion in 1.59.

[89] See 3.17.

[90] See 3.09.

compulsory rules in clauses 3, 37(F) and 38. Clause 38, in fact, makes the "Warsaw Statement" necessary whenever a forwarder agrees to provide international carriage of goods by air.[91]

Note finally clause 11 which seeks to protect the forwarding company's employees and to provide the company with an indemnity should it face claims in excess of its liability under the conditions.[92]

RIGHTS OF THE FORWARDER

Remuneration 2.12

Where a forwarder acts as a principal in relation to his customer he will normally charge a price for the service which will include his profit. Even where the customer demands the delivery of his goods before the service is completed (as he has every right to do, see 1.76) the forwarder will still be entitled to full payment.[93] Where the forwarder is an agent, various methods of charging the customer with whom he contracts[94] may be employed, such as an inclusive rate, but in common with other agents, forwarders frequently charge a commission or agency fee normally as a percentage of the cost of freight or value of the cargo. As an agent however, a forwarder could not charge for work that was not performed.

It is common for forwarders to receive commissions, allowances, etc. from other persons, such as carriers,[95] in addition to what they contract for with their customer. In strict law the forwarder is not entitled to retain them except with the customer's knowledge and approval.[96] To avoid dispute however, clause 42 of the I.F.F. Conditions purports to permit a company contracting under them to retain and be paid all "brokerages commissions allowances and other remunerations customarily retained by or paid to freight forwarders."

Indemnity 2.13

At common law, an agent such as a forwarder, has a right to be indemnified by his principal if he incurs an expense or liability within the proper exercise of his authority. This will apply if he is expressly authorised to incur the expense, but it can also be implied if such expense, etc. arises as a necessary incident of carrying out the principal's instructions. Thus, if a statutory body such as a port authority, requires the forwarder to make some payment before the goods can be exported he can recover this sum from his principal.[97] It

[91] See 6.25.

[92] See 1.87 for an explanation of this type of indemnity clause. The wording of the clause in these conditions seems more likely to achieve the desired object than the equivalent clause in the R.H.A. Conditions.

[93] *Troy* v. *Eastern Company* (1921) 37 T.L.R. 837.

[94] See 2.09 above. See also clause 40 of the I.F.F. Conditions. See the discussion in 1.109 in respect of this type of clause.

[95] Especially where, as happens sometimes in carriage by sea, the forwarder acts as a loading broker on behalf of the shipowner.

[96] Since they are "secret profits," see *Brown* v. *I.R.C.* [1965] A.C. 224.

[97] *P.S.A. Transport Ltd.* v. *Newton Landsdowne & Co. Ltd.* [1956] 1 Lloyd's Rep. 121.

seems that, in addition, a forwarder can recover an indemnity for expenses which were not in the original contemplation of the parties but which are reasonably incurred by the forwarder in the performance of his duties, *e.g.* warehousing goods due to unforseen delays in transporting them.[98] Similarly, an indemnity is obtainable where an expense or liability is directly incurred by reason of the customer's actions or fault.[99]

It is not sufficient, however, for the expense or liability of the forwarder to arise simply because the forwarder incurs it in the course of carrying out his customer's instructions. If the forwarder, *e.g.* delivers or withholds delivery of goods on the instructions of his customer but in doing so incurs a liability towards some other person who is in fact the owner of the goods he will not necessarily obtain an indemnity from his customer. It will be a question of fact whether an agreement to indemnify the forwarder can be implied in the circumstances.[1] A forwarder who faces such a potential liability would be advised to obtain an express agreement to indemnify him from his principal.[2] Similar difficulties can arise if the forwarder accepts a personal liability to a third party which he has no authority to accept as an agent.[3]

The I.F.F. Conditions contain several indemnities and warranties to protect the forwarder. Clauses 7 and 9 are of particular importance in this context. These provisions both consolidate and expand the protection afforded by the common law.[4] To obtain their protection a forwarder will need to ensure that they are, in fact, incorporated into his contract with the customer.[5]

Note finally that if a forwarder purports to act for someone with whom he does not have privity of contract and incurs a liability by doing so he will need to prove an agreement between them for an indemnity before he can recover for such liability. This is a particular source of difficulty where forwarders incur liabilities in the course of delivering goods to a consignee and then fail to recover an indemnity from such consignee because the courts find that there is no agreement between them in respect of it.[6]

2.14 **The forwarder's rights of lien and sale**

Where a forwarder acts as a principal in relation to his customer he will have whatever rights of lien and sale are available at common

[98] *Per* Greer J. in *Immediate Transportation Co. Ltd* v. *Speller, Willis & Co.* (1920) 2 Ll.L. Rep. 645 at p. 647.

[99] As occurred in the *Immediate Transportation* case, n. 98 above.

[1] *Donald Stewart & Co.* v. *John Lofthouse & Co.* (1921) 9 Ll.L. Rep. 386.

[2] As in *Lund* v. *A.O.T.* [1955] 1 Lloyd's Rep. 142.

[3] See 2.10 above.

[4] Clause 7 is important in providing the forwarder with protection where his customer is not, in fact, the owner of the goods.

[5] See *Von Traubenberg* v. *Davies, Turner & Co.* [1951] 2 Lloyd's Rep. 462 for the difficulties that forwarders often face in this respect by reason of the nature of their operations. See also 1.43.

[6] See *Angelo Casteletti* v. *Transmaritime* [1953] 2 Lloyd's Rep. 440. See further n. 13 below.

law, in respect of the service he provides. Thus where he acts as a carrier by land he will have any rights discussed in 1.100 and 1.110-1.111. Where the forwarder acts as an agent he has at common law, a particular lien,[7] as against his principal, over such property of his principal as he has rightfully in his possession for charges incurred in relation to that property.[8] If the forwarder is not in possession of the goods any attempt by him to interfere with the transit of the goods, *e.g.* by inducing a carrier to prevent delivery to a consignee, will put him in breach of contract with his principal.[9] Even if he has the goods in his possession, where the property has passed in them to someone other than his principal, he will only be able to exercise the rights, if any, that his principal has against that person.[10]

Clause 41 of the I.F.F. Conditions purports to give a general lien[11] on goods and documents in the forwarder's possession, custody or control for all sums due from the "customer"[12] or owner. It also gives a right to sell the goods on 28 days' notice in writing to the customer. Note, however, that a right of sale is also given by clause 19(B) in respect of uncollected goods and this can be exercised on 21 days notice in writing to the customer, or after holding the goods for 90 days if the customer cannot be traced. These contractual rights can normally only be exercised against a person with whom the forwarder is in privity of contract[13] and only if they are properly incorporated into the contract.

[7] See 1.111.

[8] See generally Markesinis and Munday, *An Outline of the Law of Agency* (2nd ed., 1986). See also *Angelo Casteletti* n. 6 above, *per* Devlin J. at p. 449.

[9] *Langley, Beldon & Gaunt Ltd.* v. *Morley* [1965] 1 Lloyd's Rep. 297.

[10] *Brunton* v. *Electrical Engineering Co.* [1892] 2 Ch. 434. See further Hill, p. 221 for the complexities where the forwarder is a sub-agent. See also 1.114.

[11] See 1.112.

[12] Compare the use made of the word "Trader" in the R.H.A. Conditions, see 1.16.

[13] See clause 8 of the I.F.F. Conditions which seeks to apply the conditions to persons other than the initial customer. This may only be effective if a contract can, in fact, be proved to have been made with them. See further, however, 1.114. See also clause 7.

Chapter Three

INTERNATIONAL CARRIAGE BY ROAD

INTRODUCTION

3.01 **Contents**

In this Chapter we examine the law governing international carriage of goods by road, as well as outlining briefly that relating to the international carriage of passengers and luggage by road. Later chapters will deal with other modes of international carriage but some matters of general relevance, such as the interpretation of international carriage conventions, are also considered in this Chapter.

International carriage differs from carriage within the United Kingdom because the legal position largely tends to be governed by international conventions rather than by the common law or the terms of any particular contract that the parties have made. Thus most contracts for the international carriage of goods by road to or from the United Kingdom are governed by the C.M.R. Convention,[1] which must be considered in detail. We refer in the footnotes to leading texts on C.M.R.[2]

To become part of English law such international rules must be given effect by an Act of Parliament. In the case of C.M.R. the relevant Act is the Carriage of Goods by Road Act 1965, which is reproduced in Appendix 3.A.[3]

3.02 **Conflict of laws**

C.M.R., like other international conventions which regulate contracts of carriage, lays down a standardised "regime" of liability. The reason for this is the international nature of such contracts; *e.g.* A in England sends goods to B in Spain by C a French carrier. Any court dealing with a claim is faced with a problem of "conflict of laws" because of the international nature of the contract. This means that the court would have to decide whether it can take jurisdiction[4] and whether to apply English, Spanish or French law. Such problems are largely overcome if an international convention applies to govern the case.

Such conventions do not necessarily cover every point of law that might arise in a case or, alternatively, the relevant convention might

[1] The Convention on the Contract for the International Carriage of Goods by Road. The initials C.M.R. are taken from the French title: *Convention Relative au Contrat de Transport International de Marchandises par Route.*

[2] The principal texts in English are: Clarke, *International Carriage of Goods by Road: C.M.R.* (1982); Hill and Messent, *C.M.R.: Contracts for the International Carriage of Goods by Road* (1984); and Haak, *The Liability of the Carrier under the C.M.R.* (1986).

[3] The Convention is set out in the Schedule to the Act.

[4] *i.e.* hear the case. See further 3.78.

not apply at all. In that case a court will have to turn to English law to deal with the point provided that English law is the "proper law" of the contract.[5] Thus if an issue is not governed by C.M.R. an English court will normally apply common law or the provisions of the contract.[6] If therefore an international road carrier were, as is possible, held to be a common carrier[7] he could be sued under the common law for refusing to carry, but would be liable under C.M.R. for any loss or damage in transit if he does carry.

International carriage conventions and the Unfair Contract Terms Act 3.03

Where C.M.R. or other conventions apply *there is no question* of applying the Unfair Contract Terms Act 1977.[8]

The C.M.R. Convention 3.04

C.M.R. was drafted in 1956 by the Economic Commission for Europe.[9] The need for such a convention reflected the growth of international road haulage in Europe after the Second World War. It was first adopted by nine European states in 1961 but it is now widely adopted throughout Europe.[10] It was adopted by the United Kingdom in 1967, and was amended by a protocol in 1979.[11] The reader is advised to refer where necessary to the Convention, which is reproduced in Appendix 3.A.

The interpretation of international carriage conventions 3.05

The courts recognise that a more flexible and liberal approach to the interpretation of the wording of international conventions is possible than might be permitted when dealing with purely domestic United Kingdom legislation. Such conventions are often more loosely drafted than are Acts of Parliament which are drafted to meet the strict English rules of interpretation. The courts of this country also recognise the need for consistency with the decisions of continental courts so that, as far as is possible, such conventions are applied uniformly throughout the states which adopt them.

This more flexible approach was first adopted in carriage by sea,[12] and has since been applied to carriage by road and by air.[13] The leading case in relation to C.M.R. is *Buchanan* v. *Babco.*[14] In this case the question for decision was whether damages payable by the carrier in consequence of the theft of a container load of whisky should

[5] The law which has the closest connection to the contract.

[6] See generally Chap. 1.

[7] See 1.21-1.32.

[8] Excluded by s.29 of the Unfair Contract Terms Act 1977, as to which see 1.45. See also s.26.

[9] A United Nations Organisation.

[10] Presently by 24 states.

[11] Brought into effect by the Carriage by Air and Road Act 1979, see 3.60. Future amendments can now be made under s.9 of the International Transport Conventions Act 1983.

[12] See, *e.g. Stag Line* v. *Foscolo Mango* (1931) 41 LL.L.Rep. 165.

[13] *Fothergill* v. *Monarch Airlines* [1981] 2 A.C. 251. See 3.06.

[14] [1977] 1 All E.R. 518, affirmed [1978] A.C. 141.

include the amount of excise duty paid by the claimant, *i.e.* the plaintiff,[15] in respect of the stolen whisky. If the whisky had been exported, no duty would have been payable. However since the loss was due to theft (possibly in the United Kingdom) it was impossible to prove that it had been exported and so excise duty was payable to the customs authority. Recovery of the excise duty paid was possible under C.M.R. if the duty could be considered as a "charge incurred in respect of the carriage of the goods."[16] This could mean either "expenses specifically incurred in respect of carriage," or "expenses incurred by reason of the way the goods were carried." Only on the latter wider interpretation could the claimant succeed. The Court of Appeal and a majority of the House of Lords accepted this wider interpretation, thus reflecting a more liberal approach than might have been possible had the court been concerned with purely domestic legislation.

3.06 **Interpretation, the "purposive" approach**

Lord Wilberforce said in *Buchanan,*[17] that the correct aproach to take towards the wording of an international convention was to interpret it "in a normal manner . . . unconstrained by technical rules of English law, or by English legal precedent but on broad principles of general acceptation." The majority of the House of Lords were prepared to take the view that the wording of Article 23(4) was unclear, and this permitted the court to consider the reasons for the provision, and so come to a view about its meaning based on what could be considered as its object. All the judges rejected the approach of Lord Denning in the Court of Appeal,[18] which was that the Convention had left a "gap" which could be filled by considering the "object" of the provision in question.

The decision of the House of Lords in *Fothergill* v. *Monarch Airlines*[19] also illustrates the flexible approach.[20] This case involved the interpretation of Article 26(2) of the Warsaw Convention[21] concerning carriage by air. Taking a "purposive" view, the House held that the partial loss of contents from baggage could be considered as "damage" and not simply as "loss." Article 26(2) required the claimant to give seven days' notice of "damage." The question was whether the loss of part of the contents of a suitcase amounted to such "damage." The object of the provision was, it was decided, to ensure that the carrier had adequate notice of a claim in circumstances where it would not be obvious to him that things had gone wrong during the carriage. The loss of an entire suitcase would be obvious, but this would not be so in the case of partial loss of contents with the result that notice of such partial loss should be required.

[15] It is usual to refer to the plaintiff as the "claimant" in C.M.R. cases.

[16] Under Art. 23(4), see 3.63.

[17] [1978] A.C. 141, 152.

[18] [1977] 1 All E.R. 518, 523.

[19] [1981] 2 A.C. 251.

[20] See further Munday, "The Uniform Interpretation of International Conventions" (1978) 27 I.C.L.Q. 450, and Megaw L.J. in *Ulster Swift* v. *Taunton Meat Haulage* [1977] 1 Lloyd's Rep. 346, 351. See also *The Morviken* [1983] A.C. 565.

[21] See 6.54.

Interpretation, using the foreign language text

Under Article 51 of C.M.R. both the English and French texts are equally authentic. However, unlike the Carriage by A 1961 which implements the Warsaw Convention,[22] the French te not reproduced in the Schedule to the 1965 Act. Thus in *Fothergill*[23] was quite natural to refer to the French text to aid interpretation of the Warsaw Convention. In *Buchanan*[24] there was some difference between Lord Wilberforce,[25] who thought it "perfectly legitimate . . . to look for assistance, if assistance be needed, to the French Text" of C.M.R., and the other Law Lords[26] who generally took the view that this would only be legitimate when there is a doubt as to the meaning of the English text.

Where reference can in fact be made to the French text by the courts, the extent to which expert guidance in respect of translation should be obtained, depends on the level of difficulty involved.[27]

Interpretation, using decisions of foreign courts and "Travaux Préparatoires" 3.08

In *Buchanan*,[28] it was accepted that in the interests of uniformity[29] reference could be made to continental decisions on the Convention but that the English courts are not forced to do so when no consistent interpretation of the relevant provision of the Convention emerges from an examination of them. The student must therefore be aware of this continental dimension and the fact that some issues may effectively be resolved where there is a consistent body of continental case law.[30]

In *Fothergill*,[31] the issue arose of whether reference was permissible to official documentation such as the proceedings of the diplomatic conference at which the Convention was drafted (usually termed "Travaux Préparatoires") to discover the likely intention of those who drew up the Convention. This was stated by the House of Lords to be permissible provided a court proceeded with caution and that such material was readily available. There are "Travaux Préparatoires" to the Warsaw Convention[32] but not to C.M.R. There is a commentary on C.M.R. by R. Loewe based on the conference papers,[33] but although referred to on occasion, it is not treated with quite the same authority as "Travaux Préparatoires."

[22] See generally Chap. 6.
[23] See 3.06.
[24] See 3.05.
[25] At p. 152.
[26] See in particular Viscount Dilhorne at p. 158.
[27] See Lord Wilberforce in *Fothergill* at p. 274.
[28] See 3.05.
[29] Consistency between the courts of different countries in respect of the same provisions.
[30] The chief and most easily available set of reports containing European decisions is European Transport Law. Note also that many cases reported in the Uniform Law Review and Uniform Law Cases are reproduced in Hill and Evans, *Transport laws of the World*. (1988).
[31] See above n. 19.
[32] See Chap. 6.
[33] See (1976) XI E.T.L. 311.

APPLICATION OF C.M.R.

3.09 Introduction

Section 1 of the Carriage of Goods by Road Act 1965 provides that the Convention, as set out in the Schedule, "shall have the force of law so far as it relates to the rights and liabilities of persons concerned in the carriage of goods by road under a contract to which the Convention applies." This provision means that domestic rules are displaced when C.M.R. applies and also means that the rules concerning conflict of laws (see 3.02) do not apply to an issue governed by it. Once C.M.R. applies, Article 41 prohibits the parties to a contract of carriage from writing into the contract any term which derogates from the Convention. Thus, they cannot alter the rights and responsibilities set out in it.[34]

3.10 Application, the basic rules

Article 1(1) lays down the main rules for the application of the Convention:

(a) There must be a contract for the carriage of the goods by road for reward. The mere fact of carriage is insufficient. So purely gratuitous, *i.e.* unpaid, carriage, even though international, is not covered by C.M.R.

(b) There must be carriage of "goods." "Goods" is undefined. It is unclear whether an English court would refer to the various domestic statutory definitions of the word "goods," such as those in the Sale of Goods Act 1979, or the Theft Act 1968. The word should not be interpreted too narrowly, especially as there are specific exclusions set out in Article 1(4), which would not be necessary if "goods" meant merchandise sent by way of trade.[35] These exclusions are goods carried under the terms of any International Postal Convention, funeral consignments, and furniture removal.[36] It is said[37] that passenger's luggage is not "goods" for the purposes of C.M.R.[38]

(c) The place of taking over the goods and the place designated, for delivery, as specified in the contract, must be in two different countries of which one at least must be a party to the Convention. The fact that the goods never arrive at the destination (or even leave the country of departure) makes no difference so long as the contract contemplates international carriage and the specified place of depar-

[34] Unless the Convention itself permits this as in Art. 24, see 3.66.

[35] Although this might be suggested by use of the word "marchandises" in the French text. See further Loewe, para. 25. Note that tanks belonging to the consignor have been held not to be goods, see the decision of the District Commercial Court, Antwerp, (1977) XII E.T.L. 420. See also (1972) VII E.T.L. 1054. Compare *Acme Transport* v. *Betts* [1981] 1 Lloyd's Rep. 131.

[36] Art. 1(4). Use of the word "déménagement" in the French text suggests that removal of household effects as well as furniture may be included in the exclusion of furniture removal. The mere carriage of furniture as such without some element of "removal" is not within this exclusion, District Commercial Court, Antwerp, (1980) XV E.T.L. 461. See further, Loewe, para. 36.

[37] By Loewe, para. 25.

[38] It is not "marchandises."

ture or contemplated destination are in a Contracting State. The places of residence or nationality of the parties are also irrelevant. Thus if a contract of carriage, *e.g.* provides for carriage by road between England and Morocco (which is not a party to the Convention) or vice versa, it is subject to C.M.R. because the carriage is international and England is a party to the Convention. This would be so (and any claim could be brought in England) even if none of the persons involved in the contract of carriage were English or even resident in England.[39]

(d) The carriage must be in "vehicles." This means motor vehicles, articulated vehicles, trailers and semi-trailers.[40]

Application, frontier traffic 3.11

Article 1(5) permits Contracting States to exclude C.M.R. from their "frontier traffic." Note that Britain and Eire have made it inapplicable to carriage between them. Presumably therefore where the contract is for carriage solely between these two countries then C.M.R. is not applicable. However if, *e.g.* a contract provided for carriage between Eire and France (which is a Contracting State), and this involved transit through England, the contract would still be governed by C.M.R. and English courts would apply it.[41]

Application, the "contract" of carriage 3.12

Article 1 refers to every "contract" of carriage. A carrier might make a series of separate contracts of carriage for the same goods and claim that those which do not cross international frontiers are not covered by C.M.R., *e.g.* by issuing separate consignment notes for different stages of the journey. Naturally the courts require that these are genuinely different contracts and not really part of the same contract. Thus in *Moto Vespa* v. *MAT (Britannia Express) Ltd.*,[42] goods originally meant for Barcelona were directed instead to Madrid. Since the instruction to send on to Madrid was received before the goods arrived at Barcelona this second stage could not be considered as a second contract so that the whole of the carriage was governed by C.M.R.

Application, other means of transport 3.13

Article 2 deals with the application of C.M.R. to a certain type of "combined transport." Where the goods are carried on a road vehicle, which is then itself carried on another mode of transport, Article 2 ensures that C.M.R. continues to govern the contract with the road carrier even while his vehicle is being carried, *e.g.* on a roll on-roll off ferry. Article 2 also provides that sometimes the road carrier's liability in these circumstances is to be the same as the liability of the carrier by the other mode of transport.

Article 2 is not an easy provision to interpret. It refers for instance to the court applying the "conditions prescribed by law for the

[39] Subject to Art. 31, see 3.70. Note that Jersey is not a different country from the United Kingdom. See *Chloride Industrial Batteries Ltd. and the State of Jersey Telecommunications Board* v. *F & W Freight Ltd.*, reported in Lloyd's List, October 29, 1988.

[40] Art. 1(2).

[41] Subject to Art. 31, see 3.70.

[42] [1979] 1 Lloyd's Rep. 175.

carriage of goods by that means of transport." Does this refer to the international conventions applicable to different forms of carriage or does it include purely national rules, *e.g.* the common law, which are not based on an international convention? What if these "rules" of national law normally apply but can easily be excluded by the parties? What if different rules would be applied depending on whether it is the sender or the consignee suing in their respective countries?

The difficulties of applying Article 2 are illustrated by the case of *Thermo Engineers* v. *Ferrymasters*,[43] in which a steam heat exchanger being carried on a trailer was damaged when it hit the deckhead of a ship whilst the trailer was being loaded on board. Neill J., applying Article 2, held that the Hague-Visby Rules[44] were relevant to determine the liability of the road carrier. He broke the requirements of Article 2 into three conditions:[45]

(a) The damage must occur during the carriage by the other means of transport, which, he held, begins not when the carriage by road ends but when the other means of transport as contemplated by the relevant rules begins. Here carriage by sea had begun since the damage occurred in the course of loading the trailer on to the ship.[46]
(b) The damage must not be caused by an act or omission of the carrier by road. Article 3 makes the road carrier responsible for his servants and agents and anyone else he makes use of to perform the carriage.[47] However, for the purposes of Article 2, Neill J. held that the words "carrier by road" only included the servants and agents of the road carrier himself, otherwise the provision would be largely meaningless.[48]
(c) The damage must be caused by some event which could only have occurred in the course of and by reason of the carriage by the other means of transport. Neill J. held that this applied here because the event could only be sensibly described by stating that it occurred on a ship, *i.e.* colliding with the bulkhead of a ship could only occur on a ship.[49]

However Neill J. also held that not only therefore did the standard limitation provisions of the Hague-Visby Rules apply, but also that part of the Rules which allow for the limits of liability to be increased. Thus it was possible to claim that the sender,[50] had he made a contract with the carrier by sea, would have exercised his right to increase the limit of liability in accordance with the Rules.[51] We suggest, however, that the right to claim damages in excess of the limits of liability laid down, *e.g.* by the Hague-Visby Rules should depend on the sender having given the road carrier some indication (and any necessary

[43] [1981] 1 All E.R. 1142.
[44] Which applies a lower limit than C.M.R., see 5.46.
[45] At p. 1147.
[46] See 5.29.
[47] See 3.16.
[48] A wide interpretation would also have been inconsistent with Art. 2(2).
[49] It does not have to be a type of damage peculiar to the carriage by the other means as, *e.g.* peril of the sea in respect of carriage by sea, see 5.42.
[50] The term "sender" is used in place of "consignor" in C.M.R.
[51] Under Art. IV(5)(a), see 5.46.

information) that he wants the normal limits increased. If this is not done the ability of the road carrier to obtain a full indemnity from the other carrier would be seriously prejudiced. If there are no "conditions prescribed by law in respect of the other means of transport"[52] then Article 2 says that C.M.R. is to apply.

What if the goods are unloaded from the vehicle? 3.14

Article 2 applies if the goods are not unloaded from the road vehicle. If they are in fact unloaded and transhipped on to another means of transport this potentially breaks the application of Article 2 and thus C.M.R. The Article itself creates an exception by reference to Article 14. If circumstances prevent the carriage by road from being carried out according to the consignment note, and provided the carrier attempts to obtain instructions from the sender and does not receive any, he can tranship the goods to some other means of transport, and C.M.R. will continue to apply in accordance with Article 2.[53]

If the contract itself expressly or impliedly contemplates the use of other modes of transport, thus breaking the application of Article 2, then C.M.R. will only apply to those sections of the journey which involve international road carriage and not to the whole carriage. The rules applicable to the other sections of the carriage will depend on what the national law says, which may well leave room for the operation of standard trading conditions.[54] For instance, a contract may provide for the carriage of goods in a container from England to Germany and may permit the container to be off-loaded from the road vehicle at the sea port, loaded on to a ship, and then reloaded on to a fresh road vehicle in Holland and finally carried to Germany by road. The last section will be covered by C.M.R.,[55] the sea carriage by the Hague-Visby Rules, but the initial period of road carriage will not be governed by C.M.R.[56] However the parties could make C.M.R. applicable by contract between themselves.[57]

The contract may contemplate the use of a road vehicle throughout the journey, but the carrier may break the contract by using a different mode of carriage, *e.g.* by unloading his vehicle and then shipping them by sea. Under common law such a repudiatory breach would be a deviation[58] and would deprive the carrier of the right to rely, *e.g.* on contract terms which exclude or limit his liability. Whether and how this would affect the application of C.M.R. which depends on there being a contract of carriage is a difficult question. Since this issue is also relevant, in the law of carriage by sea, as to

[52] Which is inconceivable unless these words are construed as referring to such compulsory rules as are contained in international conventions.

[53] See Art. 14(2) and 3.34.

[54] Such as are discussed in 1.54-1.59.

[55] Because it is international road carriage between two different countries.

[56] Because it is not international road carriage. Common law or standard trading conditions may apply to this stage, see generally Chap. 1.

[57] See further 3.19.

[58] Explained and discussed in 1.46-1.53, and also in 5.23-5.26, and 5.34-5.36.

whether the Hague-Visby Rules continue to apply after a deviation, the reader is referred to the discussion of this issue in 5.36.[59]

3.15 **Other types of combined transport**

Article 2 deals with only one type of combined transport and various types of contractual arrangement are possible where the use of more than one form of transport is contemplated.[60] Some contracts for combined transport give the carrier an option as to choice of mode of carriage so that he might be free to choose carriage by land, sea or air, or some combination of them as he wishes. Arguably, under this type of contract, even if the carrier decides to carry by road, he has not actually "contracted" to carry by road and so is not subject to C.M.R. In Belgium, however, a combined transport operator who chose to perform part of his contract by subcontracting to a road haulier was held to be subject to C.M.R.[61]

3.16 **Who is subject to C.M.R? The *Ulster Swift* case**

It is the carrier by road whose potential liabilities are most affected when C.M.R governs his contract, but identifying the "carrier/s" who are subject to this liability gives rise to difficulties. Article 3 makes the carrier responsible for the acts and omissions of his agents and servants and of any other persons whose services he makes use of to perform the carriage provided they act within the scope of their employment. Thus, whilst a carrier is free to subcontract, he cannot free himself from liability by doing so. This is so even if he subcontracts the entire carriage to another carrier. Thus in *Ulster Swift and The Pig Marketing Board (N.I.)* v. *Taunton Meat Haulage and Fransen Transport*,[62] a carrier was held responsible as a C.M.R. carrier even though he had subcontracted the entire carriage, and the subcontractor was named as the carrier in the consignment note. It was sufficient that the first carrier had in fact contracted to carry.[63]

3.17 **Freight forwarders**

The position where the entire carriage is subcontracted is not always so clear as is illustrated by cases involving freight forwarders. Although forwarding has been treated more fully in Chapter 2, note here the basic distinction between the position where a forwarder acts as an agent and where he contracts as principal. Where acting as a principal he will be treated as a C.M.R. carrier. The factors discussed in 2.04, which we have seen are relevant in considering this question when dealing with forwarding operations generally, are just as relevant when dealing with this issue under C.M.R. Thus in *Tetroc* v.

[59] After such a breach a court would be unlikely to apply Art. 2 in such a way as to give the carrier any benefit from it, *e.g.* by allowing him to rely on any lower limit of liability provided by the rules governing such means of transport he may have adopted.

[60] See Chap. 7.

[61] District Commercial Court, Antwerp, (1976) XI E.T.L. 279.

[62] [1977] 1 Lloyd's Rep. 346, hereinafter called *Ulster Swift*.

[63] Based on a combined application of Arts. 4 & 9, see 3.18 & 3.22. Note also the use made by the Court of Appeal of s.14(2) of the Carriage of Goods by Road Act 1965, at p. 360.

Cross Con,[64] forwarders arranged the carriage of machines by road to Copenhagen. The fact that they charged the plaintiff on an all-in basis and did not tell him what arrangements had been made for carriage was sufficient to mean that they were acting as principals and thus liable as C.M.R. carriers. This was despite the fact that the delivery instructions asked them to arrange transport, and the fact that they had only one vehicle.

DOCUMENTATION

The consignment note, Articles 4 & 5 3.18

Article 4 states that the contract of carriage shall be confirmed by the making out of a consignment note. However it qualifies this statement by indicating that its "absence, irregularity or loss shall not affect the existence or the validity of the contract of carriage."[65] Despite this the consignment note is an important document, and every care should be taken to comply with the relevant Convention requirements. Article 5 requires the document to be made out in three copies, signed by the sender and carrier. The first copy should be handed to the sender, the second accompanies the goods, and the third is retained by the carrier. Both parties should co-operate in drawing it up since each may suffer penalties if it is defective, as we indicate below. Although normally it is not a document of title,[66] its use in connection with the performance of the carriage under Article 12[67] gives it a limited role in controlling delivery of the goods.

Article 5(2) gives a right to the sender or carrier to require more than one consignment note where the goods are loaded on to more than one vehicle, or where they are of different kinds or are divided into different lots. Although C.M.R. lays down no particular form of consignment note, it does provide for certain details to be put in it,[68] and standard forms are available such as that approved by the International Road Transport Union (I.R.U.), and one designed for use in the United Kingdom approved by the F.T.A.,[69] R.H.A.[70] and S.I.T.P.R.O.[71] A copy of this consignment note is reproduced in Appendix 3.B.

Contents of the consignment note, Article 6 3.19

Article 6(1)(a)-(k) indicates the particulars which must appear on the consignment note, such as the place where it was made out, the place and date of taking over the goods, the names and addresses of the various parties, etc. Particular (k) is of special importance,

[64] [1981] 1 Lloyd's Rep. 192. See also *Elektronska Industija* v. *Transped* [1986] 1 Lloyd's Rep. 49.

[65] Compare the position under the Hague-Visby Rules, see 5.29.

[66] As is a bill of lading, see 5.11. See also, however, Art. 1(5).

[67] See 3.30.

[68] See 3.19.

[69] The Freight Transport Association.

[70] The Road Haulage Association.

[71] The Simplification of International Trade Procedures Board.

because including a statement that the carriage is subject to C.M.R. will usually ensure that the Convention is applied as a matter of contract even where the action is brought in a country which is not a party to the Convention. It will also inform people involved that their rights, etc., may well be affected by it. Article 7(3) makes the carrier responsible for failure to include the statement and liable for expenses, etc. Most writers[72] say that this gives a remedy to a party who has been unable to sue the carrier in a non-Contracting State because of the omission of particular (k).

Article 6(2)(a)-(g) indicates those particulars to be included on the consignment note when appropriate, *e.g.* an agreed time limit within which delivery is to be made. Article 6(3), permits the parties to include other particulars they consider useful. Thus, the consignment note is used both to record the essential details of the goods and parties, and also to record any special obligations undertaken by the carrier in his agreement with the sender, such as a duty not to tranship,[73] or to collect "cash on delivery" charges from the consignee.[74]

3.20 **Sender's responsibility for information provided by him, Article 7**

Article 7 makes the sender responsible for all expenses, etc., (*i.e.* unlimited by the Convention) caused by any inaccuracy in those particulars supplied by him. This is so even if, at the request of the sender, the carrier himself enters those particulars on the consignment note. He is considered to be the sender's agent for this purpose, unless this is shown not to be the case.[75] An obvious example of this would be where the sender gives an incorrect delivery address and the carrier is put to expense finding the right one. The carrier is required to check some of the particulars in any event,[76] so if he could have discovered the inaccuracy he will be unable to show that any loss or expense was "sustained by reason of the inaccuracy."

3.21 **The effect of omissions from the consignment note**

The effect of any omission of any particular, instruction, etc., will vary depending on the circumstances. Obviously difficulties of proof will arise in this context, since the consignment note will not in these circumstances act as a receipt for the goods. Thus, *e.g.* if it is claimed that five packages were delivered to the carrier, but only four arrived, and there is nothing on the consignment note to indicate the number of packages, the claimant will have to provide some other evidence that five packages were in fact delivered to the carrier.

The difficulty arises as to whether a claimant will be allowed to prove that something, such as a time limit for delivery of the goods, was in fact agreed with the carrier when it does not in fact appear on the consignment note. Conflicting decisions on this can be found

[72] Such as Loewe, para. 94. Compare the more drastic consequences of such an omission in carriage by air conventions, see 6.26, and 6.72.

[73] In this context transhipment means transferring the goods to a different road vehicle. See further 7.11.

[74] See 3.58.

[75] Art. 7(2).

[76] Under Art. 8, see 3.22.

among continental cases.[77] The courts, however, do tend to be lenient in this respect, except where the provisions of C.M.R. itself appear to emphasise the importance of the consignment note.[78]

Statements on the consignment note, Articles 8 & 9 3.22

Articles 8 and 9 should be read together. Under Article 9(1), the consignment note is prima facie evidence[79] of the making of the contract of carriage, its conditions, and the receipt of the goods. If there is no consignment note a claimant will need other proof to establish a case against the carrier, *e.g.* for loss of the goods. Article 8 requires the carrier, when he takes over the goods, to check the accuracy of the consignment note in respect of the stated number of packages, their marks and numbers, as well as to check the apparent condition of the goods and their packaging. If the carrier has no reasonable means of checking accuracy of the Consignment note he should put a "reservation" in it indicating his doubts and the reason for them.[80] Likewise, he must specify the grounds for any reservation he may make in respect of the apparent condition of the goods and their packaging.

The carrier might state on the consignment note "sender's load and count"[81] which, it would seem, would not be a sufficient "reservation" unless he also puts in the consignment note an explanation of why he has been unable to check the "load and count," such as the fact that once the vehicle was loaded it was no longer possible to count the goods. Much depends in this context on the practicalities of the situation, and it may not be reasonable to expect the carrier to check the goods if the sender has already loaded them, *e.g.* into a container so as to make it no longer practicable for the carrier to check the contents. As regards "apparent condition," a comment on the consignment note such as "packages frail and dirty" would be the type of "reservation" envisaged here.

If there are no reservations on the consignment note then Article 9(2) creates a presumption that the statements as to number of packages, and the marks and numbers are correct, and that the goods and packaging are in apparent good condition. The burden will then be on the carrier to prove that the consignment note is in fact incorrect in this respect. If there is a reservation a claimant will need to prove to the court that the details as originally indicated on the consignment note were in fact correct, or that the goods or packaging were in good condition, as the case may be. If the sender expressly agrees with the reservation, *e.g.* by putting his signature next to it, then he will be bound by it.[82] This may, however, only amount to him having agreed that the carrier had no reasonable means of checking the quantity. It

[77] See the cases cited in Libouton, "Review of Court Decisions 1965-1971" (1973) VIII E.T.L. 2, para. 26.

[78] As does Art. 34 for example, see 3.74.

[79] Since it is only *prima facie* evidence it is possible for contradictory evidence to be put forward in court, *e.g.* that the parties named in it are not the true contracting parties. See *Ulster Swift*, discussed in 3.16.

[80] Art. 8(2).

[81] Compare "weight and quantity unknown" clauses in bills of lading, see 5.09.

[82] Art. 8(2). Presumably the consignee will be bound by such an agreement made by the sender.

is not clear what is supposed to happen if the carrier does check, and then simply disagrees with the quantity stated by the sender. He could refuse to issue an uncorrected consignment note, but it would be simpler to enter a "reservation" and for this to qualify the statement of quantity, thus putting the burden on the claimant to prove that it was in fact correct.[83]

3.23 **Checking the quantity and condition of the goods**

As explained in 3.22 the carrier is only required to check the quantity and condition of the goods if he has reasonable means of doing so. This will depend on the circumstances. A driver turning up to find a huge quantity of goods in a tightly packed trailer could hardly be expected to waste valuable time on a fruitless effort to count them. Likewise, the carrier can only normally be expected to give a reasonable visual inspection to the goods and their packaging. However in one case,[84] where the carriage involved a refrigerated load, the carrier was held to be liable for failure to test the internal temperature of the goods by means of a temperature probe. This decision may go too far, but, perhaps where there is such an obvious risk and an apparently obvious means of testing it, the carrier should be penalised if he fails to use it.

The consignment note is only evidence of the apparent condition of the goods on taking over by the carrier. Where the claim is in respect of hidden damage, the claimant will have to give some proof that the goods were in good condition when they were delivered to the carrier, otherwise the carrier may find it an easy matter to persuade the court that the cause of the loss was, *e.g.* "inherent vice."[85]

3.24 **Checking the weight of the goods**

To save costs and time, the carrier is not obliged to check the weight of the goods, unless he is asked to do so by the sender.[86] The sender can also require the carrier to check the contents of packages, but must pay the costs of these various checks. The results of the check are to be entered in the consignment note which will then presumably be conclusive evidence, *e.g.* of the weight of the goods, unless there is an indication of a lack of agreement about the result. If there is no check the burden will be on the claimant to prove the weight of the goods.

Responsibilities of the Sender

3.25 **Introduction**

Several articles in the Convention impose responsibilities on the sender. Determining who is the "sender" for these purposes is not as easy as it might seem. Normally the person who signs the consignment note (if there is one) will be concluding a contract of carriage with the carrier, so there will be no problem about making him

[83] Loewe, para. 98.
[84] Appeal Court, Karlsruhe, October 18, 1967, cited in Hill and Messent, p. 44.
[85] See 1.28 and 3.46.
[86] Art. 8(3).

responsible. However, this is not always so. The person signing might be a forwarding agent, or a seller sending the goods to a purchaser and really contracting as his agent.[87] Article 9[88] opens up the possibility of looking beyond the consignment note to find the person who actually makes the contract with the carrier.[89] However, despite this, we suggest that, for the purposes of these rules,[90] whoever delivers the goods to the carrier (other than as a mere employee), or who fills in the consignment note and signs himself as sender, should be considered to be the "sender," whether he is acting as principal or agent.

The sender's responsibility for defective packing, Article 10 **3.26**

Article 10 makes the sender liable to the carrier for "damage to persons, equipment or other goods, and for expenses due to the defective packing of the goods, unless the defect was apparent or known to the carrier at the time of taking over the goods and he made no reservations concerning it." If the carrier makes a reservation on the consignment note that the goods are improperly packed, this clearly puts the risk of damage in transit on the sender. Otherwise the carrier takes the risk of damage if he could have seen the defect, whether or not he actually examined the packing. Presumably the absence of packing is also covered by this provision if such absence amounts to a "defect." The sender is liable without limit, whenever the damage or expense is caused by the defective packing, regardless of whether the sender was negligent.[91]

The liability under Article 10 is apparently owed only to the carrier personally. No action under Article 10 is given to anyone else such as the carrier's employees or the owners of other goods. However, the provision implies that the carrier can be a channel for compensation to others, although this might be limited by a requirement that the carrier himself was under a duty to compensate the person harmed (perhaps because of a statutory or contractual duty, etc.,) and so needs an indemnity from the sender. Examples might be where the carrier is made liable to an employee for failure to provide him with a safe place of work, or to the owner of other packages damaged by the defects in the packaging of the sender's goods.[92]

If damage is caused by the carrier's failure, during the carriage, to remedy a defect in the goods of which he has become aware, or to obtain instructions in accordance with Article 14,[93] he cannot sue the sender under Article 10.[94] Article 10 only deals with defective packing, yet the sender may cause damage in other ways, *e.g.* damaging the vehicle by negligent loading. This is omitted from C.M.R., although

[87] See 3.32.
[88] See 3.22.
[89] And to treat that person as the sender, see Haak, p. 253.
[90] Since they are for the protection of the carrier.
[91] See also the consignor's warranty of fitness at common law, 1.94-1.97. For dangerous goods under C.M.R. see 3.28.
[92] At common law the carrier has a right anyhow to sue on behalf of his customers, see 1.96.
[93] See 3.34.
[94] Appeal Court, Saarbrüken, (1976) XI E.T.L. 261. See Clarke, para. 94.

no doubt the carrier will have his normal common law rights to sue in the tort of negligence.

3.27 **Customs formalities, Article 11**

Article 11 makes the sender responsible for supplying the necessary documents and information, so as to enable customs and other formal requirements to be carried out without delay or difficulty. Again, the sender may find himself liable to pay any expenses involved, *e.g.* for any ensuing delay at a frontier post. Relevant instructions and a list of the documents to accompany the goods should appear in the consignment note.[95] Any attempt to make the carrier responsible, *e.g.* for failing to advise the sender of the required documents, or for not supplying a document will fail, and any term in the contract imposing such a responsibility on the carrier, it seems, will be void under Article 41.[96] However, the carrier will be liable, as an agent, up to the limit in Article 23,[97] for any loss of or incorrect use of the documents.[98] Presumably this means that the carrier is only liable for negligence in respect of the correct use of the documents. Strict liability is not imposed.[99]

3.28 **Dangerous goods, Article 22**

Article 22 requires the sender, when handing dangerous goods to the carrier, to inform him of "the exact nature of the danger and to indicate, if necessary, the precautions to be taken." Any failure to do so may again result in the sender being liable for expenses or damage, etc., and may involve the carrier having the right to destroy the goods without compensation.[1] Where the carrier has full knowledge of the nature of the goods it seems that he must take the risk of dangerous goods upon himself. The duty to inform the carrier is also reinforced by Article 6(1)(f), which requires the "generally recognised description" of the dangerous goods to be stated on the consignment note. This duty should be taken seriously by the sender,[2] who should not assume too readily that the carrier knows about the kinds of precaution to be taken, unless they have dealt together before in respect of the same type of goods.

The United Kingdom is party to the European Agreement Concerning the Carriage of Dangerous Goods by Road (the A.D.R. Agreement), which came into force in 1968, and which has been adopted by several European countries.[3] It is applied indirectly, in that if it is complied with, international carriage involving this country will be exempt from regulations that would otherwise apply to govern the

[95] See Arts. 6(1)(j) and 6(2)(g).

[96] See 3.09 and Court of Appeal, Paris, 1971, U.L.C. 151, see Clarke, para. 75.

[97] See 3.62.

[98] Under Art. 11(3).

[99] Hill and Messent, p. 50.

[1] Under Art. 22(2). The wording of this provision suggests that there is no right to destroy the goods where the carrier knows that they are dangerous but is unfamiliar with the relevant precautions. It is unclear whether there is an obligation on the carrier to act reasonably. See Hill and Messent, p. 124.

[2] See Federal Supreme Court, Germany, (1987) XXII E.T.L. 56.

[3] Presently 19 states.

transport of dangerous goods in this country.[4] However any failure to comply with the requirements of A.D.R.[5] will mean that a criminal offence is committed under one or other of these regulations. C.M.R. consignment notes contain a section for the relevant A.D.R. class and number,[6] and compliance with the requirements of A.D.R. by the sender should normally satisfy the requirements of C.M.R. However, A.D.R. does not necessarily cover every conceivable type of dangerous goods, nor does C.M.R. contain a definition of them. A useful rule of thumb would seem to be to say that goods should be considered dangerous, "if, in normal road transport, they present an immediate risk."[7]

THE RESPECTIVE RIGHTS OF THE SENDER AND CONSIGNEE IN THE PERFORMANCE OF THE CARRIAGE

Introduction, Articles 12-16 3.29

During the course of the carriage, events may occur which affect its course, or which require the original contract to be altered in some way. The sender may, for example, wish to change the destination, or a strike or natural disaster may make it impossible for the goods to be carried as originally intended. C.M.R. contains a series of interconnected provisions which deal with these problems. They also raise the question as to who has the right to sue the carrier if loss, damage or delay occurs.

The right of disposal of the goods, Articles 12 & 13 3.30

Article 12(1), gives a "right of disposal" initially to the sender. By using this right he can change the destination of the goods, or have them delivered to a consignee other than the person named as consignee in the consignment note. Several conditions set out in Article 12(5) must first be satisfied before these rights can be exercised. The first copy of the consignment note originally handed to the sender and stating the new instructions must be presented to the carrier who has the right to be indemnified for his expenses in carrying them out. It must be possible to carry out the new instructions when they reach the person who is to carry them out. They should not unduly interfere with the carrier's business or prejudice other consignments and they must not result in a division of the consignment. Thus there must be a consignment note in order for the sender to exercise this right.[8] The consignment note thus performs a limited role as a "control" document.[9] Article 12(7), makes the carrier liable to "the person entitled to make a claim" if he fails to carry out

[4] Such as the Corrosive Substances (Conveyance by Road) Regulations 1971, (S.I. 1971 No. 618). See Regulation 12.

[5] It contains a list of dangerous goods and conditions for carriage of those goods permitted to be carried.

[6] See Appendix 3.B.

[7] Loewe, para. 186.

[8] An exception to the normal rule in Article 4, see 3.18.

[9] Compare bills of lading, see 5.11, and carriage by air, see 6.29-6.33.

the new instructions or fails to require production of the first copy of the consignment note. This liability is not subject to the limit of liability in Article 23(3).[10] Article 12(6) requires the carrier to notify the sender if he cannot carry out the new instructions (presumably for one of the reasons mentioned above).

Should the sender wish the carrier in effect to take on further carriage the wording of Article 12(1) seems to suggest that technically he can impose it as of right. However the existence of the conditions would seem to give the carrier scope to negotiate, and to charge additional freight.[11] Nothing is said about the original freight which presumably remains payable.[12] The right given to the sender is more generous than the right of stoppage in transit under the Sale of Goods Act 1979, which applies only as against an insolvent buyer and where the seller is unpaid.[13] This generosity is quite amazing since a consignee buyer may well have paid for the goods in advance, yet under Article 12 the sender could redirect delivery to someone else.[14] This seems to be because C.M.R. makes an assumption that the sender is the person making the contract with the carrier which may well not be the case in English law.[15] However, the sender must produce the first copy of the consignment note, a requirement that is not necessary under the statutory right of stoppage. A buyer who has paid the seller could therefore protect himself by insisting that he is sent the first copy immediately the goods are despatched, or by requiring the seller to ensure that he (the buyer) is given the right of disposal in accordance with Article 12(3).[16]

It is unclear to what extent the right of stoppage in transit granted by the Sale of Goods Act 1979, ss.44-46,[17] is displaced by these rules. Since however, C.M.R. has the "force of law," a carrier will be protected if he follows the instructions he receives from the sender in accordance with the conditions laid down in C.M.R.

3.31 The right of disposal of the consignee

The right of disposal of the sender ends when the right passes to the consignee. This may happen in two ways. Firstly, the sender may have given the right of disposal to the consignee at the outset. This can be done by stating that the consignee has this right in the consignment note,[18] and then sending the first copy of the consignment note to him so that he can exercise the right in accordance with Article 12(5). However by Article 12(4), if the consignee exercises the right of disposal by naming a new consignee, this new consignee cannot name further consignees. This prevents the consignment note from being used like a bill of lading to transfer rights against the carrier down a chain of sellers and buyers.[19] No such restriction

[10] See 3.62 and Hill and Messent, p. 54.

[11] A duty to "indemnify" the carrier is imposed by Art. 12(5)(a).

[12] As at common law, see 1.75. We are not concerned here with who has to pay the freight, see 3.31 and the discussion in 1.106 and 6.38-6.39.

[13] See 1.73-1.74.

[14] See also 6.31.

[15] See 3.32.

[16] See 3.31.

[17] See 1.73-1.74.

[18] Art. 12(3).

[19] See 5.11.

applies to the sender when he has the right of disposal. He can name as many new consignees as he likes.[20]

Secondly, if the consignee is not given the sole right of disposal then he has no right of disposal until the sender's right ceases. This happens when the consignee receives the second copy of the consignment note (which accompanies the goods). From then onwards the carrier must obey the orders of the consignee.[21] Furthermore, when the goods reach the destination, the consignee is given, by Article 13(1), the right to demand against a receipt, the second copy of the consignment note and the goods. The consignee must pay the charges shown to be due on the consignment note.[22] Thus, regardless of any agreement between sender and consignee as to who should pay, if, in fact, the carrier was not paid in advance he has the right to get his money from the consignee, or if there is a dispute about who should pay, deliver the goods against a security given by the consignee.[23] This is so, even if the goods arrive damaged. The consignee must make a separate claim for loss or damage.[24]

If the goods are lost, or delayed beyond the time for delivery indicated in Article 19,[25] the consignee is given the right to sue the carrier in his own name *i.e.*, without having to bring in the sender as a party to the action. The wording of Article 13 therefore seems to envisage two distinct situations. The first is where the goods have arrived at the place designated for delivery. Here the consignee can demand the goods and the consignment note. From that point onwards he has the right of disposal and by implication the right to sue for any damage to the goods. The second is where the loss of the goods is established or they are delayed, Article 13 expressly gives the consignee the right to sue the carrier, regardless of whether the consignee has received any consignment note. Presumably this is to safeguard the consignee where perhaps the second copy of the consignment note has also been lost (which may well be the case if the goods have been lost), or has not yet arrived because there has been a delay in delivery. However, these rights of the original consignee are subject to the possibility that the sender may already have defeated them by exercising his prior right of disposal, *e.g.* by ordering delivery to a different consignee.[26]

[20] See further 6.33.

[21] Art. 12(2).

[22] Art. 13(2).

[23] C.M.R. therefore gives the carrier a statutory lien, as in carriage by air, see 6.33. For other issues in respect of freight see 1.106 and 6.38-6.39.

[24] Note that it was held that there is no right of set-off under C.M.R. in *R.H. & D. International Ltd.* v. *I.A.S. Animal Air Services Ltd.* [1984] 1 W.L.R. 573, despite the recognition of the possibility of exercising such a right in Art. 32(4).

[25] See 3.56.

[26] See also 6.31.

3.32 **Who can sue the carrier?**

Apart from Article 13(1) this issue is not dealt with directly by C.M.R.[27] It is important to decide whether the position under C.M.R. is different from that at common law.[28] Two broad sets of views exist on this question:

(a) Whoever has the right of disposal at any particular time is the person who has the sole right to sue the carrier under the contract of carriage for loss, damage or delay. This view has the support of cases in Germany and Belgium.[29] It has the attraction of seeming simple and of allowing the parties to use the documentation to reflect their relationship. If, *e.g.* a seller is sending goods at the risk of the buyer, he can give the buyer the right of disposal (and thus the right to sue) from the outset, but if he is taking the risk during transit then he can keep the right of disposal until the goods reach the destination. The problem is that the parties might not use the consignment note in a way that truly reflects their intentions. Also if, *e.g.* a buyer were to reject the goods after delivery by the carrier, perhaps for some perfectly valid reason, the sender on this view, having lost the right of disposal, would be unable to sue. Furthermore it ignores the fact that Article 13(1) seems to give a right to the consignee to sue once the goods are lost, regardless of who has the right of disposal at that point.[30]

(b) The second view is that it depends on who has the right to sue under the contract as determined by national law. Thus, as in England, the owner of the goods will normally have the right as the person who is assumed to have made the contract.[31] This view has the support of Dutch case law.[32] It emphasises the fact that although Article 13(1) gives a right to the consignee, it does not necessarily take away anyone else's rights so that other claims under the contract are possible.[33] These cases also seem to accept that a right to sue can also be exercised by an agent (such as a forwarding agent), provided that they are named as sender or consignee.[34]

The main danger is that of allowing a multiplicity of potential claimants so that more than one person is given the right to sue, thus leaving the carrier exposed to double liability. Fortunately, this difficult problem does not often arise in practice in England, due to the tendency for joint claims to be made on behalf of those interested in the action.[35] A possible compromise would be to recognise that

[27] Compare C.O.T.I.F., see 4.20. [28] See 1.04-1.16.

[29] Germany: Provincial Appeal Court, Karlsruhe, 1967, U.L.C. 289, *cf.* Federal Supreme Court, Germany, (1980) XV E.T.L. 863. Belgium: Court of Appeal, Brussels, (1976) XI E.T.L.238, *cf.* District Appeal Court, Antwerp, (1987) XXII E.T.L. 443.

[30] See Supreme Court, Belgium, (1980) XV E.T.L. 851.

[31] See 1.05.

[32] Supreme Court, Holland, (1974) IX E.T.L. 724.

[33] A similar view is taken by Prichard J. in *Tasman Pulp and Paper* v. *Brambles* [1981] 2 N.Z.L.R. 25 in respect of the Warsaw Convention, see 6.34.

[34] Supreme Court, Holland, 1977, N.J. 521, cited in Haak, p. 271. English courts are unlikely to hold this unless the forwarder has the "immediate right to possession of the goods."

[35] See Hardingham, "C.M.R.: Safeguarding the Parties' Interests" [1981] 2 L.M.C.L.Q. 306, 310.

Articles 12 and 13 in effect provide guidance to the carrier who, given that he may not know what is the exact relationship between the sender and consignee, should be safe in the case of loss or delay if he accepts a claim from the consignee, and in any other case, from the person with the right of disposal. Any further right of action depends on national law, which as a minimum should protect the carrier from having to pay twice if faced with the possibility of more than one right of action.

A possibility likely to be adopted by English courts is to deny a claim for more than nominal damages by a party who has no real interest in the goods.[36] This would not necessarily be inconsistent with C.M.R. The rights recognised in Articles 12 and 13 are in reality formal rights, seemingly based on the assumption that the contract of carriage is made initially with the sender and incorporating the consignee at the stage when his rights become fixed under the terms of Article 13.[37] C.M.R. does not deny the rights of others to claim substantial damages if their interest is recognised by the law of the country whose courts hear the case. This is acknowledged by Article 28(1) which contemplates the possibility that an "extra-contractual" claim may be made against the carrier and which permits him to "avail himself of the provisions . . . which exclude his liability or which fix or limit the compensation due." This clearly includes the case where say the owner of the goods who has not been named in the consignment note exercises a right of action in tort or bailment for loss or damage to the goods.

Circumstances arising in the course of transit, Articles 14-16 **3.33**

Many things can go wrong during the carriage of goods apart from the simple case of loss, or damage to goods. Events such as strikes, or natural disasters, etc., may occur which disrupt the expected course of the journey. Similarly, problems may arise at the point of destination to prevent the smooth delivery of the goods. The consignee might refuse to accept the goods, or might even have gone out of business by the time the goods arrive. Articles 14-16, are designed to deal with such problems. Unfortunately they are neither clear nor wholly satisfactory in dealing with them. The meaning of "delivery," though referred to many times, is left undefined, although we attempt in 3.40 to decide what is meant by delivery and so determine the period of responsibility of the carrier. Also the possibility that the contract might not require delivery direct to the consignee's premises, but rather that the goods should be collected from the carrier's depot, does not seem to fit easily into the scheme.

Circumstances affecting the course of transit **3.34**

Article 14 deals with situations in which it becomes "impossible" during transit to carry out the contract "in accordance with the terms of the consignment note." Thus if a contemplated route, or method of

[36] As in *The Albazero*, see 1.13. Compare Supreme Court, Belgium, see n.30 above.

[37] Supreme Court, Holland, see n.32 above. The continental view is that C.M.R. creates a stipulation in favour of a third party, see Haak, p. 254. It may not therefore be strictly correct to apply common law principles.

carriage, or destination as indicated in the consignment note[38] ceases to be feasible, as opposed to simply being more difficult or expensive, the provision will apply. It must have become impossible to perform the carriage in the way contemplated initially. In such a case the carrier must attempt to obtain instructions[39] from the person with the right of disposal, (*i.e.* normally the sender).[40] If no instructions are forthcoming within a reasonable time, but it is, however, possible to continue the carriage under different conditions, then Article 14(2) requires the carrier to act in the best interests of the person entitled to dispose of the goods, which may well involve continuing with the carriage under the new conditions, *e.g.* by the use of a different vehicle or other mode of transport. One writer[41] suggests that, if this involves "on-carriage" by a new carrier then the original carrier acts as a forwarding agent, but we suggest that the original carrier remains responsible as the C.M.R. carrier.

3.35 **Circumstances affecting delivery on arrival**

If delivery is prevented, whether by extraneous circumstances, or because the consignee refuses to accept the goods, Article 15 requires the carrier to ask the sender for instructions. This provision must envisage that the carrier has attempted to deliver to the consignee, or tried to contact him first but without success, otherwise the right given to the consignee to demand the goods, by Article 13, would be meaningless.[42] Also, where the consignee refuses to accept the goods, the sender need not produce the first copy of the consignment note in order to give the carrier fresh instructions. This makes sense because this copy may be lost or have been sent on to the consignee, whether in accordance with Article 12(3),[43] or because the consignee has insisted on having it. This suggests that in the other cases of "impossibility" envisaged by Article 14 the sender should have to produce the first copy of the consignment note before he could issue fresh instructions, which would be awkward if the sender no longer has it! Where the consignee has been given the right of disposal in accordance with Article 12(3), the carrier will have to seek instructions from him, so the same problem does not arise. However, where the consignee has been sent the first copy of the consignment note, but without having been given the right of disposal in accordance with Article 12(3) the strange result is that nobody has the right to give the carrier fresh instructions. Under Article 15(2) if the consignee refuses the goods, he can still change his mind and ask for them, provided that the sender has not already given fresh instructions for their disposition elsewhere.[44]

[38] The position is unclear where there is no consignment note.

[39] Art. 14 (1).

[40] See 3.30.

[41] Hill and Messent, p. 59.

[42] A duty to send a notice of arrival might be implied under common law since C.M.R. is silent on this, see 1.67.

[43] See 3.31.

[44] See also Art. 15(3) which provides for where a consignee with the right under Art. 12(3) names a new consignee.

The carrier's expenses 3.36

Article 16(1) gives the carrier the right to claim the cost of seeking and carrying out instructions but not where the need to obtain them is due to his own fault, or if the real reason for the expense is his negligence in carrying out the instructions.

The carrier's option of unloading the goods 3.37

In cases where circumstances prevent the carriage being carried out as originally intended, or where they prevent delivery (see 3.34 and 3.35), the carrier is given the option of unloading the goods and thus bringing the carriage to an end.[45] This will bring his liability under C.M.R. to an end, although presumably he will remain liable, as a bailee under common law,[46] if he decides to store the goods himself. If he stores the goods with a third party then, under Article 16(2), he only has to exercise reasonable care in his choice of such a third party and is under no further liability. If the carriage could be continued under different conditions and the carrier asks for instructions, the duty imposed by Article 14(2) prevents him from exercising a free choice, with the result that he can only unload the goods if it is in the best interest of the person entitled to dispose of them.[47] However, it seems that this only affects the carrier if he chooses to ask for fresh instructions since, apparently, he has the right to unload the goods without seeking such instructions if he wishes.

Taken literally, these provisions suggest that there is no duty to inform anyone at all if the carrier unloads the goods, let alone to seek instructions before he does so! Since, however, he becomes a bailee at common law at that point, he should at least be under a duty to inform his bailor of the whereabouts of the goods. The point may be that since the circumstances are completely different from the contract that was originally contemplated, the carrier should not be required to continue with the contractual carriage. If he were required to seek instructions that would imply a duty to obey them, and so force him to continue with the "contract."

Article 16(2) concludes by stating that: "The charges due under the consignment note and all other expenses shall remain chargeable against the goods." It is thought that this means that a court is left free to apply any domestic rules about carriers' liens.[48]

The carrier's right to sell the goods 3.38

Article 16(3)-(5) allows the carrier, without having to await instructions, to sell the goods if they are perishable, or in such condition as to justify this, or if storage costs would exceed their value. He can also do this with other types of goods, if they have been left on his hands, and he has not received instructions within a reasonable time (which implies at least in respect of these other types of goods that he must ask for instructions). Obviously these provisions are meant to tie in

[45] Art. 16(2).
[46] See 1.33-1.34.
[47] See Hill and Messent, p. 60.
[48] See 1.110-1.114.

with Articles 14 and 15, and so are available to the carrier only in those situations where it is no longer possible to perform the contract as originally agreed. This may well include, for example, a case where perishable goods are giving cause for concern, and can no longer be carried safely unless something is done. Nothing is said about the need for the carrier to show that selling the goods was necessary or reasonable. Possibly this can be implied,[49] especially since the carrier will, in any event, have to show that the carriage or delivery was prevented and not made merely more difficult. This may mean that the carrier will not be able to justify a sale if, *e.g.* by taking a step to preserve the goods, the carriage could have been continued. Certainly, if the need for a sale is caused by his actions, *e.g.* because the goods have been damaged by his negligence, then the carrier will be liable anyway.[50]

By Article 16(4) any proceeds of sale, less expenses, are to be paid to the person entitled to dispose of the goods. If, however, the proceeds are insufficient to cover the carrier's charges and expenses he is entitled to recover the difference. Article 16(5) says that the procedure of the sale shall be determined by the law or custom of the place where the goods are situated.[51]

Liability of the Carrier

3.39 Introduction, Articles 17-21

Articles 17 to 21 set out the main rules governing the liability of the carrier. These provisions deal with loss, damage and delay, and, where applicable, the duty to collect cash on delivery charges. They are not the only provisions in C.M.R. to deal with the liability of the carrier, but are, however, the main ones. C.M.R. does not regulate every aspect of a carriage contract so some liabilities of a carrier may fall outside its scope and depend instead upon national law, *e.g.* total non-performance of the contract of carriage.

C.M.R. creates a system of liability which has some similarity to that of the common carrier at common law,[52] although it is more complicated. This is because some of the concepts used are unfamiliar to English law and because it has a complex structure, largely to enable different rules about the burden of proof to be applied to different circumstances. Firstly we must deal with the period of time during which this system of liability is meant to operate. This is considered in 3.40.

3.40 The period of the carrier's responsibility

Article 17(1) makes the carrier liable for the "total or partial loss of the goods and for damage thereto occurring between the time when he takes over the goods and the time of delivery, as well as for any delay in delivery." The goods are "taken over" once they are in the

[49] See 1.100.

[50] See 3.39-3.58.

[51] Which in England would mean that the carrier would have a duty to obtain a reasonable price based on the duty of an agent of necessity, see 1.100.

[52] See 1.27.

control of the carrier for the purposes of carriage.[53] They do not have to be on the move provided the carrier has possession of them for the purpose of carriage. However, if they have been left with him for a period of storage prior to being carried, C.M.R. will not apply to this period, but will only begin to operate once actual transit has begun.[54] The precise point in time when the goods actually pass from the control of the sender to that of the carrier will depend on the circumstances. If, therefore, the sender loaded the goods, they will have been "taken over" by the carrier at a later time than if the carrier had loaded them himself.[55] The defence available to the carrier under Article 17(4)(c),[56] is also relevant in this context.

When delivery to the consignee takes place is not always clear.[57] Note that this is relevant not just to the question of when the carrier's liability ceases, but also to other issues such as when the time limit begins to run.[58] Normally delivery will only occur when the carrier hands the goods over to the consignee or places them under his actual control.[59] This will be so even if the carrier tenders delivery but is unable to effect delivery because the consignee refuses to take the goods or, for whatever reason, is unable to take control over them.[60] Delivery in such cases will only take place at the time they are ultimately received by the consignee.[61] The carrier does however have the option in such circumstances of bringing his C.M.R. liability to an end by unloading the goods in accordance with Article 16(2).[62]

Problems arise where the goods arrive at the original destination and the consignee orders the carrier to deliver to a fresh destination. The court must determine whether this forms part of the original contract of carriage, or constitutes a fresh contract of carriage.[63] Ultimately this must depend on the intention of the parties, but a number of factors seem to be relevant. These include:

(a) Whether the change of destination was communicated to the carrier before the goods reached the original destination.[64]
(b) Whether on the goods reaching the original destination the consignee had a reasonable opportunity to examine them.[65]

[53] Loewe, para. 149. Compare transit at common law, 1.66-1.67.
[54] Hill and Messent, p. 69.
[55] Clarke, para. 27.
[56] See 3.51.
[57] Although "delivery" is left undefined by C.M.R. it is not possible simply to apply common law. Delivery has a C.M.R. meaning which can be derived from its use in the relevant provisions of the Convention. See Haak, p. 180.
[58] See 3.71.
[59] Although allowing the consignee to unload the vehicle does not amount to delivery. See Loewe, para. 149. Compare the cases cited in Haak, p. 184.
[60] This possibility is contemplated by Art. 15, see 3.35.
[61] Supreme Court, Holland, 1980, N.J. 518, cited in Haak p. 138. This is so even if a notice of arrival has been sent to the consignee.
[62] See 3.37. See District Court, Rotterdam, (1971) VI E.T.L. 417 cited in Hill and Messent, p. 71. Compare District Appeal Court, Arnhem, December 6, 1978, criticised by Haak, p. 184.
[63] Thus accepting that the consignee has taken actual control of the goods.
[64] As in *Moto Vespa* v. *MAT (Britannia Express) Ltd.*, see 3.12.
[65] So that he can make reservations in accordance with Art. 30, see 3.69. This factor was emphasised by the District Appeal Court, Hertogenbosch, 1966, U.L.C. 119. See Clarke, para. 40.

(c) The length of the further carriage required by the consignee. Obviously where only a short distance is involved it is easier to view such on-carriage as part of the original contract of carriage.

3.41 **The system of liability, Articles 17 & 18**

The carrier is made liable for all loss, damage or delay occurring within this period, unless he can bring himself within one of the defences. These defences are of two types. The first type, which we will term the "primary" defences, are contained in Article 17(2). These are the basic defences open to the carrier, such as the "wrongful act of the claimant" or "inherent vice." Under Article 18(1) these defences will absolve the carrier from liability upon proof by him that they caused the loss. The second type, or "secondary" defences, are to be found in Article 17(4). They consist of "special risks" arising from various circumstances, such as the use of an "open unsheeted vehicle." If one of these more limited "risks" apply to the case, the carrier may get the benefit of the easier burden of proof provided by Article 18(2).

Thus the splitting up of the defences is largely due to the difference in the burden of proof, and, for that reason, there is some overlap between the two types as there may well be indeed between any two defences. Thus a set of facts can often be viewed as covered by a primary defence, (*e.g.* wrongful act of the claimant), as well as by a secondary defence, (*e.g.* the risks involved in sending goods defectively packed). It may be wrong, however, to see these two types of defences simply as completely covering the same ground and yet divided into two separate provisions in order to attach different burdens of proof to them. On occasion the secondary defences seem to involve a subtle development from the primary defences which, it is hoped, will appear from the discussion of both sets of defences in 3.44-3.55. Before discussing them further two other provisions should first be considered.

3.42 **The defective condition of the vehicle, Article 17(3)**

Article 17(3) imposes an absolute liability on the carrier in respect of the vehicle used by him to perform the carriage. Thus, if the cause of the loss is due to a defect in the vehicle, the carrier is liable whether or not he is at fault. Furthermore he cannot escape liability by pointing to the "wrongful act or neglect of the person from whom he may have hired the vehicle or of the agents or servants of the latter."[66] This provision prevents the carrier from relying on the defence of "unavoidable circumstances" within Article 17(2) wherever a defective vehicle is involved.[67] However, if the cause of the loss is *e.g.* a breakdown in the vehicle due to some external factor such as a blow-out caused by nails in the road, the carrier may have a defence.[68] Where the issue really involves the suitability of the vehicle to carry

[66] Although he could sue the supplier at common law for an indemnity.
[67] See 3.47.
[68] Loewe, para. 155.

the particular goods, the liability of the carrier depends on the extent of his knowledge of what treatment the goods require.[69]

It is said[70] that defects in the vehicle must be distinguished from defects in any special equipment used to protect the goods from the effects of "heat, cold, variations in temperature, or the humidity of the air." This is because Article 18(4)[71] refers to such equipment, suggesting that C.M.R. means to treat such equipment separately from Article 17(3). Note however, that in Belgium the courts have held a carrier liable under Article 17(3) for defects in refrigeration equipment.[72] In *Ulster Swift*,[73] however, Donaldson J. disregarded Article 17(3) when considering such equipment. However in *Walek & Co. v. Chapman and Ball (International) Ltd.*,[74] the canvas covering of a trailer (which could have been considered to be "equipment" used to protect the goods from the effects of the weather) which was defective was dealt with under Article 17(3), without reference to the possibility of instead applying Article 18(4).

Apportioning liability, Article 17(5) 3.43

The carrier will escape liability when he can prove that one of the exceptions is the sole cause of the loss or damage. Where different causes have combined to produce the resulting damage, Article 17(5) permits the court to apportion liability so that the carrier is only liable "to the extent that those factors for which he is liable . . . have contributed to the loss, damage or delay." A typical case is where the goods are defectively loaded or stowed by the sender, but then the carrier commits some act for which he would be liable, such as driving the vehicle too fast, and this either combines to produce the damage or causes additional damage.[75] Under the common law, the rule seems to be that a carrier in these circumstances has to prove how much damage was done by the cause which gives him a defence or be liable for the full amount.[76] This can be difficult to prove. However, under Article 17(5) the court can apportion liability even if the amount of damage which each individual cause has produced is not proved.

In such a case the courts must make an assessment of the factors which have produced the loss. This may be based on some view as to the contribution made by each cause to the loss,[77] or on the view that the court takes as to the degree to which either party can be said to be at fault.[78] In one case,[79] a vehicle overturned in a storm with the result

[69] Loewe, para. 157. If, however, the carrier's lack of knowledge is due to the sender's failure to inform him of the special requirements of the goods he can rely on the defences described in 3.44-3.46.

[70] By Clarke, para. 80.

[71] See 3.53.

[72] District Commercial Court, Brussels, (1987) XXII E.T.L. 582.

[73] See 3.53.

[74] [1980] 2 Lloyd's Rep. 279. See further [1981] 3 L.M.C.L.Q. 384.

[75] Provincial Appeal Court, Saarbrücken, (1976) XI E.T.L. 261. See Clarke, para. 74.

[76] See Clarke, para. 74 n. 15.

[77] District Court, Roermond, (1969) IV E.T.L. 1005.

[78] Court of Appeal, Lyon, 1977, B.T. 110. Similar principles might be applied in England by analogy with the Law Reform (Contributory Negligence) Act 1945.

[79] Court of Appeal, Reims, 1977, B.T. 406.

that a press packed in a case was damaged. The press had not been wedged and stowed as it should have been by the sender. In addition the floor of the vehicle was slippy due to oil escaping out of the press. The carrier was at fault for not doing something about the faulty stowage, but could not be blamed for the oil which would not have been visible at the time of taking over the goods. The court apportioned liability two-thirds against the sender and one-third against the carrier and awarded damages accordingly.

THE PRIMARY DEFENCES ARTICLE 17(2)

3.44 **The wrongful act or neglect of the claimant**

We suggest that this defence is open to the carrier even if the actual claimant is not the person who has committed the "wrongful act," etc. Thus if the sender is at fault this still provides the carrier with a defence where he is sued by the consignee.[80] This interpretation is more consistent with the way this type of defence usually operates in national law,[81] and is supported by the fact that only a limited indemnity is given to the carrier for liabilities imposed on him through the acts of the sender.[82] Most of the types of circumstances which might fall within this primary defence are more likely to be dealt with under Article 17(4), since carriers will be anxious to get the benefit of the easier burden of proof if possible.[83] Thus, if damage might have resulted say from defective loading performed by the sender, the issue in court will most likely revolve around Article 17(4)(c)[84] rather than Article 17(2).

Some situations will still fall wholly into this defence of wrongful act or neglect, *e.g.* an inaccuracy in the documents supplied by the sender might cause delay. It is said that the act must be "wrongful" in the sense that any loss, etc., must be traceable to the fault of the claimant.[85] If, *e.g.* the weight of heavy goods is inaccurately stated the carrier could rely on this defence, but presumably if the correct weight is given the carrier must take the risks of difficulties arising from carrying that weight. The wrongful act must be a real cause of the loss. Thus simply because the vehicle is delayed at a customs post due to faulty documents supplied by the sender, that does not excuse the carrier for theft of the goods from the vehicle which could have been avoided.[86]

3.45 **Instructions of the claimant**

Where a sender or consignee gives an instruction to the carrier which results in loss, damage or delay, the carrier is not liable, unless

[80] Loewe, para. 151. See also Rodiere, "The Convention on Road Transport" (1970) V E.T.L. 620 and (1971) VI E.T.L. 306, para. 71. Compare Hill and Messent, p. 72.
[81] See 1.28.
[82] See 3.26.
[83] See 3.48.
[84] See 3.51.
[85] Loewe, para. 151.
[86] Supreme Court, Belgium, (1981) XVI E.T.L. 250. See Clarke, para. 73.

the instruction was only necessary because of some "wrongful act or neglect of the carrier." The damage, etc., must clearly result from the instruction. Thus the simple instruction to "carry the goods" would not, in itself, provide any defence if various things went wrong thereafter. However, an instruction, *e.g.* to carry by a particular route should relieve the carrier from liability for delay due to that route being longer than the one that would otherwise have been taken by the carrier.

Can the carrier rely on this defence when it is obvious that obeying the instruction could lead to problems, or perhaps where the carrier should have realised this? In one case,[87] the carrier realised that loading a large quantity of goods on to a single vehicle could cause difficulties with the authorities at some stage. He was proved to be correct and delay resulted when the goods had to be redistributed on to two lorries. Here the carrier was held liable, because although he had pointed this out to the sender, the sender then left it up to the carrier who should have done something about it before the carriage started. This implies that the carrier is liable for not warning of the danger if he is aware of it.[88] He is, however, relieved from liability, if having been warned, the sender (or consignee) clearly takes the risk. In another case,[89] a driver upon reaching the destination, placed his vehicle near a mobile bridge in preparation for unloading. The consignee told him to move his vehicle which then struck a cable which the driver could not see. The carrier was held not liable for the damage which resulted from the accident because it was caused by the instuction given by the consignee.

Unlike the previous defence, this defence does not depend on there being any question of fault or "wrongfulness" on the part of the person giving the instruction.[90]

Inherent vice 3.46

As at common law,[91] the defence of inherent vice is available to the carrier where he can prove that it was not the way he carried the goods, but rather something in the goods themselves which was in fact the source of their destruction or damage, such as their unfitness for the contemplated carriage. The burden of proof is on the carrier to establish the inherent vice.[92] There is also a more specialised secondary defence in Article 17(4) which concentrates on the general nature of certain types of goods which makes them susceptible to harm.[93] The defence in Article 17(2) is of more use where the carrier is trying to show that the goods he carried had a defect in them which is not necessarily always present in goods of the same type.[94]

[87] Supreme Court, France, 1977, II U.L.C. 204. See Hill and Messent, p. 74.

[88] There might, however, be a case for apportionment under Art. 17(5) in such cases, see 3.43.

[89] Court of Appeal, Paris, 1978, B.T. 66.

[90] Loewe, para. 151.

[91] 1.28.

[92] On the balance of probabilities, see the *Ulster Swift* case, 3.53.

[93] See 3.52.

[94] Loewe, para. 152.

3.47 **Unavoidable circumstances**

The carrier has, by virtue of Article 17(2), a defence if he can show that the loss, etc., was due to "circumstances which the carrier could not avoid and the consequences of which he was unable to prevent." This is the most important defence in C.M.R. and often one that a carrier will try to rely on if he can think of nothing else. By this defence C.M.R. effectively imposes a system of strict, but not absolute, liability. Thus the carrier is not responsible for everything that happens to the goods in the course of the carriage. Certain risks are outside his responsibility and in the usual type of strict liability system such risks are spelt out as exceptions to liability, *e.g.* the common law defence of "Act of God."[95] However, rather than spell them out, C.M.R. makes use of the "unavoidable circumstances" formula, in order to get away from concepts used in national laws which might not be familiar in all nations or be subject to too many variations of interpretation.[96]

This wording of the defence suggests some standard by which the carrier's actions are to be judged since the court is required to consider whether the event which caused the loss was in fact "unavoidable." This inevitably involves some discussion of the steps taken by the carrier to avoid the loss and whether any further step could have been taken which might have prevented it. It is not however, a simple matter of whether the carrier has been negligent[97] but involves a higher standard of care which requires him to show that the event which caused the loss was beyond his capacity to avoid. This approach is illustrated by the leading case of *Silber Trading* v. *Islander Trucking*,[98] in which armed robbers stole a load of goods from a lorry parked at a toll gate whilst its driver was resting in the cab. There was little that could have been done in any immediate sense to avoid the loss, and Mustill J. rejected criticisms put forward by the plaintiff as to the alarm system and locking devices employed on the vehicle. He did find, however, that if two drivers had been employed, it would have been possible to drive the vehicle to a guarded lorry park without breaching E.E.C. drivers' hours regulations, and since there was no proof that had this been done the loss would still have occurred, he held that the carriers were unable to show that the loss was unavoidable and so held them liable for the loss.

The judge considered that Article 17(2) sets a standard "somewhere between, on the one hand, a requirement to take every conceivable precaution, however extreme, within the limits of the law, and on the other hand a duty to do no more than act reasonably in accordance with prudent current practice." This standard, he felt, is best expressed by treating the words "could not avoid" as comprising the rider "even with the utmost due care."[99] This will include considera-

[95] See 1.28.

[96] Such as the concept of "force majeure." See Loewe, para. 153.

[97] *Michael Galley Footwear Ltd.* v. *Laboni* [1982] 2 All E.R. 200.

[98] [1985] 2 Lloyd's Rep. 243.

[99] This is in line with important continental decisions, see Federal Supreme Court, Germany, (1975) X E.T.L. 516, and Provincial Appeal Court, Düsseldorf, (1983) XVIII E.T.L. 89.

tion of the practicality of the precautions which it is suggested should have been taken by the carrier. In this case it was possible to identify a practical step which, had it been taken, might well have prevented the loss, and which the carrier could have taken despite the extra expense. To require the carrier to take impractical or unreasonable steps to avoid all imaginable risks would be too much to expect.

Note that the burden of proving this defence falls on the carrier. In *Silber*,[1] however, Mustill J. suggested that the plaintiff should suggest ways in which the carrier could have avoided the loss, leaving the carrier to answer these if he can. Presumably this would only be the case if the carrier has given evidence of facts sufficient to bring the defence into play. If there is no proof of how the loss occurred, it is impossible to say that it was "unavoidable." In *Silber*,[2] it was at least proved that the goods were stolen and thus perhaps lost unavoidably.[3]

The Secondary Defences Article 17(4)

Introduction

Article 17(4) & Article 18(2) **3.48**

The secondary set of defences are set out in Article 17(4), which provides that the carrier "shall be relieved of liability when the loss or damage arises from the special risks inherent" in certain specified circumstances. These circumstances involve risks which the potential claimants have to bear rather than the carrier. This may be so because they have agreed to a method of carriage which carries a risk, *e.g.* use of an open unsheeted vehicle. Alternatively it may be because they have created the risk themselves, *e.g.* by sending the goods defectively packed, or because carriage of the particular goods carries a risk of loss or damage against which it would be unreasonable to expect the carrier to guarantee, *e.g.* the carriage of animals.

These risks must be read alongside special rules about the burden of proof. Under Article 18(2) where the carrier "establishes that in the circumstances of the case, the loss or damage could be attributed to one or more of the special risks referred to in Article 17(4), it shall be presumed that it was so caused." Thus the carrier gets the benefit of a presumption if he can satisfy Article 18(2). It is however only a presumption in his favour and not conclusive since Article 18(2) goes on to provide that it is still open to the claimant "to prove that the loss or damage was not in fact attributable either wholly or partly to one of these risks."

The object of the presumption in favour of the carrier seems to be that the carrier needs help to establish a defence where these special risks are relevant. Once the goods have arrived damaged it may be impossible or difficult to reconstruct what happened and to deter-

[1] See above n. 98.

[2] *Ibid.*

[3] Continental cases reveal a conflict of views as to the amount of proof required of the carrier. Compare District Court, Amsterdam, (1966) I E.T.L. 718 with District Court, Rotterdam, (1966) I E.T.L. 305.

mine exactly when and how the damage occurred.[4] Furthermore, where a type of carriage carries a risk of damage, and damage consistent with the risk actually occurs, it is natural to say that the carrier has proved his case unless there is further proof to show that the real cause was some act or fault on his part. C.M.R. is simply recognising this by creating a presumption in favour of the carrier in these circumstances.[5]

In *Ulster Swift*[6] it was accepted that to establish a primary defence under Article 17(2) the carrier must prove his case on the balance of probabilities.[7] Something less than this must be required of the carrier to obtain the benefit of the presumption in Article 18(2) as regards the secondary defences. As Megaw L.J. said[8] in the Court of Appeal the words "could be attibuted to" in Article 18(2) "presumably connotes something less than a balance of probabilities." He also felt that the further burden placed on the claimant by Article 18(2) is not higher than a balance of probabilities. However the precise degree of proof required of the carrier to get the benefit of the presumption is unclear and has caused considerable difficulty in continental cases.[9] At the very least we suggest that the carrier should establish the possibility that the special risk caused the damage by showing that the risk was in fact present and that the damage which occurred is consistent with the type of damage which might be expected to arise from that risk.[10]

The risks specified in Article 17(4) are risks against which the carrier does not guarantee. Thus he is given a defence even though these risks may not be "circumstances which the carrier could not avoid" as under Article 17(2).[11] The carrier, however, still has a duty of care to carry the goods properly. If, therefore, the true cause of the loss is his negligence and not the special risk the carrier will be held liable. Indeed all that the claimant has to prove is that another cause is responsible for the loss, whether it is the negligence of the carrier or not, to defeat the carrier's defence under Article 17(4).[12] The duty of care on the part of the carrier in these circumstances includes a duty to mitigate damage caused by one of the special risks once it comes to his attention.[13]

THE SPECIAL RISKS

3.49 **Article 17(4)(a), open unsheeted vehicles**

The first "special circumstance" involves the "use of open unsheeted vehicles, when their use has been expressly agreed and specified in the consignment note." This will clearly apply to a vehicle

[4] Loewe, para. 170.

[5] This is similar to the shifting of the burden of proof in bailment, see 1.28.

[6] [1975] 2 Lloyd's Rep. 502, affirmed [1977] 1 Lloyd's Rep. 346.

[7] [1975] 2 Lloyd's Rep. 502, 506. Continental courts may take a stricter view. See Hill and Messent, p. 104.

[8] [1977] 1 Lloyd's Rep. 346, 354.

[9] See Wijffels, "Legal Interpretations of C.M.R.: The Continental Viewpoint" (1976) XI E.T.L. 208.

[10] This seems to be a middle way through the varying interpretations.

[11] Loewe, para. 165.

[12] Court of Appeal, Liege, (1971) VI E.T.L. 541. It may still be possible to prove that this cause was unavoidable.

[13] See 3.50.

with an open top, but might also apply to a vehicle with only the sides open.[14] The use of such a vehicle must be both expressly agreed and specified in the consignment note.[15] The types of risks envisaged here are the effects of wind, rain and atmosphere, and perhaps, just the simple movement of the vehicle if the goods are such that small quantities are likely to blow off in the wind. In one case,[16] however, goods being carried from Belgium to France in an open vehicle were badly damaged by heavy rain while the vehicle was left at a frontier post for two days. The carrier was held liable for failing to take steps to protect them, perhaps reflecting the continuing duty of care noted in 3.48.

Article 18(3) provides that the carrier does not receive the benefit of the presumption in Article 18(2) if there has been an abnormal shortage, or a loss of any package, so that he will have to explain how such loss occurred. This is said to be the case because such loss is more likely to be the result of theft for which the carrier would normally be liable.[17] Perhaps, however, the point is that abnormal shortages etc. are more likely to be due to negligence rather than being a "risk" involved in open carriage.

Article 17(4)(b), defective packing 3.50

The carrier has a defence in respect of the risks due to "the lack of, or defective condition of packing in the case of goods which, by their nature, are liable to wastage or to be damaged when not packed or when not properly packed." This will provide a defence only if the goods actually need to be packed.[18] Much will depend on what is usual in the trade, and whether the method of packing used was satisfactory in the light of the contemplated carriage. The sender should anticipate the normal dangers of the carriage in choosing his packing, but he does not have to anticipate the negligence of the driver or abnormal delay. Thus the fact that the packing is not strong enough to prevent damage to the goods in a road accident caused by the driver falling asleep at the wheel will not relieve the carrier from liability.[19]

Where all the facts have been brought out in court, it may be possible for the court to come to a view that the goods were not in fact defectively packed. In *Tetroc Ltd.* v. *Cross-Con (International) Ltd.*,[20] delivery of a machine was greatly delayed and arrived damaged by rust. It was held that the machine had been packed in the usual way which would have protected it against rust, that it had been tampered with, and that this coupled with the delay, was the cause of the damage.

Even if defective packing was, or may have been present at the beginning of the carriage it may in fact, be difficult for the carrier to rely on this. Article 8 requires the carrier to check the packing on

[14] Haak, p. 154.
[15] See cases cited in Haak, p. 155 n. 175.
[16] District Commercial Court, Coutrai, 1973, U.L.C. 438.
[17] Loewe, para. 171.
[18] Provincial Appeal Court, Düsseldorf, (1970) V E.T.L. 446 (motor cars).
[19] District Appeal Court, Hertogenbosch, 1966, U.L.C. 119.
[20] [1981] 1 Lloyd's Rep. 192.

taking over the goods.[21] If the defect in packing should have been noticed at that point, then the absence of a reservation may defeat the carrier's attempt to prove that the goods were defectively packed. Some continental decisions[22] have held that the failure of the carrier to make a reservation in respect of an apparent defect prevents the carrier from relying on this defence. Once a defect in packing has begun to produce damage during the carriage the carrier has a duty to take steps to preserve the goods.[23]

3.51 **Article 17(4)(c), handling, loading, stowage, etc.**

The carrier has the defence of risks arising from the "handling, loading, stowage or unloading of the goods by the sender, the consignee or persons acting on behalf of the sender or the consignee." This covers both risks of damage occurring during any of these operations, as well as damage occurring during carriage due to the way these operations have been carried out.[24]

The basic idea is that since the sender or consignee or their agent have carried out these operations they should bear the risks of damage resulting from them, and that, because it is often difficult in these cases to identify the precise circumstances in which the actual damage occurred, the carrier should receive some help in discharging the burden of proof. Such a seemingly simple provision has, however, spawned a host of differing interpretations in continental courts.[25] Three central issues can be identified:

(a) Who is responsible for carrying out the operations referred to in Article 17(4)(c)? C.M.R. does not lay down any specific rules on this and the simplest approach is to ask who in fact carried out a particular task and then apply the presumption accordingly. Some national laws impose an obligation on one of the parties to carry out a particular task, *e.g.* an obligation to stow the goods may be imposed on the carrier.[26] This can in fact confuse matters, since even if the sender's employees do the task, they might be deemed to be doing so on the carrier's behalf. The contract of carriage might similarly attempt to impose the duty to load on the carrier or the sender and strictly speaking C.M.R. should not affect a clear agreement that certain tasks should be performed by a particular party. In one case,[27] a carrier was held not to be liable when his driver carried out the loading at the request of, and under the instructions of the sender, and damage resulted because the goods were packed too tightly into the vehicle. It must be absolutely clear, however, that the sender is undertaking the risk otherwise it could prove to be too easy an avenue of escape for the carrier.[28]

[21] See 3.22.
[22] District Appeal Court, Brussels, (1969) IV E.T.L. 948.
[23] Provincial Appeal Court, Saarbrücken, (1976) XI E.T.L. 261.
[24] Loewe, para. 164.
[25] See Wijffels, above n. 9.
[26] Loewe, para. 160. See also Haak, p. 161.
[27] Provincial Appeal Court, Hamm, (1974) IX E.T.L. 753.
[28] He may not, in fact, be taking the risk of negligence of the driver. See District Commercial Court, Brussels, (1973) VIII E.T.L. 516.

(b) When does the carrier receive the benefit of the presumption in Article 18(2)? Continental cases range between two extremes. There are those which say that the carrier only has to prove that an operation, such as the loading of the goods, was carried out by the other party to gain the benefit of the presumption.[29] In that case the burden passes to that party to show that his actions were not responsible for the damage. At the other extreme are those cases which require the carrier to prove that the operation was in fact carried out defectively before being allowed to rely on the presumption.[30]

We suggest that it is going too far to require the carrier to give at the outset definitive proof that the operation was in fact carried out badly, *e.g.* by having to prove that an inadequate method of stowage was used by the sender. It should be sufficient for him to show that the operation was carried out by, *e.g.* the sender, and that the damage which occurred was of the type which might be expected to arise from such an operation.[31] The burden will then pass to the claimant to prove that the operation was carried out correctly or that bad loading, etc., was not the cause of the loss. Where, however, there is in fact evidence that there has been some negligence on the part of the carrier, or of the existence of another possible cause, it may lead a court to say that the carrier has not "established" that the risk involved was a possible cause "in the circumstances of the case."[32] However, where the possibility is that both factors are likely to have contributed to the loss or damage it is open to the court to apportion liability.[33]

(c) Does the carrier have a duty to inspect the operation performed by the other party? Some continental decisions[34] require the carrier to check that, *e.g.* the loading, even though performed by the sender, has in fact been carried out properly. If he discovers that it is patently defective then he should either refuse to carry or remedy the defect himself. If he does not check or does nothing about a patent defect these continental cases say that he will not be able to rely on this defence. This seems to go too far since the object of Article 17(4)(c) is to put the risk arising from the operation squarely on to the party performing it. However, since the carrier is responsible for the safety of his vehicle and must comply with relevant regulations, *e.g.* weight restrictions, he should at least check that the load is safe to be carried and take steps to remedy any defect which affects the safety of the vehicle.[35] If, on checking that his vehicle is safe, the carrier observes some other defect, such as the use by the sender of poor shoring materials which do not, however, affect the safety of the vehicle, it is

[29] District Commercial Court, Antwerp, (1966) I E.T.L. 314.

[30] Supreme Court, France, (1970) V E.T.L. 57.

[31] As in Court of Appeal of the Hague, (1974) IX E.T.L. 319, where a machine slipped off the blocks to which the sender had fixed it.

[32] Court of Appeal, Liege, (1971) VI E.T.L. 541.

[33] District Court, Roermond, (1969) IV E.T.L. 1005.

[34] District Commercial Court, Verviers, (1968) III E.T.L. 1240; District Commercial Court, Corbeil Essones, (1969) IV E.T.L. 988.

[35] See Court of Appeal, Brussels, (1969) IV E.T.L. 931.

advisable for him at least to make a reservation. If, however, a defect which was not visible on loading begins to cause damage during the carriage the carrier has a duty of care to remedy it, or at least to contact the sender in accordance with Article 14.[36]

3.52 **Article 17(4)(d), the nature of certain kinds of goods**

The carrier has a defence where loss or damage is due to "the nature of certain kinds of goods which particularly exposes them to total or partial loss or to damage, especially through breakage, rust, decay, desiccation, leakage, normal wastage, or the action of moth or vermin." This is really a special form of "inherent vice"[37] but it will only apply where there is something in the nature of all goods of the type being carried which creates a risk of the damage which in fact occurs. Thus, *e.g.* bulk loads usually carry some risk of wastage. Where goods of the type carried would normally arrive undamaged, the carrier will not be able to rely on their general nature but will have to prove that there was something wrong with the particular goods he is carrying which accounts for the damage.[38] This general nature must be considered in the light of the actual circumstances, *e.g.* fresh vegetables may be expected to arrive in perfect condition when carried for a short distance in winter, but it would not be surprising if they suffer some deterioration when carried for long periods in midsummer.[39]

The claimant has, however, the option under Article 18(2), of showing that it was not in fact the nature of the goods but rather some other factor, such as a failure by the carrier to take some precaution or to follow an instruction given by the sender, that was the true cause of the loss. In one case[40] a carrier was held liable for eggs damaged by frost. The weather was so cold that it must have been obvious to the carrier that something had to be done to protect the goods, the carriage of which was delayed at a frontier post.

Where the claimant's real complaint is that the vehicle should have been specially equipped to deal with a risk, he will not be able to defeat this defence where he has failed to request it or has not given the carrier special instructions.[41] Where special equipment is in fact used by the carrier to protect the goods from the elements, special considerations arise which are considered in 3.53.

3.53 **Article 17(4)(d) and Article 18(4), special equipment**

Article 18(4) provides that "If the carriage is performed in vehicles specially equipped to protect the goods from the effects of heat, cold, variations in temperature or the humidity of the air, the carrier shall not be able to claim the benefit of Article 17(4)(d), unless he proves that all steps incumbent on him in the circumstances with respect to

[36] Provincial Appeal Court, Saarbrücken, (1976) XI E.T.L. 261.

[37] See 3.46.

[38] Libouton, 3.21 n. 77 above, para. 28.

[39] District Court, Roermond, (1969) IV E.T.L. 1012 (cauliflowers).

[40] Court of Appeal, Paris, 1988, B.T. 59.

[41] Court of Appeal, Versailles, 1984, B.T. 249 (pineapples carried in an unrefrigerated vehicle in July). In the Paris case, n. 40 above, the court said that the carrier should have made a reservation.

the choice, maintenance and use of such equipment were taken and that he complied with any special instructions issued to him." This refers to the use of such equipment as chilling, refrigeration, heating machinery, etc., used to protect the goods, although some cases have gone quite far and held even simple sheeting to be "special" equipment.[42] The carrier will only get the benefit of the presumption in Article 18(2) if he can show that this equipment was adequate and working normally. The courts tend to interpret this provision strictly with the result that the carrier will be liable, *e.g.* if the temperature gauge of the vehicle does not give a reliable guide to the temperature inside the vehicle,[43] or if any criticism can be made of the driver failing to keep a watch on the temperature.[44]

The decision in *Ulster-Swift and Pig Marketing Board (Northern Ireland)* v. *Taunton Meat Haulage Ltd. and Fransen Transport N.V. (Third Party)*[45] is of particular importance. In this case pork sides were carried in a refrigerated trailer from Northern Ireland to Basle in Switzerland. They arrived in bad condition, but the carriers claimed that this was due either to inherent vice or the nature of the goods. The possibility of inherent vice was rejected. This would have applied if the pork had been loaded at too high a temperature but the evidence showed that the meat was properly cooled before carriage began. This left some period of "uncovenanted," *i.e.* unexplained, heating during transit as the likely cause. Although this could be a risk within Article 17(4)(d), and the carrier had given evidence of proper care of the equipment, it was held in effect that the carrier needed to prove the exact cause of the loss before he could escape liability and as he was unable to, he had not given the proof required by Article 18(4).

This case has been criticised on the grounds that it imposes too high a burden of proof on the carrier.[46] However, it clearly illustrates that where the object of using the special equipment is to protect the goods from their own tendency to deteriorate, the carrier is not likely to escape liability if he cannot adequately explain how the goods still managed to deteriorate even though such equipment was used. The facts will inevitably point to some breakdown of the equipment as the most likely cause of the damage. It will be easier for the carrier to establish this defence, however, if the facts are such that even when special equipment is used, there remains a real risk that the nature of the goods will produce damage. For example chilled meat will eventually deteriorate even if kept in proper conditions if there is unavoidable delay and the carriage is taking place during an exceptionally hot spell.[47]

[42] Court of Appeal, Paris, 1973, U.L.C. 274.

[43] District Court, Rotterdam, (1971) VI E.T.L. 830.

[44] Court of Appeal, Toulouse, (1971) VI E.T.L. 131.

[45] [1975] 2 Lloyd's Rep. 502, affirmed [1977] 1 W.L.R. 625. See further Glass, "The Divided Heart of C.M.R." (1979) XIV E.T.L. 687. Compare *Centrocoop* v. *British European Transport* [1984] 2 Lloyd's Rep. 618.

[46] Haak, p. 170. See also Clarke, para. 81.

[47] Cantonal tribunal of Delft, 1966, U.L.C. 104. Note that the UN Agreement on the International Carriage of Perishable Foodstuffs (A.P.T.) may be relevant where special equipment is used. This Agreement is given effect by the International Carriage of Perishable Foodstuffs Act 1976 and Regulations made thereunder. It regulates the standards and use of such equipment.

3.54 **Article 17(4)(e), insufficiency of marks or numbers**

The possibility of loss due to "insufficiency or inadequacy of marks or numbers on the packages," is also a special risk. Thus, if the goods are not properly marked for ease of identification they run the risk of being mislaid, a risk for which the carrier should not be held liable. Under Article 8, however,[48] the carrier is required to check the accuracy of the marks and numbers on the consignment note (which he will do by checking them against those on the goods). Thus if he could have discovered that the marks were inadequate he will have difficulty convincing a court that this special risk was the cause of the loss unless he made a reservation on the consignment note at the time of taking over the goods.

3.55 **Article 17(4)(f), livestock**

Live animals are almost impossible to carry without some risk of loss or injury, even when carried in the usual manner and with every degree of care. The carrier therefore, is given a defence if damage is due to the risk of carrying them. He also gets the benefit of the presumption in Article 18(2), but before he can get this benefit, he must prove that "all steps normally incumbent on him in the circumstances were taken and that he complied with any special instructions issued to him."[49]

3.56 **Delay, Article 19**

Under Article 17, the carrier is made liable for any delay in delivery. The purpose of Article 19 is to define what amounts to delay. There is delay if "the goods have not been delivered within an agreed time limit." As long as a limit has actually been agreed, it seems that it can still be binding on the carrier even though it is not stated in the consignment note.[50] Where there is no agreed time limit, the court must examine the circumstances of the case, and decide whether the carrier has exceeded "the time it would be reasonable to allow a diligent carrier."[51] Delay may cause financial loss or may be a factor in producing physical damage or deterioration to the goods. In either case, the carrier can rely on the defences in Article 17(2),[52] where the carriage exceeds an agreed time limit, or use them as factors to indicate that he has been diligent, so that in the circumstances of the case, he has still delivered in a reasonable time.[53] He cannot, however, rely on the special risks in Article 17(4)[54] if sued for delay in delivery.

3.57 **Delay treated as equivalent to loss, Article 20**

A lengthy delay can also result in the goods being treated as lost. Article 20(1) provides that where the goods have not been delivered

[48] See 3.22.

[49] Art. 18(5).

[50] See Hardingham, "The Delay Provisions of C.M.R." [1979] 2 L.M.C.L.Q. 193.

[51] As under common law, see 1.37. Note the allowance of time given by Art. 19 in respect of partial loads.

[52] See 3.44-3.47.

[53] Hardingham, above n. 50, p. 194.

[54] Since Art. 17(4) applies them to loss or damage only.

within 30 days of an agreed time-limit, or if there is no time-limit, within 60 days from the time when the carrier took over the goods, this is conclusive evidence of the loss of the goods. The person entitled to make a claim may then treat them as lost. The claimant then becomes entitled to compensation on the same basis as if the goods have been lost and he is not limited to compensation simply for delay.

The rest of Article 20 deals with the possibility that the goods may turn up at a later stage. The person to whom compensation is paid can request in writing to be notified if the goods are recovered within a year of the payment.[55] If they are recovered within that time the claimant can, within 30 days of being notified, require that the goods be delivered to him.[56] He must then pay the charges, *i.e.* freight, shown to be due on the consignment note and refund any compensation he received less any charges which were included in it. He can still, however, claim compensation for delay under Article 23 and, where applicable, Article 26.[57]

Cash on delivery, Article 21 3.58

The carrier is liable if he delivers the goods without collecting any agreed "cash on delivery" charge from the consignee. This enables the sender to make sure that the consignee does not get the goods until he has paid any agreed charges. These may include the cost of carriage and even the price of goods. Although, under Article 6(2)(c), the amount of such a charge should appear on the consignment note, it is likely that the carrier would still be liable even if it does not appear, provided that his agreement to collect it and the amount can be proved.[58] Article 21 only applies to arrangements under which the goods are to be delivered upon payment of money, not to those under which the carrier agrees to deliver the goods against a document or proof of payment.[59] Where Article 21 does apply, and the carrier fails to collect the charge, he is liable to the sender "for compensation not exceeding the amount of such charge without prejudice to his right of action against the consignee."

Compensation

Calculating the C.M.R. limits, Articles 23-29, introduction 3.59

C.M.R. contains detailed rules which determine the amount of compensation which a claimant can recover from a carrier for loss, damage or delay.[60] As in other carriage conventions the main object is to limit this amount. The limits represent an officially imposed

[55] Art. 20(2).
[56] Art. 20(3).
[57] See 3.64 and 3.66.
[58] Hill and Messent, p. 117.
[59] *Eastern Kayam Carpets Ltd.* v. *Eastern United Freight Ltd.* (1984) reported on Lexis.
[60] Art. 27 provides for interest on the calculated amount and Art. 28 deals with currency conversion.

compromise between carriers and the owners of goods. In return for loss of the freedom of the carrier to exclude liability by contract, the carrier receives the protection of a limit of liability. The limits reflect to some extent the realities of the mode of transport used. Thus in carriage by sea,[61] a fairly low limit operates in comparison with other forms of transport.[62] This is because ships carry large quantities of goods, and a high level of liability would require an uneconomic level of insurance which would result in higher freight rates. The limit in carriage by air[63] is relatively high and thus reflects the high value of the goods normally carried by air and appropriately high freight levels.

C.M.R. has intermediate limits of liability, higher than those in sea carriage but lower than those in carriage by air and by rail.[64] As with the other carriage regimes it is possible for the limits to be increased or for further compensation to be payable. The rules, however, permit the carrier to charge above the usual rate in such cases, thus enabling him to purchase extra insurance cover.

3.60 **Limits of liability, gold or S.D.R.'s**

When setting the limits of liability, most original versions of carriage conventions stated the limits in terms of a value in gold.[65] For many years gold was an official medium of exchange with a fixed value into which currencies could be converted, and thus provided a means of ensuring reasonably uniform limits regardless of where an action was brought. This system began to break down from 1968 when the price of gold began to float freely on world markets and was no longer tied to the official rate laid down by the International Monetary Fund (I.M.F.).[66] This change created difficulties in the interpretation of convention limits expressed in gold. Should the limit be converted into national currency on the basis of the official value of gold, or the market value of gold? This problem was resolved in respect of some conventions in the United Kingdom by giving the appropriate Minister power to issue "Sterling Equivalent Orders," enabling him to fix the value of the limits in sterling.[67]

Since gold ceased to provide a stable unit of value against which individual currencies could be expressed, the I.M.F. developed the Special Drawing Right (S.D.R.) as a unit for converting currency values. It is based on a "basket" of the currencies of key Member States of the I.M.F. In recent years this has been used increasingly in new conventions as a means of expressing limits of liability, and a

[61] See 5.46.

[62] On a comparison of the limits by weight.

[63] See 6.45.

[64] See 4.19.

[65] Expressed in numbers of gold francs, as defined in terms of weight and fineness. Two types, with differing values, were used: The "Poincare" franc used for air and maritime conventions, and the "Germinal" franc used for rail, road and inland navigation conventions.

[66] See Bristow, "Gold franc—Replacement of the Unit of Account." [1978] 1 L.M.C.L.Q. 31.

[67] See, *e.g.* 6.45.

process of converting older conventions' limits of liability to S.D.R.'s is taking place. In 1979, a protocol was adopted in order to introduce S.D.R.'s into C.M.R. It is in force in the United Kingdom by virtue of the Carriage by Air and Road Act 1979. Not all countries, party to C.M.R., have adopted the protocol, with the result that actions in such countries will be subject to the original limits expressed in gold. The original limit under C.M.R. was 25 gold francs per kilo. The new limit is 8·33 units of account (*i.e.* S.D.R.'s) per kilo (approx. £6). See 3.62.

The value of goods, Article 23(1) & (2) 3.61

Where there is total or partial loss of goods,[68] Article 23(1) requires that compensation "shall be calculated by reference[69] to the value of the goods at the place and time at which they were accepted for carriage." Common law bases liability on the value of the goods at destination, so that compensation for wasted carriage charges if they have been paid to the carrier is effectively included in this.[70] C.M.R. on the other hand, begins with the value at the starting point of the carriage, so that wasted carriage charges, etc., are not recovered as part of the value of the goods. It is, however, possible to recover the carriage charges under Article 23(4) which deals with charges and expenses rendered useless because of the failure to perform the carriage properly.[71] An important difference between these two provisions is that only the compensation based on the value of the goods is subjected to the limit of liability imposed under Article 23(3). The charges and expenses recovered under Article 23(4) are not subject to this limit.

Under Article 23(2), the value "shall be fixed according to the commodity exchange price or, if there is no such price, according to the current market price," or if there is no such price, "by reference to the normal value of the goods of the same kind or quality." If there is no commodity exchange price or current market price, the tendency is to refer to the invoice sale price, if there is one, to find the "normal" value.[72] Otherwise cost or replacement value would presumably be relevant.

In *James Buchanan* v. *Babco Forwarding & Shipping*,[73] the liability of a carrier for loss of a stolen load of whisky was in issue. The price to the buyer in Iran was £7,000, but the loss to the seller, who was suing the carrier, was £30,000, because as the whisky had probably not left the country, excise duty was payable on the goods. The House of Lords were eventually to find in favour of the plaintiff under Article 23(4), but held that £7,000 was the market value for the purposes of Article 23(1). In deciding what was the "current market price," it was necessary to decide on what was the appropriate market. Here there was both a domestic market (including the duty), and an export

[68] For damage see 3.65.

[69] This suggests that, if the actual loss is less, then only the actual loss must be taken as a basis.

[70] See 1.40.

[71] See 3.63.

[72] *William Tatton* v. *Ferrymasters* [1974] 1 Lloyd's Rep. 203.

[73] [1978] A.C. 141. See Hardingham, "Damages under C.M.R.—the decision of the House of Lords" [1978] 1 L.M.C.L.Q. 51.

market (excluding it, a fact reflected in the invoice), and it was the export price which was more appropriate.

3.62 **The limit of liability, Article 23(3)**

Once the value is determined, the limit in Article 23(3) must be applied. So far as loss of value is concerned the claimant will only receive compensation up to the limit. The new limit, applicable by virtue of the 1979 Act,[74] is 8·33 S.D.R.'s per kilogram of gross weight short (approx. £6). This is converted into national currency on the day of judgment, and can easily be calculated since the value of one S.D.R. in sterling is published daily in the financial press. The Carriage by Air and Road Act 1979, s.5 provides that a treasury certificate stating the value for that day shall be conclusive.

A single consignment may consist of goods of different weights and values. If there is a loss of the entire consignment, the weight of each of the goods might be taken separately and the limit applied to the value of each of the goods individually. Alternatively the weight of all the goods in the consignment could be combined and the limit applied to the combined value of all the goods in the consignment. Continental cases[75] suggest that the weight of the entire consignment is alone relevant and not the individual weights of the goods which make it up. However, where the carriage involves a groupage or consolidation of goods belonging to different persons, the individual weights of the goods can be considered separately.[76] Where there is a partial loss, it is the weight of the goods lost which is relevant, although there is a case for saying that where the whole consignment has in fact diminished in value, then the weight of the whole consignment can be brought into account.[77]

3.63 **Additional charges, Article 23(4)**

Apart from compensation based on the value of the goods, the claimant can also recover "the carriage charges, customs duties and other charges incurred in respect of the carriage of the goods." These are to be refunded in full, *i.e.* not subject to the limit in Article 23(3), in the case of total loss, and in proportion to the loss sustained in case of partial loss. Thus if the goods are lost, any carriage charges are in effect wasted, and the claimant is able to recover this wasted expenditure from the carrier. Difficulty arises in respect of the words "other charges incurred, etc." What is envisaged by this phrase? The use of the word "refunded" in Article 23(4) might suggest that it means that the claimant should get back any further charges that he has had to pay to the carrier, such as a cash on delivery charge. Alternatively it could have a wider meaning and could include other costs to the claimant in dispatching the goods whether or not paid to the carrier, such as insurance costs. It might even mean that the claimant can recover other expenses incurred because of the way the

[74] See 3.60.
[75] Supreme Court, Germany, (1981) XVI E.T.L. 455.
[76] Supreme Court, Belgium, (1977), II U.L.R. 220.
[77] See Haak, p. 217. Compare carriage by air, 6.46.

carrier performed the carriage, such as costs of return carriage and warehousing after an accident involving the goods.

The House of Lords in *James Buchanan* v. *Babco Forwarding & Shipping*,[78] faced with conflicting continental cases, by a majority, accepted that these words were wide enough to cover excise duty which the claimant had had to pay because of the theft of whisky. The excise duty became payable because of the way the goods had been carried and it was possible to construe the words "in respect of" as meaning "in consequence of," so that a charge such as this, arising as a consequence of what occurred during the carriage, could be recovered. This leaves open the position in respect of more directly related charges such as wasted costs of packing.[79] It also creates the danger that the carrier could be liable for all sorts of costs, unlimited by Article 23(3), simply because they arise from the way the goods were carried, such as a penalty clause payable by the sender to the consignee in the event of non-delivery of the goods. Some restriction must therefore be imposed. Lord Denning in the Court of Appeal thought that "consequential damage which is not in the nature of an expense" is excluded.[80] A better approach, perhaps, is to say that any such expense should be clearly foreseeable by the carrier before he can be liable for it.[81]

Delay, Article 23(5) 3.64

Where there is delay under Article 19,[82] and the claimant proves that "damage" has resulted from it, he can claim compensation from the carrier up to the amount of the carriage charges. Only the carriage charges are relevant, not customs duties or other charges indicated in Article 23(4).[83] The carriage charges provide a limit, so the claimant must still prove the "damage" for which he requires compensation. The weight of opinion[84] is to the effect that the word "damage" in Article 23(5) means economic loss rather than physical damage or deterioration caused by delay for which the claimant can recover under Article 25.[85]

Damage, Article 25 3.65

Article 25(1) makes the carrier liable for "the amount by which the goods have diminished in value." The value is fixed by reference to Article 23(1), (2), and (4). There is German authority that repair costs

[78] [1978] A.C. 141.

[79] Allowed in *William Tatton* v. *Ferrymasters* [1974] 1 Lloyd's Rep. 203. See, however, Viscount Dilhorne in *Buchanan*, n. 78, at p. 158, who felt that insurance premiums may not be recoverable on the construction adopted by the House of Lords and doubted whether the costs of packing or of obtaining certificates of quality can be said to be charges incurred "in consequence" of the carriage. See also *I.C.I.* v. *MAT Transport* [1987] 1 Lloyd's Rep. 355, which held a damage survey fee to be recoverable.

[80] [1977] 1 All E.R. 518, 523.

[81] Hill and Messent, p. 137. Note that the decision in *William Tatton* v. *Ferrymasters*, n. 79 above, that the costs of return carriage were not recoverable was disapproved by the Court of Appeal in *Buchanan*, n. 80 above. See also *Thermo Engineers* v. *Ferrymasters* [1981] 1 W.L.R. 1470.

[82] See 3.56.

[83] Loewe, para. 194.

[84] Hill and Messent, p. 141.

[85] See 3.65.

higher than the amount by which the value of the goods has diminished are not recoverable.[86]

Article 25(2) states that compensation may not exceed:

(a) the amount payable for a total loss, if the whole consignment has been damaged;
(b) where part of the consignment has been damaged, the amount payable in the case of loss of the part affected.

Thus the amounts recoverable in respect of loss act as a ceiling to the compensation that can be awarded in the case of damage. This also means that the limits in Article 23(3) are applicable to damage.[87] Similar considerations arise in respect of damage as arose in relation to loss as to how the weight of the goods in a consignment is to be regarded, see 3.62.[88]

No matter how serious the damage, if the case is still truly one of damage and not loss the claimant can only recover under Article 25 and not Article 23. In *William Tatton* v. *Ferrymasters*,[89] Browne J. held that a machine worth £32,700, but damaged to such an extent that it had only a residual value of £9,000, could not be treated as effectively lost, so that compensation had to be determined under the damage rules. Thus carriage charges, etc., are refunded in proportion to the diminution in value of the goods, and not in full, if the goods retain some residual value after damage has occurred to them.[90]

3.66 **Breaking the limit by agreement, Articles 24 & 26**

Article 24 permits a sender "against payment of a surcharge to be agreed upon," to "declare in the consignment note a value for the goods exceeding the limit laid down in Article 23(3)."[91] This enables a sender to recover sums higher than the normal C.M.R. limit laid down in Article 23(3). He is not allowed to recover more than the goods are worth,[92] but can use this provision to make the carrier pay the full value, and thus perhaps reduce his insurance costs, especially where the goods are of high value. The actual payment of a surcharge is not necessary for the limits of liability to be increased if the carrier does not require the sender to pay it.[93] Article 24 simply permits the carrier to require extra payment if he wishes in return for the increased limit of liability. The new limit must, however, be stated in the consignment note.[94]

[86] Federal Supreme Court, 1980, I U.L.C. 260.
[87] See *William Tatton* v. *Ferrymasters*, n. 79 above.
[88] See generally Loewe, paras. 201-202.
[89] See n. 79 above.
[90] This means that the principle of "constructive total loss" in the law of marine insurance, which enables an assured to recover a full indemnity for the goods where they are so badly damaged that it would be too expensive to repair them, is not applicable to C.M.R. See also *Worldwide Carriers* v. *Ardtran* [1983] 1 All E.R. 692 and Hardingham, "Aspects of Limitation of Actions under C.M.R." [1979] 3 L.M.C.L.Q. 362. Compare *Thermo Engineers* v. *Ferrymasters*, n. 81 above.
[91] See 3.62.
[92] Since the actual value will be determined in accordance with Art. 23(1).
[93] Loewe, para. 198.
[94] Loewe, para. 196.

Article 24 is not suitable for potential claims for economic loss as opposed to loss or damage to the goods. Article 26(1), however, permits the sender against the payment of an agreed surcharge, to "fix the amount of a special interest in delivery in the case of loss or damage or of the agreed time-limit being exceeded, by entering such amount in the consignment note." Once there is a declaration, Article 26(2) provides that "compensation for the additional loss or damage proved may be claimed, up to the amount of the interest declared, independently of the compensation provided for in Articles 23, 24 and 25." Such a declaration might, for example, fix an amount representing the anticipated loss of profit on a resale should the goods fail to arrive as a special interest in delivery.

Presumably the sender can cover both his own interest and that of the consignee if that is appropriate. The carrier is protected by his ability to impose a surcharge. The provision clearly requires that such consequential loss, which is the object of the declaration, must still be proved in fact to have been suffered before it can be recovered.

Extra-contractual claims, Article 28 3.67

Article 28(1) provides that where there is an extra-contractual claim against the carrier, "arising out of carriage" under the Convention, "the carrier may avail himself of the provisions . . . which exclude his liability or which fix or limit the compensation due." This means that a claimant cannot evade the limits of liability laid down by the Convention by suing in tort or bailment rather than contract. It also ensures that the carrier can take advantage of the limits if he is sued in tort or bailment by someone who is not a party to the contract of carriage.

As we have seen,[95] it can be a difficult matter to determine who has the right to sue the carrier under the terms of the Convention. Despite this, Article 28(1) will clearly cover a carrier where he is sued by an owner of goods not named as sender or consignee in respect of goods entrusted to him by a bailee who was not acting on behalf of the owner when he made the contract of carriage.

Article 28(2) affords the same protection to "persons for whom the carrier is responsible under the terms of Article 3." The servants, agents and others whose services the carrier makes use of for the performance of the carriage can then rely on these provisions if they are sued by the claimant. They will only be able to do so, however, where the C.M.R. carrier is responsible under Article 3.[96] This is only the case where these persons act within the scope of their employment. It seems that the provision would not cover someone from whom the carrier had hired the vehicle,[97] but would certainly cover a road carrier to whom the contracting carrier had subcontracted the whole or part of the carriage. If the words "performance of the carriage" were given a wide meaning it might even cover the owner of a secure compound within which the carrier's vehicle was parked.

[95] At 3.32.
[96] See 3.16.
[97] Since the carrier is liable for this under Art. 17(3) (see 3.42), not Art. 3.

3.68 Breaking the limit, wilful misconduct, Article 29

Under Article 29 where the damage is caused by the wilful misconduct of the carrier, or of the persons for whom he is responsible under Article 3,[98] neither the carrier, or those persons, can avail themselves of the provisions which exclude or limit liability or which shift the burden of proof.[99] The meaning of "wilful misconduct" is outlined in 1.60. Wilful misconduct also has an effect on time limits under Article 32.[1]

The case of *Sidney Jones* v. *Martin Bencher*,[2] involved the issue of whether, in respect of carriage governed by C.M.R., the longer time limit available for claims in cases involving wilful misconduct was applicable. In this case a lorry was driven off the road causing damage to its load when the driver went to sleep as the result of deliberately driving too long in breach of the drivers' hours regulations. The court held that this was wilful misconduct as the driver appreciated the increased risk of an accident in such circumstances.

Claims and Actions Articles 30-33

3.69 Reservations at the end of transit, Article 30

Article 30 is the first major provision to deal with the making of claims against the carrier for loss, etc. When the goods are delivered to the consignee he may check them with the carrier. If he does so then Article 30(2) provides that the results of the check are conclusive unless the loss or damage was not apparent, *i.e.* could not reasonably be discovered by the check. If not apparent the consignee must send a "reservation" within seven days of the check or lose any right to contradict the apparent result of the check.[3] If there is no check then Article 30(1) requires the consignee to give a reservation of any apparent loss or damage at the time of delivery.[4] This can be given orally, or by other means such as a note on the consignment note.[5]

If the loss or damage could not have been discovered at the time of delivery, then the consignee must send a "reservation" in writing to the carrier within seven days of delivery, excluding Sundays and public holidays.[6] Again this can include the return of the consignment note to the carrier with a note in respect of loss or damage on it. Clearly "loss" in this context does not mean total loss since there will have been no delivery in such a case. If there are no reservations

[98] See 3.16.

[99] Compare the Hague-Visby Rules where such conduct by servants, etc., does not deprive the carrier of the right to rely on the limits of liability, see 5.48.

[1] See 3.71.

[2] [1986] 1 Lloyd's Rep. 54.

[3] Loewe, para. 229.

[4] See also Art. 30(5).

[5] Despite the use of the word "send." See Hill and Messent, p. 161.

[6] See also Art. 30(4).

where these were in fact required, the taking of delivery amounts to prima facie proof that the goods were received in the condition described in the consignment note. This means that the claimant would need to produce fairly convincing evidence that the loss or damage occurred while the carrier had charge of the goods.[7]

Under Article 30(1) the reservation should give a "general indication of the loss or damage," which suggests that a detailed claim is not required but rather sufficient information to put the carrier on notice of a possible claim so that he can investigate it in good time.[8] In the case of delay, Article 30(3) requires a reservation to be sent to the carrier within 21 days from the time the goods were placed at the disposal of the consignee, otherwise no compensation shall be payable.

Where to sue? Article 31 **3.70**

Article 31(1) lays down the places in which the parties are entitled to bring their claims. The object of this provision is to provide both the carrier and the claimant with convenient places to sue. It applies to "legal proceedings arising out of carriage under this Convention."[9] Under Article 31(1) the "plaintiff"[10] "may bring an action in any court or tribunal of a state which is a party to the Convention which is designated by agreement between the parties and in addition, in the courts or tribunals[11] of a country within whose territory:

(a) the defendant is ordinarily resident, or has his principal place of business, or the branch or agency through which the contract of carriage was made, or
(b) the place where the goods were taken over by the carrier or the place designated for delivery is situated."

The parties have a free choice in respect of these various places, since any term in the contract which attempted to cut down this choice would be contrary to Article 41, as would any clause which designated the courts of a state which had not adopted C.M.R.[12]

Where there is an agreement between the sender and the carrier, there is some doubt about whether this is binding on the consignee if he does not know about it, and in particular if it is not stated on the consignment note.[13] As stated in 1.10 the sender is often considered as the agent of the consignee so that this may mean that the consignee will be bound. However this only has much relevance when it is the carrier who is suing the consignee (*e.g.* for freight), since if the consignee is claiming against the carrier, he is free to choose one of the other jurisdictions if he wishes.

[7] Loewe, para. 228.
[8] Hill and Messent, p. 160. Compare Loewe, para. 222. Compare also the requirements of Art. 32(2), below 3.72.
[9] As well as extra contractual claims under Art. 28 (see 3.67). See Loewe, para. 238.
[10] As opposed to "claimant" since it covers the carrier as well.
[11] Which court or tribunal depends on the law of the country where the action is brought.
[12] Loewe, para. 240.
[13] See Hill and Messent, p. 166. It will be binding on the sender, Loewe, para. 242.

"Ordinary residence" makes sense only in respect of natural persons. If the defendant is a company it is not "ordinarily resident" simply because it has a branch in the country concerned.[14] It must either have its principal place of business,[15] in the country concerned, or the company must have a branch or agency in the country and through which the contract of carriage was made.

3.71 **The time limit on claims, Article 32**

Under Article 32(1) the time for "an action arising out of carriage under this Convention shall be one year." However, in the case of wilful misconduct,[16] the time limit is three years. These limits are applicable to both claims by and against the carrier. In addition the persons mentioned in Article 28[17] can "avail" themselves of these time limits. Thus a claim by the carrier for freight is limited to one year, as also is a claim against a sender for an indemnity under Article 7,[18] unless the carrier establishes that the sender is guilty of wilful misconduct, in which case the time limit is three years. The same applies to any claim against the carrier and Article 32(4) expressly provides that "a right of action which has become barred by lapse of time may not be exercised by way of counter-claim or set-off."

Once the time limit begins to run, apart from the suspension provided for by Article 32(2), it will continue to run until the plaintiff brings an action, which in English law means the date of issue of the writ.[19] A counter-claim is exercised when it is formally served under rules of court.[20] These steps must be taken within the time period, otherwise the right to claim will be lost. Any agreement made between the parties to extend the time limit will be null and void as being contrary to Article 41 if made before the claim arises, but there is no objection to a voluntary agreement for an extension once a claim has arisen.[21]

Article 32(1) sets out points in time from which the period starts to run. These are:

(a) in the case of partial loss, damage or delay in delivery, from the date of delivery;
(b) in the case of total loss, from 30 days after the expiry of the agreed time limit or if there is no agreed time limit 60 days from the date of taking over the goods by the carrier;

[14] *Rothmans of Pall Mall (Overseas) Ltd.* v. *Saudi Arabian Airlines Corporation* [1980] 3 All E.R. 359.

[15] Which could mean either the statutory or actual place of business or both. See Hill and Messent, p. 165.

[16] See 3.68.

[17] See 3.67.

[18] See 3.20.

[19] *Impex Transport* v. *Thames Holdings* [1981] 2 Lloyd's Rep. 566.

[20] See n. 19 above.

[21] Hill and Messent, p. 188. Art. 32(3) refers other procedural matters, such as what should happen if the time limit expires on a Sunday, etc., to national law. See further *Pritam Kaur* v. *S. Russell & Sons* [1973] Q.B. 336.

(c) in all other cases, from three months after the making of the contract of carriage.

These "starting points" were considered in *Worldwide Carriers Ltd.* v. *Ardtran International Ltd.*[22] In this case goods were exposed to the weather during carriage and thus rendered virtually useless. They were returned to the sender who made a claim three years later. Parker J. considered the possible application of (a), (b) and (c), but also held that whether or not (a) or (b) applied to the case it would be possible to apply (c) which could be applied whenever it was not possible to bring a case within (a) or (b). Thus, *e.g.* if the goods are damaged but not delivered due to their being refused by the consignee, the fact that there is no date of delivery may mean that paragraph (a) cannot be applied but this will not prevent the time limit running in accordance with paragraph (c).[23]

In respect of paragraph (a), following the decision of Browne J. in *Tatton* v. *Ferrymasters,*[24] he held that despite the fact that the goods only retained a scrap value, they had to be considered as damaged rather than lost. He felt that it was possible to argue that the point of delivery was the return of the goods to the sender, based on the application of Article 12(1) which gives the sender the right to dispose of the goods. However, he also held, as the main basis of his decision on these points, that if there was no delivery in accordance with (a) then the goods were in fact lost, because applying Article 20,[25] the goods were deemed to be lost if they were not delivered within the period specified in that Article. This seems a strange application of Article 20, which seems to be largely concerned with missing goods rather than goods which, though damaged, can still be disposed of because their whereabouts are known.[26]

Suspending the time limit, Article 32(2) **3.72**

Article 32(2) provides that "a written claim shall suspend the period of limitation until such date as the carrier rejects the claim by notification in writing and returns the documents attached thereto." Clearly it is only claims against the carrier which suspend the time limit, not claims by the carrier, *e.g.* for the carriage charges. The object is to ensure that the claimant is not prejudiced whilst the carrier takes time considering the claim.

What form should the claim take? Should it be a formal fully detailed claim, must it be by letter, etc.? It seems that a claim made by telex will be sufficient.[27] A series of cases in England have established that it does not have to be a formal and quantified claim,[28] but that a

[22] [1983] 1 All E.R. 692.
[23] Compare *Moto Vespa* v. *MAT (Britannia Express) Ltd.* [1979] 1 Lloyd's Rep. 175.
[24] [1974] 1 Lloyd's Rep. 203.
[25] See 3.57.
[26] See also *I.C.I.* v. *MAT Transport* [1987] 1 Lloyd's Rep. 355.
[27] District Commercial Court, Antwerp, (1977) XII E.T.L. 437.
[28] *William Tatton* v. *Ferrymasters* [1974] 1 Lloyd's Rep. 203; *Moto Vespa* v. *MAT (Britannia Express) Ltd.* [1979] 1 Lloyd's Rep. 175.

"general intimation of intention to hold the carrier liable,"[29] will be sufficient. In *I.C.I. Fibres Ltd.* v. *MAT Transport Ltd.*,[30] a letter which referred to the accident and said "We must hold you responsible for any losses we incur" was held to be sufficient to suspend the time limit. Some continental decisions have however required the claim to be specific and quantified,[31] the idea being that the carrier should be given enough information to enable him to decide whether to accept or reject it. It would seem sensible to do this in any event since unless he knows how much he is being asked to pay, the carrier will not know whether it is reasonable. Thus he is likely to reject the claim out of hand, and any further claim will not suspend the limit since Article 32(2) also says that "the running of the period of limitation shall not be suspended by further claims having the same object."

Note also that Article 32(2) envisages that some parts of a claim may be accepted whilst other parts are rejected, and the effect of this would be that the limit would start to run again only in respect of those parts of a claim which have been rejected by the carrier. The claim does not have to be sent by the claimant personally provided that it is sent by someone on his behalf who has his authority under the principles of agency.[32] This probably includes an insurer who is "subrogated"[33] to the claimant's rights and who makes the claim under his name. Likewise the sending of a claim to an agent of the carrier authorised to receive it will be sufficient.[34]

The time limit is suspended from the time when the written claim is received. Under Article 32(2) the burden of proving that the claim, or the reply, or the return of documents, was in fact received is on the party who wishes to rely on their having been received. The fact that the provision refers to the return of documents attached to the claim does not mean that the claim has to be supported by documents before it will suspend the time limit.[35] This wording is intended to ensure that time does not start to run against a claimant until documents which he needs to start proceedings are back in his hands again. The written claim will have the effect of suspending the time limit as soon as it is received by the carrier whether or not the time limit has in fact begun to run against the claimant.[36]

3.73 Arbitration, Article 33

C.M.R. permits the parties to make agreements for any dispute to be submitted to arbitration.[37] Such agreements, if made before any

[29] See Browne J. in *William Tatton*, n. 28 above, at p. 207.
[30] [1987] 1 Lloyd's Rep. 354.
[31] Provincial Appeal Court, Düsseldorf, (1970) V E.T.L. 446.
[32] See *Moto Vespa*, n. 23 above.
[33] Where the insurer, having paid on the policy, takes over the claim of the claimant.
[34] Hill and Messent, p. 184. See also *Poclain S.A. and another* v. *S.C.A.C. S.A. and others* [1986] 1 Lloyd's Rep. 404, where the carrier's insurer was held to have authority to receive a claim for this purpose.
[35] *Moto Vespa*, n. 23 above. Compare *Muller Batavia Ltd.* v. *Laurent Transport Ltd.* [1977] 1 Lloyd's Rep. 411.
[36] *I.C.I. Fibres* v. *MAT Transport Ltd.*, n. 30 above.
[37] See also the Carriage of Goods by Road Act, s.7.

claim has arisen, must expressly provide that the arbitration tribunal shall apply the Convention, otherwise they will be null and void under Article 41.[38] Similar problems arise as to who is bound by such agreements as were discussed in relation to jurisdiction clauses.[39]

Successive Carriers

Introduction, Articles 34-40 3.74

Carriers often subcontract the whole or part of the carriage without this necessarily being a breach of their contract with the customer,[40] and such subcontractors might themselves in turn subcontract the carriage. Article 3[41] and Article 28[42] have already been noted in this context. The original contracting carrier will remain liable to the customer under C.M.R., but a subcontracting carrier is not necessarily liable to the customer under C.M.R.[43] However, C.M.R. contains special rules under which a subcontracting carrier can find himself subject to the Convention by means of being "drawn into" the original contract. Thus Article 34 provides that where a single contract[44] "is performed by successive road carriers, each of them shall be responsible for the performance of the whole operation, the second carrier and each succeeding carrier becoming a party to the contract of carriage, under the terms of the consignment note, by reason of his acceptance of the goods and the consignment note."

The idea is that, when a subcontractor takes over the goods, if he also takes over a C.M.R. consignment note, he should realise that the carriage is covered by the Convention and should be prepared to take on C.M.R. responsibilities. Thus, if there is no consignment note, or if it is not taken over by him, or perhaps, if the consignment note does not state that it is subject to C.M.R., the subcontractor will probably not be subjected to C.M.R. liability. Continental cases support this view,[45] and although not directly in point the decision of Goff J. in *SGS-Ates Componenti Elettronici S.p.A.* v. *Grappo Ltd.*[46] is relevant. In this case a subcontractor accepted the goods and the C.M.R. consignment note, but did not enter his name and address on the consignment note. Article 35(1) requires a carrier accepting the goods from a previous carrier to give him a dated and signed receipt. The judge held that this failure could not be cured by applying Article 4,[47] since Article 4 does not apply to successive carriers.[48] Nevertheless

[38] *A.B. Bofors* v. *Skandia Transport* [1982] 1 Lloyd's Rep. 410.

[39] See 3.70.

[40] See 1.77.

[41] See 3.16.

[42] See 3.67.

[43] But may be liable at common law, see 1.78.

[44] An undivided contract between a customer and carrier normally evidenced by one consignment note. See also carriage by air, 6.37.

[45] District Commercial Court, Antwerp, (1977) XII E.T.L. 411.

[46] [1978] 1 Lloyd's Rep. 281.

[47] See 3.18.

[48] Since, unlike Art. 9 (see 3.22), Art. 4 was not made expressly applicable to relations between successive carriers.

he held that the words "acceptance of the consignment note" in Article 34 should be given "their natural and ordinary meaning" and could be satisfied whether or not Article 35 was complied with. Thus Article 35 was not mandatory and a carrier could still be a successive carrier even though he had not complied with its provisions. However by implication Article 34 must be complied with. Thus, since a failure to take over the goods and the consignment note cannot be cured by applying Article 4, this suggests that a subcontractor who did not "take over" the consignment note would not become a succesive carrier.

Clearly Article 34 applies to the case where the consignment note is made out by one carrier and then accepted by another. However, in *Ulster Swift Ltd.* v. *Taunton Meat Haulage Ltd.*,[49] the carrier subcontracted the entire carriage and it was the subcontractor who issued the consignment note. Nevertheless the subcontractor was held to be a successive carrier. By issuing the consignment note the subcontractor binds himself by its terms and also binds the contracting carrier under Article 3. This can, perhaps, apply down a chain of carriers, *e.g.* if carrier A contracts to carry with the customer and then subcontracts the whole of the carriage to B, who performs part of the carriage and subcontracts part to C who further subcontracts to D who actually performs that part of the carriage.[50] C could still be a successive carrier, even though he does not carry, because the goods and consignment note are accepted by D acting on C's behalf, and on his own behalf with the result that D also is a successive carrier.

The fact that a carrier carries only within national boundaries does not prevent him from becoming a successive carrier if he comes within Article 34.[51] Once a carrier becomes a successive carrier he becomes jointly liable for the whole operation to the claimant together with the contracting carrier and other successive carriers. He is thus bound by their acts and omissions. The claimant is limited, however, as to which carriers he can sue. See 3.75.

3.75 **Which carriers can be sued? Article 36**

Under Article 36 action can only be brought against the first carrier, the last carrier or the carrier who was performing that portion of the carriage during which the event causing the loss, etc., occurred.[52] These carriers can all be sued at the same time,[53] although obviously they could not together be made liable for more than the actual loss. The jurisdiction rules in Article 31[54] apply in such a way that although each of them may have a different place of business, etc., they could all be sued either in the place where the goods were originally taken over, or the place designated for delivery under the original contract.[55] The last carrier is the person who actually delivers or loses the

[49] [1977] 1 Lloyd's Rep. 346.
[50] See the facts of *SGS-Ates*, n. 46 above.
[51] Loewe, para. 275.
[52] Although the claimant can raise a counterclaim against any of them if they should sue him, Art. 36.
[53] Art. 36.
[54] See 3.70.
[55] Loewe, para. 281.

goods (providing he is a successive carrier[56]), and not someone who is merely named as a successive carrier but who never in fact becomes one because the goods are lost before they reach him.[57]

The claimant must comply with the rules as to time limits in respect of each carrier he wishes to sue. Thus he will have to issue a writ against each of them separately within the time limits. It seems also, that to suspend the time limit under Article 32(2),[58] a claimant must send a written claim to each of the carriers he intends to sue. A claim sent to one will only have the effect of suspending the time limit in respect of that carrier only and will not have the effect of suspending the time limit in respect of the others.[59]

Rights as between successive carriers, Articles 37-40 3.76

C.M.R. provides rules which determine how liability is to be divided between successive carriers and the relevant time limit, etc. These rules only apply to carriers who are successive carriers under one and the same consignment. In *Arctic Electronic* v. *McGregor*,[60] carrier A split the consignment into three lots and gave them to carriers B, C and D under separate consignment notes. He failed in his claim that each of these carriers were successive carriers in respect of each other.

Under Article 40 successive carriers are free to agree different methods as among themselves of apportioning liability from those provided for in Articles 37 and 38, (but not as regards the rules in Article 39 which are considered in 3.77). Apart from such special agreements Article 37 provides that the carrier who has paid compensation can recover it from the others on the following principles:

(a) the carrier responsible for the loss or damage shall be solely liable;
(b) where more than one carrier is responsible, each shall pay according to their share of liability, or if an apportionment on that basis is impossible, in proportion to the carriage charges due to them;
(c) if it cannot be ascertained which of them is liable, again in proportion to their respective shares of the carriage charges.

If any one of the carriers becomes insolvent then Article 38 provides that the share of the compensation due from that carrier is to be divided among the others in proportion to the carriage charges due to them.

Compulsory rules applicable to successive carriers, Article 39 3.77

Article 39(1) prohibits successive carriers from contesting the validity of any payment made by a carrier claiming from them if the amount of compensation was determined by judicial authority, *i.e.* a court or arbitrator applying C.M.R., and if they had been given notice of the proceedings and an opportunity to attend. This is to prevent the reopening of a decision against the carrier who originally

[56] Otherwise it is the carrier who is responsible for his actions provided that this carrier is a successive carrier.

[57] Hill and Messent, p. 211.

[58] See 3.72.

[59] *Worldwide Carriers* v. *Ardtran* [1983] 1 All E.R. 692.

[60] [1985] 2 Lloyd's Rep. 510.

defended the claim. Successive carriers are not prohibited however, from disputing their own liability to the carrier claiming against them, perhaps on the basis of the rules set out in Article 37.

Article 39(2) provides that a carrier making a claim for an indemnity against another carrier or carriers "may make his claim before the competent court or tribunal of the country in which one of the carriers concerned is ordinarily resident, or has his principal place of business or the branch or agency through which the contract of carriage was made." It also states that "all the carriers concerned may be made defendants in the same action." The carrier making the claim can thus force the other successive carriers to defend his claim in one place provided that place is the residence, etc., of one of them. However the carrier making the claim cannot include his own place of residence, etc., within this rule. It has to be a place of residence etc. of one of the other carriers, as was decided in *Cummins Engine Co. Ltd.* v. *Davis Freight Forwarding (Hull) Ltd.*[61]

Article 39(3) applies Article 31(3) and (4)[62] to judgments made under Articles 37 and 38, and Article 39(4) applies the time limits in Article 32.[63] Thus one carrier making a claim against a successive carrier has only one year to make the claim or three years if he can prove wilful misconduct. Article 39(4) also provides that "the period of limitation shall, however, begin to run either on the date of the final decision fixing the amount of compensation payable under the provisions of this Convention, or if there is no such judicial decision, from the actual date of payment." In *Muller Batavier Ltd.* v. *Laurent Transport Co. Ltd.*,[64] May J. held that this provision only applies to claims by one carrier against another in respect of money paid or payable to the claimant because of loss or damage to the goods etc. It does not cover a claim by one carrier against another for freight. Nor, he held, can a written claim for freight have the effect of suspending the time limit under Article 32(2).[65]

INTERNATIONAL CARRIAGE OF PASSENGERS AND LUGGAGE BY ROAD

3.78 Outline of position

The legal position in respect of the carriage of passengers and their luggage can be stated simply. As stated in 3.10 it seems that luggage is not covered by C.M.R. Presumably luggage means items carried by a passenger or accompanying him on the vehicle used to convey him or other passengers.[66] Consequently the liability of a carrier towards both passengers and their luggage and vice versa will be governed either by the common law, or by any contract terms agreed subject to

[61] [1981] 1 W.L.R. 1363. See also *ITT Schaub-Lorenz* v. *Birkart Johann Internationale Spedition* [1988] 1 Lloyd's Rep. 487, where the application of a defendant carrier to join other carriers to the proceedings brought by the claimant was accepted.

[62] See 3.70.

[63] See 3.71.

[64] [1977] 1 Lloyd's Rep. 411.

[65] See 3.72.

[66] For discussion of the meaning of luggage at common law see 1.118.

the Unfair Contract Terms Act 1977.[67] This will be the position if English courts are able to take jurisdiction, and if English law is applicable according to the principles of conflicts of laws.[68]

An English court can exercise jurisdiction over a non E.E.C. national if he is in the country[69] and over an E.E.C. national if he is domiciled, *i.e.* based here.[70] In addition it is also possible for the court to hear claims in respect of an English contract,[71] or a contract containing a clause granting the court jurisdiction as well as claims in tort if the harm occurred here.[72] For contractual claims the court will apply the "proper law of the contract,"[73] with the result that, if English law is the proper law, it will be the law applied. If a claim is made in tort against a carrier for, *e.g.* negligently injuring a passenger, English law will be applied. This is true wherever the tort was committed if it would constitute a tort if committed in England and would be subject to civil liability in the place where the tort was in fact committed.[74]

The C.V.R. Convention 3.79

There is also, in fact, an International Convention in existence in this area, namely the Convention on the Contract for the International Carriage of Passengers and Luggage by Road (C.V.R.) 1973, and a protocol of 1979. The Carriage of Passengers by Road Act 1974 exists to give effect to the Convention but it is not yet in force. The Convention is contained in the schedule to the Act. Likewise the Carriage by Air and Road Act 1979 contains provisions to enable the protocol to be brought into effect.[75] When brought into effect the Convention, as amended, will replace the common law provisions discussed briefly in 3.78.

Briefly, the Convention if and when it is brought into force, will apply to passengers and their luggage when carried in vehicles by road (other than taxis or hired vehicles) when the contract provides that the carriage shall take place in the territory of more than one state and that either the place of departure or destination or both of them are in a Contracting State.[76]

The Convention makes the carrier liable for death or injury caused to a passenger while inside the vehicle, or while entering or alighting from it, or which occurs in connection with the loading or unloading of luggage.[77] The carrier has a defence if he can show that the accident was caused by circumstances which a carrier, using the diligence

[67] See generally Chap. 1.
[68] See generally J. H. C. Morris, *The Conflict of Laws*. (3rd ed., 1984)
[69] Under the Rules of the Supreme Court, Order 11.
[70] Civil Jurisdiction and Judgments Act 1982.
[71] R.S.C., Order 11, rr. 1(1)(f) & (g).
[72] R.S.C., Order 11, r. 1(h).
[73] The law with the closest connection with the contract. It is possible to make an express choice of law in the contract.
[74] *Chaplin* v. *Boys* [1971] A.C. 356.
[75] s.4.
[76] Art. 1.
[77] Art. 11(1).

which the particular facts called for, could not have avoided and the consequences of which he was unable to prevent.[78] Likewise the carrier is liable for loss or damage to luggage handed to him, *i.e.* unaccompanied luggage from the time he takes charge of it until delivery or deposit in a safe and convenient place on arrival.[79] The carrier is only liable for other luggage (including personal effects[80]) while it is in the vehicle.[81] If however, such luggage is stolen or cannot be found, the carrier is responsible only if it had been placed in his care or if it is stolen or lost in the course of an accident occurring to the road vehicle.[82] The carrier also has the same general defence of "diligence" for luggage as he has in relation to passengers but also has additional defences of inherent vice and special risks inherent in its dangerous or perishable nature.[83]

The limits of liabilty as laid down in the protocol are:

(a) for death or injury 83,333 S.D.R.'s (approx. £60,000) for each victim[84] (although Contracting States can set a higher limit and Section 3 of the Act provides that this limit shall not apply to United Kingdom carriers);
(b) loss or damage to luggage is limited[85] to 166·67 S.D.R.'s (approx. £110) for each piece or 666·67 S.D.R.'s (approx. £500) per passenger;
(c) for personal effects[86] 333·33 S.D.R.'s (approx. £250).[87]

The exclusions or compensation limits cannot be relied on where there has been wilful misconduct.[88] The time limit for claims is three years for death or personal injury and one year for other claims.[89] There are provisions concerning the issue of passenger tickets and "luggage registration vouchers" as well as provisions concerning notice of claims and jurisdiction many of which are similar to C.M.R.

[78] Art. 11(2).
[79] Art. 14(1).
[80] Presumably this means items carried about the passenger's person including his clothes.
[81] Art. 14(1).
[82] Art. 14(1). The meaning of "accident" is considered in 6.58.
[83] Art. 14(2).
[84] Art. 13(1), as amended by the protocol, Art. 2.
[85] Art. 16(1), as amended.
[86] See above n. 80.
[87] Art. 16(1), as amended.
[88] Art. 18(2). For the meaning of wilful misconduct see 1.60.
[89] Art. 22(1).

Chapter Four

INTERNATIONAL CARRIAGE BY RAIL

INTRODUCTION

Contents and background 4.01

In this chapter we consider the regimes of liability which govern international carriage by rail. These respectively cover the carriage of goods, passengers and luggage. Fortunately we now need only to refer to one international convention when explaining the law in this area. This is the Convention Concerning International Carriage By Rail (the C.O.T.I.F. Convention), signed at Berne in 1980. It has been given effect in the United Kingdom by the International Transport Conventions Act 1983,[1] which was brought into force on May 1, 1985. The provisions of the Convention are set out in a Command Paper,[2] and consists of general provisions and a series of more specific provisions. These include: in Appendix A of C.O.T.I.F., a set of uniform rules concerning the contract for international carriage of passengers and luggage by rail abbreviated to C.I.V., and in Appendix B, uniform rules concerning the contract for international carriage of goods by rail abbreviated to C.I.M. A review of the main features of the rules governing carriage of goods will be given in 4.03-4.22, and then a brief outline of the position in respect of passengers and luggage in 4.23-4.25.

C.O.T.I.F. is in fact the latest in a series of conventions governing this area. The first C.I.M. Convention was produced in 1890 on the initiative of the Swiss government.[3] The first C.I.V. Convention on carriage of passengers was produced in 1923. The last major revision of these conventions came in 1970. In addition, because C.I.V. did not deal with liability for death or injury to passengers, an Additional Convention was produced in 1966, coming into effect in 1973. This was implemented in the United Kingdom by the Carriage by Railway Act 1972 which also gave effect to the liability rules in C.I.M./C.I.V. Other parts of these conventions were given effect by contract by virtue of the British Rail consignment notes issued for international rail carriage.[4] C.O.T.I.F. is in effect a consolidating and reorganising revision of the rules made with the major object of introducing

[1] s.1. For a more detailed review of C.O.T.I.F. see N. Palmer, *Bailment*. (2nd ed., 1989).

[2] Cmnd. 8535. See also Hill and Evans , *Transport Laws of the World*, (1988) Vol. 2.

[3] See Hill and Evans, *Transport Laws of the World*, (1988) Vol. 2, 1/B/v for the historical background to the Convention.

[4] The latest consignment notes were introduced in 1985. These have replaced the previous consignment notes which contained a clause designed to make the contract of carriage expressly subject to C.I.M. This clause is no longer necessary and has been removed. An example of a consignment note presently in use is given in Appendix 4. See also 4.07-4.08.

S.D.R.'s[5] into them. The 1983 Act brings the whole convention into English law. The C.I.M. rules were in fact used as a model for the C.M.R. Convention,[6] and many of its provisions are similar, so that only a fairly brief review of these rules is necessary in this Chapter.[7]

4.02 **Administration of C.O.T.I.F.**

The C.O.T.I.F. Convention, as did the previous versions, contains elaborate machinery for the administration and revision of the Convention. The Contracting states together form the Intergovernmental Organisation for International Carriage by Rail (O.T.I.F.) which has a secretariat in Berne called The Central Office for International Carriage by Rail (O.C.T.I.). The Central Office maintains and publishes the list of lines registered under the Convention,[8] publishes relevant information,[9] and provides administrative services. Complex provisions provide machinery for revision of the Convention with a Revision Committee having responsibility for certain matters.

CARRIAGE OF GOODS

4.03 **Application of C.O.T.I.F. in respect of goods**

The uniform rules concerning the carriage of goods set out in Appendix B of the Convention (the C.I.M. rules)[10] apply under Article 1 of these rules to "all consignments of goods for carriage under a through consignment note made out for a route over the territories of at least two States and exclusively over lines or services included in the list provided for in Articles 3 and 10 of the Convention," *i.e.* the list maintained by the Central Office. Thus the carriage must be international in that the goods must be carried over the territories of at least two different States. Where however, the stations of sending and of destination are in the same State, and the line passes through the territory of another State, the carriage may not be subject to C.I.M.[11] The carriage must be exclusively over lines registered with the Central Office.[12] Thus although, unlike C.M.R. (see 3.10), C.I.M.

[5] See 3.60.

[6] See Chap. 3. Note that Art. 28 of C.O.T.I.F. states that the French text of the Convention alone shall prevail. Compare Art. 51 of C.M.R. and the discussion in 3.07.

[7] Note that in Eastern Europe international rail carriage is also covered by special international rules, the S.M.G.S. regime for goods, and the S.M.P.S. regime for passengers. Some States such as East Germany and Poland are parties to both C.O.T.I.F. and to these regimes.

[8] See 4.03.

[9] Note especially its publication, *Bulletin des Transports Internationaux Par Chemin de Fer*.

[10] Which will be referred to simply as C.I.M.

[11] If the line is operated exclusively by the railway of departure, or the States or railways concerned have agreed not to regard such carriage as international, Art. 2(1). By Art. 2(2) it is possible for C.I.M. to be excluded where a line between two adjacent States or between two States in transit through a third State is operated solely by the railway of one of them. The sender can elect to have the goods carried solely by the internal regulations governing that railway.

[12] Two lists are kept, one each for C.I.M. and C.I.V. The Department of Transport is responsible for registration. The whole of the railway system operated by British Rail is registered.

does not refer to either the State of departure or of destination or both of them being a party to the Convention, the effect of this requirement is that the whole of the carriage must take place over the railway lines of countries which have adopted the Convention. Finally, a through consignment note must be issued.[13]

Combined transport, complementary services 4.04

It is possible to include in the list maintained by the Central Office, in addition to services on railway lines, complementary land and sea services and inland waterways operated by or on behalf of the railways, and thus apply C.I.M. to them.[14] Thus, *e.g.* ferry services can be brought in and C.I.M. made applicable to the whole carriage and not just the periods of rail carriage. Article 3 of C.O.T.I.F. allows adjustments to be made to the rules to make allowance for the different mode of transport, but no adjustment can be made to the rules concerning liability. However there is an exception in the case of rail-sea traffic. Article 48 of C.I.M. allows a State to include a note in the list of services to the effect that the sea carriage excepted perils[15] shall apply to the service.[16]

The obligation to carry 4.05

Article 3 places the railway under a duty to carry goods presented to it if various conditions are satisfied. A cause of action is provided[17] for compensation for loss or damage caused by breach of this obligation. The railway is thus placed under a similar duty to carry as is a common carrier,[18] but see 4.06 below.

Acceptable articles for carriage 4.06

The rules[19] identify some articles as not being acceptable for carriage. These are: (i) those prohibited in any of the territories through which they would be carried; (ii) those within the monopoly of postal authorities; (iii) those unsuitable for carriage because of dimensions or weight, etc., and (iv) those not acceptable under dangerous goods regulations.

Other goods are identified[20] as acceptable for carriage but only subject to conditions. These are: (i) dangerous goods; (ii) funeral consignments; (iii) railway rolling stock running on its own wheels; (iv) live animals, and (v) consignments the carriage of which presents special difficulties by reason of their dimensions, etc. Dangerous goods are subject to special regulations set out in Annex 1 of C.I.M. known as the R.I.D. regulations.[21] Live animals must normally be accompanied by an attendant provided by the consignor.

[13] See Appendix 4 and 4.07-4.08.

[14] Art. 2(2) of C.O.T.I.F. The Department of Transport monitors this and updates the list from time to time.

[15] Similar to those contained in the Hague-Visby rules, see 5.27-5.43.

[16] In addition to those provided for in Art. 36, see 4.17.

[17] Art. 3(6). [18] See 1.23.

[19] Art. 4. [20] In Art. 5.

[21] Similar in type to the A.D.R. regulations governing the international carriage of goods by road, see 3.28.

4.07 **Making the contract of carriage**

Article 11(1) states that "the contract of carriage shall come into existence as soon as the forwarding railway has accepted the goods for carriage together with the consignment note." Acceptance is established by the application to the consignment note and where appropriate, to any additional sheet, of the stamp of the forwarding station or accounting machine entry, showing the date of acceptance. The stamping of the consignment note should take place once all the goods have been handed over for carriage and, where this is required, any carriage charges are paid.[22] Thus, unlike C.M.R.,[23] the existence of a consignment note is vital to the existence of a contract subject to C.I.M. Furthermore it is the details which appear on the consignment note which will determine much of how the carriage is to be performed (see, *e.g.* 4.12). Thus it has a central place in the operation of the rules.

4.08 **The consignment note**

The consignor is required to present a consignment note duly completed,[24] which will travel with the goods. After acceptance of the consignment he must receive a duplicate.[25] The consignment note must be printed in at least two, or where necessary, three languages one of which must be a language of a member State.[26] The railways must establish a standard consignment note for each of fast traffic and slow traffic.[27] An example of a C.I.M. consignment note used by British Rail is given in Appendix 4.[28] Article 13 requires the consignment note to contain details of the destination station, the names and addresses of the consignor and consignee, the description of the goods, weight, and number of packages, and a list of customs and other documents. For wagon loads the number of the wagon must be included. The consignor can also include information relating to the consignment for the consignee. The operation of other rules in the Convention may require further details to appear on the consignment note, *e.g.* instructions as to route as permitted by Article 14 (see 4.11).

4.09 **The consignment note as evidence**

Article 11(3) states that the consignment note shall be evidence of the making and content of the contract. Presumably this means that the consignment note will be prima facie evidence of the particulars contained on it.[29] Where the loading of the goods is the responsibility of the consignor, the particulars as to weight and number of packages

[22] Art. 11(2).
[23] See 3.18.
[24] Art. 12(1).
[25] By Art. 11(5) the duplicate shall not have affect as the consignment note accompanying the goods, nor as a bill of lading.
[26] Art. 12(3).
[27] Art. 12(2). These are termed *grande vitesse* and *petite vitesse*.
[28] British Rail use form number BR 20105/114 for *grande vitesse* and BR 20105/113 for *petite vitesse*. The example given in Appendix 4 is for *petite vitesse*.
[29] Note however that there are no equivalent provisions to Arts. 4, 8 and 9 of C.M.R., see 3.18 and 3.22.

shall only be evidence against the railway when they have been verified by it and certified on the consignment note.[30] If they have not been, then these facts must be proved by other evidence. It is open to the railway, if it so wishes, to verify the particulars on the consignment note by, *e.g.* examining the contents, whether at the forwarding or destination station, and charge the costs of such an examination to the customer if the consignment note should prove to be incorrect.[31] National provisions may lay down when the railway must determine for itself the weight or number of packages.[32] Note that regardless of the particulars on the consignment note, if it is obvious that there is no deficiency in the actual weight or number of goods on arrival, despite an apparent discrepancy between the consignment note and the amount actually delivered, the consignment note shall not be evidence against the railway.[33] This applies, in particular, when a wagon is handed over to the consignee with the original seals intact.

The railway may indicate on the consignment note any obvious signs of damage to the goods when it accepts them.[34] If the goods are insufficiently or badly packed the railway can either refuse them or require the sender to acknowledge the bad packing in the consignment note.[35] In the absence of such an acknowledgement the railway has the burden of proving that the goods were badly packed.[36] As under C.M.R.,[37] the consignor is made responsible for the consequences of bad packing,[38] as well as for the correctness of details inserted by him in the consignment note.[39]

Loading and carriage of goods 4.10

The handing over and loading of goods at the place of departure are governed by the "provisions in force at the forwarding station."[40] These may require loading to be performed by the consignor, or by the railway or subject to special agreement between the consignor and the railway. If the consignor loads the goods, he must comply with whatever load limit is in force,[41] and be liable for the consequences of defective loading.[42] He must also state in the consignment note the number and description of the seals affixed to wagons by him.[43] C.I.M. contemplates that normally goods will travel in

[30] Art. 11(4).
[31] Art. 21.
[32] Art. 22. Presumably British Rail byelaws and regulations deal with this.
[33] Art. 11(4).
[34] Art. 19(1).
[35] Art. 19(3).
[36] Art. 19(4). By implication there is no such burden in respect of bad external condition. Thus the consignment note is not an acknowledgement of the good condition of the goods. Compare 3.22, 5.10, and 6.27.
[37] See 3.26.
[38] Art. 19(4). The consignor must comply with any provisions in respect of packing in force at the forwarding station (Art. 19(2)) and may be required to label packages (Art. 19(5)).
[39] Art. 18. This includes putting details in the wrong space in the consignment note!
[40] Art. 20(1), *i.e.* in the U.K., the byelaws and regulations laid down by British Rail.
[41] Art. 20(2).
[42] Art. 20(3).
[43] Art. 20(5).

railway wagons, whether privately owned,[44] or supplied by the railway.[45] They may however be carried in containers and subject to the special regulations (R.I.Co.) laid down in Annex 111. Express parcels traffic is also subject to special regulations (R.I.Ex.) laid down in Annex 1V.[46] They are normally carried in the luggage vans of passenger trains.

4.11 **Route and speed of transit**

The consignor may stipulate in the consignment note the route to be followed by reference to frontier points or frontier or transit stations, provided they are open to traffic between the stations of forwarding and destination.[47] If no route is chosen, the railway must choose that which appears to be most favourable to the consignor.[48] The consignor must also choose whether to send by fast transit, known as *grande vitesse*, or by slow transit, known as *petite vitesse*. He does this by choosing the appropriate consignment note,[49] and although transit periods can be determined by agreement between railways they must not exceed the periods laid down in Article 27. Thus for fast traffic, a period of 12 hours is permitted for despatch, after which time the goods must travel 400 kilometres every 24 hours in the case of full wagon load consignments, and 300 km every 24 hours for less than wagon load consignments. With slow traffic a period of 24 hours is allowed for despatch, and then a rate of 300 km every 24 hours for wagon loads, and 200 km every 24 hours for less than wagon loads.

4.12 **Tariffs and charges**

Carriage charges must be laid down in tariffs published in each State.[50] They must be applied to all users on the same conditions.[51] The route chosen will affect the amount of carriage charges and it can sometimes be possible to choose a route by reference to the tariffs.[52] Supplementary charges, such as those for warehousing or weighing are also laid down in the tariffs. In addition customs duties will be payable and other charges that may arise in the course of carriage.[53] Article 15 sets out who must pay the charges. This depends on what the consignor has undertaken to pay. He may undertake to pay all or part or none of the charges. Different phrases are set out[54] for inclusion in the consignment note to indicate what the consignor has agreed to pay, such as "carriage charges paid to X." The charges

[44] In which case the regulations concerning international haulage of private owners' wagons (R.I.P.) contained in Annex II of C.I.M. will apply. Art. 8 makes provision for special regulations to deal with specialised types of traffic.

[45] As to which note Art. 20(4) which refers to the types of wagons to be used. Note that goods are often consolidated into wagonloads either by forwarders or by the railway itself when it accepts a consignment which is less than a full load.

[46] Note the Rail Express Europe service operated by British Rail with its own consignment note, BR 20105/13. The liability provisions of C.I.M. of course continue to apply.

[47] Art. 14(1).

[48] Art. 14(6).

[49] See 4.08.

[50] Art. 6(1).

[51] Art. 6(3).

[52] Art. 14(2)(b).

[53] *e.g.* demurrage charges. See 5.75 as to the meaning of demurrage.

[54] In Art. 15(2).

which the consignor has not agreed to pay are deemed payable by the consignee.[55] However if the consignee does not take delivery or control of the goods, the charges become payable by the consignor.[56] Charges incurred by reason of acts or requests of the consignee are payable by him.[57] The forwarding railway can, however, require the consignor to prepay charges in the case of goods which are liable to rapid deterioration or which, by reason of their low value or nature, do not provide sufficient security for the charges.[58] Where the consignor has undertaken to pay charges, but they cannot be ascertained exactly at the start of the carriage, *e.g.* customs duties, the railway can demand that a deposit be paid.[59] As under C.M.R.[60] the consignor can require the railway to collect any cash on delivery payment.[61]

Customs 4.13

The consignor must attach to the consignment note the documents required by customs and other administrative authorities,[62] and is responsible for their sufficiency, etc.[63] He is also responsible for packing the goods, etc., in accordance with the relevant customs regulations.[64] The railway then acts as an agent in completing the necessary formalities so that the goods can be cleared through customs points without the involvement of customers unless they wish to be involved.[65]

Modification of the contract of carriage 4.14

Similar rules to C.M.R.[66] deal with the right to modify the contract of carriage, although they are set out in more complex detail in C.I.M. The consignor has the right to modify the contract by, *e.g.* stopping the goods in transit, changing the destination or consignee, etc.[67] To exercise the right he must give a written declaration in the form required by the railway, reproduce it on the duplicate of the consignment note, which must be signed by him, and then the duplicate must be stamped by the railway and returned to the consignor.[68] All of this is subject to the ability of the railway to carry out the order.[69] Once the goods have entered the customs territory of the country of destination the consignee takes over the right to give such orders to the railway.[70] That is so unless the consignor has undertaken to pay

[55] Art. 15(4).
[56] Art. 15(4).
[57] Art. 15(5).
[58] Art. 15(6), presumably regardless of whoever undertakes to pay them.
[59] Art. 15(7).
[60] See 3.58.
[61] Art. 17.
[62] Art. 25(1).
[63] Art. 25(3). See 3.27 for discussion of the equivalent rule under C.M.R.
[64] Art. 25(4).
[65] Art. 26.
[66] See 3.29-3.31.
[67] Art. 30(1).
[68] Art. 30(2).
[69] Art. 32. The railway must comply unless one of the reasons set out in Art. 32 are applicable.
[70] Art. 31. The consignee must make use of a prescribed form.

charges relating to carriage in the country of destination, and has inserted in the consignment note the words "Consignee not authorised to give subsequent orders." Both the consignor's and consignee's right to modify the contract of carriage are extinguished once the consignee has taken possession of the consignment note, or accepted the goods or asserted his rights under Article 28.[71]

4.15 **Delivery**

Under Article 28 the railway must hand over the consignment note and deliver the goods to the consignee at the destination station against a receipt and payment of amounts chargeable to him. The provisions in force at the destination station determine whether the railway is entitled or obliged to hand over the goods to the consignee elsewhere than at the railway station, whether at a private siding, at his domicile, (*i.e.* private address) or at a depot, and "delivery" does not occur until the goods have been handed over at one of these points.[72] However where, in accordance with the provisions in force at the destination station, the goods have been handed over to customs or other authority, or have been deposited for storage with the railway, or with a forwarding agent, or in a public warehouse, this is deemed to be delivery.[73] If the loss, (*i.e.* total loss) of the goods is established or they are delayed beyond 30 days from the expiry of the transit period,[74] the consignee may assert in his own name any rights he may have acquired under the contract of carriage.[75]

4.16 **Circumstances preventing carriage or delivery**

Where circumstances prevent the carriage of the goods, the railway has the choice of modifying the route or asking the consignor for instructions.[76] The consignor can give his instructions to the forwarding station or to the station where the goods are being held. If he wishes to change the consignee or the destination station, or to give the instructions to the station where the goods are being held, he must enter these details on the duplicate of the consignment note.[77] If no instructions are forthcoming within a reasonable time, the railway must act in accordance with "provisions in force at the place where the goods have been held up."[78] Thus the sale of the goods may be permitted by local regulations.[79] If, however, the consignee has modified the carriage by virtue of Article 31[80] before such circumstances arise the railway must apply instead to him for instructions.[81]

[71] Arts. 30(4) and 31(3). For a discussion of Art. 28 see 4.15 below.
[72] Art. 28(3).
[73] Art. 28(2).
[74] As specified in Art. 39(1) as the time from when the goods can be presumed to be lost. As to transit periods see 4.11.
[75] Art. 28(4).
[76] Art. 33(1).
[77] Art. 33(4). Prior instructions anticipating such circumstances may be given under Art. 33(3).
[78] Art. 33(6).
[79] Art. 33(6). The proceeds are to be paid over to the consignor.
[80] See 4.14.
[81] Art. 33(8).

When circumstances prevent delivery of the goods, the station of destination must notify the consignor through the forwarding station and ask for his instructions.[82] The consignor may have indicated beforehand in the consignment note a desire to have the goods returned to him in such circumstances, but otherwise they can only be returned to him with his express consent.[83] If the consignee has in fact refused the goods the consignor can give fresh instructions without having to produce the duplicate of the consignment note.[84] Again the "provisions in force" at the destination station can deal with the situation where these rules do not provide a satisfactory result and may provide for the sale of the goods.[85]

Liability and Compensation

The scheme of liability 4.17

The scheme of liability set out in the C.I.M. rules follows a similiar pattern to that of the C.M.R. Convention.[86] The railway which has accepted goods for carriage together with the consignment note is responsible for any loss, etc., over the entire route up to delivery.[87] It is also liable for its servants and for any other persons whom it employs to perform the carriage.[88] If, however, such servants or other persons, at the request of an "interested party," (*e.g.* the consignor), make out consignment notes, make translations or render other services which the railway itself is under no obligation to render, they shall be deemed to be acting on behalf of the person to whom the service is rendered.[89]

The railway is liable for loss or damage to the goods between the time of acceptance for carriage and the time of delivery and also for loss or damage resulting from the transit period being exceeded.[90] As with C.M.R. two sets of defences are open to the carrier. Article 36(2) sets out the four primary defences. Thus the railway is relieved of liability if such loss, etc., is caused by (i) a fault on the part of the person entitled; (ii) by an order given by the person entitled otherwise than as a result of a fault on the part of the railway; (iii) by inherent vice of the goods (decay, wastage, etc.), or (iv) by circumstances which the railway could not avoid and the consequences of which it was unable to prevent.[91] In addition Article 36(3) provides the railway with a defence if loss or damage arises from the special risks inherent in one of the following circumstances:

[82] Art. 34(1).
[83] Art. 34(4).
[84] Art. 34(3).
[85] Art. 34(6).
[86] See 3.39-3.58.
[87] Art. 35(1). The position of other railways which may be involved in the carriage is dealt with in 4.22.
[88] Art. 50. This is not expressly limited to acts within the scope of their employment. Compare Art. 3 of C.M.R. in Appendix 3A.
[89] Art. 50.
[90] Art. 36(1). The transit period is determined in accordance with Art. 27, see 4.11.
[91] These primary defences and those which follow are similar to those set out in C.M.R. See 3.44-3.55 for a more detailed consideration of them.

(a) carriage in open wagons under the conditions applicable thereto or under an agreement made between the consignor and the railway and referred to in the consignment note;[92]
(b) absence or inadequacy of packing in the case of goods which by their nature are liable to loss or damage when not packed or when not properly packed;
(c) loading operations carried out by the consignor or unloading operations carried out by the consignee under the provisions applicable thereto or under an agreement made between the consignor and the railway and referred to in the consignment note, or under an agreement between the consignee and the railway;
(d) defective loading, when loading has been carried out by the consignor under the provisions applicable thereto or under an agreement made between the consignor and the railway and referred to in the consignment note;
(e) completion by the consignor, the consignee or an agent of either, of the formalities required by customs or other administrative authorities;
(f) the nature of certain goods which renders them inherently liable to total or partial loss or damage, especially through breakage, rust, interior and spontaneous decay, dessication or wastage;
(g) irregular, incorrect, or incomplete description of articles not acceptable for carriage or acceptable subject to conditions, or failure on the part of the consignor to observe the prescribed precautions in respect of articles acceptable subject to conditions;
(h) carriage of live animals;
(i) carriage which, under the provisions applicable or under an agreement made between the consignor and the railway and referred to in the consignment note, must be accompanied by an attendant, if the loss or damage results from any risk which the attendant was intended to avert.

In addition to these two sets of defences Article 41 provides a special recognition of goods which "by reason of their nature, are generally subject to wastage in transit by the sole fact of carriage." This is a special kind of inherent vice and an allowance is made for such inevitable wastage. Thus for liquid goods and certain specified goods such as hides, tobacco, vegetables, etc., the railway is only liable to the extent that any wastage exceeds 2 per cent. of these goods. For all other dry goods with this nature, a tolerance of 1 per cent. is specified.

4.18 **The burden of proof**

Again, as with C.M.R.[93] there is a double scheme of proof required in establishing the defences. Thus the railway has the normal burden of proving that one of the primary defences in Article 36(2) is the cause of the loss.[94] However when the railway "establishes that, having regard to the circumstances of a particular case, the loss or

[92] A particularly important exception in the days of coal-fired steam trains!
[93] See 3.48.
[94] Art. 37(1).

damage could have arisen from one or more of the special risks referred to in Article 36(3), it shall be presumed that it did so arise."[95] In that case the burden passes to the claimant to prove that "the loss or damage was not attributable wholly or partly to one of those risks." Similarly the allowances specified in Article 41 are subject to the possibility of proof that the loss was not due to causes which would justify an allowance.[96]

The presumption in favour of the carrier in respect of the special risks does not apply in the case of carriage in open wagons if an abnormally large quantity has been lost or if a package has been lost.[97] This is the equivalent to Article 18(3) in C.M.R.[98] Note however that there is no equivalent in C.I.M. to Article 18(4) or 18(5)[99] of C.M.R. nor is there any equivalent to Article 17(5).[1]

Compensation 4.19

By Article 40 in the case of total or partial loss[2] compensation is to be calculated on the basis of the "commodity exchange quotation," or according to the "current market price," or "according to the normal value of goods of the same kind and quality at the time and place at which the goods were accepted for carriage."[3] Such compensation shall not exceed 17 S.D.R.'s[4] per kilogramme,[5] approx £13.[6] Note however that tariffs can provide for carriage at reduced rates with correspondingly lower limits of liability.[7] In addition the railway must refund carriage charges, customs duties and other amounts incurred in connection with carriage of the lost goods.[8]

Compensation for damage is based on the loss of value of the goods,[9] *i.e.* the difference between the value as determined under Article 40 and the actual value as damaged goods at the destination subject to a limit based on the amount which would have been recoverable had the goods been lost. A proportionate amount of the carriage charges, etc., can also be recovered.

Where "loss or damage"[10] has resulted from the transit period being exceeded, the railway must pay compensation up to a limit of

[95] Art. 37(2). Compare 3.48.

[96] Art. 41(2). Compare 3.48.

[97] Art. 37(2).

[98] See 3.49.

[99] See 3.53 and 3.55.

[1] See 3.43.

[2] Under Art. 39(1) there is a presumption that the goods are lost if they have not arrived after 30 days from the expiry of the transit periods (similar to C.M.R., see 3.57).

[3] For a discussion of these words see 3.61.

[4] For the meaning of S.D.R.'s see 3.60.

[5] Art. 40(2).

[6] About twice the C.M.R. limit, see 3.62.

[7] Art. 45.

[8] Note the difference in wording to C.M.R., see 3.63. The wording used in C.I.M. seems to suggest sums directly incurred in carriage rather than incurred as a consequence of carriage. Compare *Buchanan* v. *Babco* [1978] A.C. 141 in respect of C.M.R. discussed in 3.63.

[9] Art. 42.

[10] This would seem to mean economic loss or damage rather than physical damage or deterioration caused by delay which would fall under Art. 42. See the decision of the Federal Supreme Court, Germany June 14, 1976, XI E.T.L. 787. *cf.* the decision of the Court of Justice, Amsterdam, November 21, 1974, [1976] I U.L.R. 265. See also 1.58 and 3.64.

three times the carriage charges.[11] Where such compensation is claimed in addition to compensation for loss or damage[12] the total amount payable may not exceed the amount payable for total loss. However Article 16 provides for the possibility of declaring an amount as representing an interest in the delivery of the goods subject to charges laid down in the tariffs. Where there is such a declaration Article 46 allows further compensation to be claimed in addition to that normally allowed by Article 40.

Where the loss, damage or delay has been caused by wilful misconduct[13] on the part of the railway,[14] full compensation is payable for proven loss, etc.[15] If the loss, etc., has been caused by "gross negligence" the railway is liable up to twice the amounts specified in the various limits, *e.g.* 34 S.D.R.'s in the case of loss.[16]

CLAIMS AND ACTIONS

4.20 **Persons who may bring an action**

The C.I.M. rules are quite specific as to who is entitled to make a claim and to bring an action against the railway. Under Article 54(3) actions arising from the contract of carriage may be brought in the first instance by the consignor. However once the consignee takes possession of the consignment note, or accepts the goods, or exercises his rights under Article 28 or 31,[17] an action may then be brought by him.[18] An action for recovery of a sum paid under the contract may only be brought by the person who made the payment,[19] and in respect of cash on delivery payments by the consignor.[20]

Before bringing an action, a claimant would be well advised to first make a claim which must be in writing.[21] In making a claim or bringing an action the consignor must produce the duplicate of the consignment note, or failing this produce an authorisation from the consignee or furnish proof that the consignee has refused to accept

[11] Art. 43(1). For transit periods see 4.11.

[12] *e.g.* where the goods are both delayed and arrive damaged.

[13] For discussion see 1.60 and 3.68.

[14] Including its servants or persons whom it employs to perform the carriage since the railway is made liable for these persons by Art. 50. See also 3.68 and 6.49.

[15] Art. 44.

[16] Art. 44. Presumably "gross negligence" means a serious failure to take proper care of the goods but without the element of intention or recklessness required for wilful misconduct.

[17] See 4.15.

[18] The continental courts apply these rules strictly so that someone not named in the consignment note cannot sue, nor can the consignor sue once the consignee has taken possession of the consignment note: District Commercial Court, Paris, September 29, 1971, [1973] II U.L.R. 451; Supreme Court, France, May 15, 1974, [1975] II U.L.R. 381. Note also that by Art. 51 any action brought against the railway on any grounds is subject to the conditions and limitations laid down in the rules. See also 3.32, 5.12, and 6.34.

[19] Art. 54(1).

[20] Art. 54(2).

[21] Art. 53(1). Failure to do so may mean loss of the right to sue, see 4.21.

the consignment.[22] The consignee likewise must produce the consignment note if it has been handed to him.[23]

Extinction of rights of action and time limits 4.21

Article 57(1) states that acceptance of the goods by the person entitled to them shall extinguish all rights of action against the railway in case of partial loss, damage or delay. Fortunately this drastic provision is qualified in a number of ways. Firstly, if the person entitled on receiving the goods can see that there is partial loss or damage, he should require the railway to draw up a report on the loss or damage.[24] If he does not he will lose the right to sue. If the loss or damage is not apparent the person entitled has seven days (or earlier if he discovers the loss or damage before seven days have passed) to ask for a report or risk loss of the right to sue.[25] With delay the person entitled has 60 days from the ending of the transit period to make a claim.[26] However there is no loss of the right to sue where the loss or damage is proved to have been caused by the wilful misconduct or gross negligence of the railway.[27]

Under Article 58 the normal period of limitation is one year.[28] However this period is extended[29] to two years for (i) a cash on delivery charge collected by the railway; (ii) for the proceeds of a sale effected by the railway; (iii) for loss or damage caused by wilful misconduct; (iv) for fraud; and (v) for an action arising from a previous contract of carriage when the goods were reconsigned with the railway under the rules.[30] The rules[31] governing the time when the period begins to run are complex. Basically for most claims against the carrier, time runs from the date of delivery. However in the case of a claim for total loss time runs from the thirtieth day after the expiry of the transit period.[32] For recovery of charges time runs from the day of payment.[33] Once a written claim is sent to the railway with the necessary supporting documents[34] the period of limitation is suspended until the railway rejects the claim.[35]

Who and where to sue 4.22

By Article 55(1) an action for recovery of a sum paid to the railway, *e.g.* freight, may be brought against the railway which has collected it

[22] Arts. 53(3) and 54(4).
[23] Arts. 53(3) and 54(4).
[24] Art. 57(2)(a). The procedure for this is governed by Art. 52.
[25] Art. 57(2)(b).
[26] Art. 57(2)(c).
[27] Art. 57(2)(d).
[28] For both claimant and railway.
[29] By Art. 58(1)(a)-(e).
[30] Provided for by Art. 38(1).
[31] Set out in Art. 58(2).
[32] As also a claim relating to cash on delivery.
[33] And for recovery of proceeds from a sale from the date of sale. Claims for carriage charges run from the day the goods were accepted for carriage or from when a charges note is submitted to the consignor, although for charges payable from the consignee time runs from the date when he accepted the consignment note. In any case not provided for, time runs from the day when the cause of action arises.
[34] Such as the duplicate of the consignment note.
[35] Art. 58(3). See also 3.72.

or on whose behalf it was collected. An action in respect of cash on delivery payments may only be brought against the forwarding railway.[36] Other actions arising from the contract of carriage may be brought against the forwarding railway, the railway of destination or the railway on which the event giving rise to the proceedings occurred.[37] The railway of destination can be sued even if it has received neither the goods nor the consignment note.[38] However once the plaintiff has brought an action against any one of them he cannot sue any of the others.[39] The railway can only be sued in the State to which it belongs.[40] Several rules govern the rights as between railways[41] including rights of recourse so that the railway which caused loss or damage, etc., will ultimately have to pay the railway which compensated the plaintiff.

CARRIAGE OF PASSENGERS AND LUGGAGE

4.23 The C.I.V. rules

Appendix A of the C.O.T.I.F. Convention contains the Uniform Rules Concerning the Contract for International Carriage of Passengers and Luggage by Rail (C.I.V.). Naturally it shares many features in common with the C.I.M. rules but with appropriate differences bearing in mind that it is concerned with passengers and not goods. A brief outline is given below.

The C.I.V. rules apply to any carriage of passengers and luggage under international transport documents, (*i.e.* a specially marked passenger ticket[42]) made out for a journey over the territories of at least two States and exclusively over listed lines.[43] They do not apply to death or injury to passengers occurring on other modes of transport connected with an international rail carriage, *e.g.* a "pick-up" service by bus. However, where an event causing such injury occurs on a ferry and is due to an accident arising out of the operation of the railway and happens while the passenger is in, entering or alighting from a railway vehicle, the rules apply.[44] The C.I.V. rules also apply to death or personal injury caused to persons accompanying goods consigned under C.I.M.[45] Luggage is categorised as either hand luggage which accompanies the passenger[46] or

[36] Art. 55(2).

[37] Art. 55(3). The collective responsibility of the railways involved in the carriage is stated in Art. 35(2).

[38] Art. 55(3), Compare C.M.R., see 3.75.

[39] Art. 55(4). However a counterclaim may be brought by the plaintiff if any railway chooses to sue him, *e.g.* for unpaid carriage charges (Art. 55(5)). Compare C.M.R., see 3.75.

[40] Art. 50.

[41] Arts. 59-64.

[42] The requirements for which are set out in Art. 11.

[43] Art. 1.

[44] Art. 33.

[45] Art. 1.

[46] Under Art. 15. Hand luggage is carried without extra charge. Art. 15 specifies certain articles which are not acceptable as hand luggage such as bulky items.

registered luggage carried under a luggage registration voucher.[47] Live animals are also covered if they accompany the passenger where permitted by the tariffs.[48] Special provision is made for accompanied motor vehicles.[49] Each passenger is entitled only to the space above and below his seat for hand luggage unless the carriage is the type which contains a luggage area.[50]

Liability of the railway 4.24

Article 26(1) makes the railway liable for the death of, personal injuries to, or any other bodily or mental harm to a passenger caused by an accident[51] arising out of the operation of the railway which happens while the passenger is either in or entering or alighting from railway vehicles. Thus, an accident occurring to a passenger while on the platform or other part of the station and not while he is travelling on or getting into or off the train would be covered in the United Kingdom by the common law (see 1.115-1.117) and not C.I.V. Damages for death include the costs of transport of the body, burial and cremation.[52] Those deprived of the support of the dead person when that person had a legal duty to maintain them can also obtain compensation.[53] Damages for personal injury or other bodily or mental harm include treatment and transport costs as well as compensation for "financial loss due to total or partial incapacity to work, or to increased needs."[54]

The railway is not liable[55] if the accident was (i) due to circumstances not connected with the operation of the railway and which, having taken the care required in the particular circumstances, it could not avoid and the consequences of which it was unable to prevent; or (ii) was due to the passenger's fault; or (iii) to behaviour on his part not in conformity with the normal conduct of passengers; or (iv) was due to the behaviour of a third party which the railway, having taken the care required in the particular circumstances, could not avoid and the consequences of which it was unable to prevent. In essence therefore the railway would seem to be subject to a "fault" liability similar to the liability of a carrier of passengers at common law (see 1.115).

[47] See Arts. 17-21.

[48] Art. 15(2)(d).

[49] By Art. 41.

[50] Art. 15(1).

[51] The meaning of an "accident" is left undefined. See however the definition adopted in 6.58 which perhaps can be applied also to carriage by rail.

[52] Art. 27(1).

[53] Art. 27(2). Consequently their right to sue under the Fatal Accident Act 1976 is removed by section 3 of the International Transport Conventions Act 1983. However any right of other persons to sue, or any right to sue for bereavement under the Fatal Accident Act is preserved. Any award must take into account damages recoverable under C.I.V.

[54] Art. 28. Under Art. 29 it is left up to national law to determine whether damages for other injuries such as pain and suffering or disfigurement can be recovered and to what extent.

[55] Under Art. 26(2).

The railway is also liable[56] for total or partial loss of, or damage to, any hand luggage or animals subject to the same defences as in the case of carriage of passengers.[57] However the passenger is made specially responsible for the care of such hand luggage, etc., unless they are placed in the luggage area of a special carriage.[58] Furthermore, in the case of accompanied hand luggage, etc., Article 47(2) states that the railway will not be liable unless the loss or damage is caused by its fault.[59] Presumably this puts the burden of proof on to the passenger. Article 35(1) makes the railway liable for loss or damage to registered luggage occurring between the time of acceptance and delivery as well as for delay in delivery.[60] The railway has the defences[61] of (i) fault or orders of the passenger; (ii) inherent vice; (iii) unavoidable circumstances; (iv) the special risks arising from the nature or packing of the registered luggage and (v) the despatch of unacceptable items.[62]

4.25 **Limits on liability and actions**

The limit of liability for death or personal injury is 70,000 S.D.R.'s[63] per passenger, approx £50,000.[64] For hand luggage and animals it is 700 S.D.R.'s per passenger, *i.e.* about £500.[65] With registered luggage, where the amount of loss or damage is established, the limit is 34 S.D.R.'s per kilo (approx £25), or 500 S.D.R.'s per item (approx £380).[66] Where however, the amount of the loss or damage to registered luggage is not established the amount to be paid is 10 S.D.R.'s per kilo (approx £7.50), or 150 S.D.R.'s per item (approx £115).[67] Where registered luggage is delayed, if the claimant can prove the damage caused to him by the delay, a limit of 0.40 S.D.R.'s per kilo (approx 30p) or 7 S.D.R.'s per item (approx £5) is imposed.[68] If the amount of damage arising from the delay is not proved, the amount payable is specified as 0.07 S.D.R.'s per kilo (approx 5p) or 1.40 S.D.R.'s per item (approx £1.06p).[69] In the case of motor vehicles a

[56] Under Art. 26(1).

[57] It is implicit in Art. 32, that the burden of proof is on the railway. This Article prohibits tariffs or special agreements from exempting liability for death or personal injury, or reversing the burden of proof on the railway, or setting lower limits than those laid down in Arts. 30(2) and 31.

[58] Art. 15(5).

[59] The same applies to articles left inside motor vehicles, Art. 41(4). There is no liability at all for articles left on top of vehicles.

[60] Otherwise liability for delay is left up to the law of the State in which the incident causing the delay occurred, Art. 47(1).

[61] Under Art. 35(2) and (3).

[62] A burden of proof similar to that in Art. 37(2) of C.I.M. (see above 4.18) is attached to these special risks by Art. 36(2). A presumption of loss arises after 14 days from a request for delivery (Art. 37(1)).

[63] See 3.60.

[64] Art. 30(2).

[65] Art. 31.

[66] Art. 38(1)(a).

[67] Art. 38(1)(b).

[68] Art. 40(1)(a).

[69] Art. 40(1)(b).

limit of 4,000 S.D.R.'s (approx £3,000) is specified,[70] and a total of 700 S.D.R.'s for articles left inside the vehicle.[71] These limits cannot be relied upon by the carrier in the event of gross negligence or wilful misconduct, although in the case of registered luggage the limits are only doubled in cases involving gross negligence.[72] The time limit for claims is three years for death or personal injury,[73] and one year for other actions, *e.g.* luggage claims.[74]

[70] Art. 41(3).
[71] Art. 41(4).
[72] Art. 42.
[73] Art. 55(1). Counted in most cases from the date of the accident.
[74] Art. 55(2). Increased to two years in cases involving wilful misconduct or fraud.

Chapter Five

ELEMENTS OF CARRIAGE BY WATER

Carriage by Sea, Introduction

5.01 Scope and contents

The law relating to the carriage of goods by sea is huge in content and complex in many of its provisions. A vast body of case law has accumulated on the subject, much of it decided on the specific terms of very complex contracts. In addition carriage by sea is more than adequately covered in both reference[1] and elementary textbooks.[2] Therefore, in this Chapter, we give only a relatively brief summary of the law relating to carriage by water.

There are two types of contract of carriage of goods by sea or "contract of affreightment." Firstly there are contracts by which it is agreed that certain goods will be carried to a named destination. Secondly there are contracts for the hire of a ship or charterparties. In the first type a bill of lading is usually, but not always, issued to the consignor or "shipper." As we shall see below this document has important implications. The second type of contract, *i.e.* charterparties, can be divided into three main types, namely "voyage charters," "time charters" and "bareboat charters" (or "charters by demise"). The nature of bills of lading and charterparties is outlined in 5.04. An example of a bill of lading is given in Appendix 5.A., of a voyage charter in Appendix 5.B and of a time charter in 5.C. The two most important statutes relating to carriage of goods by sea, namely the Bills of Lading Act 1855 and the Schedule to the Carriage of Goods by Sea Act 1971 will be found in Appendices 5.D. and 5.E. respectively. A brief outline of the law relating to the carriage of passengers and their luggage will be found in 5.84-5.89 and that relating to carriage by inland waterway will be found in 5.82-5.83.

In this Chapter, as in other Chapters, we concentrate mainly on the liability for loss and damage of the carrier. Therefore more coverage is given to bills of lading[3] and we give only a brief examination to technical matters that only arise in relation to charterparties such as laytime and demurrage.

5.02 C.I.F. contracts

In order to understand the law of carriage by sea and especially the functions of a bill of lading[4] it is necessary to have a rudimentary understanding of the types of international contracts for the sale of

[1] Carver, *Carriage by Sea*, (13th ed., 1982); *Scrutton, On Charterparties*, (19th ed., 1984).
[2] *Payne and Ivamy's Carriage of Goods by Sea*, (12th ed., 1985); *Chorley and Giles' Shipping Law*, (8th ed., 1987).
[3] See 5.07-5.50.
[4] See 5.07-5.11.

goods. Such contracts vary enormously and the duties of the buyer and seller will depend on the precise terms of their individual contract of sale. However there are two main types of contract in common use, namely C.I.F. contracts and F.O.B. contracts.

C.I.F. stands for Cost, Insurance and Freight. Under sections 17(1) and 18 of the Sale of Goods Act 1979[5] the seller and buyer can make any contract they wish as regards the passing of property and/or risk in the goods and thus rebut the presumptions laid down by the Rules in Section 18. A C.I.F. contract is precisely such a contract. It is performed not just by the delivery of the goods to the carrier but essentially by the delivery to the buyer of documents, namely:

(1) The bill of lading which is evidence of the contract of carriage, a receipt for the goods and a document of title.[6] Note that the bill must normally be a "shipped" Bill, *i.e.* one stating that the goods have been shipped on board.[7]
(2) An insurance policy covering the goods while they are in transit.
(3) An invoice, customs documents, etc.

Unlike land carriage[8] the seller under a C.I.F. contract makes the contract of affreightment not as an agent for the buyer but in his own right as principal. It is his duty to contract as principal to have the goods delivered to the port of destination by means of a reasonable contract of carriage[9] and to pay the freight.[10] He must also insure the goods and within a reasonable time deliver the documents to the buyer. If the documents are in order and are delivered to the buyer then the seller has performed his side of the contract of sale. The goods are then the buyer's property and at his risk from the moment of shipment. If the goods are lost or damaged in transit after delivery of the documents the buyer must still pay the price.[11] His remedy, if any, in these circumstances is to sue the carrier or claim on the insurance policy. Nevertheless the documents must be accurate, *e.g.* they must show the correct date of shipment. The buyer has the right to reject the documents and the separate right to reject the goods and refuse to pay for them if they are not as per the contract of sale.[12]

C.I.F. contracts are often combined with a particular method of financing international sales. For example, if A, in England, sells goods C.I.F. to B in Nigeria, B may get a bank in Nigeria to issue an irrevocable "letter of credit" in favour of A, *i.e.* a document promising to pay A upon production of the bill of lading and other documents. The Nigerian bank will then get an English bank to "confirm" the letter of credit, *i.e.* guarantee it. Once the goods are shipped A will present the documents to the English bank and get paid. The English bank will then send the documents to the Nigerian bank. The

[5] Compare the position in carriage by land outlined in 1.08.
[6] See 5.07-5.11.
[7] See 5.07.
[8] See 1.10.
[9] Sale of Goods Act 1979, s.32(2).
[10] See 5.58.
[11] *C. Groom Limited* v. *Barber* [1915] 1 K.B. 316.
[12] *Kwei Tek Chao* v. *British Traders and Shippers* [1957] 2 Q.B. 459.

Nigerian bank will then in turn give them to B if he pays the price to the bank. With the documents B can collect the goods at the port of destination. If the buyer, B, does not pay up then the Nigerian bank still have the documents as security (they are said to have a "pledge" over them) and they can collect the goods themselves instead.[13]

5.03 **F.O.B. contracts**

The other main type of international sale contract is an F.O.B. or Free On Board contract. There are many types of F.O.B. contract. However under most of them it is the duty of the buyer to arrange for the carriage, to ensure that the vessel is at the port of departure at the agreed time and, if he wishes, to insure the goods. Under section 32(3) of the Sale of Goods Act 1979[14] however it is the seller's duty to give the buyer sufficient information so that the seller can insure the goods. If the seller does not do so then the goods are at his risk during transit. When the seller delivers the goods to the ship it is a question of fact whether he also becomes bound by the terms of the contract of affreightment.[15] In a classic F.O.B. contract the risk and also normally the property, (*i.e.* ownership) in the goods passes to the buyer when they pass over the ship's rail.[16]

5.04 **Types of contract of affreightment**

As mentioned in 5.01 the two most common types of contract of affreightment are under a bill of lading and under a charterparty. What are known as "general ships," carry cargo for a number of customers. If a businessman sells a small volume of goods to an overseas customer on a C.I.F. basis[17] he will, either directly or through an agent, contract with the owners of a general ship to have the goods carried and he will receive a bill of lading from the shipping company. The Bill of lading is a receipt for the goods, is evidence of the contract and may be a transferable document of title or ownership.[18] An example of a bill of lading, the "Conline" bill, is given in Appendix 5.A. and the law relating to them is outlined in 5.07-5.60. Carriage under a bill of lading is often, but not always, subject to the Hague-Visby Rules implemented into English law by the Carriage of Goods by Sea Act 1971. The Hague-Visby Rules will be found in Appendix 5.E. and their provisions are discussed in 5.27 to 5.49. *Do not confuse the Hague-Visby Rules with the ("Hague Protocol") on carriage by air discussed in Chapter 6.*

The other type of contract of affreightment is called a "charterparty." A charterparty is a contract for the hire of the use of a ship. This contract would be used by someone, *e.g.* who wanted to deliver a bulk cargo and who therefore required the whole of the ship. There

[13] See 5.11.
[14] See Appendix 1.C.
[15] Compare the dubious decision of *Pyrene* v. *Scindia Navigation* [1954] 2 Q.B., which should have been decided on the grounds of a bailment on terms (see 1.84), and *The Roselyne* [1987] 1 Lloyd's Rep. 18 (Canada).
[16] *Pyrene* v. *Scindia Navigation* [1954] 2 Q.B. 402.
[17] See 5.02.
[18] See 5.08-5.11.

are three types of charterparty: a voyage charter, a time charter and a charter by demise (otherwise known as a bareboat charter). In a voyage charter the owner or seller of the cargo may hire, *i.e.* charter, a vessel to go, for example, from London to New York and, perhaps, back again. The Gencon voyage charter reproduced in Appendix 5.B. is an example of such a contract. Voyage charters are discussed in 5.61-5.75. In a time charter the vessel is hired for a certain length of time, *e.g.* one year. The Baltime charter in Appendix 5.C. is an example. Time charters are discussed briefly in 5.76-5.81. With both time charters and voyage charters the charterer may in turn let out space to other cargo owners who may be given bills of lading. This can lead to legal difficulties, discussed in 5.15-5.16, in deciding whether the contract of the holder of the bill of lading is with the shipowner or the charterer.

In both voyage and time charters the ship remains in the possession of, and under the control of, the shipowner. The charterer merely hires the use of the ship. In the third type of charterparty, the charter by demise or bareboat charter, this is not so. The charterer in such a contract takes possession and virtually full control of the vessel and its crew who become his temporary employees. A bareboat charter is thus an example of a bailment for reward[19] of a ship and not a contract of affreightment. A discussion of such contracts is therefore outside the scope of this chapter.

In contracts of affreightment, except perhaps time charters (see 5.76-5.81), there are three essential common law duties that fall on the shipowner. These are:

(1) The duty to supply a seaworthy ship.[20]
(2) The duty not to deviate from the agreed voyage.[21]
(3) The duty to load, carry and unload with due dispatch, *i.e.* without undue delay.[22]

The Unfair Contract Terms Act 1977 and contracts of affreightment 5.05

Any term in a contract of affreightment that purports to exempt liability for negligently causing death or injury is null and void.[23] It is difficult to conceive of any such clause ever appearing in a Bill of lading or a charterparty which are contracts for the carriage of goods not persons. Obviously one cannot challenge the provisions of the Carriage of Goods by Sea Act 1971 under the "reasonableness test" in the Unfair Contract Terms Act 1977.[24] Apart from where there is an exclusion of liability for death and injury and, perhaps, where the goods are not actually on board the ship[25] contracts of affreightment can only be challenged as unreasonable under the Unfair Contract Terms Act 1977 if made with "consumers" as opposed to business

[19] See 1.03.
[20] See 5.17-5.12.
[21] See 5.23-5.26.
[22] See 1.36 and 5.68.
[23] Unfair Contract Terms Act 1977, s.2(1) and Sched. 1(2)(c).
[24] See 1.45.
[25] See below.

customers.[26] Needless to say, private persons only rarely have goods carried under a Bill of lading and virtually never charter cargo carrying vessels. Nevertheless the Carriage of Goods by Sea Act 1971, which implements the Hague-Visby Rules, only applies to the period from the loading of the cargo to its discharge.[27] In addition Schedule 1 of the Unfair Contract Terms Act states that the Act's provisions do not normally apply to "any contract for the carriage of goods by ship." It is arguable that a clause in a bill of lading[28] or a charterparty excluding liability for negligent loss or damage before loading or after discharge could be challenged under the reasonableness test[29] in the 1977 Act.

5.06 Are carriers by sea common carriers?

There is no reason in principle why a carrier by sea should not be a common carrier.[30] In fact in *Bennett* v. *Peninsular Steamboat Co.*[31] the defendants were held liable as common carriers for refusal to carry the plaintiff and his luggage by sea. It is very unlikely however, that a shipowner who lets out whole vessels on charter would be held to have held himself out as prepared to carry for all and sundry.[32] There is no reason, however, why the owners of general ships who issue Bills of lading to all and sundry should not be common carriers and such carriers by sea have been held to be common carriers in other Commonwealth countries.[33] This matter is however only of importance as regards actions for refusal to carry[34] as opposed to actions for loss or damage to cargo. This is because the best view is that whether a carrier by water is a common carrier or not he is by "custom of the realm" under the same liability for loss or damage as if he were a common carrier.[35] In fact the case of *Liver Alkali* v. *Johnson*[36] may be express authority for this proposition. In other words all carriers, whether common or private, by water as opposed to land, are, at common law, strictly liable for loss or damage irrespective of negligence. This point is of importance when construing exclusion clauses in a contract of affreightment.[37] Nevertheless nearly all carriage by sea is subject to the Carriage of Goods by Sea Act 1971 or the express terms of the contract of affreightment rather than the common law.

[26] Sched. 1(2).
[27] Art. I(e). See *Rambler Cycle Company* v. *Pacific and Orient* [1968] 1 Lloyd's Rep. 42 (Malaysia).
[28] See 5.07 for an outline of the nature of a bill of lading.
[29] See 1.45.
[30] See 1.21-1.29.
[31] (1848) 6 C.B. 775.
[32] This is the test of whether a person is a common carrier. See 1.22.
[33] *e.g. Hearle* v. *Ross* (1857) 15 U.C.R. 259 (Canada).
[34] See 1.23.
[35] Although there are *dicta, i.e.* comments, to the contrary the majority of the *dicta* favour this view. See, *e.g.* Brett J. in *Nugent* v. *Smith* (1876) 1 C.P.D. 423.
[36] (1872) L.R. 7 Ex. 267, affirmed (1874) L.R. 9 Ex. 338.
[37] Compare the position in land carriage discussed in 1.29.

Functions of a Bill of Lading

Introduction 5.07

When goods are delivered to a ship to be carried subject to a Bill of lading a receipt called a mate's receipt is usually issued. A mate's receipt is not normally (as a bill of lading usually is),[38] a document of title or transferable although it may become so by local custom.[39] Any defects in the goods will be noted on the mate's receipt. If any such defects have been noted on the receipt these will be copied on to the bill of lading. If the bill of lading thus contains, for example, the statement "some barrels broken and leaking" then it is known as a "claused" bill of lading. If, on the other hand, it says "received in apparent good order and condition" it is known as a "clean" bill of lading.

The bill of lading is usually a document signed by the shipowner, his agent or the ship's master stating that goods have been received for shipment, *i.e.* a "received for shipment" bill, or have actually been shipped aboard. The latter is called a "shipped Bill." Once signed it is delivered to the shipper who may be the seller of the goods or who may be the buyer either personally or, more probably, acting through an agent. A bill of lading has three functions. These are:

(1) As good evidence of the terms of the contract of affreightment.
(2) As a receipt for the goods as to
 (i) Quantity,
 (ii) Condition.

(3) As a possible document of title.

These three functions are outlined in the following paragraphs:

The bill of lading as evidence of the contract 5.08

The actual contract of carriage is nearly always made before the bill of lading is issued, for example, when the customer books space on the ship. However the understanding will almost always be that the contract will be subject to the shipowner's standard bill of lading. Thus the bill of lading is very strong evidence of the terms of the contract. Nevertheless it is possible to bring evidence even to contradict the written terms of the bill of lading by, for example, proving that the agreed contract was to sail directly without deviation to a certain port[40] thus overriding a liberty to deviate clause[41] in the bill of lading. However where the bill is transferred to a third party[42] *it becomes the contract* between the shipowner and the transferee of the bill and its contents cannot be challenged.[43]

[38] See 5.11.
[39] *Kum* v. *Wah Tat Bank* [1971] 1 Lloyd's Rep. 439.
[40] *The Ardennes* [1951] 1 K.B. 55.
[41] See 5.24.
[42] See 5.11.
[43] *Leduc* v. *Ward* (1888) 20 Q.B.D. 475.

5.09 **The bill of lading as a receipt as to quantity**

The second function of a bill of lading is, as a receipt for the cargo as regards quantity, condition and quality. As regards quantity if, for example, the bill of lading states that 150 bales of rubber have been shipped then this is strong evidence that 150 bales were in fact shipped. The burden of proving that, for example, only 125 bales were received would fall on the shipowner. However, at common law, under the rule in *Grant* v. *Norway*[44] if the shipowner can prove that *no cargo* at all has been shipped or only part of the cargo then a transferee[45] for value of the bill of lading will have no remedy against the shipowner as regards goods never taken on board. This is because, surprisingly, the captain has no apparent authority to sign for cargo he never received and the shipowner is not liable for his wrongful act in signing for non-existent cargo.[46] The transferee could, in these circumstances, sue the ship's master under section 3 of the Bills of Lading Act 1855[47] but the master may not be worth suing. The position under contracts subject to the Hague-Visby Rules is discussed in 5.38.

To overcome *Grant* v. *Norway*[48] some bills of lading provide that statements on the Bill as to the quantity of cargo shall be conclusive evidence that that the stated quantity has in fact been shipped. On the other hand some Bills, such as the Conline Bill in Appendix 5.A. state "weight and quantity unknown" or suchlike. Where there is such a clause the burden is on the cargo owner to prove that the stated cargo was in fact shipped.[49]

5.10 **The bill of lading as a receipt as to quality and condition**

The master of a ship has no authority to bind the shipowner as to the quality of the shipped goods[50] because because he cannot as an unskilled person judge such matters. If on the other hand the bill of lading states, as does that in Appendix 5.A., that the cargo was "shipped in apparent good order and condition" then as against the transferee[51] of a bill of lading the shipowner is estopped, *i.e.* prevented, from denying that they were in apparent good condition. The courts have been very hostile to clauses saying for example, "quality and condition unknown" and have interpreted them *contra proferentem*[52] as exemption clauses and virtually prevented shipowners from relying on them.[53]

[44] (1851) 20 L.J.C.P. 93.

[45] *Thorman* v. *Burt* (1886) 54 L.T. 349. As to transfer of Bills of lading, see 5.11.

[46] *Grant* v. *Norway* (1851) 20 L.J.C.P. 93. However a charterer or ship's agent does have apparent authority to state on a bill that cargo has been shipped below deck when it has, in fact, been shipped on deck, *Nea Tyhi* [1982] 1 Lloyd's Rep. 606. Likewise he has apparent authority to state that goods have been shipped on a certain day when in fact they were not shipped till a later date, *The Saudi Crown* [1986] 1 Lloyd's Rep. 261.

[47] See Appendix 5.D.

[48] See n. 44, above.

[49] *New Chinese Antimony* v. *Ocean Steamships* [1917] 2 K.B. 664.

[50] *Cox* v. *Bruce* (1886) 18 Q.B.D. 147.

[51] See 5.11.

[52] See 1.44 and *Compagnia Vascogranda* v. *Churchill & Sim* [1906] 1 K.B. 273.

[53] See, *e.g. The Tromp* [1921] P. 337.

The bill of lading as a document of title 5.11

As explained in 5.02, where goods are sold on C.I.F. terms the delivery of the bill of lading, together with other documents, normally passes the ownership of the goods to the buyer. Thus a bill of lading may act as a document of title and like the "key to a warehouse"[54] gives the buyer the right to collect the goods from the ship at the port of destination. If the bill is an "order bill" then, by the "custom of merchants," it is also transferable.[55] Examples of "order bills" are "deliver to A or order" and "deliver to A or his assigns." Where there is an order bill the named consignee can sell the goods in transit to someone else by means of endorsing the bill, *i.e.* signing it on the back, over to a new person. This new person can then, by surrendering the bill to the shipowner, collect the goods from the ship at the port of destination. Delivery to someone without the bill of lading amounts to the tort of conversion even if he is the named consignee[56] or even the true owner.[57] If the consignee has pledged the bill to a bank as security for a loan then the pledge does not pass the ownership of the cargo to the bank.[58] However, if the shipowner delivered the cargo to the consignee without production of the bill of lading, the bank could sue the shipowner in conversion because a "pledgee"[59] has sufficient title to bring such an action.[60] Once a bill of lading is transferred by the buyer to a third party the seller loses his right of stoppage in transit.[61] House "bills of ladings" issued by freight forwarders are not transferable nor perhaps are "received for shipment" bills as opposed to "shipped on board" bills. However a "received for shipment bill" can become a "shipped bill," and thus transferable both at common law and under the Hague-Visby Rules,[62] if the cargo is shipped on board and the bill is subsequently endorsed, *i.e.* marked, by the shipowner to that effect.

Note that although a bill can be a document of title and may be transferable it is not negotiable in the true legal sense, *i.e.* that a transferee of the bill gets a better title than the transferor. Say that A sells goods C.I.F. to B and B receives the bill of lading and endorses it to C. When C collects the cargo it transpires that some of it has deteriorated in transit due to inherent vice.[63] If sued by C, the shipowner can still successfully plead inherent vice just as he could if sued by A or B. Nevertheless an order bill of lading is a document of title for the purposes of the Factors Act 1889 and section 25 of the Sale of Goods Act 1979.[64] So if X obtained a bill of lading and endorsed it to

[54] See *Sanders* v. *Maclean* (1883) 11 Q.B.D. 327, 342.
[55] But not negotiable in the true legal sense, see below.
[56] *The Stettin* (1889) 14 P.D. 142.
[57] *The Jag Shakti* [1986] A.C. 337.
[58] *Evans* v. *Nichol* (1841) 3 M. & G. 614.
[59] *i.e.* someone with whom goods or a document of title to goods, such as a Bill of lading, are deposited as security for a loan.
[60] *Evans* v. *Nichol*, above n. 58, *The Jag Shakti* [1986] A.C. 337.
[61] *Lickbarrow* v. *Mason* (1794) 5. T.R. 683. As to stoppage in transit generally, see 1.73-1.74.
[62] See 5.39.
[63] See 1.28.
[64] See Appendix 1.C.

Y who took it in good faith and the shipowner delivered to Y in good faith then the shipowner would not be liable to the true owner of the goods.[65] In addition, Y would get a good title to the cargo.

WHO CAN SUE THE SHIPOWNER ON THE BILL OF LADING OR IN BAILMENT?

5.12 **Who can sue the shipowner under the bill of lading?**

Although the transfer of a bill of lading may transfer the ownership of the goods it did not, in the early 19th century, at common law transfer the contract so as to give the transferee the right to sue the shipowner on the contract.[66] There is now no doubt that a contract of bailment is assignable.[67] Likewise in the early 19th century the liability of the carrier in tort and bailment to an owner of goods who was not a party to the contract of carriage was unclear.[68] In any event, whether we would now consider the Act to be necessary or not, in the light of the problems, as they were perceived at that time, Parliament passed the Bills of Lading Act 1855 which is reproduced in Appendix 5.D. Section 1 of the Act removed most of the difficulties in this area and usually gives the named consignee or the endorsee the right to sue on the contract as if the contract had been made with them provided property passes to him "by reason of such endorsement or consignment." Thus the transferee of a bill of lading can sue in respect of damage done to cargo even before the bill was transferred to him.[69]

5.13 **A shipowner's liability on an implied contract or as a bailee**

Section 1 of the Bills of Lading Act 1855 did not dispense with every difficulty. Say that a bill of lading was pledged to a bank as security for a debt. This would not pass the ownership to the bank.[70] If the debtor did not pay up and the bank used the bill of lading to collect the cargo from the ship and found that some of it had been damaged in transit they could not sue the shipowner under Section 1 because the property had not passed to the bank "by reason of such . . . endorsement," but rather by reason of the fact that the debtor had not paid up! However in *Brandt* v. *Liverpool*[71] the court held that where the pledgee, *i.e.* the bank, presents the bill of lading and takes possession

[65] *Cahn* v. *Pocketts Steamships* [1899] 1 Q.B. 643.
[66] *Thomson* v. *Dominy* (1845) 14 M. & W. 403. However an assignee of a Bill could bring an action in the name of the assignor. *Blackburn on Sale,* (1st ed., 1845) p.276.
[67] *British Overseas Traders* v. *Brooks Wharf* [1967] 2 Lloyd's Rep. 51.
[68] But see *Martin* v. *Great Indian Peninsular Railway* (1867) L.R. 3 Ex. 9, discussed in 1.17, and *Lickbarrow* v. *Mason* (1794) 5 T.R. 75, "if the bill of lading transfer the property an action of trover against the captain for non delivery . . . is the proper form of action." Per Buller J. See 1.03 and 1.17.
[69] *Short* v. *Simpson* (1866) L.R. 1 C.P. 248.
[70] *Sewell* v. *Burdick* (1884) 10 App.Cas. 74.
[71] [1934] 1 K.B. 575.

of the cargo a new implied contract on the same terms as the bill of lading can come into existence giving the bank the right to sue the carrier. However, such a contract cannot automatically be implied merely by taking delivery of the cargo.[72]

If the ownership of the cargo passes to a new person during transit other than by endorsement of the Bill of lading and the court cannot imply a *Brandt* v. *Liverpool*[73] type contract then the new owner of the cargo can sue in bailment.[74] However if the new owner knows that his goods are being carried, for example, subject to the Hague-Visby Rules,[75] then if he sues the shipowner in bailment then the doctrine of bailment on terms[76] applies and the owner's action in bailment will be subject to the defences and limits of liability in the Rules.[77]

Sometimes the holder of a bill of lading will surrender the bill to the shipowner in return for what is known as a "delivery order" requiring the shipowner to deliver all or part of the cargo to the holder thereof. Such delivery orders, may, like bills of lading, be documents of title and give the holder the legal right to possession of the cargo. Also it seems that if the holder of the delivery order indorses it in favour of a third party then this acts as an assignment of the contract of carriage and gives the right to the new holder to sue the carrier.[78]

Difficulty may arise if someone has, for example, agreed to buy part of a bulk cargo on C.I.F. terms. Even if the bill of lading is delivered to him he cannot become the owner of any part of the cargo until it is ascertained (see 1.07-1.08). It is impossible to pass the ownership of unascertained goods.[79] As he is not the owner he cannot sue under Section 1 of the Bills of Lading Act, nor in bailment or the tort of negligence[80] because he is not the owner or a bailee with an immediate right to possess.[81] The correct person to sue is the seller of the cargo because he is still its owner. It is irrelevant that he has already been paid by the buyer or that the goods are at the buyer's risk during transit.[82] Needless to say any damages recovered by the seller must, in these circumstances, be paid over to the persons who have agreed to buy parts of the cargo and who have paid him for them.[83]

If A sells goods C.I.F. to B and contracts with C to have them delivered to B by sea then, unlike the position in land carriage,[84] A is an original party to the contract of carriage. Suppose that A delivers

[72] *The Aramis* [1988] *Financial Times*, November 22.

[73] [1924] 1 K.B. 575.

[74] See 1.03 and 1.17.

[75] See 5.27-5.50.

[76] See 1.84.

[77] *The Kapetan Marcos (No. 2)* [1987] 2 Lloyd's Rep. 321. See also Art.IV*bis*(1) of the Hague-Visby Rules discussed briefly in 5.44.

[78] *Cremer* v. *General Carriers* [1974] 1 W.L.R. 341. Compare *Cunningham* v. *Guthrie* (1888) 26 Sc.L.R. 208.

[79] Sale of Goods Act 1979, s.16.

[80] *The Aliakmon* [1986] 2 All E.R. 145.

[81] See 1.05 and *Transcontainer Express* v. *Custodian Security* [1988] 1 Lloyd's Rep. 128.

[82] *The Sanix Ace* [1987] 1 Lloyd's Rep. 321. See 1.09.

[83] See n. 82, above.

[84] See 1.05-1.10.

the documents to B and thus performs his contract of sale with B and that subsequently the carrier, C, loses the goods in breach of contract. In these circumstances if the shipper, A, sues C then he can only recover nominal damages, *e.g.* £10, because at the time of the breach of contract the goods did not belong to him.[85] If, however, in our example above the goods were carried by sea without a bill of lading having been issued, as still happens in the coastal trade, then A may be able to sue B for substantial damages on the principle outlined in 1.14.

5.14 Actions against servants or agents of the sea carrier

The owner of goods may try to circumvent any exclusion clauses in the contract of affreightment by suing the carrier's servants or agents, such as stevedores who unload the cargo, in bailment or negligence.[86] The common law principles applicable to such an action are basically the same as those discussed in relation to actions against subcontractors in carriage by land in 1.19 and 1.78-1.87. Note clause 18 of the bill of lading in Appendix 5.A. which is an example of a "Himalaya Clause" as discussed in 1.78. This clause, in its last sentence requires the cargo owner to pay over to the shipowner any damages he recovers from such servants or agents of the shipowner thus attempting to frustrate any action that the cargo owner may bring against them. It is arguable that such a clause is illegal.[87]

Bills of Lading issued where a Ship is Chartered

5.15 Bills of lading given to a charterer

If a person hires the use of a ship under a voyage or time charterparty[88] then in addition to the main written contract, *i.e.* the charterparty, he may also require the shipowner to issue him a bill of lading in respect of all or parts of the cargo. The charterer may wish to sell the cargo in transit and without a bill of lading he will find this very difficult. Where the bill of lading is received by the charterer directly from the shipowner then the contract between them is governed by the charterparty and not by the bill of lading.[89] The bill of lading in these circumstances is a receipt for the cargo and not evidence of the contract of affreightment. The only exception is when it is agreed that the bill of lading shall vary the terms of the charterparty.[90] Say, on the other hand, that the bill of lading was originally issued to someone other than the charterer, for example, to the seller of goods and that the seller has subsequently endorsed the

[85] *The Albazero* [1977] A.C. 774.

[86] See 1.17-1.19.

[87] But see the *Elbe Maru* [1978] 1 Lloyd's Rep. 206 in which the contract imposed a promise not to sue a subcontractor and the court upheld the provision.

[88] The nature of such contracts is outlined in 5.04.

[89] *Rodocanachi* v. *Milburn* (1886) 18 Q.B.D. 67.

[90] *The Jocelyne* [1977] 2 Lloyd's Rep. 121. See also *Gullishen* v. *Stewart* (1884) 13 Q.B.D. 317.

bill of lading over to the charterer. In these circumstances the charterparty still generally prevails over the bill of lading.[91]

A bill of lading issued to a charterer may be endorsed by him to someone who buys the cargo from him while it is in transit. In that instance a new contract comes into effect between the shipowner and the transferee of the bill of lading on the terms of the bill of lading. The transferee is not bound by the terms of the charterparty even if he knew about it unless the bill of lading incorporates the terms of the charterparty.[92] If the bill does incorporate the terms of the charterparty then to what extent it binds the transferee of the bill is a very complex matter.[93] Essentially it depends on the nature of the term and the words which attempt to incorporate it.

Bills of lading given to a person other than the charterer 5.16

When a seller of goods on F.O.B. terms delivers goods to a ship chartered by the buyer the seller may receive a bill of lading from the shipowner and he will normally deliver this bill to the charterer/buyer. The charterer may then in turn transfer the bill to someone who buys the cargo from him. Similarly where a person time-charters or voyage-charters a ship then he himself may let out space on the ship to other cargo owners. These persons will usually require bills of lading for their respective cargos. If cargo belonging to these bill of lading holders is lost or damaged in transit then who should they sue for breach of contract, the charterer or the shipowner?

Obviously the question of who has made the contract with the cargo owner is a question of fact but there is a strong presumption that the contract is made with the shipowner rather than the charterer. This is especially so if the bill of lading is signed by the master of the ship who is, of course, the servant of the shipowner. So strong is this presumption that a shipowner has been held bound by a bill of lading signed by the charterer rather than the master.[94] Charterparties often contain what is called an "employment and indemnity clause" under which the charterer must compensate the shipowner in respect of claims brought against him by, for example, the holders of bills of lading. These clauses, however, do not stop the holders of bills of lading suing the shipowner and merely concern the relationship between the charterer and the shipowner.

BILLS OF LADING AND SEAWORTHINESS AT COMMON LAW

Seaworthiness as an intermediate term of the contract 5.17

Where goods are carried under a bill of lading or a voyage charter at common law rather than under the Hague-Visby Rules as imple-

[91] *President of India* v. *Metcalfe Shipping* [1970] 2 Q.B. 289.
[92] *The Miramar* [1984] A.C. 676.
[93] See Chap. 6 of *Scrutton, On Charterparties*, (19th ed., 1984) and *The Miramar*, above.
[94] *Nea Tyhi* [1982] 1 Lloyd's Rep. 606.

mented by the Carriage of Goods by Sea Act 1971[95] there is an absolute duty upon the shipowner to supply a seaworthy ship. The precise nature of this duty is unclear.[96] In fact there is some authority[97] that a sea carrier can be sued in tort for unseaworthiness by a cargo-owner with whom he has no contract. If this is correct then the duty cannot be purely contractual in nature. Nevertheless, the duty is usually described as arising upon an implied term of the contract of affreightment. In fact it is often described as the "implied warranty of seaworthiness" but this is *most misleading*.

The express or implied terms, *i.e.* promises, that make up a contract can be divided into conditions, intermediate terms and warranties depending upon their importance. If there is a breach of condition then the injured party has the right, but not the duty, to repudiate the contract and claim damages. If there is a breach of warranty he cannot repudiate and must continue with the contract but he can claim damages. Intermediate terms are sometimes also called "composite clauses" or "complex terms." If there is a breach of an intermediate term then whether the injured party has the right to repudiate the contract or not depends on the seriousness of the breach. If the breach of an intermediate term substantially deprives the injured party of what he has bargained for then he may repudiate the contract, if it does not then he cannot repudiate. There is no doubt that the implied term as to seaworthiness is an intermediate term[98] and not a warranty. Thus if the vessel is only technically unseaworthy in some minor respect then that does not substantially deprive the cargo owner of what he has bargained for and he cannot repudiate the contract[99] but must be satisfied with an action for damages.[1] So if the vessel can speedily be repaired the cargo owner has no right to repudiate.

5.18 Nature of the duty to supply a seaworthy vessel

The law relating to seaworthiness is different from the equivalent duty as regards "roadworthiness" in the case of a private carrier by land.[2] A sea carrier is under an *absolute duty* at common law to supply a seaworthy vessel.[3] For an outline of the position under the Hague-Visby Rules see 5.32-5.33. It is no defence at common law for a shipowner to say that he took all reasonable care to ensure that the vessel was seaworthy and/or that he could not reasonably have detected the defect in the vessel.[4]

Although the duty is absolute, in the sense that it does not depend on negligence, only a reasonable degree of fitness is required. The duty is an absolute duty to provide a reasonable degree of fitness. A

95 See 5.32-5.33.
96 But see *Kopitoff* v. *Wilson* (1876) 1.Q.B. 377, 382, *per* Field J.
97 *The Termagent* (1914) 30 T.L.R. 377.
98 *Hong Kong Fir Shipping* v. *Karasaki* [1962] 2 Q.B. 26.
99 *Kish* v. *Taylor* [1912] A.C. 604.
1 See 1.39-1.42.
2 See 1.35.
3 *Stanton* v. *Richardson* (1875) L.R. 9 C.P. 390.
4 *The Glenfruin* (1885) 10 P.D. 103.

shipowner does not guarantee that his vessel will survive every calamity. "She must be fit . . . to encounter the ordinary perils of the voyage."[5] When assessing whether a vessel is fit for the voyage and thus seaworthy one must take into account the particular voyage, the type of cargo and the time of the year. Thus a vessel may be perfectly fit to sail in Arctic waters in Summer but be unfit for such a voyage in winter.

Seaworthiness does not only include the vessel herself and her tackle, *e.g.* her cranes. A ship is also unseaworthy if she has an alcoholic or incompetent master,[6] does not have a full crew, has inadequate charts, (*i.e.* maps), instruments or fuel, (*i.e.* "bunkers") on board. The test of seaworthiness is whether the vessel has *"that degree of fitness which an ordinary, careful and prudent owner would require his vessel to have at the commencement of her voyage having regard to all the probable circumstances."*[7]

"Cargoworthiness" as seaworthiness 5.19

In order to be seaworthy within the above definition the vessel must also be fit to take, stow, carry and discharge the cargo. Thus in a contract to carry frozen meat a vessel is not cargoworthy if her refrigeration is faulty[8] or, if she is to carry animals, if she has not been disinfected with the result that the animals die of foot and mouth disease.[9] If the ship is fit to carry cargo but the goods are damaged through bad stowage then that does not normally amount to uncargoworthiness.[10] The cause of the damage in that case is bad stowage not uncargoworthiness. However if the bad stowage endangers the safety of the ship then this can make her unseaworthy. Thus in *Kopitoff* v. *Wilson*[11] the shipowner negligently stowed on board armoured steel plates which broke free during the voyage, went through the side of the ship and sank her. The court held that the negligent stowage made the vessel unfit for the journey and she was therefore unseaworthy.

The doctrine of stages 5.20

The shipowner does not guarantee that the vessel will remain seaworthy throughout the voyage. Obviously he would not be liable for unseaworthiness if she was disabled by a collision during the voyage. Nevertheless the vessel must be seaworthy at the beginning of every "stage" of the voyage. Say that a vessel is to travel part of the journey by river and part by sea. As regards the river stage she need only be fit to encounter the normal incidents of river navigation rather than those of the open sea. When she reaches the sea stage she must be made fit for incidents of the sea voyage. If a vessel is to call at various ports during the agreed voyage then she must be seaworthy

[5] See n. 3, above.
[6] *Moore* v. *Lunn* (1923) 39 T.L.R. 526.
[7] *McFadden* v. *Blue Star Line* [1905] 1 K.B. 697, 706.
[8] *Rowson* v. *Atlantic Transport* [1903] 2 K.B. 774.
[9] *Tattersall* v. *National Steamship Company* [1915] 2 K.B. 774.
[10] *Elder Dempster* v. *Paterson Zochonis* [1924] A.C. 522.
[11] [1876] 1 Q.B.D. 377. Compare *The Thorsa* [1916] P. 257.

when she departs from each port. Thus if she calls at an intermediate port and fails to take on sufficient bunkers, *i.e.* fuel, to reach the next port then she would be unseaworthy for the next stage of the journey.[12]

5.21 **The burden of proof and consequences of unseaworthiness**

The burden of proof of unseaworthiness falls on the cargo owner. Thus the fact that a vessel disappears for no apparent reason is not prima facie evidence of unseaworthiness.[13] However, if it is proved that she has sunk in normal heavy weather this is rebuttable evidence of unseaworthiness.[14] In addition the cargo owner must prove that the unseaworthiness was at least one of the causes of the loss or damage.[15] If the vessel would, *e.g.* have sunk in any event, whether unseaworthy or not, then the loss has not been caused by unseaworthiness.

If the unseaworthiness is sufficiently serious at the commencement of the voyage so as to substantially deprive the cargo owner of a safe ship[16] then he can repudiate the contract, refuse to give the cargo to the shipowner, and can claim damages for non performance of the contract of affreightment.

Any exclusion clauses in the contract will not normally be interpreted as covering a breach of the duty to supply a seaworthy vessel.[17] If the goods are actually delivered via an unseaworthy vessel then the carrier is still entitled to the contract freight.[18]

5.22 **Clauses excluding liability for seaworthiness**

A shipowner may, in principle, exclude the common law warranty of seaworthiness by an express term to this effect in the Bill of lading. Nevertheless the courts are in practice very hostile to such clauses and always interpret them *contra proferentem*.[19] A clause reducing the absolute liability to one to take all reasonable care to provide a seaworthy vessel may be acceptable.[20] However a clause purporting to completely exclude the duty to provide a seaworthy vessel must be drafted very comprehensively and in clear and unambiguous terms. If there is any alternative meaning that can be given to the clause other than that it totally exempts seaworthiness then this other interpretation will be adopted and the shipowner will remain liable if the vessel is unseaworthy.[21] In addition a generally worded clause, *e.g.* excluding liability for all losses "however caused" will not be interpreted as covering unseaworthiness.

[12] *The Vortigern* [1899] P. 140.
[13] *Ajum Goolam* v. *Union Maritime Assurance* [1901] A.C. 362.
[14] *The Torenia* [1978] 2 Lloyd's Rep. 210.
[15] *The Europa* [1908] P. 84.
[16] See 5.17.
[17] *Nelson* v. *Nelson Line* [1908] A.C. 108; *The Glenfruin* (1885) 10 P.D. 103.
[18] *Atlantic Shipping* v. *Dreyfus* [1922] 2 A.C. 250, 257.
[19] See 1.29 and 1.44.
[20] *Cargo Ex Laertes* (1877) 12 P.D. 187.
[21] *The Christel Venen* [1924] P. 208.

BILLS OF LADING AND DEVIATION AT COMMON LAW

What amounts to a deviation? 5.23

The basic principles of deviation in land carriage have been discussed in 1.46-1.53 and they equally apply to carriage by sea. The carrier must carry by the agreed or normal route.[22] Some voluntary departures are justifiable and therefore in law not strictly deviations but part of the agreed voyage. A departure to save life is justifiable but not one to save property. Thus in *Scaramanga* v. *Scamp*[23] a ship deviated to assist a vessel in distress. She agreed to give her a tow for £1000 and while doing so the towing vessel ran aground and sank. It was held that if she had merely saved the crew then the departure would have been justified but she had no right to attempt to save the ship and thus the deviation was not justified. A departure to avoid the perils of war is justified[24] and indeed obligatory because it would be a breach of contract to unnecessarily enter perilous waters. A departure to further the voyage, *e.g.* by putting into a port for necessary repairs[25] even if these repairs are necessitated by the unseaworthiness of the vessel is justified.[26] However it is not justifiable to deviate purely for the convenience of the shipowner. It may be that a carrier who unjustifiably stows cargo on deck also deviates from the terms of the bailment.[27] In addition in carriage by sea a delay amounting to a repudiation of the bailment, and thus the contract, may also amount to a deviation.[28]

Liberty to deviate clauses 5.24

A contract of affreightment may contain what is known as a "liberty to deviate" clauses. An example is clause 5 of The Conline Bill in Appendix 5.A. Another common such clause gives the shipowner the "liberty to call at any port in any order." These clauses are interpreted *contra proferentem*[29] as giving the shipowner the right to visit *any ports that are naturally or usually ports of call on the agreed voyage* for the purposes of furthering the voyage or to discharge or take on cargo or bunkers. So, if a vessel goes off on an entirely different voyage from that contemplated then the shipowner cannot rely on the "liberty to deviate."[30] The approach of the courts to such clauses is that "the two parts of the bill of lading, the described voyage and the liberty to deviate clause must be read together and reconciled, and . . . a liberty to deviate however generally worded would not frustrate but must be subordinate to the described voyage."[31]

[22] *Frenkel* v. *Macandrews* [1929] A.C. 545.
[23] (1880) 5 C.P.D. 295.
[24] *The Teutonia* (1872) L.R. 4 P.C. 171.
[25] *Phelps* v. *Hill* [1891] Q.B. 605.
[26] *Kish* v. *Taylor* [1912] A.C. 604. The shipowner would, of course, be liable in damages for undue delay in such circumstances.
[27] *Newall* v. *Royal Exchange* (1885) 33 W.R. 342.
[28] *Brandt* v. *Liverpool* [1924] 1 K.B. 575, 597 and 601.
[29] See 1.29 and 1.44.
[30] *Leduc* v. *Ward* [1883] 20 Q.B.D. 475.
[31] *Frenkel* v. *Macandrews* [1929] A.C. 545, 562, *per* Viscount Sumner.

5.25 **Deviation and exclusion clauses**

As in carriage by land[32] a carrier who deviates repudiates the terms of the bailment. Normally as a matter of construction he cannot therefore rely on the terms of the bailment to exclude liability. Thus in *Thorley* v. *Orchis*[33] a sea carrier who unjustifiably deviated was precluded from relying on a clause exempting him from the negligence of stevedores. Of course if the cargo owner confirms the contract of bailment with knowledge of the deviation then the bailment and its exclusion clauses still stand.[34] However the mere fact that the cargo owner has received the cargo or endorsed the bill of lading over to another person does not amount to a confirmation of the contract.[35] Even if the cargo owner has waived the deviation on his own behalf this waiver does not bind a transferee of the bill of lading who takes the bill unaware of the deviation.[36]

5.26 **Deviation and liability for loss and damage**

We argued in 1.51 that a carrier by land who unjustifiably deviates is liable as a wrongful possessor. One view as regards deviation in carriage by sea is that the deviating carrier is liable as if he were a common carrier. Presumably this is on the basis that he is thrown back on his common law liability which is, we suggested in 5.06, the same as that of a common carrier. However a close reading of the cases[37] that are quoted in support of this proposition does not seem to bear out this view. In fact the legal position of a sea carrier who deviates was expressly left open by Fletcher Moulton L.J. in *Thorley* v. *Orchis*.[38] In this case he said of a deviating carrier by sea "the most favourable position which he can claim to occupy is that he has carried the goods as a common carrier. . . . *I do not say in all cases he would be entitled as of right to be treated even as favourably as this*." It would be unsatisfactory if carriers and other bailees who deviated were under different liability depending upon the mode of carriage or the type of bailment. We suggest that a sea carrier who deviates becomes a wrongful possessor and is liable on the principles discussed in 1.51. This issue is discussed in more depth in Chapter 15 of the Second Edition of *Bailment* (1989) by N. Palmer.

It seems that it has never been decided whether a deviating carrier can rely on exclusion clauses as regards loss or damage that occurred before he deviated or, similarly, whether he is strictly liable as a wrongful possessor for such loss or damage. The writers suggest in principle that he cannot rely on such exclusion clauses and he is strictly liable for such loss or damage. This is because the consequences of deviation should be retrospective.

As explained in 1.53 if the carrier actually delivers the goods after deviating then, unless the cargo owner has confirmed the contract, *i.e.* the terms of the bailment, he is not entitled to the contract freight

[32] See 1.46-1.51.
[33] [1907] 1 K.B. 660.
[34] *Hain* v. *Tate and Lyle* [1936] 2 All E.R. 597.
[35] *United States Shipping Board* v. *Masters* (1922) 14 Lloyd's Rep. 208.
[36] See n. 34, above.
[37] *International Guano* v. *Macandrews* [1909] 2 K.B. 360.
[38] [1907] 1 K.B. 660, 669.

but rather to a *quantum meruit, i.e.* a reasonable sum, as a reward for his services.[39]

HAGUE-VISBY RULES. INTRODUCTION

Historical background 5.27

In the nineteenth century many carriers by sea commenced putting all embracing exclusion clauses in Bills of lading. This was particularly true of English carriers who had a virtual monopoly at the time of much of the world's shipping. The hostility of the cargo owning countries led to some of them passing their own legislation to attempt to defeat unfair exclusion clauses, a famous example being the United States "Harter Act" of 1890. This hostility, plus the usual difficulty as regards "conflict of laws"[40] led to the Hague Rules which were implemented into English law by the Carriage of Goods by Sea Act 1924. The Rules were compulsory upon carriers who were not permitted to contract out of them and were in effect a compromise between the interests of cargo owners and those of shipowners. The Hague Rules were not a comprehensive code and were silent on some matters such as freight, in relation to which English law still applied.

The Rules, which should not be confused with the Hague Protocol on carriage by air,[41] gained wide acceptance amongst the international community. Nevertheless, as with the Warsaw Convention on carriage by air,[42] over the years defects were found in the Hague Rules, particularly in relation to the position of the carrier's servants and agents, containerisation and limits of liability. These difficulties led to the Brussels Protocol, better known as the Hague-Visby Rules, which was implemented into English law by the Carriage of Goods by Sea Act 1971. The Act came into effect in 1977 and repealed the 1924 Act. Since then the Merchant Shipping Act 1981 has altered the limits of liability in the Rules so that they are now expressed in S.D.R.'s[43] rather than gold francs. The Hague-Visby Rules as they appear in the Schedule of the 1971 Act, as amended by the Merchant Shipping Act 1981, together with section 1 of the Act itself are reproduced in Appendix 5.E. Note that Article III(8) usually forbids the shipowner from excluding liability under the Rules. In other words if the 1971 Act applies its provisions are mandatory.

Some countries, such as the United States, are not high contracting parties to the Hague-Visby Rules. Thus it is possible that a dispute coming before the English courts concerning a contract subject to a Bill of lading might be covered by the common law or the original unamended Hague Rules rather than the Carriage of Goods by Sea Act 1971.

[39] *Weiss* v. *Northern Traffic* (1919) 1 Lloyd's Rep. 241.
[40] See 3.02.
[41] See Chap. 6.
[42] See 6.03.
[43] See 3.60.

Since the Carriage of Goods by Sea Act 1971 a new set of Rules has been drafted called the Hamburg Rules 1978. These Rules are much more generous to cargo owners than the Hague-Visby Rules. Essentially, if and when these Rules come into effect, the liability of the carrier will be very similar to that of a carrier by air under the Hague Protocol as discussed in Chapter 6. The carrier will be presumed liable unless he can prove he took all reasonable measures to avoid the loss or damage. The limits of liability for loss or damage are 25 per cent. higher than those in Hague-Visby Rules as outlined in 5.46. The limit of liability for delay is the same as that in the draft Multimodal Transport Convention as outlined in 7.17. The Hamburg Rules are not yet in force, have not been ratified by the United Kingdom, and are unlikely to be in the near future.

5.28 Hague-Visby Rules, interpretation

The Hague-Visby Rules are interpreted subject to the principles of interpretation of international conventions as outlined in 3.05-3.08. All references in the Rules, for example in Article IV(1), to "loss or damage" include loss or damage caused by delay, misdelivery, etc. as well as literally the physical loss of, or damage to, the goods.[44]

Article I provides that the Rules apply only to the carriage of goods under Bills of lading or similar documents including those issued under a charterparty (but see 5.31). "Goods" are defined in Article I(c), and Article I(d) makes the Rules applicable to carriage in "ships." Perhaps therefore the Rules do not apply to carriage by small boats.[45] Article I(b) refers to carriage by "sea." "Sea" in this context probably includes all navigable waters and thus presumably includes rivers and canals.[46] However the Hague-Visby Rules would only apply to carriage on such inland waterways if they would also apply if the vessel was on the high seas.

As the result of Orders in Council issued under the Hovercraft Act 1968 carriage of cargo by hovercraft is also subject to a version of the Hague-Visby Rules.

5.29 When the Hague-Visby Rules apply under articles I and X

Article X provides that the Rules may apply to every Bill of lading for the carriage of goods by sea between ports in two different states. So Article X does not make the Rules applicable to the coastal trade, *i.e.* between ports in the same country, *e.g.* London to Southampton.[47] Thus the carriage must be international for it to be covered by Article X. In addition, for the Rules to apply the carriage must fall

[44] *Anglo Saxon Petroleum* v. *Adamastos Shipping* [1957] 2 Q.B. 273, [1959] A.C. 133, *Renton* v. *Palmyra* [1957] A.C. 149.

[45] In *The Acadia Forest* [1974] 2 Lloyd's Rep. 563 (U.S.A.) it was held that a barge was not a "ship" for the purposes of the Rules but the authority of the case is weakened by the fact that it was reversed on other grounds on appeal at 537 F. (2d) 1272. However, it has been held that if a barge is used as part of the process of discharging the cargo, then the Rules still apply, *Falconbridge Nickel* v. *Chimo Shipping* [1973] 2 Lloyd's Rep. 469 (Canada).

[46] See *Scrutton, On Charterparties,* (19th ed., 1984) p. 428.

[47] But Section 1 of the Act, as opposed to the Convention itself, makes the Rules applicable to such carriage. See 5.29.

into one of three categories. Firstly the Bill could be issued in a country which is a high contracting party. Secondly the carriage could be from a high contracting country. Thus it can be seen that the Rules apply essentially to outgoing voyages, not necessarily incoming voyages to the United Kingdom, *e.g.* Lagos to London. However the third category listed in Article X(c) permits the parties to state that the Rules apply. Normally a voyage from the United States to London would not be subject to the Rules because the United States is not a party to them. However if the Bill stated that "this contract is subject to the Hague-Visby Rules" or "this contract is subject to the British Carriage of Goods by Sea Act 1971" then the Rules would have statutory force. This clause would not merely act as a contractual term incorporating the Rules, *i.e.* a "Clause Paramount," and allow the parties to contract out of parts of the Rules they disliked. The Rules would be mandatory. It seem, however, that if, in a Bill covering a voyage from the United States to England, the parties put a clause saying "this contract is subject to English law" then this would incorporate the Rules by Clause Paramount and the Rules would not be mandatory. Thus the parties could in their contract exclude some of the provisions of the Rules if they wished.

Note that, while Article X refers to "Bills of lading," Article I(b) refers to contracts "covered" by a Bill of lading. Thus it has been held[48] that the Rules apply where goods have been received for shipment on the understanding that a Bill of lading will be issued even though at the time of the damage it had not yet been issued. Also where a document such as a mate's receipt is "by the custom of merchants" a document of title[49] then the Rules may apply. Note that Article I(c) states that the Rules do not apply to the carriage of live animals,[50] or to the carriage of cargo on deck provided the Bill of lading states that the cargo is being carried on deck and provided that it is, in fact, carried on deck.[51]

"Carriage" of goods is defined in Article I(e) and includes the acts of loading[52] and discharging the ship. If the shipowner, *e.g.* delivers the cargo to someone without the Bill of lading after discharging the cargo then the Hague-Visby Rules do not apply and he will be unable, for example, to rely on the limitation period in Article 3(6).[53] Article I(e) must be read together with Articles II and III(2). These show that the Hague-Visby Rules control the liability of the shipowner during "carriage" but they do not prevent the parties defining for themselves what the agreed voyage, *i.e.* "carriage," is to be. Thus it was held in *Renton* v. *Palmyra*[54] that a clause allowing the shipowner to discharge the cargo at an intermediate port in the event of strikes was not forbidden by the Rules.

[48] *Pyrene* v. *Scindia Navigation* [1954] 2 Q.B. 402.
[49] *Kum* v. *Wah Tat Bank* [1971] 1 Lloyd's Rep. 439.
[50] But see 5.30, below.
[51] *Svenska Traktor* v. *Maritime Agencies* [1953] 2 Q.B. 295.
[52] See n. 48, above.
[53] *Rambler Cycle Company* v. *P. & O.* [1968] 1 Lloyd's Rep. 42 (Malaysia).
[54] [1957] A.C. 149.

5.30 **When the rules apply under section one of the Act**

Section 1 of the Carriage of Goods by Sea Act 1971, purely for the purposes of British domestic law, applies the Hague-Visby Rules to other contracts besides those covered by Articles I and X. So section 1(3) and 1(4) of the 1971 Act, for the purposes of English law only, make the Rules applicable to the coastal trade[55] provided a Bill of lading or similar document is issued. Section 1(6)(a) seems to add little to Article X(c) except that it makes the Rules applicable to coastal as well as international voyages. Section 1(6)(b) makes the Rules also applicable to non-negotiable documents marked as such if they expressly incorporate the Rules. This provision again provides for the mandatory application of the rules in such an instance rather than by Clause Paramount. So if goods were, for example, carried under a mate's receipt marked "non-negotiable" but which said "this contract is subject to the Hague-Visby Rules" then the 1971 Act would apply by force of law and its provisions could not be excluded.

5.31 **The Hague-Visby Rules and charterparties**

Articles I(b) and V of the Rules state that the Rules apply to Bills of lading issued under a charterparty. However this is rather misleading because, as explained in 5.15, a Bill of lading given by a shipowner to a charterer is a mere receipt for the goods and not evidence of the contract of carriage. The Hague-Visby Rules only therefore apply mandatorily by statute to Bills of lading issued under a charterparty if the Bill is transferred by endorsement to a third party. If the third party collects the cargo at the port of discharge and finds it damaged then his claim against the shipowner is subject to the Hague-Visby Rules.

The Hague-Visby Rules only apply to charterparties themselves if the charterparty contractually incorporates the Rules. If it does then this is contractual incorporation, *i.e.* incorporation by Clause Paramount, and the parties can exclude any provisions of the Rules that they wish because the rules have no mandatory application.

SEAWORTHINESS UNDER THE HAGUE-VISBY RULES

5.32 **No absolute duty of seaworthiness**

Article III(1) and IV(1), together with Section 3 of the Carriage of Goods by Sea Act 1971 make it clear that under the Hague-Visby Rules, unlike the common law,[56] there is no absolute "warranty" of seaworthiness. The absolute duty is replaced by a duty to "exercise due diligence to make the vessel seaworthy."[57] So if a shipowner buys a new ship from an apparently reputable shipyard and defects in the vessel cannot be detected by due diligence the shipowner is not liable.[58] However from the time that the shipowner takes possession

[55] *i.e.* where the ports of loading and unloading are in the same country.
[56] See 5.17-5.19.
[57] Art. (III)(1).
[58] *Angliss and Company* v. *P. & O.* [1927] 2 K.B. 456.

and control of the vessel the duty is a *personal non-delegable duty*. In other words he becomes liable for the lack of due diligence on the part of his servants and agents. Thus he is liable for the negligence of those who survey the vessel for him[59] and of those who repair the ship on his account.[60] He is also obviously liable if he fails to use due diligence to appoint competent officers and crew.[61] If the shipowner fails to exercise all due diligence to provide a seaworthy ship and the unseaworthiness is the cause of the loss then he cannot rely on any of the excepted perils in Article IV(2).[62]

The doctrine of stages 5.33

Article III(1) requires the shipowner to use due diligence to make the vessel seaworthy "before and at the beginning of the voyage." It may be that this rule replaces the common law doctrine of stages discussed in 5.20.[63] It is inconceivable, however, that a shipowner who negligently allowed a vessel to depart from an intermediate port in an unseaworthy condition could escape liability. We suggest that in such circumstances he would be liable under Article III(2) for failure to "properly . . . care for" the cargo.[64]

DEVIATION UNDER THE HAGUE-VISBY RULES

What deviations are permitted by Article IV(4)? 5.34

Article IV(4) gives the shipowner the right to deviate to "save life or property" and to make any other "reasonable deviation." Thus under the Hague-Visby Rules a deviation is permitted to save property whereas at common law it is not.[65] As to what is a reasonable deviation the test is whether the deviation is one which a prudent person would make bearing "in mind all the relevant circumstances existing at the time, including the terms of the contract and the interests of all parties concerned, but without obligation to consider the interests of any one as conclusive."[66] Thus it is "reasonable" to deviate to avoid imminent danger, to further the joint interests of the shipowner and cargo owners[67] or where matters of national importance require the carrier to deviate. It is not reasonable however to deviate purely for the convenience of the shipowner.

Liberty to deviate clauses 5.35

Some doubt has been expressed as to whether Article IV(4) and Article III(8) forbid liberty to deviate clauses. However the case of *Stag*

[59] *The Muncaster Castle* [1961] A.C. 807.
[60] See n. 59, above.
[61] *The Makedonia* [1962] P. 190.
[62] *Maxine Footwear* v. *Canadian Government Merchant Marine* [1959] A.C. 589.
[63] See *The Makedonia* [1962] P. 190 and *Leesh River Tea Company* v. *British India Steam Navigation* [1966] 1 Lloyd's Rep. 450.
[64] See 5.40.
[65] See 5.23.
[66] *Stag Line* v. *Foscolo Mango* [1932] A.C. 328, *per* Lord Atkin.
[67] *The Daffodil B.* [1983] 1 Lloyd's Rep. 498.

Line v. *Foscolo Mango*[68] shows that such clauses are not forbidden. They merely define the agreed voyage and do not exclude liability so are not made void by Article III(8).

5.36 **The effects of unjustified deviation**

Much argument has been expressed as to whether the shipowner can still rely on the excepted perils in Article IV(2) if he has unjustifiably deviated. One view is that he cannot. It is argued that because it was held in *Maxine Footwear* v. *Canadian Government Merchant Marine*[69] that a carrier cannot rely on Article IV(2) if he fails to exercise due diligence to provide a seaworthy ship then equally he cannot do so if he commits an even graver repudiatory breach by deviating. In addition it is suggested that the case of *Stag Line* v. *Foscolo Mango*[70] is authority for the proposition that a deviating shipowner cannot rely on Article IV(2) even though the point did not arise precisely in that case and therefore opinions expressed to that effect were technically *obiter*. It is argued that Article II states that the Rules apply to "contracts." If the shipowner repudiates the terms of the bailment and thus the contract then the contract goes, the Rules do not apply and the carrier loses their protection. Nor, it is suggested, does he have to prove that the deviation is the cause of the loss or damage. Once the carrier unjustifiably deviates the contract goes and he is liable as a wrongful possessor on the principles outlined in 1.51 and 5.26.

The second view is that he can rely on the perils if he deviates. It is argued that because the Hague-Visby Rules are given the "force of law" by The Carriage of Goods by Sea Act 1971 the Rules are mandatory and apply even where the shipowner has unjustifiably deviated with the result that he can still rely on the perils in Article IV(2). This view is given some support by the recent case of the *Antares*.[71]

Almost certainly, however, a shipowner who unjustifiably deviates can still rely on the limitation period laid down in Article III(6) because this applies "in any event," *i.e.* even if the contract is repudiated (see 5.49). In the *Antares*[72] a carrier wrongfully carried goods on deck. The court was dubious as to whether this was a deviation in the full sense but decided that his actions did not prevent him from relying on Article III(6).

Hague-Visby Rules. Bill of Lading Provisions

5.37 **Contents of the bill of lading**

Article III(3) gives the right to the shipper to demand from the shipowner, provided that the shipowner can verify these facts, a bill of lading stating:

[68] [1932] A.C. 328.
[69] [1959] A.C. 589.
[70] See n. 68, above.
[71] [1987] 1 Lloyd's Rep. 424.
[72] *Ibid.*

(1) the "leading marks" on the goods so as to identify them.
(2) the number of packages or weight, etc.
(3) the apparent order or condition of the cargo.

It seems that this provision does not mean that every cargo owner can demand a bill of lading as of right but rather that, if a bill is issued, the shipper can demand that these particulars appear on it. The main defect of Article III(3) is that the right to demand these details on the bill is only given to the shipper and not to the consignee. The shipper could demand that, for example, a "weight and condition unknown" clause[73] be removed from the bill of lading. In practice he may not do this and the transferee will presumably be bound by the clause. One could argue that this failure to insist on his rights under Article III(3) would amount to a breach of Section 32(2) of the Sale of Goods Act 1979[74] by the shipper if he was a seller under a C.I.F contract.

Article III(3)(a) and (b) state that the shipper can only demand that the leading marks and weight, etc., should appear on the bill if these details are given to the shipowner in writing. Article III(5) requires in return that the shipper guarantees the accuracy of the written information. If the shipowner suffers loss as a result of their inaccuracy then the shipper must indemnify him. Presumably if the goods are dangerous and cause damage then the shipowner can also sue on the consignor's warranty of fitness at common law.[75]

Grant v. _Norway_ made inapplicable under the Hague-Visby Rules 5.38

Article III(4) provides that the "bill of lading shall be prima facie evidence of the receipt by the carrier of the goods" as it is at common law.[76] However it also provides that as regards the transferee of a Bill of lading, provided he takes the bill in good faith, the statements enumerated in Article III(3) shall be conclusive. So the shipowner could not bring evidence to prove that all or part of the cargo had never been shipped on board. Thus Article III(4) makes the rule in *Grant* v. *Norway*[77] inapplicable to carriage under the Hague-Visby Rules.

Received for shipment bills of lading 5.39

If goods are delivered to a shipowner or his agent and not immediately loaded the shipper will probably be given a "received for shipment" bill of lading. This acts as a receipt for the goods but, perhaps, is not a transferable document of title. Article III(7) deals with this matter. It permits the shipper, after the goods have been loaded, to exchange his received for lading bill for a "shipped on board" bill or to have his received for shipment bill turned into a shipped on board bill by an endorsement to this effect. Once this is done then the shipper can transfer the bill to the buyer or pledge it to a bank.

[73] See 5.09-5.10.
[74] See 1.10.
[75] See 1.94-1.97.
[76] See 5.09-5.10.
[77] (1851) 10 C.B. 665. See 5.09.

HAGUE-VISBY RULES. LIABILITY FOR LOSS AND DAMAGE

5.40 **The duty of care under Article III(2)**

Article III(2) provides that subject to Article IV the "carrier shall properly and carefully load, handle, stow, carry, keep, care for and discharge" the cargo. "Properly and carefully" means that all the listed operations must be carried out in accordance with a sound system and with reasonable care. Thus if the loading system is unsound the shipowner is in breach of Article III(2).[78] The duty imposed by Article III(2) is, as with that under the Rules to exercise due diligence to provide a seaworthy vessel,[79] a personal non-delegable duty. Thus the shipowner is liable for the negligence of his independant contractors acting in the scope of their employment.[80]

5.41 **The burden of proof**

The burden of proof in bailment in common law has been discussed in 1.17 and 1.89. The burden of proof under the Hague-Visby Rules is complicated by the fact that the liability of a carrier by water is at common law probably not that of an ordinary bailee for reward but that of a common carrier.[81] This branch of the law is a matter of controversy. We propose the view of Hunter.[82] He argues that the burden is on the shipowner to prove that he has not been negligent, *i.e.* in breach of Article III(2). If he proves a loss due to one of the excepted perils then he may, depending upon the peril, have in effect disproved negligence. Say that the carrier proves that the cause of the loss was peril (p) of Article IV(2), *i.e.* "latent defects not discoverable by due diligence." If he proves that the loss was caused by this peril then he has in effect disproved negligence, and thus a breach of Article III(2). Say, on the other hand, he proves that the cause of the loss was peril (e), *i.e.* Act of war, in that his ship was sunk by an enemy vessel. In this case he has only proved a *possible* cause of the loss other than by negligence. It would now be open to the cargo owner to prove that the ship had, for example, sailed too near the enemy vessel and that thus the shipowner had in fact been negligent.

5.42 **Excepted perils (a) to (c) in Article IV(2)**

The shipowner's defences or excepted perils under the Rules are listed in Article IV(2). He cannot rely on them if he has not exercised due diligence to supply a seaworthy vessel[83] and the unseaworthiness is the cause of the loss. Perhaps, also, he cannot rely on the perils if he has unjustifiably deviated.[84] The perils will now be considered:

[78] *The Farrondoc* [1967] 2 Lloyd's Rep. 276 (Canada).

[79] See 5.32.

[80] *International Packers* v. *Ocean Steamships* [1955] 2 Lloyd's Rep. 218.

[81] See 5.06.

[82] In a monograph entitled *Inherent Vice*, in the City of London Polytechnic Library. See also the lucid article by F. Cadwallader in *Current Legal Problems* [1967] 13. Compare *Albacora* v. *Westcott and Laurance* [1966] 2 Lloyd's Rep. 53.

[83] *Maxine Footwear* v. *Canadian Government Merchant Marine* [1959] A.C. 589.

[84] See 5.36.

(a) Act, neglect or default of the master, etc., in the navigation or the management of the ship. Normally, of course, negligence is a grounds of liability. Here, however, it is a defence. Not every form of negligence, however, is included. Thus the negligence of the shipowner or his agents as opposed to the master, etc., is not included. Note also that it is not all negligence of the master, etc., that is excepted but only neglect or default in the *navigation or management of the ship.* "Navigation" means that the vessel must be moving. "Management" presents more difficulties but we can draw the following conclusions:

(1) If the negligence is primarily neglect of the cargo rather than the ship then the shipowner cannot plead the peril. Thus in *Gosse Millard* v. *Canadian Government Merchant Marine*[85] a ship put into an intermediate port for repairs. The crew opened the hatches to let in the workmen but did not bother to close them when it rained. The House of Lords held that this was neglect of the cargo rather than neglect of the ship and that the shipowner was liable for ensuing rain damage to the cargo. If the carrier was not liable in these circumstances then Article III(2)[86] would be valueless to cargo owners.

(2) If the negligence is primarily neglect of the ship rather than the cargo, then peril (a) applies and the shipowner is not liable. Thus it has been held that negligent failure of the crew to maintain the ship's pumps was negligence in the management of the ship and the shipowner was not liable.[87]

(3) Negligent failure to use the apparatus of the ship for the protection of the cargo is not negligence in the management of the ship and the shipowner cannot rely on the peril.[88]

(b) Fire unless caused by the actual fault or privity of the carrier. The meaning of "actual fault or privity" is discussed in the context of peril **(q)** in 5.43. Where there has been fire on board a *British* registered vessel the carrier can plead section 18 of the Merchant Shipping Act 1979 as an alternative to Article IV(2)(b). Section 18 states that the carrier is not liable "for any property on board the ship" if she "is lost or damaged by reason of fire on board." Various points should be noted. First the shipowner can still rely on section 18 even if the vessel is unseaworthy whereas he cannot under the Hague-Visby Rules.[89] Secondly the defence in section 18 is only available if the property is on board the vessel. Thus if the cargo caught fire while aboard a "lighter" the shipowner could not plead section 18 whereas he could still rely on the Rules by virtue of Article I(e).[90] Thirdly the

[85] [1929] A.C. 233.
[86] See 5.40.
[87] *The British King* (1898) 89 Fed.Rep. 872 (U.S.A.).
[88] See *International Packers* v. *Ocean Steamships* [1955] 2 Lloyd's Rep. 218.
[89] See n. 83, above.
[90] *i.e.* a small vessel that carries goods to or from a ship.

shipowner cannot rely on section 18 "if it is proved that the loss resulted from his personal act or omission, committed with the intent to cause such loss, or recklessly and with knowledge that such loss would probably result." This provision is almost identical to Article 25 of the Hague Protocol on carriage by air discussed in 6.50 and almost certainly has the same meaning. Such "misconduct" is more difficult to prove than "actual fault or privity" under the Hague-Visby Rules because, *e.g.* the test of "misconduct" is subjective whereas the test of "fault or privity" is objective. Therefore if there is a fire on board a British registered vessel it is to the advantage of the shipowner to rely on section 18 of the 1979 Act rather than Article IV(2)(b) of the Rules.

(c) Perils of the sea, etc. This may include events occuring during loading and unloading and accidents in harbours and rivers. "Perils of the sea," it would appear, essentially denote events peculiar to carriage by water as opposed to other modes of carriage. However if the action of the winds blew a vessel on to the rocks that would be "perils of the sea" even though one might argue that high winds could equally blow a lorry off the road. It includes storm damage, collision with rocks or icebergs or other vessels, going aground and, perhaps, the acts of pirates. Things that have no particular connection with the sea such as accidental fire on board, the cargo being eaten by rats and lightning are not included. As with all the perils if the main cause of the loss is the negligence of the shipowner, master or crew then the shipowner cannot rely on (c).

5.43 **Excepted perils (d) to (q) in Article IV(2)**

(d) Act of God. This has the same meaning as it does at common law. See 1.28.

(e) Act of war. This is wider than (f) discussed below and includes, *e.g.* the sinking of a neutral vessel whose country of registration is not at war with that of its aggressor. Apparently it is not necessary that war should have been formally declared. It may, perhaps, include acts of aggression by rebels if their uprising is sufficient to amount to a civil war.

(f) Act of public enemies. This has much the same meaning as "Acts of the Queen's enemies" discussed in 1.28, *i.e.* it means in this context "the acts of the enemies of the state in which the cargo carrying vessel is registered." In addition to perhaps being within (c), the acts of pirates may also be included because pirates are the enemies of every state.

(g) Restraints of Princes and Rulers, etc. This amounts to forcible interference with the voyage by a government or its agents. It includes blockades of ports, quarantine restrictions, confiscation of the cargo, etc. The restraint may be indirect as where, for example, a vessel is delayed because she puts into a port and finds she cannot take bunkers on board because they have all been requisitioned by the authorities. If the master of a ship reasonably refuses to put into a port because he believes that the authorities will impound the cargo then the shipowner can rely on (g). On the other hand if a shipowner deliberately courts danger by illegally taking on board cargo belonging to enemy aliens then he cannot rely on (g).[91]

(h) Quarantine restrictions. This is unnecessary as they are already covered by (g) above.

(i) Acts or omissions of the shipper, etc. This is the maritime equivalent of "consignor or consignee's own fault or fraud" discussed in 1.28.

(j) Strikes, etc. This probably includes strikes by the shipowner's own crew. It is suggested that the words "from whatever cause" in this context do not extend to cover a strike caused by the shipowner's own negligence, *e.g.* by his failure to pay the crew's wages. This is because to do so would conflict with the shipowner's duty under Article III(1)(b) to use due diligence to "properly man" the ship.

(k) Riots and civil commotion. Riot is a criminal offence that has a technical meaning. Civil commotion connotes something beween a riot and civil war.

(l) Saving life and property. This would be a defence if damage was caused while deviating to save life or property.[92] In addition it would justify throwing cargo overboard in extreme emergencies to lighten the vessel and thus save her and the crew.

(m) Inherent vice, etc. For a discussion of inherent vice see 1.28, 1.88 and 1.92.

(n) Bad packing. For a discussion of bad packing, which probably is already covered by (i) or (m) in any event, see 1.28 and 1.92-1.93. In the context of the Hague-Visby Rules the shipowner can also rely on this peril if the damage is caused by the bad packing of goods other than those actually damaged.[93]

(o) Inadequacy of marks. This covers such things as inadequate addressing of the goods and seems superfluous in the light of (i).

(p) Latent defects. As inherent vice and bad packing are covered by (m) and (n), this obviously covers defects in the ship not discoverable with due diligence (see 5.32). It probably also covers defects in her

[91] *Dunn* v. *Bucknall* [1902] 2 K.B. 814.
[92] See 5.34.
[93] *Goodwin Ferreira* v. *Lamport and Holt* [1929] All E.R. 623.

equipment and possibly cargos which, *e.g.* leak and damage adjacent cargo.

(q) Any other cause without the actual fault or privity of the carrier, etc. The second use of the words "fault or privity" in (q) have been held to mean "fault and privity."[94] "Actual fault or privity" is difficult to apply now that nearly all ships are owned by companies rather than individuals or partnerships. In such a case the courts examine the fault or privity of the person actually in control of the company.[95]

Actual fault or privity involves a degree of blameworthiness on the part of the shipowner. Thus if he fails to give proper instructions to the master[96] this is an example of (q). The test is objective not subjective. So the test is "has the owner acted in a blameworthy way?" It does not matter that he does not realise that his actions were wrong.[97]

Much difficulty has been caused by the use of the words "without the fault or neglect of the servants or agents of the carrier." Essentially they imply that the shipowner is not liable for the acts of independant contractors as opposed to servants. It may be that in this context, as in Article IV(bis)(2),[98] the word "agents" does not include independant contractors. Thus the shipowner is not normally liable for the acts of stevedores not acting under his control because they are independant contractors, not servants or agents. So in *Leesh River Tea Co.* v. *British India Steam Navigation Co.*[99] a stevedore stole the cover plate from a storm valve and this theft was not discoverable during the voyage. The cargo was thus damaged by sea water. The Court of Appeal held that the shipowner was protected by (q). On the other hand if the stevedores are acting under the control and supervision of the shipowner they become his temporary servants and if they do in a wrong way that which they are employed to do in a correct way then the shipowner is liable.[1] Thus in *Heyn* v. *Ocean S.S. Co.*[2] stevedores stole the cargo that was entrusted to them[3] and the shipowner failed in his attemps to rely on Article IV(2)(q).

5.44 **Other liability provisions affecting the shipowner**

The shipowner is not liable to anyone for loss or damage if he has been misled as to the nature or value of the goods.[4] Under section 18 of the Merchant Shipping Act 1979 unless there has been what we term "intentional or reckless misconduct"[5] the shipowner is not liable for the theft, etc., of gold, silver, watches, jewels or precious stones

[94] *Leesh River Tea Company* v. *British Indian Steam Navigation Company* [1967] 2 Q.B. 250.
[95] *Lennard Carrying Company* v. *Asiatic Petroleum* [1915] A.C. 705.
[96] *Standard Oil* v. *Clan Line* [1924] A.C. 100.
[97] *The Lady Gwendolen* [1965] P. 294.
[98] See 5.45.
[99] [1967] 2 Q.B. 250.
[1] *i.e.* they are acting in the scope of their employment. See 1.18 and 1.116.
[2] (1927) 137 L.T. 158.
[3] Therefore they are acting in the scope of their employment. See 1.18.
[4] Art. IV(5)(h).
[5] For the meaning of this provision, see 6.50.

unless their value and nature has been declared to him.[6] Nor is he liable if he is forced to discharge or destroy inflammable, explosive or dangerous goods.[7]

The shipowner is entitled to exclude liability for loss or damage to goods before they are loaded and after they have been discharged.[8] Presumably his common law liability for goods in transit[9] that are not on board the ship is that of a common carrier.[10] Once goods are discharged and the consignee has had a reasonable time to collect them then transit has ceased[11] and the shipowner's liability is that of a warehouseman, *i.e.* a bailee for reward.[12] Apparently there is no common law duty to tell the consignee that the goods have arrived.[13] However most contracts of affreightment impose this liability on the shipowner. Note however the draconian provisions in clauses 4 and 8 of the bill of lading in Appendix 5A. It is possible that such clauses excluding liability for negligent loss or damage before loading or after discharge can be challenged under the "reasonableness test"[14] in the Unfair Contract Terms Act 1977.[15]

Article VI permits the shipowner to exclude the provisions of the Rules where no transferable bill of lading is issued and the cargo is not of an ordinary commercial nature. Presumably this includes such cargos as explosives and dangerous goods.

If the cargo owner is not a party to the contract of affreightment and he sues in tort or bailment[16] then the shipowner can still rely on the defences and limits of liability in the Rules.[17]

Actions against the servants and agents of the shipowner 5.45

If the cargo owner sues the servants or agents of the shipowner in tort then under Article IV(bis)(2) they also can normally rely on the defences and limits of liability in the Rules. However if they are guilty of "intentional or reckless misconduct"[18] then they lose the benefits of the Rules.[19] Article IV(bis)(2) expressly does not extend to independent contractors, *e.g.* stevedores unless perhaps they are under the direct control of the shipowner and thus his temporary "servants"[20] as suggested below. It is difficult to conceive in English law of an "agent" who is not by definition an independent contractor. Perhaps a person can be self employed but under the control and direction of the shipowner and thus in a sense a "servant."[21]

[6] Compare the provisions of the Carriers Act 1830 in carriage by land. See 1.30-1.32.
[7] Art. IV(6).
[8] Art. VII. It is possible, however, that such clauses are subject to the "reasonableness test" in the Unfair Contract Terms Act 1977. See 5.05.
[9] As to the meaning of "transit," see 1.66-1.68.
[10] See 5.06.
[11] See 1.68. [12] See 1.71.
[13] *Houlder* v. *General Steam Navigation* (1862) 3 F. & F. 170.
[14] See 5.05.
[15] See 1.45.
[16] See 1.17-1.20, 1.84 and *The Kapetan Marcos (No. 2)* [1987] 2 Lloyd's Rep. 321.
[17] Art. IV*bis*(1).
[18] See 6.50.
[19] *e.g.* the defences in Art. IV(2) and the limits of liability in Art. IV(5).
[20] See the discussion of peril (q) of Art. IV(2) in 5.43.
[21] Thus making his employer vicariously liable for his acts.

The cargo owner cannot double the limits of liability under the Rules by suing both the shipowner and his servants.[22]

Hague-Visby Rules. Limits of Liability and Limitation of Actions

5.46 **Limits of liability and declarations of value**

The amount of damages a carrier is liable to pay, if he is liable under the Hague-Visby Rules, is determined by the value of the goods at the port of discharge[23] and by the principles of remoteness of damage discussed in 1.39-1.42. If the shipper has declared the value of the goods on the bill of lading then under Article IV(5)(a) the shipowner is normally liable for the declared amount. However under Article IV(5)(f) the shipowner has the right to prove that the goods do not in fact bear the declared value. In addition if the shipper has "knowingly mis-stated" the value or the nature of the goods the shipowner is not liable at all.[24] Provided the shipowner was not a common carrier[25] he could refuse to carry the goods if they were of a high declared value. In addition, even if he were a common carrier, he could apparently refuse to carry goods of a high value for which he had no safe facilities.[26]

If the value of the goods has not been declared then under Article IV(5)(a), as amended by section 2(3)(a) of the Merchant Shipping Act 1981, there are two alternative limits of liability. The shipowner's liability is limited to whichever is the higher of 666.7 S.D.R.'s,[27] about £500, per package or unit or 2 S.D.R.'s, about £1.70p, per kilo. Note also that section 17 of the Merchant Shipping Act 1979 also limits the liability of shipowners, charterers and others. These limits of liability are based on the tonnage of the ship and apply both to cargo claims and claims for death and injury.

5.47 **Limits of liability for containers and pallets, etc.**

Much difficulty was occasioned under the original Hague Rules[28] as to the meaning of the words "package or unit" in Article IV(5)(a) particularly in regard to container traffic. Most of this difficulty has been removed by Article IV(5)(c) of the revised Hague-Visby Rules. This provides that "the number of packages or units enumerated in the bill of lading as packed" in the container or pallet shall govern the limit of liability. So if a bill of lading states "one container containing television sets" the maximum liability for the whole container is 666.7 S.D.R.'s or 2 S.D.R.'s per kilo. If on the other hand the bill states "one container containing 500 television sets" then the limits attach to each

[22] Art. IV *bis*(3).
[23] Art. IV(5)(a).
[24] Art. IV(5)(h).
[25] See 1.21-1.23 and 5.06.
[26] *Batson* v. *Donovan* (1820) 4 B. & A. 21, 32.
[27] See 3.60.
[28] See 5.27.

television set and not to the container. Difficulty arises if the bill states "one container said to contain 500 television sets."[29]

The effect of intentional and reckless misconduct 5.48

Under Article IV(5)(e) the shipowner loses the limits of liability if he is guilty of what we describe as "intentional and reckless misconduct." The meaning of the identical provision in the Hague Protocol on carriage by air is discussed in 6.50. An example of such misconduct in carriage by sea would be if the shipowner deliberately scuttled the ship in order to make a fraudulent claim on an insurance policy.

Time limits for claims 5.49

Under Article III(6) the shipowner must be notified in writing of loss or damage to the cargo before or at the time of its delivery to the consignee. If the damage is not apparent then the period of notice is extended to three days. The written notice is not required if the goods have been jointly surveyed. If the consignee does not notify the shipowner within these time limits then receipt of the cargo is prima facie evidence of a good delivery. The burden now falls on the consignee to prove the loss or damage and also, of course, that the loss or damage occurred during the sea carriage and not after delivery of the cargo to the consignee or his agent.

Limitation of actions 5.50

Under Article III(6) the shipowner is discharged from liability "in any event" if the cargo owner does not sue him within one year of the date upon which the goods were delivered or should have been delivered. Thus it seems that the cargo owner loses the right to sue the shipowner after one year even if the ship was unseaworthy or there has been an unjustified deviation.[30] In the event of an arbitration clause in the contract then provided the arbitrator is appointed within one year this is sufficient.

Article III(6) applies even if the shipowner sues for the freight after one year. The cargo owner cannot even claim a "set off" for any loss or damage to the cargo as a defence. This can lead to manifest injustice as happened in the *Aries Tanker*.[31]

FREIGHT AND LIENS

Introduction 5.51

The liability to pay freight is not dealt with by the Hague-Visby Rules but rather by the common law. The word "freight" is used in this Chapter to denote the carriage charges in respect of carriage

[29] See 7.05, esp. 7.34. Compare the "weight and quantity unknown" clause discussed in 5.09.

[30] *The Antares* [1987] 1 Lloyd's Rep. 424.

[31] [1977] 1 Lloyd's Rep. 334. The same principles apply to a counterclaim for a repudiation of the contract, as opposed to damage to the goods in transit. *Colonial Bank* v. *European Grain and Shipping* [1989] *The Times*, February 3, (House of Lords).

under a bill of lading or a voyage charter. The word "hire" is used in the context of time charters.[32] Because this area of the law of carriage by sea is not controlled by legislation the parties can make any contract they like as to what sum may be payable and when it is earned.

5.52 **When freight is payable at common law**

If the contract is silent as to when freight is earned the following common law principles apply. Freight is earned when the contract is substantially performed. In other words it is payable when the shipowner is ready to deliver at the agreed or normal place of destination and the consignee has had a reasonable time to collect it from the carrier. Unlike the position that probably obtains in carriage by land[33] a sea carrier is under no common law duty to tell the consignee that the goods have arrived.[34] However most shipowners undertake such a duty by contract, although the Bill of lading in Appendix 5.A. has no such provision. In *Duthie* v. *Hilton*[35] the consignee of a cargo of cement was given three days under the contract in which to collect the goods. Within that period the vessel caught on fire and had to be scuttled with the result that the cargo was a total loss. The court held that the consignee was not bound to pay the freight. Likewise if the ship is sunk during the voyage, even by an excepted peril, then the freight is not earned.[36]

However even if the cargo is delivered in a damaged condition then the freight is payable.[37] If sued for the freight the cargo-owner cannot even claim a "set off" for damage to the cargo as a defence. Under the Rule in the *Aries Tanker*[38] he must bring a separate claim against the shipowner. However, if the "cargo" is delivered in such a condition that it has lost its *commercial identity* then there is no substantial performance of the contract and the freight is not earned. Thus in *Asfar* v. *Blundell*[39] a cargo of dates was sunk in the Thames. The vessel was refloated but the dates were no longer fit for human consumption even though the consignees took possession of them and they retained some commercial value. The court held that the cargo was no longer a cargo of dates, had thus lost its commercial identity, and that therefore no freight was payable. If the cargo owner wrongfully refuses to take delivery or frustrates the voyage by his own wrongful acts, *e.g.* by allowing someone with a claim to the cargo to seize it in transit, then he is still liable to pay the freight.[40] If the ship is disabled in transit and the cargo is trans-shipped to another vessel and

[32] See 5.80.
[33] See 1.67.
[34] *Houlder* v. *General Steam Navigation* (1862) 3 F. & F. 170.
[35] (1868) L.R. 4 C.P. 138.
[36] *Liddard* v. *Lopes* (1809) 10 East 526.
[37] *Dakin* v.*Oxley* (1864) 15 C.B. 646; *The Aries Tanker* [1977] 1 Lloyd's Rep. 374. Compare *The Olympic Brilliance* [1982] 2 Lloyd's Rep. 205.
[38] [1977] 1 Lloyd's Rep. 374.
[39] [1896] 1 Q.B. 123. See also *The Caspian Sea* [1980] 1 Lloyd's Rep. 91.
[40] *Cargo in re Galam* (1863) BR. & L. 167.

delivered within a reasonable time then the freight is payable.[41] If the cargo owner voluntarily takes possession of the cargo at an intermediate port then again the full freight is earned.[42]

Pro rata freight 5.53

Although the full freight is earned if the cargo owner prevents delivery or demands delivery at an intermediate port there is no right in principle to a proportion of the freight, (*i.e. pro rata* freight) if the goods are delivered short of their destination because this is not substantial performance of the contract. Of course, however, if the shipowner has the right under the contract to deliver at an intermediate port in certain emergencies then this would be a substantial performance and full freight would be earned. The courts will not imply a promise to pay *pro rata* freight merely because the consignee at the *shipowner's* request takes delivery at a port other than the port of destination.[43] Even if the shipowner has to sell the goods under an agency of necessity[44] then there is no right to *pro rata* freight.[45] However, if the cargo owner negligently delivered goods to the shipowner in such a condition that the shipowner was forced to dispose of them during the voyage then the cargo owner would be liable to the carrier for depriving him of the opportunity to earn freight. If the shipowner, however, *e.g.* delivers half the agreed cargo then he is entitled to freight *pro rata, i.e.* 50 per cent.[46]

Lump sum freight 5.54

In some voyage charters the full freight is payable regardless of the amount of cargo actually loaded provided the ship reaches the port of destination.[47] This is known as "lump sum freight." A charter providing for payment on "intake quantity" is much of the same nature.[48]

Advance freight 5.55

Sometimes, as in clause 11 of the Bill of lading in Appendix 5.A., the contract will provide for "advance freight." In other words the freight is payable in advance and earned whether the cargo is delivered or not. It is not recoverable even if the cargo is lost through an excepted peril.[49] although it would not be payable if the cargo was lost in breach of contract. It is important in this context to distinguish between advance freight and a *loan* of money. The mere fact that all or part of the freight has to be paid in advance does not necessarily mean that this payment is "advance freight." Such a payment may merely be a loan or prepayment. So a clause saying "½ of freight . . .

[41] *Shipton* v. *Thornton* (1838) 9 A. & E. 314.
[42] *Troy* v. *Eastern Company* (1921) 37 T.L.R. 837.
[43] *The Solomsten* (1866) 1 A. & E. 293.
[44] See 1.100.
[45] *Vlierblom* v. *Chapman* (1844) 13 M. & N. 230.
[46] *Nordborg* v. *Sherwood* [1939] P. 121.
[47] *Thomas* v. *Harrowing Steamship Company* [1915] A.C. 58.
[48] *The Metula* [1978] 2 Lloyd's Rep. 5.
[49] *Allison* v. *Bristol Marine* (1876) 1 App.Cas. 209.

to be advanced" is merely a clause requiring a loan and is recoverable if the ship is lost due to an excepted peril.[50]

5.56 **Dead "freight"**

In many voyage charters the freight is payable per ton carried. In return the charterer will guarantee to ship a full cargo so that the shipowner can earn full freight on his ship. If the charterer fails to supply a full cargo as promised then he is liable in damages to the shipowner. These damages are rather misleadingly called "dead freight."

5.57 **Freight to whom payable**

When a ship is chartered and bills of lading are issued to cargo owners other than the charterer himself then the bill may be silent as to who is to receive the freight, the shipowner or the charterer. This is a complex matter largely depending upon the construction of the contract. It is discussed in detail in *Scrutton, On Charterparties*.[51] If the cargo owner is in doubt as to who to pay then he should interplead, *i.e.* go to court and request its directions.

5.58 **Freight by whom payable**

Most bills of lading and charterparties state that both the shipper and the consignee are liable to pay the freight. If the contract is silent on this point then in theory the common law applies as discussed in 1.106. The difficulty is to apply the common law principles of carriage by land to contracts of affreightment. As explained in 5.02 if goods are sold on C.I.F. terms by A to B then at the time of the delivery of the goods to the carrier the goods still belong to A. As owner, he is presumed to be a party to the contract and thus liable to pay the freight. Thus in *Dommett* v. *Beckford*[52] the defendant was the owner of the goods throughout the voyage and was rightly held liable to pay the freight. If the goods are sold F.O.B.[53] then they usually belong to the seller when they are delivered to the carrier and do not belong to the buyer until they pass over the ship's rail. Thus one might argue that the seller is prima facie liable to pay the freight as owner at the time the goods are delivered to the shipowner. This however ignores the fact that in a classic F.O.B. contract it is the buyer who contracts to have the goods carried, not the seller. Indeed the mere act of giving the goods to the shipowner does not make the seller in any real sense the "shipper" or "consignor." This is especially true where the ship has been chartered by the buyer. In any event if the goods are sold not on a F.O.B or C.I.F. basis but subject to the common law as codified in section 18 of the Sale of Goods Act 1979 and carried by water not under a bill of lading then we certainly submit that the

[50] *Great Indian Railway* v. *Turnbull* (1885) 53 L.T. 325.
[51] (19th ed., 1984). Arts. 38 and 170.
[52] (1833) 5 B. & A. 521.
[53] See 5.03.

seller/ "shipper" is not prima facie liable to pay the freight[54] because he is not a party to the contract of carriage.[55]

Section 2 of the bills of Lading Act 1855 states that the Act does not affect any right of the shipowner to sue the original consignor for the freight. Obviously this section does not impose any liability on the consignor to pay freight unless such a liability already exists at common law or under a collateral contract.

Depending on the wording of the bill of lading the consignee is normally presumed to be the owner of the goods and therefore prima facie the owner of the goods and thus liable to pay the freight. This is confirmed by section 1 of the bills of Lading Act 1855 which also makes the indorsee of the bill liable to pay the freight. If A endorses a bill to B, and B in turn re-endorses it to C then B is no longer liable to pay the freight.[56] If the endorsement of the bill does not pass the property because, for example, it is pledged to a bank as security for a loan,[57] then section 1 of the bills of Lading Act[58] does not apply. However, it may be possible, upon appropriate facts, to imply a new contract to pay the freight if the bank realise their security and use the bill to take delivery of the cargo.[59] However such a contract cannot automatically be implied merely because somebody takes delivery of the cargo.[60]

Many voyage charters contain what is known as a "Cesser Clause." These clauses attempt to dispense with the charterer's liability to pay the freight on cargo in respect of which bills of lading have been issued to third parties. In return the charterer purports to give the shipowner a lien on the cargo. Such cesser clauses are only essentially effective to discharge the charterer from his liability for freight if the shipowner is given an effective lien.[61] Whether a contract between A and C to give C a lien on B's property is effective to achieve that aim was discussed briefly in 1.114. In addition to any contractual lien the shipowner may have a lien on the cargo for unpaid freight against a transferee of the bill of lading. This issue is discussed at 5.59.

The shipowner's lien 5.59

Whatever the theoretical objections[62] there is no doubt that carriers by sea have a common law lien for unpaid freight.[63] Whether this common law lien can be exercised against the true owner of goods who is not a party to the contract of affreightment never seems to

[54] *Dickenson* v. *Lano* (1860) 2 F. & F. 188.

[55] See 1.106.

[56] *Smurthwaite* v. *Wilkins* (1862) 11 C.B.(N.S.) 842.

[57] See 5.13.

[58] See Appendix 5.D.

[59] *Sanders* v. *Vanzeller* (1843) 4 Q.B. 260.

[60] *Furness* v. *White* [1895] A.C. 40.

[61] *The Tropwave* [1981] 2 Lloyd's Rep. 159.

[62] See 1.110.

[63] This has been assumed rather than decided in numerous cases, *e.g. Montgomery* v. *Foy Morgan and Company* [1895] 2 Q.B. 321.

have been decided.[64] The common law lien only exists if the freight is payable on delivery. There is no common law lien for advance freight,[65] "dead freight,"[66] or if the freight is not payable until after delivery. Under section 1 of the bills of Lading Act 1855 an endorsee of the Bill of lading is liable to pay the freight[67] and therefore the shipowner can exercise his common law lien for the freight against the endorsee. In addition to his common law lien the shipowner may also have a contractual lien for "dead" or advance freight. As to contractual liens and their exercise against persons who are not parties to the contract of carriage see 1.112-1.114.

5.60 **Liens for general average contributions**

In addition to any lien for unpaid freight a shipowner may also have a lien on the cargo for general average contributions. General average is a complex topic outside the scope of this work. Essentially, however, general average arises where a shipowner is forced to jettison part of the cargo, *e.g.* in a hurricane, to save the ship and other cargo or is forced to spend money to save all or part of the cargo, *e.g.* by hiring a tug to tow the vessel into port. Such sacrifices or expenditures are known as "general average acts." In these circumstances the cargo owner who has lost his cargo is entitled to a *pro rata* contribution from the shipowner and other cargo owners. Likewise the shipowner who has incurred the cost of the tug can recover a contribution from the cargo owners. The shipowner, but *not* the cargo owner, has a lien on the cargo for any general average contribution owed to him.

VOYAGE CHARTERPARTIES. INTRODUCTION

5.61 **The law applicable**

The nature of voyage charters was explained in 5.04. Bills of lading issued to the charterer of a vessel, as explained in 5.15-5.16, do not normally prevail over the charterparty unless they are endorsed to a third party. The Hague-Visby Rules, as implemented by the Carriage of Goods by Sea Act 1971, therefore have no mandatory application to charterparties. It is, however, open to the parties to a charterparty to incorporate the Rules by Clause Paramount.[68] If they do so then, because the Rules have no mandatory application, the parties can partially exclude their terms. *The common law rules relating to seaworthiness and deviation, as discussed in 5.17-5.22 and 5.23-5.26 respectively, apply equally to voyage charterparties as they do to Bills of lading unless the*

[64] If a carrier by water is by custom of the realm under the liability of a common carrier (see 5.06) then perhaps he has the privileges of such a carrier, *e.g.* a lien against the whole world, see 1.111.
[65] *How* v. *Kirchner* (1857) 11 Moore P.C. 21.
[66] *Phillips* v. *Roche* (1812) 15 East 547.
[67] See Appendix 5.D.
[68] See 5.31.

parties have contracted to the contrary. The same is true of the law relating to freight and liens discussed in 5.51-5.60.

The description and whereabouts of the vessel 5.62

Most charterparties will describe the vessel as being of a certain class[69] and nationality. Obviously she must correspond to her description in these respects. The contract will also state the tonnage of the ship. This is an intermediate term[70] of the contract. Thus if the vessel is of a substantially different tonnage then the charterer can repudiate the contract.[71]

A statement in the contract that the vessel is at a named place is a condition of the contract,[72] a breach of which gives the charterer the right to repudiate. A statement that, *e.g.* the vessel is "expected ready to load at Amsterdam on January 13" is of a similar nature.[73] If the shipowner has no such reasonable belief the charterer can repudiate.[74]

Liability for loss, damage or delay to the cargo 5.63

The liability of the shipowner to the charterer[75] for loss of or damage to the cargo depends on the terms of the contract. The contract may, for example, contractually incorporate the Hague-Visby Rules.[76] On the other hand clause 2 of the "Gencon" voyage charter in Appendix 5.B. only imposes minimal liability on the shipowner for loss or damage. Such a clause cannot be challenged under the Unfair Contract Terms Act 1977.[77]

VOYAGE CHARTERS. THE PRELIMINARY VOYAGE

Due dispatch 5.64

It is an implied intermediate term[78] of the contract that the ship will proceed to the port of loading, load the cargo and carry out the voyage with "due dispatch," *i.e.* all reasonable speed, or by a stated date. Most charters contain a "cancellation clause" to the effect that the charterer can abandon the contract, if the vessel has not arrived by a given date. In addition even if there is no express cancellation clause in the contract if the vessel has not arrived after a reasonable time and the venture is thus frustrated commercially the charterer may repudiate.[79] The shipowner is then liable in damages to the charterer unless the delay was caused by a contractual excepted peril.

[69] If she is of this class then the shipowner is not liable. There is no implied promise that she is rightly classed. *Hurst* v. *Usborne* (1856) 18 C.B. 144.

[70] See 5.17.

[71] *Barker* v. *Windle* (1856) 6 E. & B. 675.

[72] *Behn* v. *Burness* (1863) 3 B. & S. 751. As to the meaning of "condition," see 5.17.

[73] *The Mihalis Angelos* [1971] 1 Q.B. 164.

[74] See n. 73, above.

[75] As to liability to holders of bills of lading, see 5.15 and 5.31.

[76] See 5.28 and 5.30.

[77] See 5.05

[78] See 5.17.

[79] *Universal Cargo Carriers* v. *Citati* [1957] 2 Q.B. 401. Compare *Hong Kong Fir Shipping* v. *Kawasaki* [1962] 2 Q.B. 26.

5.65 **Safe port or berth**

Sometimes a voyage charter does not name the ports of loading and discharge. In such cases there is invariably a contractual term that the charterer will nominate, *e.g.* "good and safe ports." Such a clause also appears in time charters.

A port is not "safe" unless the ship can safely reach it, use it and leave it if she is navigated with proper skill.[80] The port must be "safe" at the time it is nominated and be expected to remain safe but there is no guarantee that it will remain so.[81] The following factors should be noted:

(1) A port can be "safe" if in all human probability it is expected to be safe, when the vessel is likely to arrive there, even though at the time of nomination it is temporarily unsafe.[82]
(2) The size and type of vessel must be taken into account.
(3) A port may be politically unsafe, *e.g.* on account of the nationality of the ship.
(4) The vessel must be able to enter and leave the port fully laden.[83]
(5) A port can be safe even though it is occasionally unsafe in very high tides.[84]
(6) To be safe a port must have at least one safe approach.[85]

If the charterer nominates an unsafe port he is liable for any ensuing damage[86] unless the main cause of the loss is the owner's default or the master's negligence.[87] It is not negligence to make reasonable efforts to get into a difficult port.[88] In time charters if the port is unsafe the charterer must nominate another safe port.[89] Whether this also true of voyage charters is unclear. If a vessel finds herself in an unsafe port the shipowner must minimise his loss by making all reasonable efforts to get out of it. Any reasonable expense thus incurred is recoverable from the charterer.[90]

5.66 **"So near as she can get"**

Sometimes the contractual duty on the shipowner is to get as near as he reasonably can to the port. Having done so the vessel must wait a reasonable time.[91] After a reasonable time the shipowner can require the charterer to bring the cargo out to him in lighters.[92] Often the shipowner is alternatively given the contractual option, in the case of delivery of the cargo, of delivering at the nearest alternative reasonable port.

[80] *The Eastern City* [1958] 2 Lloyd's Rep. 153.
[81] *The Evia* [1983] 1 A.C. 736.
[82] See n. 81, above.
[83] *The Alhambra* (1881) 6 P.D. 68.
[84] *AKt. Eriksen* v. *Foy Morgan* (1926) 25 Lloyd's Rep. 422.
[85] *Gracie* v. *General Steam Navigation Company* [1950] 2 K.B. 383.
[86] See n. 85, above.
[87] *The Dagmar* [1968] 2 Lloyd's Rep. 563.
[88] See n. 85, above.
[89] *The Evia* [1983] 1 A.C. 736.
[90] *The Medolanum* [1984] 1 Lloyd's Rep. 129.
[91] *Parker* v. *Winlow* (1857) 7 E. & B. 942.
[92] *i.e.* small vessels, *Dahl* v. *Nelson* (1881) 6 App.Cas. 38.

The charterers duty to provide a cargo 5.67

If the vessel is chartered for lump sum freight[93] then there is no duty on the charterer to provide any cargo. If the vessel is to earn freight per ton carried then there is invariably a term in the contract to the effect that the charterer must provide a full cargo unless he is expressly excused from this liability in some exceptional circumstances stated in the contract. If no such full cargo is provided then the charterer is liable in damages called "dead freight."[94]

Loading and unloading, by whom and how long is allowed? 5.68

At common law, it is the charterer's duty to bring the cargo alongside the ship. The duty and expense of loading then fall on the shipowner. If, however, as provided by clause 5 of the Gencon Charter in Appendix 5B the contract is on F.I.O.S Terms, *i.e.* "free in, out and stowed," then these duties fall on the charterer. *The comments made in the remainder of this paragraph and in 5.70-5.75 only apply to contracts on F.I.O.S. Terms.* If there is a contractual duty upon the charterer to load and unload the vessel then the common law allows him a reasonable time to do so. If he fails to do so then he is liable in damages to the shipowner for any subsequent delay to the vessel. However, all modern F.I.O.S. voyage charters grant the charterer, *e.g.* "seven weather working days"[95] to load or unload. This time is called "laytime" or lay-days. Once the laytime, *i.e.* time allowed, has expired the charterer must pay an agreed sum of damages to the shipowner for delay to the ship. These liquidated, *i.e.* fixed, damages are called demurrage. Sometimes in order to encourage speedy loading and discharge the contract may provide for "dispatch money." This means, for example, that if there are 10 lay days but the charterer loads or unloads the vessel in eight days he will be paid by the shipowner for the saving in time.

Commencement of laytime 5.69

Before the lay days can start to run three things are required at common law:

(1) The vessel must be fit to load[96] or unload.
(2) She must be an arrived ship.[97]
(3) Notice of readiness to load or unload, otherwise called "N.O.R.," must be given to the charterer.

At common law notice only need be given at the port of loading and

[93] See 5.54.
[94] See 5.56.
[95] See 5.73.
[96] See 5.71.
[97] See 5.72-5.73.

not at the port of discharge. However most voyage charters provide also for N.O.R. to be given at the discharge port.

5.70 **Fitness to load**

For laytime to commence the vessel, at the time of notice of readiness, must be fit to load. She will not be fit if, for example, her holds are infected.[98] The fact that a ship has not complied with mere routine port formalities[99] such as customs clearance or has not been cleared on health grounds (called "free pratique") will not prevent her from being fit to load.

5.71 **Arrived ship, berth and dock charters**

Normally for laytime to commence the vessel must be an "arrived ship." To be an arrived ship she must have completed her previous voyage[1] and be at the agreed place. What is the "agreed place" depends on the type of charterparty contact. Voyage charters are of three kinds:

(1) Berth charters. Examples would be where the vessel was to proceed to "Number Ten Berth, Victoria Docks, London" or "to a safe named berth at Lagos."

(2) Dock charters. An example would be "Tilbury Docks in the Port of London."

(3) Port charters. An example would be the "Port of London."

In relation to berth or dock charters it is usually tolerably clear when a vessel has "arrived" at the agreed place. Port charters present great difficulties which are briefly summarised in 5.72.

5.72 **Arrived ship, port charters**

Ports are often crowded and a vessel may be held up for months awaiting a berth. Enormous difficulty has arisen in modern times with port charters and the necessity that for laytime to commence the vessel must be an "arrived ship." Some ports are huge in area and it is often not clear when the vessel is within the port especially if the normal "waiting area" is outside the "port" in its normal geographical sense. Common sense would suggest that if the vessel got as near to the port as she could that this would be sufficient for her to be an "arrived" ship but this is not the law.[2] This area of law is still in some confusion and we can only give a brief summary. Readers are referred to a series of articles by one of the country's leading shipping arbitrators in which the late writer examines this area with clarity and in detail.[3]

[98] *The Tres Flores* [1974] Q.B. 264.
[99] *The Albion* [1953] 1 W.L.R. 1026.
[1] *Maratha Envoy* [1978] 1 A.C. 1.
[2] See n. 1, above.
[3] H. S. Keswani, *City of London Law Review*, Michaelmas 1975, 17; Lent 1976, 17; Spring 1979, 11. *Charterparty International*, Vol. I, No. 1, 5 (Nov. 1984); Vol. I, No. 3, 35 (Jan. 1985).

Essentially the port includes all areas that are under the fiscal and administrative control of the port authority. Thus in the *Johanna Oldendorff*[4] the charterer nominated Liverpool as the port of discharge. The vessel arrived off the port but no berth was available. After clearing customs she was ordered by the port authority to wait at the Mersey Bar anchorage which was 17 miles from the nearest berth but where vessels usually waited. On arriving at the anchorage she gave notice of readiness. The House of Lords held that she was an arrived ship at this point, because the Bar anchorage was part of the administrative port of Liverpool, and laytime started to run.[5] Lord Reid said[6] that to be an "arrived ship" "she must . . . have reached a position within the port where she is at the immediate and effective disposal of the charterer. If she is at a place where waiting ships usually lie, she will be in such a position. . . . "

Laytime days 5.73

Once the three requirements outlined in 5.69 are satisfied then the lay-days, *i.e.* agreed days for loading or unloading, start to run against the charterer. A reference in a charter to "days" in the context of laytime means whole days. Thus if the contract provides for seven lay days and a ship satisfies the three requirements at one minute to midnight then in two minutes time, at one minute past midnight, she is already into her second day's laytime. However most voyage charters are more precise as regards parts of days and allow laytime to be calculated by the hour rather than by whole days. Such "days" are called "conventional days." Sometimes the charter will not state a number of lay days but will instead require the charterer to, for example, load a minimum of 200 tons of cargo per day.

Laytime expressions 5.74

If the laytime provision merely refers to, *e.g.* "seven days." Then that literally means every day and includes Sundays and holidays. The following laytime expressions are however regularly found:

(1) "Sundays and holidays excepted," (*i.e.* "S.H.E.X"). Note that in this context a day can be a "holiday" even though work is actually done in the port on an overtime basis.[7] What is a holiday depends on local law, custom and facts.

(2) "Working days." This means all days upon which work is normally done in the port, excluding Sundays and holidays. If no work is possible on a certain day because, *e.g.* of the weather then this still counts as a day.

(3) "Weather working day." This means a day which is suitable for loading or unloading taking into account the nature of the cargo.[8] It

[4] [1974] A.C. 479.
[5] See 5.73.
[6] At p. 535.
[7] *The Trevarrock* (1932) 48 T.L.R. 363.
[8] *Reardon Smith* v. *Ministry of Agriculture* [1963] A.C. 691.

seems that the words "Working Day Weather Permitting" bear much the same meaning.[9] The fact that no loading is contemplated or actually takes place is irrelevant. If part of the day is lost then the laytime is calculated *pro rata*. So if the normal working day is eight hours and two hours are lost through rain then six hours, *i.e.* three quarters of a day's laytime has been used.

Provided that a day is a lay-day for the purpose of the charterparty the duty to load or unload is *absolute* unless there is an exception in the contract or loading would be illegal.[10] So a day is still a lay day even though the charterer is prevented from loading due to, *e.g.* strikes or overcrowding in the docks.

5.75 **Demurrage**

Once the lay-days, *i.e.* agreed days for loading or unloading, have expired then the charterer becomes liable to pay demurrage, *i.e.* the agreed damages for delay to the ship. The charter may provide for, *e.g.* "Seven Weather Working Days" laytime or provide that lay-days will not count if there is a strike in the dock. However these clauses are irrelevant once demurrage has commenced. So in the above example, once the vessel is on demurrage, if the charterer cannot load on a certain day because of bad weather and/or strikes this day still counts against him and he must pay demurrage for it.[11] This rule is summarised by the phrase *"Once on demurrage always on demurrage."*

Despite this rule one should not imagine that demurrage runs for ever. If the delay becomes so serious as to amount to a repudiation of the contract by the charterer the shipowner can withdraw the vessel and claim damages[12] on common law principles.[13] Likewise if the contract provides for, *e.g.* "30 days demurrage at £2,000 per day" then, after the 30-day period has expired, the shipowner can claim damages on common law principles.

Time Charters

5.76 **Introduction**

Time charters are of relatively modern origin. An example of such a contract is the Baltime Time Charter in Appendix 5.C. Essentially such a charter is more in the nature of a contract for the use of a ship rather than a contract of carriage. In addition the liabilities of the parties depend on the exact terms of contracts which often vary greatly in their provisions and are of great complexity. For these reasons we therefore only give this complex topic a brief examination.

[9] *The Vorros* [1983] 1 Lloyd's Rep. 579.
[10] *Ralli* v. *Compania Naviera Sota* [1920] 2 K.B. 287.
[11] *The Tsukubu Maru* [1979] 1 Lloyd's Rep. 459; *The Altus* [1985] 1 Lloyd's Rep. 423; *Food Corporation of India* v. *Corras Shipping* [1983] 2 Lloyd's Rep. 496.
[12] *Universal Cargo Carriers* v. *Citati* [1957] 2 Q.B. 401.
[13] See 1.39-1.42.

Unlike a charter by demise or bareboat charter[14] in the case of a time charter the vessel remains in the possession of the shipowner and the master remains his servant. Whereas under a voyage charter most of the duties fall on the shipowner under a time charter the duties are shared between the charterer and the shipowner. The responsibility for navigation remains that of the shipowner. Although the cargo is in the possession of the shipowner once it is on board all other cargo responsibiities usually fall on the charterer. He is responsible for loading and unloading the cargo and pays for all port dues and bunkers, *i.e.* fuel. The charterer can load any cargo he likes provided (a) it is lawful, (b) it is not dangerous and (c) it is not forbidden under the contract. The shipowner usually pays for the wages of the master and crew, victualling (*i.e.* food), stores, maintenance, lubricating fuel and also is responsible for insuring the vessel.

The speed and fuel "warranty" 5.77

Invariably time charters will contain a "fuel and speed warranty," *i.e.* a clause stating the speed and fuel consumption of the ship. Despite its misleading name this term of the contract is usually an intermediate term[15] and not a warranty. Thus the charterer can only repudiate the contract if the statement as to fuel and speed is substantially incorrect. This area of law is a complex one outside the scope of this work.[16]

The maintenance "warranty" 5.78

At common law it seems that a ship that is time chartered need only be seaworthy[17] upon delivery to the charterer.[18] Most time charters, however, impose a similar duty upon the shipowner to maintain the ship in a seaworthy condition in the form of a "maintenance warranty" though the duty under the contract may not be absolute and merely one of due diligence.[19] Again this duty is in the nature of an intermediate term[20] and is not strictly speaking a "warranty."

Liability for loss, damage and delay to cargo 5.79

Sometimes a time charter will contractually incorporate the Hague-Visby Rules[21] by "Clause Paramount."[22] In that event these Rules, unless partially excluded, will govern the shipowner's liability in relation to the cargo. However, in a time or a voyage charter the parties can make whatever contract they like. For example, clause 13 of the Baltime Charter in Appendix 5.C. only places minimal liability

[14] See 5.04.
[15] See 5.17.
[16] See the illuminating series of articles by H. S. Keswani, *Charterparty International,* Vol. I, No. 11, 154 (Sept. 1985); Vol. I, No. 12,170 (Oct. 1985); Vol. IV, 51 (1986), Vol. V, 66 (1986).
[17] See 5.17-5.19.
[18] *Giertson* v. *Turnbull* (1908) S.C. 1101.
[19] See clause 3 of the Baltime Charter in Appendix 5.C. As to due diligence, see 5.32.
[20] See 5.17.
[21] See 5.27 *et seq.*
[22] See 5.28 and 5.30.

on the shipowner for loss and damage to cargo. In these circumstances a wise charterer will take care to ensure that the cargo is properly insured.

5.80 **The payment of hire**

The payment made by the charterer in respect of a time charter as opposed to a voyage charter is called "hire" rather than freight. It seems that the Rule in the *Aries Tanker*[23] mentioned in 5.50 and 5.52 does not apply in its full unjust vigour to time charters.[24]

The hire is usually payable upon a monthly basis. To be a good payment it must be in "cash," *i.e.* the money must be at the immediate effective disposal of the shipowner.[25] Under most time charters[26] non payment of the hire on time justifies the shipowner in repudiating the contract and withdrawing his vessel immediately from the service of the charterer.[27] This is thus a great temptation to shipowners to withdraw the vessel if the payment is only a day late and charter rates are going up on the market. The mere fact that the shipowner's bank have accepted late payment[28] or that the shipowner has not immediately repudiated the contract[29] do not show that the shipowner has waived his right to repudiate the contract. However if the shipowner permits payment by post and the payment is posted in good time but delayed in the post then the charterer is excused late payment.[30]

To overcome the harshness of these rules a sensible charterer will insist that the contract shall contain what is called an "anti-technicality clause." Such clauses grant some leeway to the charterer as regards payment of hire and only permit the shipowner to withdraw his vessel once he has, *e.g.* given the charterer 48 hours notice to remedy his late payment.

At common law the hire must be paid on the due date even if the ship is, *e.g.* blockaded in a port and no use to the charterer. To deal with this most time charters include an "off-hire" clause[31] which entitles the charterer to withold payment in some circumstances. These clauses are of innumerable variety and great complexity and are outside the scope of this work.

5.81 **Redelivery of the vessel**

Time charters usually provide[32] that the vessel must be returned to the shipowner in good condition at the end of the charter period

[23] [1977] 1 W.L.R. 185. See 5.50 and 5.52.
[24] *The Nanfri* [1979] A.C. 757.
[25] *The Chikuma* [1981] 1 W.L.R. 314.
[26] See, *e.g.* clause 6 of the Baltime Charter in Appendix 6.C.
[27] *The Laconia* [1977] A.C. 850.
[28] See n. 27, above.
[29] *The Mihalios Xilas* [1978] 2 Lloyd's Rep. 186.
[30] *Tankexpress* v. *Compagnie Financiere Belge* [1949] A.C. 76.
[31] See clause 11 of the Baltime charter in Appendix 5.C.
[32] See clause 7 of the Baltime charter in Appendix 5.C.

allowing for "fair wear and tear."[33] However the charterer is only liable for any damage to the vessel caused by his breach of contract or the negligence of those for whom he is responsible, *e.g.* that of stevedores whom he has appointed to unload cargo.

CARRIAGE OF GOODS BY INLAND WATERWAY

The application of the Hague-Visby Rules 5.82

As explained in 5.28 carriage by "sea" for the purposes of the Hague-Visby Rules probably includes carriage by "ships" on inland navigable waters. Therefore in appropriate circumstances[34] the Hague-Visby Rules discussed in 5.27-5.50 can apply to carriage by inland waterway. However it is most unlikely that goods to be carried only by inland waterway would be carried subject to a Bill of lading or subject to a contract incorporating the Hague-Visby Rules. Contracts for the carriage of goods only by inland waterway are therefore subject to the common law and the contract the parties have made. The question of which common law principles are applicable is discussed in the next paragraph.

Carriage by inland waterway at common law 5.83

There have been remarkably few cases on the law relating to carriage by inland waterway and it is therefore difficult to say whether in a given case the law relating to inland carriage by land or that relating to carriage by sea is applicable. It seems from the case of *Liver Alkali* v. *Johnson*[35] that carriers by inland waterway, even if they do not hold themselves out as prepared to carry for all and sundry, are by "custom of the realm" under the liability of a common carrier.[36] It apparently has never been decided whether, *e.g.* a canal barge operator has an absolute duty to supply a "canalworthy" vessel. If the carrier operated subject to his common law liability this matter would, however, be largely academic as the existence of an unfit vessel is not one of the common carrier's excepted perils.[37] It could however be important if he was carrying by contract under conditions similar to those in clause 5.A. of the British Rail Conditions as discussed in 1.63. This is because if there is a duty to supply a "canalworthy" vessel and his vessel was in fact not "canalworthy" then by analogy with the position in carriage by sea[38] he could not rely on any excepted perils in the contract.

It was held, *obiter*, in *Bryans* v. *Nix*[39] that there is no reason in principle why a canal receipt should not be a document of title as is a

[33] He cannot, however, refuse to take redelivery of the vessel in a damaged condition. *The Puerto Buitrago* [1976] 1 Lloyd's Rep. 250.

[34] See 5.28-5.30.

[35] (1872) L.R. 7 Ex. 267, affirmed at (1874) L.R. 9 Ex. 338.

[36] See 1.27-1.28 and 5.06.

[37] See 1.28.

[38] See 5.21, 5.32 and 5.36.

[39] (1839) 4 M. & W. 7754.

Bill of lading (see 5.11) if it was accepted as such by the "custom of merchants." It does seem however that they are not accepted as such by the commercial world.

Apart, perhaps, from the above questions of common carrier's liability, "canalworthiness" and documents of title we suggest that carriage by inland waterway has more in common with carriage by land than carriage by sea. Therefore we suggest that, on the whole, carriage by inland waterway is more appropriately covered by the principles outlined in Chapter 1 rather than those in this Chapter.

Carriage of Passengers and Luggage by Sea. The Athens Convention

5.84 **Introduction**

The law relating to carriage of passengers and their luggage by sea is governed by section 14 and Schedule 3 of the Merchant Shipping Act 1979 which implement into English law the provisions of the Athens Convention 1974 as amended by the Protocol of 1976. section 17 of the 1979 Act also limits the carrier's liability to passengers based on the tonnage of the ship. The Convention itself is not yet in force because an insufficient number of countries have ratified it. Therefore Schedule 3 of the 1979 Act, which contains the Convention should be interpreted as a piece of purely British legislation[40] and not in accordance with the principles used for interpreting international conventions as outlined in 3.05-3.08. Because the Convention is not yet in force, its provisions, as implemented into English law, only apply to voyages to and from Great Britain. Shipowners are forbidden from contracting out of the provisions of the Convention by Article 18.

As the result of Orders in Council issued under the Hovercraft Act 1968 the carriage of passengers and baggage by hovercraft is covered by the Hague Protocol discussed in Chaper 6 and not by the Athens Convention.

5.85 **Carriage of passengers**

A "passenger" is defined in Article 1(4) of the Convention as anyone who is carried under a contract of carriage or who, with the consent of the carrier, accompanies a vehicle or live animals. The Convention applies during the "carriage" by sea. As regards passengers, "carriage" means the period during which the passenger is either on board the ship or embarking or disembarking. This includes the carriage of the passenger to or from the ship by water but not any period during which the passenger is in the care of the carrier on land.[41] The burden is upon the passenger to prove that any accident occurred during the "carriage" by sea.[42]

[40] See 6.70 and the discussion of "particular" (q) of Art. 4 of the Unamended Warsaw Convention in 6.71.

[41] Compare the position in carriage by air under the Hague Protocol. See 6.58.

[42] Art. 3(2).

The shipowner is liable for death or injury during the "carriage" if it was caused by the "fault or neglect of the carrier or his servants agents acting within the scope of their employment."[43] Fault or neglect will be presumed in the case of "shipwreck, collision, stranding, explosion or fire, or defect in the ship."[44] Of course in such a case the shipowner could rebut the presumption by, *e.g.* proving that a collision at sea was solely the fault of the other ship. In which event he would escape liability. In other cases, *e.g.* if a passenger fell overboard, the burden of proving "neglect or default" would fall on the plaintiff.[45] If the shipowner can prove "contributory fault" on the part of the passenger then this is a partial or total defence to the shipowner.[46] Liability per passenger for death or injury is limited to 46,666 S.D.R.'s,[47] approximately £38,000, unless a higher limit of liability has been contracted for.[48]

Unaccompanied luggage 5.86

"Luggage" for the purposes of the Convention is defined as any article or vehicle carried by the shipowner under a contract of carriage.[49] However goods carried under a charterparty,[50] Bill of lading[51] or other contract "primarily concerned with the carriage of goods" are excluded from the definition as are live animals.[52] Luggage is divided into two types, namely "cabin luggage" and "other luggage." "Cabin luggage" is what a common lawyer would describe as accompanied luggage, *i.e.* luggage that stays in the possession of the passenger. Presumably the definition of cabin luggage in Article 1(5) would include "personal effects," *e.g.* the clothes a passenger was wearing. The provisions concerning such luggage are outlined in 5.87. "Other luggage" is luggage that is in the care of the shipowner,[53] in other words what a common lawyer would describe as unaccompanied luggage. As regards unaccompanied luggage the carrier is liable under the Convention during its "carriage." "Carriage" for the purposes of unaccompanied luggage is defined to mean much the same as "transit" at common law.[54] In other words the carrier is liable from the time he is given the luggage till it is redelivered to the passenger. This could include, of course, periods when the luggage was on land. As regards loss of or damage to unaccompanied luggage

[43] Art. 3(1). As to "scope of employment," see 1.18 and 1.116.
[44] Art. 3(3).
[45] *Ibid.*
[46] Art. 6.
[47] Art. 7(1). As to S.D.R.'s, see 3.60.
[48] Art. 10(1).
[49] Art. 1(5).
[50] See 5.04.
[51] See n. 50, above.
[52] Art. 1(5).
[53] Art. 1(6).
[54] Art. 1(8)(e). As to "transit," see 1.66-1.71.

then the loss or damage is presumed to be caused by the "fault or neglect" of the shipowner whenever it happens during the carriage[55] and not just when it happens in "shipwrecks," etc., as is the case with passengers.

The limit of liability for unaccompanied luggage is 1,200 S.D.R.'s, approximately £1,000, per person, and that for vehicles and their contents is 3,333 S.D.R.'s, approximately £2,700. The shipowner is under no liability whatsoever for money, gold, silver, etc., and "other valuables" unless they are deposited with the carrier.[56] Even if they are deposited then the carrier can still limit his liability to 1,200 S.D.R.'s unless a higher limit has been agreed.[57]

5.87 **Accompanied luggage**

As regards accompanied or "cabin" luggage "carriage" is defined as it is in relation to the carriage of passengers.[58] The rules as to the burden of proof of "fault or neglect" are also the same as in the case of carriage of passengers.[59] The limit of liability for unaccompanied luggage is 833 S.D.R.'s, approximately £680, per person.[60]

5.88 **Intentional and reckless misconduct**

The carrier cannot rely on the limits of liability in the Convention if it is proved that the loss, etc., was caused by an "act or omission of the carrier done with intent to cause damage, or recklessly with knowledge that such damage would probably result."[61] The meaning of the identically worded provision in the Hague Protocol on carriage by air is discussed in detail in 6.50.

5.89 **Servants, agents and subcontractors**

Any actions brought against the servants, agents or "performing carriers," *i.e.* subcontractors, of the shipowner are subject to the same principles of liability and limits of liability as are actions against the shipowner himself.[62] The plaintiff cannot increase his damages by suing more than one person.[63] The servants, agents and performing carriers will also lose the Convention limits of liability if they are guilty of intentional or reckless misconduct.[64]

[55] Art. 3(3).
[56] Art. 5.
[57] Arts. 5 and 10(1).
[58] See 5.85.
[59] See n. 58, above.
[60] Art. 8(1).
[61] Art. 13(1).
[62] Art. 11.
[63] Art. 12.
[64] Art. 13(2).

Chapter Six

CARRIAGE BY AIR

INTRODUCTION

Background and terminology 6.01

Carriage by air is largely governed by International Conventions given effect in the United Kingdom by legislation. These Conventions and other sets of rules governing the liability of carriers are called "regimes of carriage." As with the C.M.R. Convention[1] the regimes are not fully comprehensive. Where the Conventions do not deal with a point of law then the common law principles discussed in Chapters 1, 2 and 5 will apply.

In this Chapter the main Convention, *i.e.* the "Warsaw Convention as amended by the Hague Protocol," otherwise known as the Amended Warsaw Convention or, just simply, as the Hague Protocol will be discussed in 6.12-6.56. In 6.69-6.76 and 6.82-6.84 respectively we point out the variations in the other "regimes of carriage" that have the force of law in the United Kingdom, namely the unamended Warsaw Convention and the Non-International Rules. We also include a brief survey of the provisions of the various regimes as regards passengers and their "baggage" and of other Protocols (*i.e.* amendments to the Warsaw Convention) that are not yet in force in the United Kingdom. The "Americanisms" "air waybill," "cargo" and "baggage" are used in the Conventions, as implemented in the United Kingdom, rather than "air consignment note," "goods" and "luggage" respectively. These expressions will regretfully, therefore, largely be used in this Chapter.

The English text of the Hague Protocol will be found in Appendix 6.A and some of the more important provisions of the unamended Warsaw Convention as implemented in the United Kingdom (where it varies significantly from the Hague Protocol) in Appendix 6.B. These Appendices should be studied closely when their provisions are discussed in the text.[2]

It should be emphasised that the Unfair Contract Terms Act 1977 has no application to carriage by air under the Hague Protocol, the unamended Warsaw Convention or the Non-International Rules, nor indeed to any international conventions on carriage.[3]

The Warsaw Convention 1929, the unamended rules 6.02

When carriage by air was growing in importance in the 1920s there were considerable difficulties as to "conflict of laws."[4] Some diffi-

[1] See 3.02.

[2] See Shawcross and Beaumont, *Air Law* (4th ed., 1983), to which the reader is referred for a more comprehensive coverage of the law relating to carriage by air.

[3] But see 5.05.

[4] See 3.02.

culties in this context were avoided because many air carriers used standard conditions of carriage laid down by a federation of carriers called the International Air Traffic Association. However these conditions were often interpreted differently in different countries many of whose courts were hostile to exclusion clauses[5] in the conditions of carriage.

In order to create a uniform set of legal rules with the force of international law and in order to protect "fledgling" airlines from massive claims, the Warsaw Convention was signed in 1929. The Convention dealt with the carriage of cargo and also of passengers and their baggage. This Convention was implemented into English Law by the now repealed Carriage by Air Act 1932.

6.03 **The Hague Protocol 1955. the amended rules**

Over the years defects were revealed in the original Warsaw Convention. These mainly concerned the low limits of the carrier's liability for death or injury to passengers and the proof of "wilful misconduct" which presented difficulties in some countries, especially those that used a version of the Convention other than in the English language. In 1955, therefore, a new fully revised version of the Warsaw Convention was produced. This is known as "the Warsaw Convention 1929 as amended by the Hague Protocol."[6] The Hague Protocol was implemented into English law by the Carriage by Air Act 1961 but the Act did not come into force till 1967. *Do not confuse the Hague Protocol with the Hague-Visby Rules* on the law of carriage by sea discussed in Chapter 5.

6.04 **The Guadalajara Convention 1961**

Both the original Warsaw Convention and the Hague Protocol had a defect when it came to dealing with the "actual carrier." The Conventions dealt with the liability of the carrier who made the contract of carriage and any "successive carriers," *i.e.* carriers who by agreement between the customer and first carrier took over from the contracting carrier and performed part of the carriage. The Conventions did not deal with the position if the whole of the carriage was subcontracted to another carrier. In addition they did not deal with the position where part of the carriage was subcontracted without the agreement of the customer. Such "actual" carriers presumably did not have the protection of the Conventions. To deal with this defect the Guadalajara Convention was drafted and implemented into English law by the Carriage by Air (Supplementary Provisions) Act 1962. Essentially under this Convention the "actual carrier" who performs the whole of the contract of carriage is given the same rights and liabilities as the contracting carrier.[7] The provisions of the Guadalajara Convention are discussed in 6.64-6.68.

[5] As to exclusion clauses generally, see 1.43-1.44.
[6] s.1 of the Carriage by Air Act 1961.
[7] Art. II of the Guadalajara Convention.

The Montreal Agreement 6.05

The United States have never ratified the Hague Protocol mainly because it was felt that even the increased limits of liabilty in the Amended Convention in the case of death or injury were still inadequate. In fact the United States threatened to denounce, (*i.e.* withdraw from) the original unamended Warsaw Convention. An agreement was therefore made at Montreal that has the force of law in the United States. It affects all flights to, from or with an agreed stopping place in the United States. Under this agreement all carriers contract with their passengers for a higher limit of liability[8] and for strict liability irrespective of fault on the part of the carrier of passengers.[9] The Montreal Agreement does not technically act as an amendment to the original unamended Warsaw Convention but purely as a matter of contract between the carrier and his passengers. Note that the Montreal Agreement does not apply to the carriage of *cargo*. The Agreement is discussed further in 6.80.

Subsequent developments 6.06

Since the Montreal Agreement in 1966 there have been further attempts to reform the Warsaw Convention. First there was the Guatemala Protocol of 1971 that mainly dealt with the carriage of passengers and their baggage. This Protocol has never been implemented into English law and seems unlikely ever to come into effect. In addition, there were the Montreal Protocols of 1975 (not to be confused with the Montreal Agreement discussed above in 6.05). The first three Montreal Protocols expressed the limits of liability in S.D.R.'s[10] rather than gold francs. The fourth Montreal Protocol incorporated the changes made at Guatemala and made similar changes to the cargo provisions. The Carriage by Air and Road Act 1979 provided for the Montreal Protocols to be implemented into English law, but this power has not yet been exercised and thus the fourth *Montreal Protocol is not yet in force*. The reason for this is that the Montreal Protocols have not yet received the ratification of a sufficient number of countries to come into force and it looks unlikely that they will come into effect in the near future. Nevertheless in 6.86 we give a brief outline of their provisions.

The non-international rules 6.07

Flights to the U.K., from countries that have not ratified either the original unamended Warsaw Convention or the Hague Protocol (or *vice versa*)are not subject to either Convention, nor are flights purely within the United Kingdom. To deal with such cases English law has its own purely domestic legislation, namely the Carriage by Air Acts (Application of Provisions) Order 1967, Schedule 1.[11] This legislation obviously only applies to the United Kingdom and therefore to

[8] See 6.80.

[9] The carrier can still rely on the defence of contributory negligence in Art. 21 of the unamended Convention. See 6.80.

[10] *i.e.* Special Drawing Rights. See 3.60.

[11] Issued under powers granted by s.10 of the 1961 Act.

actions brought before its courts.[12] It is based largely on the Hague Protocol, (*i.e.* Amended Warsaw) and its provisions are outlined in 6.82-6.84.

6.08 **The current United Kingdom position**

The United Kingdom is a signatory to the original Warsaw Convention and also to the Hague Protocol (Amended Warsaw). Flights to the United States and some other countries and vice versa are still covered by the original unamended Warsaw Convention because these countries have not ratified the Hague Protocol. If a case involving the carriage of cargo, passengers or baggage comes before the United Kingdom courts then there are FOUR different possible "REGIMES" OF CARRIAGE that may apply. These are:

(1) International carriage under the Warsaw Convention as amended by the Hague Protocol, (*i.e.* the "AMENDED CONVENTION" or simply HAGUE PROTOCOL). This regime is implemented into English law by the Carriage by Air Act 1961 as amended by the Carriage by Air Acts (Supplementary Provisions) Act 1962, (*i.e.* the Guadalajara Convention[13]). This regime is outlined in 6.12-6.63 below and the Hague Protocol itself is reproduced in Appendix 6.A. Do not confuse the Hague Protocol with the Hague-Visby Rules on carriage by sea discussed in Chapter 5.

(2) International carriage under the original unamended Warsaw Convention. The original Carriage by Air Act 1932 which implemented this regime into English law was repealed and superseded by the Carriage by Air Act 1961. Nevertheless the unamended Warsaw Convention with some minor alterations (mainly as to wording) is still part of English law by virtue of delegated legislation[14] issued under powers granted by Section 10 of the 1961 Act. This delegated legislation is called the Carriage by Air Acts (Application of Provisions) Order 1967, Schedule 2. Some of the more important provisions of Schedule 2, where it differs from the Hague Protocol, will be found in Appendix 6.B. A brief outline of the differences between this regime and the Hague Protocol is given in 6.69-6.81 below.

(3) Non-international carriage and the carriage of mail and postal packets are covered by the Carriage by Air Acts (Application of Provisions) Order, Schedule 1. A brief outline of this regime is given in 6.82-6.84.

(4) Gratuitous carriage not performed by "an air transport undertaking." An example of such carriage would arise where a private person carried friends and their luggage in his private aircraft without payment. This is subject to the English common law. In other words the carrier is liable as a gratuitous bailee in the case of carriage of

[12] It is not an international convention or part of international law.
[13] See 6.64-6.68.
[14] *i.e.* legislation issued by a body to which Parliament has delegated legislative power, in this case to the Queen in Council.

goods[15] and for the tort of negligence in the case of carriage of passengers.[16]

The first three regimes mentioned above have been amended by the Guadalajara Convention[17] which is discussed in 6.64-6.68.

Actions against third parties 6.09

The four regimes outlined above govern the liability of the carrier[18] and in the case of the first three limit his liability for loss, damage and delay. They do not, on the whole,[19] govern the liability of third parties. The owner of goods may have alternative actions in, for example, the tort of negligence against such persons as:

(1) The operator of another aircraft that negligently collided with that in which his goods were being carried.
(2) The manufacturer or company servicing the aircraft on which his goods were being carried.
(3) An air traffic controller or his employer.

If the owner of goods successfully sued any of these persons they could not rely on any of the defences or limits of liability in the Hague Protocol, Warsaw Convention or the Non-International Rules. Note however, that these three regimes of carriage do give the benefit of their defences and limits of liability to actual and successive carriers[20] and also to the carrier's servants and agents.[21]

In addition, the carrier by air as a bailee in possession,[22] has the right to sue any wrongdoer who destroys or damages the goods for substantial damages irrespective of his liability to the owner of the goods[23] under the regimes of carriage.

As to whether a freight forwarder becomes a "carrier" for the purpose of carriage by air and therefore subject to the regimes discussed above and liable for loss or damage during transit, see 2.11.

Common Carriers by Air

Can carriers by air be common carriers? 6.10

There is no reason why a carrier by air cannot be a common carrier.[20] It was held in the Canadian case of *Nysted* v. *Wings*[25] that a carrier by air was a common carrier and it seems that the Privy

[15] See 1.03.
[16] See 1.115-1.119.
[17] Implemented by the Carriage by Air (Supplementary Provisions) Act 1962.
[18] Including "actual" and "successive" carriers.
[19] Unless they are servants or agents of the carrier under Art. 20. As to the meaning of "agent" see 6.41.
[20] See 6.64-6.68.
[21] Art. 25A of the Hague Protocol.
[22] See 1.04.
[23] See 1.04 and 1.96.
[24] *Aslan* v. *Imperial Airways* (1933) 149 L.T. 276, 278, *per* Mackinnon J.
[25] [1942] 3 D.L.R. 336 (Canada).

Council took the same view in *Ludditt* v. *Ginger Cootes Airways.*[26] The current I.A.T.A. conditions of carriage do not seem to deny common carrier status.[27] At first sight, Article 33 of the Protocol would seem to prevent the carrier from being a common carrier but the provision only refers to the "Convention" not preventing the carrier from refusing to carry; it does not stop the common law imposing a duty to carry as a common carrier.

6.11 **The liability of a common carrier by air**

There is no doubt that in principle a common carrier by air can be sued for refusal to carry just as may a carrier by land[28] and by sea.[29] Nevertheless it is clear from Article 24 of the Protocol and its equivalents in the other regimes of carriage that, whether a carrier by air is a common carrier or a private carrier, his liability for loss of or damage to the consigned goods will be governed normally either by the Hague Protocol, the Warsaw Convention or the Non-International Rules and not by the common law.

Hague Protocol. Interpretation and Application

6.12 **Hague Protocol, interpretation**

As explained above in 6.03 the Warsaw Convention as amended by the Hague Protocol, (*i.e.* the Amended Convention or simply Hague Protocol) was enacted into English law by the Carriage by Air Act 1961. The general principles of the interpretation of international conventions have been discussed above in 3.05-3.08. The original French text of the Amended Convention is given in Part II of the Schedule to the the Carriage by Air Act 1961 and an English version in Part I (reproduced in Appendix 6.A). In the event of inconsistency between the French text and the English text the French text prevails.[30]

6.13 **Carriage not covered by the Hague Protocol**

Apart from carriage which is subject to the original unamended Warsaw Convention[31] or the Non-International Rules[32] the Hague Protocol does not cover military carriage by air.[33] Nor does the Protocol cover gratuitous (*i.e.* unpaid) carriage by a non-transport undertaking. Thus, if a private person agreed without reward to deliver goods for a friend by means of his light aircraft then the common law would apply and he would be liable as a gratuitous

[26] [1947] A.C. 233.
[27] As to denial of common carrier status generally see 1.26.
[28] *Crouch* v. *London & North Western Railway* (1854) 14 C.B. 255, discussed in 1.23.
[29] *Bennett* v. *Peninsular & Oriental Steamboat Company* (1848) 6 C.B. 775.
[30] s.1(2) of the Carriage by Air Act 1961.
[31] See 6.69.
[32] See 6.82.
[33] s.7 of the Carriage by Air Act 1961. Presumably such carriage is subject to the common law.

bailee.[34] However the Hague Protocol does apply to gratuitous carriage by transport undertakings, *e.g.* airlines, and by the State.[35]

Article 1(1) refers to carriage by "aircraft." This word is not defined but presumably includes such things as hot air balloons, airships and helicopters as well as more conventional aeroplanes. As the result of Orders in Council issued under the Hovercraft Act 1968 the carriage of cargo by hovercraft is covered not by the Hague Protocol but by the Hague-Visby Rules discussed in Chapter 5. However the Orders in Council do make the Hague Protocol applicable to the carriage of passengers and their baggage by hovercraft.

International carriage, the agreement 6.14

The Hague Protocol only covers "international carriage" as defined in Article 1 (especially Article 1(2)) which should be studied closely). The word "parties" in Article 1(2) presumably includes the consignor of goods who makes the contract as agent for the consignee. The consignee is normally in English law the party to the contract of carriage.[36] The Protocol applies to "agreements" to carry and not only to actual carriage. Thus if A agrees with C that C will carry his (A's) goods from Heathrow (England) to Dublin (Ireland) by air and the plane crashes on take-off then the Hague Protocol will still apply because the agreement is for international carriage even though that agreement has been frustrated. If the agreement is for one single journey it does not matter if the goods are transhipped to another mode of carriage for part of the journey.[37] If they are damaged during the "carriage by air"[38] then the Hague Protocol still applies.

International carriage, agreed stopping places 6.15

Article 1(2) refers to the Protocol applying where there is an "agreed stopping place" outside the territory of a contracting state. A place can be an agreed stopping place even if the carrier does not in fact stop there because of an emergency, as it can also if the stopping place is not actually named on the air waybill.

International carriage, places of departure and destination 6.16

Unlike the C.M.R. Convention[39] on international carriage by road the Hague Protocol only applies if the places of departure and destination as named on the air waybill are *both* in the territories of high contracting parties, (*i.e.* states that have ratified the Protocol). The Protocol also applies to colonies and dependent territories if the colonial power has ratified the Protocol as regards those territories. In England the Privy Council issues delegated legislation known as Orders in Council which are, for the purposes of English law, conclusive proof as to which countries are high contracting parties. If the place of departure is a high contracting party to the Hague

[34] See 1.71.
[35] Art. 2(1).
[36] See 1.10.
[37] Art. 31.
[38] See 6.22-6.23.
[39] See 3.10(*c*).

Protocol but not to the original Warsaw Convention and the place of departure is a party to the original Convention only (or vice versa) then it seems that neither regime applies and the carriage would not be "international." Thus, as far as English law is concerned, the Non-International Rules would apply.[40] However it could alternatively be argued that if a country ratifies the Hague Protocol then it by implication also accepts the original Warsaw Convention.

6.17 **International carriage, illustrations**

The following are examples of what would, and would not, amount to "international" carriage for the purpose of Article 1 of the Hague Protocol. The United Kingdom, Spain and Ireland are all high contracting parties to the Protocol. The United Kingdom has also ratified the Protocol on behalf of its self-governing colony Gibraltar. The United States is a party to the original unamended Warsaw Convention only and the imaginary state of Ruritania is party to neither the Protocol nor the unamended Convention.

EXAMPLES OF "INTERNATIONAL CARRIAGE" UNDER THE HAGUE PROTOCOL

(1) Edinburgh (United Kingdom) to Dublin (Ireland).

(2) Edinburgh to Plymouth (United Kingdom) with an agreed stopping place in Ruritania. This is "international" because although the places of departure and destination are both within the United Kingdom there is an agreed stopping place outside the United Kingdom. Note that in this instance the status of Ruritania is irrelevant. The flight would still be subject to the Hague Protocol even if Ruritania was a party to the unamended Warsaw Convention.

(3) Edinburgh to Ruritania and back to Edinburgh on the same principles as discussed in example (2) above.

(4) Milan (Spain) to Heathrow (United Kingdom) where the goods are by agreement to be transhipped and delivered to another carrier for onward delivery to Edinburgh.[41]

EXAMPLES WHERE THE PROTOCOL DOES NOT APPLY

(1) Edinburgh to Ruritania. Ruritania is not a party to the Protocol so the carriage is not "international."[42]

(2) Gibraltar to Edinburgh. This counts as carriage within the territory of the United Kingdom, *i.e.* what is technically called "cabotage," and is covered by the Non-International Rules.

[40] See 6.82-6.84.

[41] Because the carriage is one operation the Heathrow to Edinburgh section of the journey is subject to the Hague Protocol and not to the Non-International Rules, as it would be if it were a purely internal flight.

[42] It is subject to the Non-International Rules, see 6.82-6.84.

(3) Edinburgh to New York (United States). The United States is a party to the unamended Warsaw Convention only. Therefore this carriage, provided there was no agreement for a return flight to the United Kingdom, is subject to that Convention[43] and not to the Hague Protocol.

(4) Ruritania to Edinburgh with an agreed stopping place in Madrid. Here the agreed stopping place is irrelevant and as the place of departure (Ruritania) is not a high contracting party the carriage is not "international."[44]

International carriage, successive and actual carriers 6.18

Article 1(3) of the Hague Protocol states that carriage performed by a "successive carrier" is deemed to be "international" and therefore covered by the Hague Protocol in the following circumstances. It must be viewed as one operation by the customer and the first carrier and must be clearly divided into separate stages to be carried out by separate carriers. Say that A gives his goods to C to be carried from Edinburgh to Dublin by air. It is agreed between them that C will carry them to Glasgow and then hand them over to D to complete the journey to Dublin. D would be a "successive carrier" for the purposes of Article 1(3). If it is agreed between A and C during the transit to substitute another carrier, E, in place of D then E would become a "successive carrier."[45] Say, on the other hand, A gives his goods to C to be carried from Edinburgh to Dublin. D subcontracts the whole of the carriage to D or, alternatively, without A's permission subcontracts the Glasgow to Dublin portion of the carriage to D. D would not be a "successive carrier" for the purposes of Article 1(3) but rather an "actual carrier." However under Article II of the Guadalajara Convention, implemented into English law by the Carriage by Air Acts (Supplementary Provisions) Act 1962, the Hague Protocol would still apply to the carriage. C would be bound by D's acts[46] and any actions brought against D by A would be subject to the defences and limits of liability in the Protocol.[47] The Guadalajara Convention is discussed further in 6.64-6.68.

Deviation in carriage by air 6.19

In carriage by land and sea at common law an unjustified deviation amounts to a repudiation of the terms of the bailment depriving the carrier of the benefit of his exclusion clauses and making him liable as a wrongful possessor.[48] Section 1 of the 1961 Act says that the Convention shall have the "force of law" to carriage by air where the Protocol is applicable. Article 1 of the Hague Protocol seems to be mandatory and applies the provisions of the Protocol to "all interna-

[43] See 6.69.
[44] See n. 42, above.
[45] *Egan* v. *Kollsman Instrument Corporation* 10 Avi.Cas. 17, 651 (1967) (U.S.A.).
[46] Art. III(2).
[47] Art. II.
[48] See 1.51.

tional carriage" and not contracts of carriage.[49] It is submitted therefore that an unjustified deviation not amounting to "intentional or reckless misconduct" (see 5.49) does not displace the provisions of the Protocol. This was the opinion of Pilcher J. in *Rotterdamsche Bank* v. *B.O.A.C.*[50] It also appears to be the position under Article III(6), *i.e.* the one-year limitation provision, of the Hague-Visby Rules in relation to carriage of goods by sea.[51] However if the Protocol had no statutory application, but was instead incorporated purely as a matter of *contract,* then we suggest that the doctrine of deviation would apply to carriage by air with the same consequences as in carriage by land and sea.

6.20 **Avoidance of the Protocol**

Any attempt to contract out of the Protocol or to reduce its limits of liability is null and void under Article 23. Article 24(1) also appears to prevent the customer avoiding the defences or limits of liability in the Protocol if he sues in bailment or tort.[52]

6.21 **Multimodal transport**

This topic is discussed generally in Chapter 7. Where carriage is to be performed partly by air and partly by some other mode of transport then Article 31 provides that the Protocol only applies to that part of the carriage that is performed by air. However Article 18(3) provides that if there is a contract for the carriage of cargo by air and the cargo is partly carried by some other mode of carriage then any loss, damage or delay is presumed to have occurred during the carriage by air unless it can be proved otherwise. When "carriage by air" commences and ceases for the purposes of the Protocol is discussed in 6.22-6.23 below. If goods on board a lorry are carried by air then the liability of the road carrier will normally be subject to the C.M.R. Convention[53] rather than the Protocol. However the liability of the carrier by air to the road carrier would in turn be subject to the Hague Protocol.

6.22 **"Carriage by air," loss or damage to cargo and luggage**

The liabilities and defences of the Hague Protocol as regards loss of, or damage to cargo and baggage only apply to the air carrier during the period of the "carriage by air." "Carriage by air" for these purposes is defined in Article 18(2) and this provision should be studied closely. The essential point is that the goods should be in the *"charge of the carrier;"* in other words they must have been delivered to the carrier. In *Swiss Bank Corp.* v. *Brinks Mat*[54] three consignments of banknotes were driven in a Brinks Mat security van to the warehouse of the air carrier (K.L.M.) at Heathrow and were unloaded by the

[49] Compare the position in carriage by sea. See 5.36-5.46 and also 6.49-6.50.
[50] [1953] 1 W.L.R. 493.
[51] *The Antares* [1987] 1 Lloyd's Rep. 424. See 5.36.
[52] As to such actions see 1.17-1.20.
[53] See 3.13.
[54] [1986] Q.B. 853.

van's crew. The first two consignments were weighed and checked in by K.L.M.'s handling agents and were therefore in the "charge of the carrier." The third consignment had been unloaded but not yet weighed or checked in, and therefore not yet in the "charge of the carrier," when a gang of armed thieves broke in and stole all three consignments. K.L.M. were only held liable for the first two consignments. If K.L.M.'s agents had unloaded the van, rather than the Brinks Mat employees then they would have been in charge of all three consignments of banknotes the moment they were unloaded. This case also seems to show that goods are "in charge of the carrier" when being handled by his agents.

Even if the owners of cargo or their employees accompany the cargo on the flight then the cargo is still in the carrier's charge and the Hague Protocol applies.[55] When the goods arrive at the airport of destination then they are probably still "in charge of the carrier" even when they are in the actual possession of the Customs authorities.[56]

If cargo to be carried by air is carried by some other mode of carriage then it is presumed that any loss, damage or delay occured during the carriage by air unless proved otherwise.[57]

"Carriage by air," delay to cargo or baggage 6.23

The liability of the carrier by air for delay under the Hague Protocol only applies, by virtue of Article 19, during the "carriage by air." "Carriage by air" in this context of delay, as opposed to loss or damage, is not defined. The best view, however, seems to be that it means exactly the same as it does in relation to loss or damage as defined in Article 18(2) discussed above. This was the opinion of the court in the Guyanan case of *Bart* v. *British West Indian Airways*.[58]

Hague Protocol. Cargo Documentation

Completing the air waybill and customs documents 6.24

Articles 5-16 deal with the documentation that should accompany the cargo. The main document is called the air waybill. Article 5(1) requires the consignor to make out the air waybill and deliver it to the carrier who must accept it. If the carrier fills out the air waybill for the consignor at his request then the carrier is presumed to do so as the agent for the consignor.[59]

The air waybill must be in three parts and be delivered with the cargo.[60] The first, or carrier's copy, has to be marked "for the carrier" and be signed by the consignor.[61] The second copy has to marked "for the consignee" and must be signed by both the consignor and the

[55] *United International Stables* v. *Pacific Western Airlines* (1967) 5 D.L.R.67 (Canada).
[56] *Guardian Assurance* v. *Sabena* (1976) 11 E.T.L. 919 (Belgium).
[57] Art. 18(3).
[58] [1967] 1 Lloyd's Rep. 239.
[59] Art. 6(5).
[60] Art. 6(1).
[61] Art. 6(2).

carrier.[62] This is the copy that accompanies the goods. The third has to be signed by the carrier and delivered by him to the consignor after the cargo has been accepted.[63] The carrier has the right to require separate air waybills for more than one package.[64]

In addition, as in C.M.R., Article 16(1) requires the consignor to supply all necessary information and all necessary customs documents to satisfy customs formalities. For a discussion of the almost identical C.M.R. provisions see 3.20-3.24.

6.25 Contents of the air waybill

Compared with those of the unamended Warsaw Convention[65] the documentation provisions of the Hague Protocol are very simple and the three requirements are listed in Article 8. The air waybill must contain:

1. The place of departure and destination.
2. Any agreed stopping place outside the state if the agreed place of departure and destination are within the same state. Thus in a flight from Edinburgh to London via Ruritania the agreed stopping place in Ruritania must be stated on the air waybill. Note that if the places of departure and destination are in different states then it is not necessary to enter the stopping places on the air waybill.
3. The "Warsaw Statement," *i.e.* a statement that the Warsaw Convention may apply and that it governs and usually limits the carrier's liability. Of course in this context the "Warsaw Convention" means the Convention as amended at the Hague, in other words the Hague Protocol.

Of course, in practice, an air waybill will contain many other particulars such as the weight, value and nature of the cargo. However under the Hague Protocol such contents are not legally necessary.[66]

6.26 Absence or irregularity of the air waybill

If there is no air waybill issued, or if it is defective in some way or is lost then the Hague Protocol still applies.[67] However if the cargo is loaded on board the aircraft without an air waybill having been made out then the carrier loses the limits of liability in Article 22(2).[68] Presumably the carrier cannot satisfy this requirement by merely "making out" an air waybill and never giving it to the customer. If the goods are lost or damaged at the airport during the "carriage by air"[69] before they were loaded on to the aircraft then presumably the carrier could still rely on the limits of liability in Article 22(2) even if no air waybill has been issued. Likewise if the air waybill does not contain

[62] *Ibid.*
[63] Art. 6(2).
[64] Art. 7.
[65] See 6.71-6.72, 6.78 and 6.81.
[66] But see 6.26, below.
[67] Art. 52.
[68] Art. 9. As to limits of liability, see 6.45-6.48.
[69] See 6.22-6.23.

the "Warsaw Statement"[70] then the carrier again loses the limits of liability in Article 22(2). However it would seem to follow that if the air waybill is only missing either or both of the first two requirements of Article 8, *i.e.* places of departure/destination and stopping places, then the carrier could still rely on Article 22(2) to limit his liability.

In addition, Article 34 excuses the carrier from all his duties concerning documentation where the carriage is "performed in extraordinary circumstances outside the normal scope of an air carrier's business." Presumably therefore if an air carrier is required to carry urgent medical supplies to a disaster area he would not be liable for failure to issue an air waybill and could still rely on the Protocol's limits of liability.

It should be noted that the provisions concerning the absence or irregularity of documentation in the unamended Warsaw Convention as regards baggage and cargo are different and more draconian. See the brief discussion of this topic in 6.72 and compare the position as regards passenger documentation under the unamended Convention as discussed in 6.78.

The air waybill as a receipt and evidence of the contract 6.27

By virtue of Article 11 the air waybill is prima facie evidence of the making of the contract and of its terms as well as a receipt for the cargo.[71] In practice, although not required by Article 8, the air waybill will state such matters as the weight and condition of the cargo. If these statements on the air waybill concern weight, dimensions, packing and number of packages then these are prima facie evidence against the carrier. In other words it is presumed these statements are true. If, for example, the air waybill states that 10 cases of glass have beeen consigned then the burden is on the carrier to prove, for example, that he only received nine cases.

Statements as to quantity, volume and condition do not normally constitute such evidence against the carrier unless:

1. They have been checked by the carrier in the presence of the consignor and;
2. Are stated on the air waybill to have been so checked.

So if the air waybill stated that a package contained 100 glass decanters this would only be evidence that the package actually contained 100 decanters if the carrier had checked the quantity and recorded on the air waybill that he had checked the quantity. Apparently, from the rather confusing last words of Article 11(2), it seems that if the air waybill stated that the cargo was "apparently in good condition" then this would be prima facie evidence against the carrier that it was in apparent good condition even if the condition had not been checked by the carrier, etc. Article 11(2) seems to be drawing a distinction between a statement as to actual condition and one as to apparent condition. If the waybill stated that the cargo was "in good condition" then the burden is upon the person suing the

[70] See Art. 8(c).
[71] Compare the functions of a Bill of lading outlined in 5.07-5.12.

carrier to prove that it was in good condition. The statement on the waybill will not assist the customer. If, on the other hand, the air waybill stated that the goods were "in apparent good condition" then the burden is on the carrier to prove that they were not apparently in good condition.

The consignor is responsible for the correctness of any particulars about the cargo that he enters on the consignment note.[72] If the particulars are incorrect then he must indemnify the carrier under Article 10(2) for any damage or liability to others that the carrier suffers as a result. Presumably, in addition to this right of indemnity given under Article 10(2), the common law consignor's warranty of fitness discussed in 1.94-1.97 would grant an alternative ground of action where dangerous goods were given to a carrier and caused death or injury.

6.28 The air waybill as a negotiable instrument?

Article 15(3) states that an air waybill may be "negotiable." "Negotiable" in this context does not mean negotiable in the strict legal sense but rather "transferable." In other words an air waybill may be a document of title or ownership as is a bill of lading in the law of carriage by sea.[73] Whether an air waybill is in fact a document of title presumably depends upon the law that governs the making of the contract. As far as English law is concerned whether a document is a document of title depends upon "the custom of merchants." In other words it depends whether the document is recognised as "negotiable" by the business community. It seems that in England the business community do not recognise an air waybill as "negotiable."

HAGUE PROTOCOL. RIGHTS OF POSSESSION TO THE CARGO

6.29 Rights of control over the cargo in transit, introduction

As stated in 1.07-1.09 where goods are sold by A to B to be delivered via C, a carrier then, by virtue of Section 18 of the Sale of Goods Act 1979, the property in the goods normally passes to the buyer/consignee at the moment the goods are delivered to the carrier. It has been held that Articles 12 and 13 of the Hague Protocol do not affect the passing of property and the relationship between the buyer and seller in English law[75] and Article 15(1) seems to confirm this. Nevertheless the philosophy of the Hague Protocol is based on Continental law which basically takes the view, contrary to English law, that the consignor is a party to the contract and can enforce it. As a result Articles 12 and 13 grant to the consignor rights of control and

[72] Art. 10(1).
[73] See 5.11.
[74] See 1.04-1.11.
[75] *Morton Norwich Products* v. *Intercen Ltd.* [1978] Restrictive Practice Cases 501.

disposition over the goods much wider than those granted by Sections 44-46 of the Sale of Goods Act 1979.[76] The consignee's rights only come into existence when the cargo arrives at the airport of destination or if the cargo is lost or delayed.[77]

The consignor's rights of control during transit 6.30

Article 12(1) grants the following rights to the consignor:

(1) To withdraw the cargo at the airport of departure.

(2) To withdraw the cargo at the airport of destination.

(3) To stop the goods in transit.

(4) To order that the goods be delivered at a stopping place or at the airport of destination to someone other than the original consignee named on the air waybill.

(5) To have the goods returned to the consignor at the airport of departure.

Article 14 allows the consignor to exercise these rights on his own behalf or on behalf of the true owner, *e.g.* the consignee, if the consignor is not the owner himself. So if the consignee sold the goods in transit he could ask the consignor to order the carrier to deliver to the new owner of the cargo.

Consignor's rights, reconciliation with English law 6.31

It should be noted that in Article 12(1) there is no requirement, as there is in English law,[78] that the consignor be an unpaid seller or that the consignee, if he is a buyer, be unable to pay his debts. In fact, at first sight, a seller-consignor could exercise his rights over the goods under Article 12(1) even though he has been paid in advance for them and they are the consignee's property. Note however that Article 14 grants these rights to a consignor acting "in his own interests or in the interests of another." A seller/consignor who has been paid in advance normally has no interest in the goods. Say that such a consignor wrongfully deprived a consignee/buyer of the goods by exercising his rights under Article 12(1). Presumably Article 12(1) would be no defence to an action brought by the buyer/consignee against the seller/consignor for breach of the contract of sale or for the tort of conversion.

Say that the consignee/buyer sued an air carrier for the tort of conversion because the carrier had obeyed the instructions of a consignor exercising his rights under Article 12(1). In that case Article 12(1) would give a statutory defence to such an action. In addition it seems that the original consignee has no right to sue the carrier for loss of the goods during transit under Articles 13(3) or 14 if the carrier has obeyed the instructions of the consignor exercising his powers

[76] See 1.73-1.74.
[77] Art. 13(1).
[78] See n. 76, above.

under Article 12(1).[79] The consignor may have no right to exercise those powers but the carrier is not to know this. If the carrier did in fact know that the consignor was acting unlawfully and that the consignor had no "interests" in the goods then the position is doubtful. The best course of action for the air carrier would be to "interplead." In other words he should go to the court and ask for the court's directions.

6.32 **Restrictions on the consignor's powers of control over goods**

The Hague Protocol sets certain restrictions on the consignor's powers of control over the goods in transit. These are as follows:

A. The rights of control over the cargo granted by Articles 12-14 can be altered by an agreement recorded on the air waybill.[80] Thus a consignor/seller could, if he wished, give the rights of control over the cargo granted by Article 12(1) to the buyer/consignee.

B. The rights granted by Article 12(1) to the consignor are "subject to his liability to carry out all his obligations under the contract of carriage." Whether this provision makes the consignor liable to pay the freight will be discussed in 6.36 below. In addition, a consignor exercising his powers of control over the cargo during transit must pay the carrier any expenses the carrier thus incurs.

C. The consignor cannot exercise his rights of control over the cargo under Article 12(1) if this would prejudice the carrier or other consignors. Presumably therefore a consignor could not withdraw the goods at the airport of departure if this would cause serious delay in the departure of an aircraft.

D. Before the consignor can exercise his rights under Article 12(1) he must produce his copy of the air waybill.[81] If the carrier obeys the instructions of the consignor without requiring the production of the copy of the air waybill then he may be liable to anybody who is in possession of that copy, *e.g.* a bank to whom it had been pledged as security for a loan.

E. If it is impossible to obey the consignor's instructions as to the disposal of the goods then the carrier should inform the consignor forthwith.[82]

F. The consignor loses his rights of control over the goods under Article 12(1) in any of the circumstances laid down by Article 13,[83] namely where:

(i) The cargo arrives at the airport of destination and the consignee requires the carrier to deliver to him the consignee's copy of the air waybill and the cargo.[84]

(ii) The carrier admits the cargo is lost.[85]

[79] It is submitted that the consignee can only sue for loss or damage under Art. 13(3) if he is entitled to delivery of the goods. To hold otherwise would create a great injustice to the carrier.

[80] Art. 15(2).

[81] Art. 12(3).

[82] Art. 12(2).

[83] See also 6.33, below.

[84] Art. 13(1).

[85] Art. 13(3).

(iii) The cargo has not arrived seven days after it is due to have arrived.[86]

However if the consignee rejects the goods or air waybill or, alternatively, cannot be communicated with then the rights of control revert to the consignor.[87]

The consignee's rights at the airport of destination 6.33

Unless the consignor has exercised his rights of control over the cargo under Article 12(1),[88] once the cargo has arrived at the airport of destination, the consignee has the right[89] to require the carrier to deliver to him the third copy of the air waybill and the cargo itself. The consignee can exercise these rights on his own account or on behalf of the true owner.[90] He can, however, only exercise these rights if he pays the "charges" and he complies with any delivery conditions set out in the air waybill. It seems therefore that Article 13(1) grants the carrier a stautory lien for the freight whether he is a common carrier or not. The word "charges" obviously includes any outstanding freight and presumably any expenses incurred under Article 12(1). Presumably the word "consignee" in Article 13(1) means the new consignee if the consignor has exercised his rights under Article 12(1) to substitute a new consignee in place of that originally named in the air waybill. The result is that the new consignee cannot obtain the cargo unless he pays these "charges" as well as the freight.

It is the carrier's duty, unless otherwise agreed, to give notice of arrival of the goods to the consignee.[91] Again presumably the word "consignee" includes a new consignee.

Hague Protocol. Who can Sue and be Sued?

Who can sue the carrier for loss of the cargo? 6.34

As explained in 1.05 at common law the contract is presumed to be between the owners of the goods and the carrier. The owner is normally the consignee and he is the correct person to sue on the contract.[92]

Article 13(3) of the Hague Protocol states that if the carrier admits the loss of the goods or the goods have not arrived within seven days after they should have arrived then the consignee can sue on the contract for the loss or delay. Obviously the original consignee can only sue the carrier under this provision if the consignor has not exercised his rights under Article 12(1) by sending the goods to

[86] *Ibid.* See also 6.33, below.
[87] Art. 12(4).
[88] See 6.32, above.
[89] Art 13(1).
[90] Art. 14.
[91] Art. 13(2).
[92] See 1.10.

someone other than the original consignee named on the air waybill.[93] The original consignee, however, if he is the true owner of the cargo, might conceivably have some other action against the carrier at common law for negligence or for breach of bailment[94] if he had obeyed the consignor's instructions knowing that he was acting dishonestly and that the goods belonged to the consignee.

If the consignee was not the owner of the goods because, *e.g.* he was merely a freight forwarder presumably Article 14 would grant him the right to sue for substantial damages on behalf of the true owner. However there is no mechanism by means of which the owner could force the consignee to sue. If the consignee refused to sue and if the owner had no right of action, the air carrier would not be liable for the loss to anyone. Note also that Article 14 grants the consignee the right to sue for loss or delay but does not at first sight give him such a right to sue for damage to the goods. However one could argue that the consignee is implicitly given the right to sue for damage by Article 13(3) or by virtue of his right to demand the goods. If Article 14 gives the only right to sue for loss or delay to the consignee and the true owner had to sue for damage the position would be absurd. However in the case of *Tasman Pulp and Paper* v. *Brambles.*[95] Prichard J. was of the opinion, although he did not have to decide the point and therefore his opinion was technically *obiter*, that Article 14 was only an enabling provision. In other words it entitled the consignor or consignee to sue for loss or delay on behalf of others but it did not mean that they were the only persons who could sue.[96] We suggest that this view is correct.

In addition, one could argue that the consignor only has the right to sue on behalf of others up to such time as the consignee demands the cargo and the air waybill at the airport of destination under Article 13(1). At that point the right to sue passes to the consignee unless, perhaps, the goods still belong to the consignor.

6.35 Who can sue the carrier for delay to the cargo?

Exactly the same comments as were made in respect of loss of the cargo in 6.34 above equally apply to its delay. Another difficulty however, arises as regards claims for delay brought by the true owner of the goods who is not in fact a party to the contract of carriage. The question is whether, if a bailor who is not the consignor or consignee sues in bailment, the bailee is liable for negligent delay as opposed to loss of or damage to the cargo. The Guyanan case of *Bart* v. *British West Indian Airways*[97] denied the plaintiff a remedy in such a case

[93] See 6.31.

[94] See 1.17-1.20.

[95] [1981] 2 N.Z.L.R. 25 (New Zealand). See now *Gatewhite Ltd.* v. *Iberia Lineas Aereas* H.Ct. (unreported), noted J.B.L. [1988] 424.

[96] Shawcross and Beaumont, *Air Law* (4th ed., 1983), at para. VII, 188 state that Art. 15(3) permitting a negotiable air waybill supports this view. However, if a negotiable air waybill was endorsed in favour of a new consignee it is suggested that he would become "the consignee" for the purposes of Art. 14.

[97] [1967] 1 Lloyd's Rep. 239.

when his football coupon was delayed by the defendants' negligence (note however, that the delay was not during the "carriage by air"[98]). However it is submitted that the decision is unjust and wrongly decided. The court did not take into account the cases of *Danish Dairies Co-operative Society* v. *Midland Railway*[99] and *Kyle* v. *Buffalo & Lake Huron Railway*[1] in both of which it seems that the defendants were held liable as bailees for negligent delay even though there was no contractual relationship between them and the plaintiffs. If the person who contracted with the carrier refuses to sue and the true owner cannot sue in bailment for delay then the negligent air carrier/bailee completely escapes liability and the unfortunate owner of the goods has no remedy. If this is the law then it is manifestly unjust and in need of reform.

Who can sue the carrier for damage? 6.36

Article 14[2] grants the right to the consignor or consignee to sue the carrier for loss or delay on behalf of the true owner though it seems that they cannot be forced to do so. What if the goods were damaged in transit? In that case Article 14 perhaps does not apply.[3] In *Tasman Pulp* v. *Brambles*[4] it was held that the owner of goods damaged in transit who was not the named consignor or consignee could sue in bailment and, if he could prove that he was a party to the contract of carriage, in contract as well. It is submitted that this case is correctly decided and if the law were not so the carrier might not be liable for substantial damages for damage to the cargo to anybody.

Actions against successive carriers 6.37

The distinction between a "successive carrier" and an "actual carrier"[5] has been discussed in 6.18. Essentially under Article 1(3) where part of carriage which is regarded as one operation is performed by more than one carrier then the carriers are called successive carriers. Article 30(1) states that a successive carrier becomes a party to the contract "in so far as the contract deals with that part of the carriage which is performed under his supervision." Presumably therefore each successive carrier can sue the appropriate person[6] for the unpaid freight owing in respect of his section of the journey and presumably must obey the consignor's instructions in relation to the cargo under Article 12.[7] Article 30(3) provides that the consignor can sue the first carrier, that the consignee entitled to delivery can sue the last carrier and that "each may take action against the carrier who performed the carriage during which the destruction, loss, damage or delay took place." The wording of Article 30(3) makes it plain that this

[98] See 6.22-6.23.
[99] (1892) 8 T.L.R. 212.
[1] (1865) 16 C.P. 76 (Canada).
[2] See 6.34.
[3] See 6.34.
[4] [1981] 2 N.Z.L.R. 25 (New Zealand), see now Gatewhite Ltd. v. *Iberia Lineas Aereas* [1989] 1 Lloyd's Rep. 160.
[5] As to actions against the "actual carrier," see 6.64-6.68.
[6] As to who is liable to pay freight, see 6.38-6.39, below.
[7] See 6.34.

provision does not mean that the consignor and consignee can sue two different carriers and recover damages twice over in two different countries. In fact Article 30(3) is difficult to reconcile with Article 14 discussed in 6.34-6.36. We suggest that a successful action against one carrier for substantial damages by either the consignor, consignee or the owner of the goods[8] would preclude any subsequent action against the same carrier or any other carrier by any other person.

6.38 **The liability of the consignor to pay the freight**

The basic principles of the law relating to freight have been outlined in 1.106-1.107 and 5.51-5.58. Whether the unjust rule in the *Aries Tanker*[9] applies to carriage by air under international Conventions has yet to be decided.[10]

In 1.10 we suggested that in a "three party" contract[11] of carriage by land the consignor normally makes the contract of carriage as agent for the consignee. Therefore, unless there is a course of dealings or a collateral contract between the consignor and the carrier by means of which the consignor has promised to pay the freight, we suggested that the consignor, as a mere agent is not *prima facie* liable to pay the freight. The person *prima facie* liable to pay the freight is the consignee. We submit that, subject to any express provisions in the Hague Protocol, where the contract is subject to English law the same principles apply to carriage by air. Admittedly there are two carriage by air cases[12] in which consignors were held liable to pay the freight but the defendant consignors foolishly did not even argue that they were not liable to pay as mere agents so these cases are not against our proposition.

If the consignor exercises his right of control over the goods granted by Article 12(1)[13] then he must "carry out all his obligations under the contract of carriage." We submit that *prima facie* the obligation to pay freight is not his (*i.e.* the consignor's) "obligation under the contract" but rather that of the consignee. However if he exercises his rights of control over the goods he should be liable to pay the freight just as he is if he has exercised his rights of stoppage in transit under section 44-46 of the Sale of Goods act 1979.[14]

A carrier by air may be a common carrier.[15] If he were a common carrier he would have a lien against the whole world for his freight charges.[16] If the consignor exercised his rights under Article 12(1) by

[8] It is submitted that a consignor is not normally entitled to substantial damages "on his own account" as he is not normally the owner of the goods. See 1.13.

[9] [1977] 1 W.L.R. 185.

[10] It is suggested that it is an anomaly and should be restricted to carriage by sea. See 1.107, 5.50 and 5.52.

[11] *i.e.* a contract of carriage in which the consignor and consignee are different persons.

[12] *Swiss Air Transport* v. *Palmer* [1976] 2 Lloyd's Rep. 604, *Panalpina International Transport* v. *Densil Underwear* [1981] 1 Lloyd's Rep. 187.

[13] See 6.29-6.31.

[14] See 1.74.

[15] See 6.10.

[16] See 1.110-1.111.

repossessing the goods it is suggested he would have to discharge the common carrier's lien. If the carrier by air were a private carrier he would probably have no common law lien for the freight.[17]

Liability of the consignee to pay freight 6.39

In a "three party" contract we submitted in 1.105 that the consignee, if the owner of the cargo, is prima facie liable to pay the freight.[18] If the consignor exercises his rights under Article 12(1) to nominate a new consignee then the original prima facie liability to pay freight on the part of the original consignee seems to be transferred to the new consignee by virtue of Article 13(1) when he demands the cargo and the air waybill at the airport of destination. If the contract was such that freight was payable even though the goods had been lost in transit and they were lost after they had been reconsigned to the new consignee then whether the new consignee would be liable to pay the freight is unknown. However, as stated in 6.38, in such circumstances it seems the consignor would be liable.

Article 13(1) creates a liability on the consignee to pay the freight when he demands the cargo and air waybill at the airport of destination. This liability under Article 13(1) would arise whether he were the true owner or not. We suggest that, in addition to the consignee's liability under Article 13(1), if the true owner were someone other than the named consignee he also would be liable for the freight upon common law principles[19] if it could be proved that he was in reality a party to the contract of carriage.

Hague Protocol. Liability for Loss, Damage and Delay

Introduction 6.40

Under the Hague Protocol, as at common law,[20] the carrier is prima facie liable under Article 18(1) for loss or damage to cargo during the "carriage by air."[21]; However, as we explain later in 6.54, the provisions of Article 26(2) may make it more difficult for the plaintiff to prove damage than loss. The carrier also appears to be prima facie liable for delay[22] under Article 19. He has, however, two defences which are available to him under Articles 20 and 21. The burden of proving these defences falls on the carrier. Presumably, as in English law, he merely has to prove these defences on the balance of probabilities.[23]

The defence of "all necessary measures" 6.41

By virtue of Article 20 of the Protocol the carrier is not liable for loss, damage or delay to cargo "if he and his servants and agents took all

[17] See 1.110.
[18] Because the owner is presumed to be a party to the contract of carriage. See 1.05.
[19] See 1.106.
[20] See 1.17.
[21] See 6.22.
[22] See 6.43, below.
[23] See 1.89.

necessary measures to avoid the damage or that it was impossible" to take such measures. The word "damage" in Article 20 means "damage to the plaintiff" and includes damage to him caused by loss of, or delay to the cargo as well as physical damage to the cargo. If one interpreted this defence of "all necessary measures" literally then it would mean that the defence would never be available! This is because if the carrier had taken all necessary measures to avoid the damage then the damage would never have happened! However, both in passenger cases[24] and the cargo case of *Swiss Bank Corp.* v. *Brinks Mat*[25] these words have been interpreted as meaning "all reasonably necessary measures" or all measures which a reasonable man would deem necessary. The cases are not entirely clear on this point but the *Swiss Bank* case seems to show that that this standard of care is a slightly higher one than that imposed by the English law of negligence or breach of bailment.[26] It does not seem as high a standard of care, however, as that required by the C.M.R. Convention[27] in relation to the carriage of goods by road.

The defence of all necessary measures is illustrated by the passenger case of *Chisholm* v. *B.E.A.*[28] in which a passenger was instructed to fasten her seat belt and remain in her seat because air turbulence was expected. She disobeyed this instruction and got up to visit the toilet. While she was doing so the aircraft was hit by turbulence and the plaintiff was thrown to the floor and injured. The court held that the carriers were not liable because they had taken "all necessary measures" to avoid the accident.

There seem to have been no cases on the word "agents" in Article 20. However, it seems that the word would encompass any independent contractors who assist in some aspects of the "carriage by air."[29] Thus it would probably include firms that prepare food for passengers, who are handling agents for cargo and those who refuel aircraft.

6.42 The defence of "contributory negligence"

Article 21 grants the carrier the partial or total defence of contributory negligence by the "injured person." At first sight one might have thought that these words limited the defence to carriage of passengers. However it seems from the decision of the High Court in *Rustenberg Platinum Mines* v. *South African Airways*[30] that the defence is also open in cargo claims as well as those brought by passengers. Thus if cargo was damaged in transit due solely to improper packing by the consignor then we suggest that improper packing is a form of contributory negligence and that the carrier would be under no liability. If the cargo was damaged partly because of improper

[24] *Grein* v. *Imperial Airways* [1937] 1 K.B. 50, *Goldman* v. *Thai Airways* [1983] 1 W.L.R. 1186.
[25] [1986] 2 Lloyd's Rep. 79.
[26] See 1.03 and 1.33-1.34.
[27] See 3.47.
[28] [1963] 1 Lloyd's Rep. 79.
[29] See 6.22.
[30] [1977] 1 Lloyd's Rep. 564, affirmed on other grounds [1979] 1 Lloyd's Rep. 19.

packing and partly by the carrier's failure to take "all necessary measures" to look after the cargo then the plaintiff's damages would be reduced. By how much the damages would be reduced is unclear in some instances because of the following difficulty. Under Article 22(2)[31] the carrier's liability is normally limited to 250 gold francs per kilogram. This is roughly equivalent to £14 per kilogram. Say that goods worth £20 per kilo were lost in transit and that the court held that the loss was caused equally by the contributory negligence of the plaintiff and equally by the failure of the carrier to take "all necessary measures." In that eventuality there are two possible interpretations of Article 21. First it could mean that the plaintiff would recover 50 per cent. of his actual loss of £20 per kilo; thus he would recover a net sum of £10 per kilo. Secondly it could mean that he recovers 50 per cent. of the maximum liability under Article 22(2), *i.e.* £14 per kilo, thus leaving the carrier with a maximum liability of £7 per kilogram. Surprisingly this point never seems to have been decided.

Liability for delay to cargo 6.43

Under Article 19 the carrier is liable for delay during the "carriage by air."[32] "Delay" in this context seems to mean the same as it does at common law,[33] *i.e.* a failure to deliver within an agreed or reasonable time. Arguably if the goods have not arrived at the airport of destination within seven days of the time they should have arrived under the provisions of Article 13(3)[34] then this would be evidence of delay. If the goods are delayed the carrier would not be liable if he could prove that he took "all necessary measures" or that the cause of the delay was the plaintiff's (or his agent's) contributory negligence.[35] Thus if cargo was delayed by weather conditions despite all diligence on the part of the carrier or was delayed by negligent addressing of the cargo by the consignor then the carrier would not be liable. Thus, apart from the fact that the defence of "all necessary measures" may create a slightly higher standard of care[36] than that imposed by the common law, the liability of a carrier by air for delay is much the same as that of a carrier by land at common law as discussed in 1.37. These principles are illustrated by the case of *Panalpina International Transport* v. *Densil Underwear*[37] in which the plaintiff carriers sued for unpaid freight and the defendant-sellers of goods counterclaimed for delay in delivery. It was held that 19 days was not a reasonable time in which to deliver a cargo of shirts by air from the United Kingdom to Nigeria. The carriers failed to prove that they had taken "all necessary measures" to avoid the delay and were held liable.

Liability of the carrier's servants and agents 6.44

Article 25A(1) provides that if an action is brought against the carrier's servants or agents then, provided they were acting in the

[31] See 6.45-6.48.
[32] See 6.23.
[33] See 1.37.
[34] Surprisingly this point never seems to have arisen in a case.
[35] See Art. 21.
[36] See 6.41.
[37] [1981] 1 Lloyd's Rep. 187.

course of their employment,[38] they also can rely on the limits of liability in Article 22.[39] What is not entirely clear is if the action is brought in tort or bailment against the servant or agent whether the basis of their liability is the same as that of the carrier under Articles 18-21.[40] Article 24(1) states that any actions for loss damage or delay under Articles 18 and 19 "however founded" are subject to the conditions and limits laid down by the Protocol. The difficulty is, however, that Articles 18 and 19 refer to the liability of the carrier and not to that of his servants and agents. Unless the word "carrier" is interpreted to include the carrier's servants and agents it could be argued that actions against a servant for the tort of negligence or against a handling agent for breach of bailment are not actions against the "carrier." Therefore Article 24(1) would not apply and the liability of servants and agents, as opposed to their limits of liability, would be governed by the common law.

Hague Protocol. Limits of Liability

6.45 **Remoteness of damage and the gold franc problem**

In actions for loss of, or damage or delay to cargo then, if the contract is subject to English law, the damages must be reasonably foreseeable[41] Thus in *Panalpina* v. *Densil Underwear*[42] the plaintiffs delivered the defendant's goods late to Nigeria. The defendant had informed the carriers that it was essential that the goods should arrive in time for the Christmas market in Nigeria. It was therefore held that the carriers were liable in damages for the difference between the price the goods were actually sold for and the price they would have been sold for if they had arrived in time. In other words this difference in price was reasonably foreseeable.

In addition the carrier's liability for loss, damage and also, rather surprisingly, for delay[43] is limited, under Article 22(2), to 250 gold francs per kilogram. However these limits can be exceeded where there has been a declaration of value[44] or the carrier is guilty of "reckless or intentional misconduct."[45] A gold "franc" is defined in Article 2(5) as a certain weight of gold. As explained in 3.60, however, gold now has no fixed price and this has caused great difficulty when attempting to calculate the limits of the carrier's liability. If and when the Montreal Protocols[46] come into effect under the Carriage by Air

[38] As to the meaning of course or scope of employment, see 1.18 and 1.116.
[39] See 6.45.
[40] See 6.40-6.43.
[41] See 1.39-1.42.
[42] [1981] 1 Lloyd's Rep. 187.
[43] Compare the C.M.R. Convention in which liability for delay is limited to the carriage charges. See 3.64.
[44] See 6.48.
[45] See 6.49-6.50.
[46] See 6.86.

and Road Act 1979 then gold francs will be replaced by Special Drawing Rights.[47] However, as regards almost all actions brought in the English courts, the value of a "gold franc" is fixed by delegated legislation known as Sterling Equivalent Orders. This legislation is issued by the Secretary of State for Transport under powers granted by Section 4(1) of the Carriage by Air Act 1961. The latest Sterling Equivalent Order, issued in 1986, fixes the limit of liability per kilo, *i.e.* 250 gold francs, as approximately £14.

Limits of liability, further problems 6.46

Where only part of the cargo is lost, damaged or delayed then the limits of liability only attach to the parts of the cargo actually lost, damaged or delayed.[48] So if five packages each weighing one kilo are given to a carrier and one package is lost then the maximum liability of the carrier will be 1 × 250 gold francs, *i.e.* approximately £14, and will not be calculated on the weight of the whole consignment, *i.e.* five kilos. However if the loss of one package affects the value of other packages, *e.g.* the loss of one of a set of packages containing the parts of a valuable antique clock, then this factor can be taken into account.[49]

Article 23(1) forbids the carrier from contractually exempting liability or limiting liability below the limits laid down by Article 22(2). However Article 23(2) allows an exception to this prohibition in the case of limits of liability for "inherent vice."[50] Thus he is permitted to reduce these limits of liability where there has been inherent vice in the cargo. At first sight Article 23(2) is incomprehensible. If cargo deteriorates because of inherent vice then the carrier surely would not be liable in any event. Could he not plead "all necessary measures" or "contributory negligence" under Article 20 and 21 respectively? Why does he need to limit liability for what he is not liable for? The only interpretation the writers can think of that makes sense of Article 23(2) is as follows:

Say a carrier put a clause in his contract limiting his liability to 125 gold francs (approx £7) per kilo where there has been inherent vice in the cargo. Cargo worth £20 per kilo is destroyed partly by inherent vice (*i.e.* contributory negligence) and equally by the carrier's failure to take "all necessary measures." Let us assume that the second interpretation of Article 21 discussed above in 6.42 is correct, namely that in these circumstances the carrier's liability would now, if there were no limitation clause, be reduced to £10 per kilo. In these circumstances, where the carrier had the 125 gold franc limitation clause he could reduce his liability further, namely from £10 per kilo to £7 per kilo.

Limits of liability. Carrier's servants and agents 6.47

If the carrier's servants or agents are sued rather than the carrier himself then the basis of their liability is unclear.[51] However by virtue

[47] See 3.60.

[48] Art. 22(2)(b).

[49] Compare *Data Card Corp.* v. *Air Express* [1984] 1 W.L.R. 198 decided under the original Warsaw Convention. Discussed below in 6.74.

[50] As to the meaning of "inherent vice," see 1.28.

[51] See 6.44.

of Article 25A(1) their liability is limited on the same basis as is the carrier's under Article 22. If, for example, the carrier has failed to issue an air waybill the carrier cannot rely on the limit of liability in Article 22.[52] Presumably therefore if the action is brought against the servant or agent of the carrier they also would be precluded from relying on Article 22 to limit liability. This seems very unjust.

If the servant or agent is guilty of intentional or reckless wrongdoing[53] then by virtue of Article 25A(3) he also loses the protection of the limits of liability in Article 22.

One cannot double the limits of liability under Article 22 by suing the carrier's servant or agent actually responsible for the loss or damage as well as the carrier himself. Article 25A(2) thus provides that the aggregate amount of damages recovered from the carrier together with his servants and agents must not exceed the limits of liability laid down by Article 22.

6.48 **Declarations of value**

The carrier's liability can be increased beyond the limits laid down by Article 22(2) if the consignor, at the time of the delivery of the goods to the carrier, has made a "declaration of interest in delivery at destination" and paid a surcharge where required. There is no requirement that this declaration should be made on the air waybill or in any particular form. So, in theory, it could be made by word of mouth which would hardly be satisfactory. Most air carriers' conditions of carriage state that the declaration must be on the air waybill. Whether such a contractual condition would be null and void under Article 23(1) is unclear. The fact that a consignor states the value of the goods, *e.g.* for customs purposes, does not necessarily mean that he has made a declaration of "special interest" for the purpose of Article 22(2)(a).[54] Note that "special interest" does not only cover the actual value of the goods. It would also cover a statement to the effect that if the goods did not arrive by a certain date the owner would lose, *e.g.* £5,000 profits on resale. If the carrier can prove that the declaration of interest is untrue, *e.g.* he can prove that the goods are not in fact worth their declared value, then he will presumably only be liable for their actual value; although the wording of Article 22(2)(a) is vague in this respect. Presumably the use of the word "consignor" in the last line of Article 22(2)(a) also includes the consignee or any other person suing the carrier.[55] If this were not so then in a "three party" contract a consignee could not recover any damages because the consignor would normally have no interest in the goods.[56]

[52] See 6.45.
[53] See 6.49-6.50.
[54] *Corocraft* v. *Pan American Airways* [1969] 1 Q.B. 616.
[55] See 6.34-6.36.
[56] See 1.13-1.14.

HAGUE PROTOCOL. "INTENTIONAL OR RECKLESS" MISCONDUCT

Introduction 6.49

Article 25 states that the carrier cannot rely on the limits of liability in Article 22 if the plaintiff can prove that the loss, damage or delay was caused by "an act or omission of the carrier, his servants or agents, done with intent to cause damage or recklessly and with knowledge that damage would probably result." The air carrier can still in theory rely on the Protocol defences, as opposed to the limits of liability, if guilty of such "misconduct." However a carrier guilty of such wrongdoing would in practice find it impossible to successfully plead the defence of "all necessary measures." In addition for the carrier to be held liable for the misconduct of a servant or agent then it must also be proved that the servant or agent was acting "within the scope of his employment."[57] It is important to emphasise in this context that the burden of proving wrongdoing under Article 25 on the part of the carrier falls on the plaintiff.

If the plaintiff sues the servants or agents of the carrier instead of the carrier himself then they also lose the limits of liability under Article 22 if they are guilty of intentional or reckless misconduct.[58]

The meaning of "intentional or reckless misconduct" 6.50

The leading case on the meaning of Article 25 is the passenger case of *Goldman* v. *Thai Airways*[59] In *Goldman* the pilot of an aircraft was told of two areas of moderate clear air turbulence on his route. Clear air turbulence is something that is not visible to a pilot and which can hit an aircraft with no warning to him. The flight manual instructed pilots to tell passengers to fasten their seatbelts when air turbulence could be expected. However on this occasion the pilot failed to do this when approaching the area concerned. The aircraft hit severe rather than the moderate air turbulence expected and the plaintiff was thrown upwards against the roof of the aircraft and injured. The Court of Appeal held that in order to satisfy the requirements of Article 25 the plaintiff must prove three things:

(1) That the damage resulted from the act or omission.

(2)(a)That the act was done with intent to cause damage or

(b) That it was done recklessly with knowledge that damage would probably result.

(3) That the damage that occurred was of the type known by the guilty person to be the probable result of his acts.

There was no doubt that the first test was satisfied and equally it was clear that the pilot had not intended to injure the plaintiff. Were, however, the pilot's acts reckless and with knowledge that injury was probable? The court decided that they were not. The test of reckless-

[57] As to the meaning of "course or scope of employment," see 1.18 and 1.116.
[58] Art. 25A(iii).
[59] [1983] 1 W.L.R. 1186.

ness was subjective and not objective. The state of the pilot's mind was the essential thing. The court was "not entitled to attribute to him knowledge which another pilot might have possessed or which he himself should have possessed." The likelihood was that the pilot had just forgotten the instructions and not deliberately ignored them. In any event the injury to the plaintiff was not the probable or likely consequence that the pilot foresaw as resulting from his acts. Severe clear air turbulence was extremely rare and even when air turbulence was forecast it was often not, in fact, encountered. Thus the defendants escaped liability because the pilot did not know that injury would probably result from his actions. This is one important difference between the unamended Warsaw Convention and the Hague Protocol.[60] Also the court held, *obiter*, and with some hesitation that the damage suffered must be of the type anticipated by the guilty person as likely to result from his wrongdoing. Thus if the expected result of wrongdoing was breaking wine glasses on board an aircraft and instead somebody was seriously injured an employee would not be guilty of misconduct such as would satisfy the requirements of Article 25.

Hague Protocol. Notification of Cargo Claims for Damage and Delay

6.51 **Introduction**

As is the case in all modes of carriage it would be unjust if the carrier was burdened with cargo claims long after the loss, damage or delay had occurred. To deal with this problem Article 26 lays down certain time limits for notification of damage or delay but not for the loss of the cargo. The contractual conditions of many air carriers however require notification of loss of the cargo to be submitted within 120 days. Decisions from the courts of other countries differ as to whether such a contractual condition is null and void under Article 23(1). If the requirements of Article 26 are not complied with then the carrier is not liable for the damage or delay unless he is guilty of fraud.[61] Presumably therefore, if the carrier had deliberately concealed the damage from the consignee or perhaps told him that written claims were unnecessary then the carrier would remain liable.

Article 26(1) states that the receipt of the cargo by the person entitled to delivery[62] without complaint is prima facie evidence of delivery in good condition. How this provision can be reconciled with Article 26(2) will be discussed in 6.53 below.

6.52 **The written notice**

Article 26(3) requires the notice of complaint to be in writing upon the air waybill or upon a separate document. An oral complaint

[60] See 6.75.

[61] Art. 26(4).

[62] The person entitled to delivery need presumably not be the person named on the air waybill as the consignee; for example where the consignor has exercised his rights under Art. 12(1) to name a new consignee.

would not satisfy this requirement. However if the carrier told the customer that an oral complaint was sufficient then the carrier would presumably be guilty of fraud under Article 26(4).[63] By analogy with the interpretation given to the equivalent provision in the C.M.R. Convention[64] presumably written notice to the carrier's agent such as an insurer appointed to receive claims would satisfy Article 26(3).

Both Article 26(1) and (2) refer to complaints by the "person entitled to delivery" of the cargo. Obviously a complaint by the consignee's agent would be sufficient. In addition it is suggested that a complaint would suffice if it was made by the true owner even though he was not the consignee named on the air waybill and so, arguably, not literally the "person entitled to delivery." Thus if cargo was delivered to a freight forwarder but the owner made the complaint then that complaint would satisfy the requirements of Article 26.

Notice of complaint after receipt without complaint 6.53

Article 26(2) requires that the person entitled to delivery[65] must make his complaint about damage (but not delay?) immediately upon discovering the damage and, at the latest, within 14 days of receiving the goods. In the case of delay the time period is 21 days from the time when the cargo has "been placed at his disposal." Difficulty arises in reconciling this provision with Article 26(1) which states that receipt of the cargo is prima facie evidence of delivery in good condition. Before the carrier can be held prima facie liable under Article 18[66] obviously the plaintiff must prove that the cargo has in fact been damaged. However receipt of the cargo without complaint, by virtue of Article 26(2), is evidence that it has not been damaged. Presumably therefore in these circumstances the plaintiff would have to bring convincing evidence of the damage and show some good reason why he had not notified the carrier of the damage "forthwith," *i.e.* upon receiving the cargo. There should be no difficulty in achieving this if he proved that he could not discover the damage because it was impossible to examine the cargo closely because it was tightly packaged or in a container.

Notification of "damage" 6.54

Article 26(2) requires written notice of complaints concerning "damage," as opposed to the loss of the goods or their destruction. What would be the position if animals died in transit? Would this be a case of damage or rather of loss or destruction? It has been held in the United States that the death of racing greyhounds was not "damage" and that no written complaint was necessary.[67] On the other hand it has been held in English carriage by road cases subject to the C.M.R. Convention[68] that the English insurance law doctrine of "constructive

[63] See 6.51.
[64] See 3.72 esp. nn. 32-33.
[65] See 6.52 above.
[66] See 6.40.
[67] *Hughes Gibb* v. *Flying Tiger* 16 Avi.Cas. 17, 492 (1967) (U.S.A.).
[68] See Chap. 3.

total loss" has no application in that field.[69] Provided the goods still have some real economic value (unlike dead greyhounds!) and have not been totally destroyed then severe damage to the goods should likewise in carriage by air amount to "damage" rather than loss.

At one time there was controversy as to whether the loss of part of a cargo amounted to "damage" for the purpose of Article 26(2). However, as regards United Kingdom law, this difficulty is largely removed by section 2 of the Carriage by Air and Road Act 1979 which states that in Article 26(2) "damage" includes "loss of part of the baggage or cargo." In other jurisdictions the House of Lords case of *Fothergill* v. *Monarch Airlines Ltd.*[70] to the same effect will be a very strong persuasive precedent. Even under the 1979 Act, however, difficulty might still arise if several cargoes being carried for different customers under different air waybills were all placed in the same container. It is tentatively suggested that, for the purposes of Article 26(2), the destruction of any of these individual cargoes would not amount to a partial loss and that therefore no written complaint would be required.

Hague Protocol. Time and Place for Litigation

6.55 Where can the plaintiff sue?

Under Article 28(1) the plaintiff can sue in any of the following countries:

1. Where the carrier is ordinarily resident.
2. Where the carrier has his principal place of residence.
3. Where the carrier has an "establishment" (*i.e.* branch?) which actually made the contract.
4. The country of destination.

In addition the country where the action is brought must also be a party to the Protocol. Apart from that requirement, which is not present in C.M.R., the provisions of Article 28(1) are very similar to those of Article 31 of the C.M.R. Convention[71] (although C.M.R. also grants two other possible venues for litigation). Therefore for a discussion of any difficulties arising in relation to the meaning of the alternative venues listed above see 3.02.

6.56 Limitations of actions

Article 29(1) provides that the "right to damages shall be extinguished if an action is not brought within two years." By virtue of Section 5(1) of the Carriage by Air Act 1961 this includes actions against servants and agents. It would seem that an action for unpaid

[69] *e.g. William Tatton* v. *Ferrymasters* [1974] 1 Lloyd's Rep. 203. See 3.71.
[70] [1981] 2 A.C. 251. Discussed in 3.06. [71] See 3.70.

freight brought by a carrier would not be an action for "damages" and would not be covered by Article 29(1). The limitation period therefore for such a claim would presumably be six years under the Limitation Act 1980. One difficulty that might arise in this context would be that the carrier could sue for freight after two years and the owner of the goods would be unable to counterclaim for loss, damage or delay.[72] If one took Article 29(1) literally a plaintiff could still sue after two years and recover the costs of litigation but recover no damages! Such an interpretation would be absurd and presumably therefore the words "action for damages" means "right to sue."

The time limit starts to run against the plaintiff:

1. From the date of arrival at the destination or
2. From the date on which the aircraft should have arrived or
3. From the date on which the carriage stopped.

If these dates are not the same then time starts to run from whichever date is most favourable to the plaintiff. Thus it was held in a United States case[73] that time ran against the carrier from the date that the cargo was delivered to the consignee and not from the date it arrived at the airport of destination. Until it was delivered to the consignee carriage had not "stopped" because the cargo was "in charge of the carrier."[74] It is submitted that this is basically the correct approach but that one must not take it too far. Say that a consignee, hearing the cargo had been seriously damaged in transit, refused to collect it from the airport. He could delay the limitation period under Article 29(1) indefinitely. We suggest that in that instance the common law should apply.[75] Transit (*i.e.* "carriage") would cease after the consignee had had a reasonable time to collect the cargo after he had been given notice that it had arrived under Article 13(2). Once a reasonable time had lapsed the limitation would start to run against him.

Another problem might arise if goods were lost in transit. Arguably if that were the case time would run against the carrier from the date on which the goods should have been delivered to the consignee, *i.e.* the date on which the carriage was expected to stop.

It seems that in English law a new plaintiff or defendant cannot be joined to the action after the two-year period.[76] Article 29 does not seem to apply to claims between carriers for an indemnity. Say that the consignee sued the contracting carrier[77] and he was held liable for the acts of his successive carrier under Article 30.[78] The contracting carrier would want to sue the successive carrier for an indemnity in respect of his own liability to the consignee and in other countries he would not be bound by the time limits in Article 29(1). However in

[72] See *The Aries Tanker* [1977] 1 W.L.R. 185.
[73] *Alltransport* v. *Seaboard World Airlines* 12 Avi.Cas. 18, 163 (1981) (U.S.A.).
[74] See 6.22.
[75] See 1.66.
[76] See *Liff* v. *Peasley* [1980] 1 W.L.R. 781.
[77] See 6.37.
[78] As he may under Art. 30(3). See 6.37.

the United Kingdom Section 10 of the Civil Liability (Contribution) Act 1978 creates a similar two-year limitation period for such actions for an indemnity.

Hague Protocol. Passenger Provisions

6.57 **Introduction**

A detailed exposition of the law relating to carriage of passengers by air is inappropriate in a work on the carriage of goods. Therefore only a cursory examination will be given to this topic. Essentially the law relating to common carriers, the application of the Protocol, intentional and reckless misconduct and place and time of litigation, equally apply to passengers. The following paragraphs contain a short discussion of the major passenger provisions that differ substantially from their cargo counterparts.

6.58 **When does the carrier's liability commence and cease?**

Article 17 provides that "the carrier is liable for damage sustained in the event of the death or wounding of a passenger or any other bodily injury suffered by a passenger, if the accident which caused the damage so sustained took place on board an aircraft or in the course of embarking or disembarking." "Wounding or bodily injury" includes mental injury. An "accident" is any "unlooked-for event" so presumably a deliberate assault on a pasenger by a member of the aircrew would amount to an "accident." The words "embarking or disembarking" have given some difficulty but perhaps the best view is that "embarking" commences when the passenger leaves the air terminal and comes under the care of the carrier or his servants or agents. So a passenger would be embarking while travelling on a bus from the passenger terminal to his waiting aircraft. "Disembarking" would similarly cease when the passenger ceased to be in the carrier's care. Another view is that a passenger is "embarking" from the moment that he goes through the security checks.

6.59 **Documentation, the passenger ticket**

The documentation provision relating to carriage of passengers is Article 3. Article 3(1) requires the "delivery" of a passenger ticket before the passenger embarks. It is suggested that delivery of a ticket to someone travelling with the plaintiff, for example his wife, or, in the case of a booking by, for example, a club, delivery to the club leader would suffice. We also tentatively suggest that the word "embarks" in Article 3(2) bears the same meaning as does "embarking" in the context of Article 17 discussed in 6.58.

We submit that the requirement in Article 3(1) that the passenger ticket must be "delivered" to the passenger does not mean that the carrier must give the passenger "reasonable notice" of its contents. Thus any ticket, the contents of which satisfy the requirements of Article 3, will suffice and the carrier will be able to limit his liability under Article 22. The ticket does not have to be given a reasonable time before embarking or in a bold or particularly legible form.[79] However the Canadian Supreme Court held, *obiter*, in *Ludecke* v. *Canadian Pacific*[80] that the word "notice" in Article 3(1)(c) meant something noticeable. Therefore the "Warsaw Statement"[81] in Article 3(1)(c), as opposed to the other requirements of Article 3(1), must be sufficiently largely printed so as to be noticeable by a reasonable passenger.

Limits of liability 6.60

Under Article 22(1) the limit of liability for death or injury is 250,000 gold francs which under the latest Sterling Equivalents Order is approximately £14,000. The carrier cannot rely on these limits if he delivers no ticket, delivers a ticket without the Warsaw Statement required by Article 3(1)(c) or is guilty of intentional or reckless wrongdoing.[82] As a matter of contract however, many carriers increase their maximum limits of liability for death or injury. In addition many countries insist that their airlines do so. Thus in the United Kingdom the Civil Aviation Authority requires that all British commercial air transport licence holders increase their liability for death and injury by contract to 100,000 S.D.R.'s,[83] which is approximately £80,000.

Hague Protocol. Baggage Provisions

Introduction 6.61

Apart from the documentation provision and limits of liability discussed below the only difference between the baggage provisions in the Protocol and those concerned with cargo is that under Article 26(2), written complaints as regards damage[84] to baggage have to be made within seven days, as opposed to the 14-day period for cargo.

Documentation, the baggage check 6.62

The documentation provision for "baggage" is Article 4. Article 4(1) requires that a baggage check be delivered[85] in respect of registered

[79] *Ludecke* v. *Canadian Pacific* [1979] 2 Lloyd's Rep. 260 (Canada).

[80] *Ibid.*

[81] Note the difference in the wording of the equivalent Art. in the unamended Warsaw Convention.

[82] See 6.49.

[83] See 3.05-3.08 for the meaning of S.D.R.'s.

[84] See 6.54.

[85] As to the meaning of "delivered," see 6.59.

baggage. However the same provision permits the issue of a combined passenger ticket/baggage check. In *Collins* v. *British Airways Board*[86] the combined passenger ticket/baggage check did not contain the number of pieces of baggage or their weight. Nevertheless the majority of the Court of Appeal held that it was still a baggage check and the irregularity did not deprive the carrier of his limits of liability under Article 22.

6.63 **Limits of liability**

Under Article 22(2)(a) the carrier's limit of liability for baggage where there has been no special declaration[87] is 250 gold francs per kilo, *i.e.* approximately £14, as it is with cargo.[88] The limit of liability in the case of unregistered baggage, *i.e.* hand luggage, is 5,000 gold francs, *i.e.* approximately £280 per passenger.

THE GUADALAJARA AMENDMENTS TO THE HAGUE PROTOCOL

6.64 **Introduction**

As explained in 6.04 the Warsaw Convention and the Hague Protocol did not apply to "actual" as opposed to "successive carriers." The distinction between these two species has been briefly outlined in 6.18. In order to give the protection of the Protocol to actual carriers the Guadalajara Convention was drafted and implemented into English law by the Carriage by Air (Supplementary Provisions) Act 1962. The Guadalajara Convention is also incorporated into the Carriage by Air Acts (Application of Provisions) Order 1967[89] that implements the Unamended Warsaw Convention and the Non-International Rules in English law.[90] Note that the 1962 Act applies to the carriage of cargo, passengers and baggage and only to actual and not to successive carriers.

6.65 **Documentation**

If the contracting carrier performs part of the contract of carriage himself and fails to issue documentation as required by the Protocol[91] then, by virtue of Article III(1) of the Guadalajara Convention, it seems that the actual carrier can still rely on the limits of liability laid down by Article 22 of the Protocol.[92] If the actual carrier performs the whole of the carriage himself and fails to comply with the documentation requirements[93] of the Protocol then it seems he cannot rely on the limits of liability in Article 22. If the contracting carrier issues proper

[86] [1982] Q.B. 734.

[87] See 6.48.

[88] As to how the weight limit is calculated per item of baggage lost when the baggage check merely states the total weight of all pieces of baggage, see *Bland* v. *British Airways Board* [1981] 1 Lloyd's Rep. 289.

[89] Extracts from Sched. Two of which will be found in Appendix 6.C.

[90] See 6.69-6.81 as to the unamended rules and see 6.82-6.84 as to the Non-International Rules.

[91] See 6.24-6.28, 6.59 and 6.62.

[92] See 6.45-6.47.

[93] See n. 91, above.

documentation then we suggest that there is no obligation on the actual carrier to duplicate these documents on his own account.

Liability of the actual carrier 6.66

The actual carrier is essentially only liable for that part of the journey *he actually performs.*[94] He is however, liable for the acts of the contracting carrier and those of the contracting carrier's servants and agents in relation to his, the actual carrier's, part of the journey.[95] Say that A gives goods to C, the contracting carrier, and C subcontracts part of the carriage to D, the actual carrier. C's employees damage the cargo while loading it into D's aircraft. D is liable for the acts of C's employees. Let us assume, however, that, in our example, C's employees were guilty of intentional and reckless wrongdoing.[96] In that event D, unlike C, could still rely on the limits of liability in Article 22 of the Protocol.[97] Similarly if the contracting carrier, by contract, undertakes a higher liability than that imposed by Article 22, or if there has been a "declaration of interest in delivery"[98] to the contracting carrier then these do not bind the actual carrier unless he has agreed to them.[99] He can still limit his liability to 250 gold francs per kilo. If the servants or agents of the actual carrier are sued on their own account then their liability is the same as that of the actual carrier as just outlined.[1]

Liability of the contracting carrier 6.67

Under Article III(1) the acts of the actual carrier and his servants or agents in relation to the portion of the journey performed by him are deemed to be the acts of the contracting carrier. Thus the contracting carrier is liable for any happenings on the whole journey whether he himself is carrying or not. So if, for example, the actual carrier is guilty of intentional or reckless wrongdoing[2] then the contracting carrier is liable without limit.

Other provisions 6.68

Complaints of damage or delay[3] can be made to either the contracting or actual carrier but orders under Article 12[4] to, for example, alter the destination can only be given to the contracting carrier.[5] In relation to carriage performed by the actual carrier the plaintiff can sue the actual carrier, the contracting carrier or both of them.[6] A plaintiff cannot, however, double his damages by suing both carriers.[7] The action for damages can be brought in any of the jurisdic-

[94] Art. II.
[95] Art. III(2).
[96] See 6.49-6.50.
[97] See 6.45-6.47.
[98] See 6.48.
[99] Art. III(2).
[1] Art. V
[2] See 6.49-6.50.
[3] Art. IV.
[4] See 6.29-6.31.
[5] Art. IV.
[6] Art. VII.
[7] Art. VI.

tions discussed in 6.55 and, in addition, in the country in which the actual carrier is ordinarily resident or carries on business.[8] This could be very unjust. Thus a small Brazilian company operating solely in that country could find itself having to defend an action in England. Presumably the two-year time limit within which actions must be commenced, laid down by Article 29[9] of the Hague Protocol, also applies to actions brought against actual carriers. The time limit certainly does apply as regards actions between contracting and actual carriers to recover an indemnity in respect of one another's acts for which they have been held liable.[10]

UNAMENDED WARSAW. INTRODUCTION

6.69 **Schedule 2 of the Carriage by Air Acts (Application of Provisions) Order 1967**

As explained in 6.08 the unamended Warsaw Convention will still apply to flights between countries that are parties to the original Convention rather than the Hague Protocol. Schedule 2 of the 1967 Order applies on the principles discussed in 6.16-6.17 to flights to, from or with an agreed stopping place in countries which are parties to the unamended Warsaw Convention as opposed to the Hague Protocol. The most important provisions of the Schedule, where they differ from those of the Hague Protocol, will be found in Appendix 6.B. It should be noted that passenger flights to or from the United States are also subject to the Montreal Agreement outlined in 6.80.

6.70 **Wording and interpretation**

The original unamended Warsaw Convention, as implemented by Schedule 2 of the 1967 Order, is not identical to the original English text of the Convention. The most obvious, but least important change, except from an aesthetic point of view, is the use of the Americanisms "air waybill" and "baggage check" rather than the English words "air consignment note" and "passenger ticket" as used in the original translation of the Convention in the 1932 Act. In addition Schedule 2 contains Article 25A of the Hague Protocol giving the protection of the Convention to the servants and agents of the carrier. This provision was not in the original Warsaw Convention. The most important change in wording, however, is the absence of Article 36 of the Convention dealing with the French text. This provision was identical to Article 36 of the Protocol.[11] The absence of Article 36, together with the absence of any provision in the 1967 Order to the effect that the French text of the Convention prevails over the English, suggests that the Order is a piece of purely English domestic legislation. It is therefore submitted that, as regards cases

[8] Art. VIII.
[9] See 6.56.
[10] s.3(2) of the Carriage by Air (Supplementary Provisions) Act 1962.
[11] See Appendix 6.A.

which are subject to the 1967 Order, as opposed to the Protocol, the courts cannot look at the French text unless, perhaps, the English text is ambiguous.[12] Therefore if the facts of *Corocraft* v. *Panam.*[13] came before the courts today it is suggested that the court would be compelled to a different decision and that *Corocraft* no longer represents the law.

Unamended Warsaw. Documentation Provisions

The "particulars" required on the air waybill 6.71

Article 4 of the unamended Convention requires no fewer than 17 particulars to be contained on the air waybill. Article 4 and its "particulars" will be found in Appendix 6.B. No doubt the complexity and number of these requirements led to their removal when the Hague Protocol was drafted. Many of them seem to serve no useful commercial purpose and their omission can lead to unfair and draconian consequences for the carrier.[14] If one investigated these individual "particulars" closely one could, no doubt, find many real or imagined ambiguities in their wording. We will however, limit ourselves to brief comments on three of the particulars that have been considered in important cases:

(1) Particular (c) as regards "stopping places." This requirement was held to be satisfied in a United States case[15] in which there was a general statement on the air waybill that as regards stopping places the customer should refer to the airline's timetables.
(2) Particular (i) as regards weight, etc. It was held in *Corocraft* v. *Panam.*[16] that the English version of this particular was a mistranslation of the original French text and that the inclusion of any one of the matters in particular (i) would suffice; *i.e.* weight or quantity or volume or dimensions. It was suggested in 6.70 that a court could no longer consult the French text unless, perhaps, words in the Schedule were ambiguous. It seems to the writers that the English translation of this particular is tolerably clear and requires that three of the four matters must be included.
(3) Particular (q), *i.e.* the Warsaw Statement. In *Westminster Bank* v. *Imperial Airways*[17] it was held that this particular was not satisfied by a statement on the air waybill that carriage was "based on" the Warsaw Convention. On the other hand in *Samuel Montague* v. *Swiss Air*[18] it was held that particular (i) was satisfied by a statement that the Convention applied *unless* the carriage was not international. The court rejected the argument that this was a statement that the

[12] As to the interpretation of international conventions generally, see 3.05-3.08.
[13] [1969] 1 Q.B. 616. Discussed in 6.71.
[14] See 6.72, below.
[15] *Kraus* v. *K.L.M.* 2 Avi.Cas. 15, 017 (1949) (U.S.A.).
[16] [1969] 1 Q.B. 616.
[17] [1936] 2 All E.R. 890.
[18] [1960] 2 Q.B. 306.

Convention *might* apply rather than a statement that the Convention did apply.

By virtue of Article 34 of the Schedule the need for documentation is removed for experimental flights and where there are "extraordinary circumstances."[19]

6.72 **Absence or irregularity of the air waybill**

Unlike Article 9 of the Hague Protocol, Article 9 of the unamended Convention appears to require, rather unfairly, that the air waybill be made out *before* the carrier accepts the cargo rather than before it is loaded. If it is not then the carrier suffers the draconian consequences stated in the remainder of the Article. Article 9 provides that, if the air waybill is not issued before the cargo is accepted, or if it omits any of particulars (a) to (i) or particular (q), *i.e.* the Warsaw Statement, then the carrier cannot rely on any provisions of the Schedule "which exclude or limit his liability." Thus he loses the benefit of *both* the defences and the limits of liability in the Convention. In the Hague Protocol on the other hand he only loses the limits of liability under Article 22[20] and can still rely on the Protocol's defences. However we suggest that the words "exclude or limit . . . liability" do not cover the time limit in Article 29 which the carrier can still rely on even if he has failed to comply with the documentation provisions in Article 9.[21]

UNAMENDED CONVENTION. LIABILITY AND LIMITS OF LIABILITY

6.73 **Liability for loss, damage or delay**

The liability of the carrier for cargo is much the same as it is under the Hague Protocol.[22] However Article 20(2) of the unamended Convention gives him the additional defence of "negligent pilotage or negligence in the handling" or navigation of the aircraft. This defence is based on Article IV, Rule 2(a) of the Hague-Visby Rules which was discussed in 5.42 and presumably has much the same meaning as that provision. Surprisingly there seem to have been no cases on Article 20(2).

6.74 **Limits of liability**

Under Article 22(2) of the unamended Warsaw Convention the basic limit of liability is 250 gold francs per kilo, *i.e.* approximately £14, as it is in the Hague Protocol. However the limit of liability can be increased upon a "declaration of value at delivery" by the customer whereas the Hague Protocol refers to a "declaration of interest in delivery." Presumably therefore, under the unamended Convention, the carrier cannot make a declaration to the effect that he will, for example, suffer £2,000 loss of profits on resale if the goods do not

[19] See 6.26. [20] *Ibid.*

[21] There are several decisions to this effect, *e.g. Lewin* v. *Air Jamaica* 14 Avi.Cas. 17, 251 (1976) (U.S.A.).

[22] See 6.40-6.44.

arrive in time, whereas under the Protocol he can. Such a declaration, we suggest, is not one of "value."

Note that there is no Article 22(2)(b) in the unamended Convention as there is in the Protocol.[23] If then part of the cargo is lost, is the carrier's limit of liability assessed by reference to the total weight of the cargo or by reference to the weight of portion lost? It was held in *Data Card Corp.* v. *Air Express International*[24] that where there was such partial loss or damage the carrier's limit of liability should be assessed by reference to the weight of the portion lost, damaged or delayed and not to the weight of the total number of packages. Therefore the position under the unamended Convention as regards partial loss is much the same as it is in the Protocol. However in the Protocol where the loss of part of a cargo affects the value of the unlost portion this can be taken into account when assessing the damages under Article 22(2)(b). Appparently this factor cannot be taken into account under the unamended Convention.

In addition the unamended Convention, unlike the Hague Protocol,[25] is silent as to whether the plaintiff can recover legal costs in addition to the maximum damages under Article 22. We suggest that the reference to "liability" in Article 22(2) refers to liability to pay damages and not to any liability to pay legal costs. Therefore such costs should be recoverable in addition to the maximum limits of liability laid down by the Article. The strange provision in Article 23(2) of the Protocol, discussed in 6.46, allowing the carrier by contract to lower the limits of liability in the case of inherent vice in the cargo is not present in the unamended Convention.

Unamended Convention. Wilful Misconduct

Meaning of, and comparison with other schemes of liability 6.75

Whereas Article 25 of the Hague Protocol refers to what we have summarised as "intentional or reckless misconduct" Article 25 of the unamended Convention refers to "wilful misconduct." This is a phrase well known to and understood by common lawyers and its meaning has been discussed in 1.61 in the context of clause 5B of the British Rail Conditions of Carriage. Although Article 25, unlike the British Rail Conditions, is not too clear it is suggested that the burden of proving wilful misconduct falls on the plaintiff. Under the British Rail Conditions it is unclear whether the servants of the carrier have to be acting in the scope of their employment in order for the carrier to be vicariously liable for their misconduct.[26] In the case of a carrier by air under the unamended Convention, however, it is clear from the provisions of Article 25(2) that such a carrier is only vicariously liable for the acts of servants or agents if they are acting "in the scope of their employment." Thus it was held in *Rustenberg* v. *South African*

[23] See Appendix 6.A.
[24] [1984] 1 W.L.R. 198.
[25] See Art.22(4) of the Hague Protocol.
[26] See 1.61.

Airways[27] that a carrier under the unamended Convention was liable when a cargo loader stole a quantity of platinum that had been entrusted[28] to the loader.

It was explained in 6.50 that for a person to be held liable for "intentional or reckless misconduct" under the Protocol he must have known that damage would probably result. It can however, be seen from the cases noted in 1.61 that this is not a necessary requirement when alleging wilful misconduct under the unamended Convention.

6.76 **The effects of wilful misconduct**

It is important to note that, despite the fact that wilful misconduct means exactly the same in carriage by air as it does under the British Rail Conditions, it has quite different effects in the two schemes of liability. In the British Rail Conditions wilful misconduct is the *only* ground upon which the carrier can be held liable when carrying at "owner's risk." Under Article 25 of the unamended Convention however, a carrier guilty of wilful misconduct loses the benefit of "the provisions of the Schedule which exclude or limit liability." The meaning of this provision has been discussed in 6.72. Essentially the air carrier loses the benefit of the "defences and limits of liability" in the Schedule.

As is the case in the Protocol the action under the unamended Convention may be brought directly against the servant or agent of the carrier rather than the carrier himself. In that event the servant or agent, under Article 25A(3), only loses the limits of liability in Article 22(2), and *not* the defences, if he is guilty of "intentional and reckless misconduct" rather than wilful misconduct.

UNAMENDED CONVENTION. PASSENGERS, THE MONTREAL AGREEMENT AND BAGGAGE

6.77 **Passengers, introduction**

The position of a carrier of passengers by air under the unamended Convention is much the same as it is under the Hague Protocol subject to the differences already pointed out in relation to cargo. However there are some other differences in the provisions of the Schedule that should be noted. The first is that the defence of "negligent pilotage,"[29] etc., in the unamended Convention does not apply to the carriage of passengers. The other two major differences are outlined below in 6.78-6.79.

6.78 **Passenger documentation**

Article 3 of the Schedule lists the requirements of the passenger ticket. The first thing to note is that the ticket must be delivered[30] before the passenger is accepted. This implies that it must be

[27] [1979] 1 Lloyd's Rep. 19.
[28] A carrier is vicariously liable in these circumstances. See 1.18.
[29] See 6.73.
[30] As to the meaning of the word "delivered," see also 6.59.

delivered before the passenger is in the carrier's care.[31] In the United States it has been held that a ticket is not "delivered" unless it is handed over in time to give the passenger adequate time to make insurance arrangements and that it is not "delivered" unless it is sufficiently boldly printed so as to give the passenger notice of its contents.[32] It is submitted that this is clearly contrary to the express wording of Article 3 and that in the United Kingdom the courts would follow the decision of the Canadian Supreme Court in *Ludecke* v. *Canadian Pacific*.[33] In *Ludecke* the court held that provided anything qualifying as a "ticket" was handed over then Article 3 was satisfied. The ticket did not have to be legible or delivered in time to take out insurance. Strangely enough there does not even seem to be a requirement in Article 3 that the ticket should contain any of the particulars listed in Article 1(3) as there is in relation to some of the particulars required for the cargo and baggage documentation. Thus the delivery of a ticket omitting even the "Warsaw Statement" would satisfy the requirements of Article 3.

Liability and limit of liability for death and injury 6.79

The maximum liability of the carrier under Article 22(1) of the unamended Convention is only 125,000 gold francs, *i.e.* approximately £7,000, which is only half the maximum sum under the Protocol. It should be noted, however, that many countries require their carriers to contractually undertake a higher liability[34] and that many carriers increase this limit voluntarily by contract without any compulsion from their governments. In addition the limit does not apply when the carriage is subject to the Montreal Agreement discussed below in 6.80.

Carriage of passengers under the Montreal Agreement 6.80

The United States is not a party to the Hague Protocol but merely to the unamended Convention. Under United States domestic delegated legislation called C.A.B. No. 18900, however, it is required that in the case of carriage of passengers, all carriers sign the Montreal Agreement as a prerequisite to obtaining permission to fly to or from that country. The Agreement applies to all flights to, from or with an agreed stopping place in the United States. As regards such flights, the Agreement requires that the carrier agrees by contract with the passenger for the following:

(1) That the maximum liability of the carrier for death or injury will be increased to $75,000 inclusive of legal costs or $58,000 plus legal costs.
(2) That the carrier will not rely on the defence of "all necessary measures".[35] Thus the carrier becomes strictly liable for death or injury. He can still rely, however, on the defence of contributory negligence of the passenger.[36]

[31] See 6.58.
[32] *Lisi* v. *Alitalia* [1968] 1 Lloyd's Rep. 505 (U.S.A.).
[33] [1979] 2 Lloyd's Rep. 260 (Canada).
[34] See 6.60.
[35] See 6.41.
[36] See 6.42.

If a carrier subject to the Agreement made such a contract with the passenger and the case came before the English courts then they would of course enforce it.

Note that the Montreal Agreement does not apply to cargo or baggage and that it should not be confused with the Montreal Protocols discussed briefly in 6.86.

6.81 **Baggage documentation**

The differences between the unamended Convention provisions concerning baggage and those of the Protocol are much the same as those outlined in 6.70-6.76 in respect of cargo. In addition, Article 4 of the Schedule concerning the baggage check is different from its equivalent in the Protocol. It will be noted that there is no specific provision in the Article permitting the issue of a joint passenger ticket cum baggage check. However if the document delivered was described as such then clearly it would be a "baggage check" for the purposes of Article 4. If the carrier does not keep a copy of the baggage check as Article 4(2) seems to require then it is suggested that if he has delivered a copy to the passenger no legal consequences would follow from his omission.

The particulars required to be on the baggage check are listed in Article 4(3). If no baggage check is delivered[37] or one is delivered that omits particulars (d), (f) or (h) then under Article 4(4) the carrier loses the Convention limits of liability and defences.[38]

The Non-International Rules

6.82 **Application of the Rules**

Schedule One of the Carriage by Air Acts (Application of Provisions Order) 1967 as amended, which implements the Non-International Rules, is a piece of purely English domestic legislation and, we suggest, should be interpreted as such.[39] The Schedule applies to:

(1) Flights to, from or within the U.K. that are not subject to the Hague Protocol or the unamended Convention including such gratuitous flights by a transport undertaking, (*e.g.* an airline) and flights by the Crown.

(2) The carriage of mail and postal packets.

This obviously includes flights purely within the United Kingdom and flights to or from colonies and dependant territories. It also covers flights to, from or with an agreed stopping place within the U.K. if the flight is to or from a country that has not ratified either the Hague Protocol or the unamended Convention. However it does not cover a flight purely within the territory of another country. Thus in

[37] See 6.78.
[38] See 6.72.
[39] See 6.70.

Holmes v. *Bangladesh Biman Corporation*[40] it was held that a flight solely within the territory of Bangladesh was subject not to the Non-International Rules but rather to Bangladesh law. Nor does it cover flights from one non-convention country to another where there is no stopping place in the U.K.

As regards carriage of mail and postal packets Section 29(3) of the Post Office Act prevents anybody other than the Post Office suing in tort in respect of the loss of postal items when the mail is in possession of the Post Office's servants, agents and subcontractors. It was held in *American Express* v. *British Airways Board*[41] that one could not avoid this legislation by suing in bailment rather than tort. This decision is, however, open to doubt because Palmer[42] convincingly argues that liability in bailment is quite separate from liability in tort.

Limits of liability 6.83

The limits of liability in the Non-International Rules are:

(1) In the case of passengers 100,000 S.D.R.'s[43] which is approximately £80,000.

(2) In the case of cargo and registered luggage 17 S.D.R.'s per kilo which is approximately £13.

(3) In the case of hand baggage, 320 S.D.R.'s, approximately £260.

The absence of documentation provisions 6.84

The second major difference between the Non-International Rules and the Hague Protocol is the complete lack of any documentation provisions in the former regime. Articles 3 to 16 of the Protocol are completely omitted from Schedule One. It follows that the Schedule's limits of liability in Article 22 can still be relied on even where there is no documentation at all. As there are no documentation requirements in the Schedule, Article 34 that dispenses with the need for documentation in "extraordinary circumstances" is omitted. Presumably as regards rights of control over the cargo are concerned, because Article 12 of the Protocol is absent, if the contract is subject to English law then Sections 44-46 of the Sale of Goods Act 1979 and the common law principles discussed in 1.75-1.76 apply rather than the Protocol. Likewise the questions of who can sue[44] and be sued by a carrier[45] are presumably subject to the common law because there is no Article 14 giving the right to sue to others.[46]

Article 28 is also omitted with the result that English courts can only hear the case if the English rules on jurisdiction apply.

[40] *The Times*, February 18, 1989.
[41] [1983] 1 W.L.R. 701.
[42] Palmer, *Bailment* 1st ed. (1978), pp. 36-50 and 139.
[43] See 3.60.
[44] See 1.04-1.20.
[45] See 1.106.
[46] See 6.36.

Regimes Not yet in Force

6.85 **The Guatemala Protocol on passengers and baggage**

The Guatemala Protocol 1971 only applies to passengers and baggage and *not* to cargo. It has not yet come into force and there is no legislation in the United Kingdom permitting its introduction. Nevertheless its provisions are incorporated in the Montreal Protocol Number Four, discussed in 6.86 below, except that the Montreal Protocol limits of liability are expressed in S.D.R.'s. There is provision for the fourth Montreal Protocol to be implemented into English law under the Carriage by Air Act 1979. The Guatemala Protocol contains three major changes from the Hague Protocol:

(1) The carrier loses the defence of "all necessary measures" in the case of death or injury but not for delay in the carriage of passengers. He retains the defence of contributory negligence.
(2) The limit of liability is 1,500,000 gold francs (approximately £84,000) for death and injury and 62,500 gold francs (approximately £3,500) for delay to passengers. As regards baggage, whether registered or not, the limit is 15,000 gold francs (approximately £820) whatever the weight of the baggage.
(3) The carrier does not lose the limits of liability if guilty of intentional or reckless misconduct or if the documentation is absent or irregular.

6.86 **The Montreal Protocols**

There were four extra Protocols introduced at Montreal in 1975. These Protocols must not be confused with the Montreal Agreement discussed in 6.80. Section 7 of the Carriage by Air and Road Act 1979 gives power to the Queen in Council to implement the Second, Third and Fourth Protocol by means of delegated legislation known as Orders in Council. There was no need to grant this power in respect of the First Protocol because there is already power to implement it in the Carriage by Air Act 1961. The United Kingdom government has only ratified the first Protocol and none of the Protocols are yet in force nor are likely to be in the near future. The first three Protocols essentially introduce Special Drawing Rights[47] (S.D.R.'s) rather than gold francs to express the limits of liability but the limits themselves are unchanged. The Fourth Protocol incorporates the amendments of the Guatemala Protocol as regards passengers and baggage but expresses the limits of liability in S.D.R.'s. It also brings the cargo provisions more into line with those of the Guatemala Protocol

Montreal Protocol Number Four appears as a Schedule to the Carriage by Air and Road Act 1979. As explained above the Schedule has not yet come into force. It incorporates the Guatemala Provisions about passengers and baggage but expresses the limits in S.D.R.'s rather than gold francs. As regards cargo, the Fourth Protocol makes

[47] See 3.60.

no changes to the limits of liability but these also are now expressed in S.D.R.'s. The provisions of the Fourth Protocol contained in the Schedule differ from the cargo provisions of the Hague Protocol in the following main ways:

(1) The defence of "all necessary measures" is removed in cases of loss and damage but not delay to cargo. The carrier therefore becomes strictly liable for loss or damage subject to the defence of contributory negligence. In addition he has four new defences, or as a common lawyer would say, excepted perils. These are inherent vice,[48] defective packing,[49] act of war or armed conflict and the acts of public authorities. The liability for delay to cargo is essentially the same as it is in the Hague Protocol. The carrier's liability, therefore, under the 1979 Act for loss, damage or delay to cargo is remarkably similar to that of a common carrier[50] at common law. However there is no defence in the Protocol of Act of God.
(2) The carrier does not have to include the "Warsaw Statement" on the air waybill, *i.e.* the statement that the carriage may be subject to the Convention.
(3) The carrier does not lose the limits of liability in the event of absence or irregularity of the documentation.
(4) The carrier does not lose the limits of liability if he is guilty of intentional or reckless misconduct.

[48] See 1.28.
[49] See 1.28 and 1.92-1.93.
[50] See 1.27-1.28.

Chapter Seven

CONTAINERISATION AND COMBINED TRANSPORT

INTRODUCTION

7.01 **Contents**

Recent years have seen the growth of international carriage contracts that permit the use of more than one mode of transport. This idea is not new. For many years there have been, *e.g.* services between Europe and North America which have offered the customer delivery of his goods to inland destinations through a combination of transport by sea and rail. What is new, however, is the development of modern techniques which have revolutionised the handling and movement of cargo and which thus have made the transfer of goods between different modes much easier. Thus from the 1950s pallets and containers have been used to "unitise" cargoes. Containers have been standardised in their dimensions[1] so as to facilitate their use by different carriers and ease their transfer between different modes of transport.[2] Other developments have included the use of roll-on roll-off ("ro-ro") ships,[3] barge-carrying vessels,[4] and piggyback systems.[5] The container however, is today the most important means of consolidating goods.

In 7.02-7.08 we examine the development of containerisation and some of its attendant legal problems, especially in respect of carriage by sea. These legal problems are not necessarily unique to "combined" transport since they can also arise when containers are carried by any single mode of transport. It is, however, convenient to deal with these problems in this Chapter since the use of the container has led to modern "through transport" contracts. The development of these contracts is considered in 7.09-7.15. An example of such a contract is reproduced in Appendix 7. Finally in 7.16-7.17 we examine the 1980 Multimodal Transport Convention.

[1] Through the work of the International Standardisation Organisation (I.S.O.). Most containers today are 8 feet 6 inches high and generally are 20 feet or 40 feet long. For the practical aspects of containerisation see Graham and Hughes, *Containerisation in the Eighties* (1985). For legal aspects see Booker, *Containers: Conditions, Law and Practice of Carriage and Use* (1987). See also; Schmitthof and Goode, *International Carriage of Goods: some legal problems and possible solutions* Vol. 1. (1988).

[2] This is less so in carriage by air where more light weight containers called "unit load devices" (U.L.D.s) are common.

[3] Compare the expression "load-on load-off" ("lo-lo") used to distinguish units requiring tackle or cranes for loading operations.

[4] *e.g.* Lash (Lighter Aboard Ship) ships.

[5] Road vehicles carried on railway wagons.

The carriage of goods in containers 7.02

During the mid-1960s the first major cross-Atlantic containerised shipping services began. Thereafter container services have spread throughout the world. They are employed both in long-distance trades where carriage by sea is normally a major component and in carriage to the Continent where carriage by other modes, such as by road or rail, tends to assume greater importance. The practical realities of containerisation have meant the introduction of new types of services both by traditional transport operators and by forwarders.[6] The ownership of the container is often in the hands of a leasing company which hires them to merchants, shipping companies or forwarders.

Where there is a containerised shipping service, the carrier by sea may agree to carry a container filled by the customer. The normal practice is for the carrier to deliver an empty container[7] to the customer at his premises. The customer packs[8] and seals it,[9] whereupon the container is carried to the container terminal at the port, shipped, and eventually delivered to the consignee who unpacks it at his premises. This is known as F.C.L.[10]/F.C.L. carriage. Since this usually involves the goods being collected from the consignor's premises and delivered direct to the consignee, it may also referred to as "house-to-house" carriage.[11] Alternatively the carrier may combine[12] the goods belonging to different customers and thus fill a container at an "inland clearance depot."[13] He will then carry the sealed container to a depot at the destination, remove the goods from the container and deliver them to their respective consignees. This is termed "depot-to-depot" or L.C.L.[14]/L.C.L. carriage.[15]

Many of the legal problems which relate to the use of containers will exist regardless of the means of transport used to carry the container. However, we concentrate on those problems which arise in the context of carriage by sea.

[6] See generally Chap. 2.

[7] Alternatively the container may be owned or leased by the customer.

[8] Sometimes termed "stuffing" the container. Unpacking is sometimes termed "de-stuffing."

[9] Usually with a seal provided by the carrier.

[10] Full Container Load.

[11] Alternatively the customer may arrange carriage to and from the container terminal himself, in which case the service provided by the carrier by sea is termed "port-to-port" or "pier-to-pier."

[12] Bringing goods together in this way is called "groupage" or "consolidation" and is a service which has long been provided by freight forwarders. See 2.02.

[13] Usually abbreviated to I.C.D.

[14] Less than "full container load."

[15] Note that further variations exist within these basic types of services.

Legal Problems Arising from the Use of Containers

7.03 **Proof of the contents of the container**

As regards most forms of carriage documents are usually issued as receipts for the goods.[16] In the context of carriage by sea, as discussed in 5.07-5.10, a Bill of lading is issued. This acts as a receipt as to the quantity and apparent condition of the goods.[17] However, where a merchant ships a container which he has himself packed and sealed the statement that the goods were "shipped in apparent good order and condition" may well be taken to refer only to the external condition of the container, and not the goods which it contains.[18] He will have to provide proof of the condition of the goods to establish any claim for damage to the goods in transit. Alternatively he would have to show by other means, such as the condition of the container on arrival, that the damage actually occurred whilst the goods were in the carrier's charge.

Similarly the fact that the bill of lading may state the contents of the container will not necessarily be proof of those contents. Thus the bill of lading may be qualified by such common statements as "shipper's load and count," or it may acknowledge receipt of a container "said to contain" a certain quantity of goods. The Hague-Visby Rules[19] give the shipper the right to demand a bill of lading indicating the number of packages received by the carrier.[20] The carrier, however, is not bound to state the number of packages on the bill of lading if he has no reasonable means of checking the statement. In *The Esmeralda I*[21] the bill of lading acknowledged receipt of 437 cartons in a container but also stated "said to contain, packed by shipper." The bill of lading was held to be not even prima facie evidence of the quantity of goods in the container. However, an alternative approach taken in France[22] is to require the carrier to refuse to indicate the quantity on the bill of lading at all. If he does not do so he is bound by the statement as to the number of packages even if he has added, *e.g.* the qualification "said to contain."

7.04 **Application of the "package" limitation to containers**

Under the original Hague Rules[23] a carrier by sea could limit his liability for loss or damage to £100[24] per package or unit. We explain in 5.47 that the advent of containerisation made the application of this

[16] See 1.06, 3.18, 4.08, 5.07 and 6.24.
[17] See 5.09-5.10
[18] See Shachar, "The container Bill of lading as a receipt" (1978) 10 J.M.L.C. 39.
[19] See 5.27-5.50.
[20] Art. III(3). See 5.37.
[21] [1988] 1 Lloyd's Rep. 206 (Australia).
[22] *The American Legacy* (1980) 15 E.T.L. 385 (French Supreme Court). See also *Coutinho, Caro & Co. (Canada) Ltd.* v. *Owners of the Vessel "Ermua"* (1979) 100 D.L.R.(3d) 461 (Canada).
[23] See 5.27.
[24] Under the British Maritime Law Association Gold Clause Agreement British shipowners agree to a limit of £400.

limit a matter of some difficulty since the question arose whether the container alone should be considered to be the relevant "package" (thus limiting the carrier's liability to £100 per container), or whether the goods inside the container could be considered to be individual packages. The Hague-Visby Rules have largely removed this problem since they provide both a weight limit as an alternative[25] as well as a test for determining when the container or its contents are to be considered as packages (the "container clause").[26] However, by no means all states have ratified the Visby amendments so that the issue is still a live one in cases, *e.g.* where the shipment is to the United Kingdom rather than from a United Kingdom port.[27]

The problem has been given considerable attention in the United States which has not yet ratified the Hague-Visby Rules. The courts of that country have struggled to find a consistent solution to this problem. Some cases have placed emphasis on the ownership of the container. Where in the case before them the container has been owned by the carrier, it has in effect been treated as a part of the ship so that the goods contained in it are considered to be the relevant packages.[28] Other cases have reached the opposite conclusion where the container has not been supplied by the carrier.[29] Yet other cases have looked to how the goods have been described on the bill of lading as a major factor,[30] in the same way as is required by the Hague-Visby Rules.[31] Some cases have however, seen this as only one of a range of factors to be taken into account.[32] This last solution, in particular, must lead to great uncertainty, but it does involve a degree of flexibility which can be contrasted with the solution imposed by the Hague-Visby "container clause" which is discussed in the next paragraph.

The "container clause" in the Hague-Visby Rules 7.05

Article IV(5)(c) of the Hague-Visby Rules refers to the number of packages or units enumerated on the bill of lading to determine the number of packages for the purposes of limitation (see 5.47). If no number is stated then the container is to be considered as the package. This limits the factors to be considered and puts an onus on

[25] Art. IV(5)(a), see 5.46.

[26] Art. IV(5)(c), see 5.47 and 7.05.

[27] In such cases the Rules are less likely to apply than when carriage is from a U.K. port, see 5.29.

[28] *Leather's Best* v. *S.S. Mormaclynx* [1971] 2 Lloyd's Rep. 476 (U.S.A.). See also *Matsushita Elec. Corp.* v. *S.S. Aegis Spirit* [1977] 1 Lloyd's Rep. 93 (U.S.A.). For a review of the U.S. cases see Armstrong, "Packaging trends and implications in the container revolution" (1981) 12 J.M.L.C. 427.

[29] *Royal Typewriter* v. *M.V. Kulmerland* [1973] 2 Lloyd's Rep. 428 (U.S.A.). This case put forward the "functional economics test" which required a court to consider whether or not the goods were packed with carriage in a container in mind. This test has since been discredited, see *Mitsui & Co.* v. *American Export Lines, The Red Jacket* [1981] A.M.C. 331 (U.S.A.).

[30] *The Red Jacket*, see n. 29 above. Note also *Allstate Insurance* v. *Inversiones Navieras Imparca* 646 F.2d 169 (1981) (U.S.A.).

[31] See 5.47 and 7.05.

[32] *Re Norfolk, Baltimore & Carolina Line* 478 F.Supp. 383 (1979) (U.S.A.).

the shipper to ensure that the bill of lading indicates the relevant number. In particular it means that the question as to who owns the container is no longer relevant to this issue. The provision is not, however, without difficulty. How is it to be applied if, *e.g.* the goods are enumerated in different ways, such as "350 machines in 10 cases" or if loose terms are used, such as "several" or "some"? Similarly is the quantity of goods sufficiently enumerated where the bill of lading only ackowledges that the container is "said to contain" a certain quantity?[33]

A distinct problem is where the number stated is incorrect or there is some other inaccuracy, *e.g.* where the goods are described as being "packed" when, in fact, they are not. We suggest that in such cases the shipper would be bound by the description in the bill of lading for the purpose of applying the limit of liability.[34] Thus if the bill of lading enumerated less goods than were contained in the container the carrier would only be liable up to the limit in respect of the number of packages stated on the bill of lading and not those proved to be in the container. However, this would not prevent a carrier from showing that the bill of lading is incorrect, *e.g.* by showing that there are more goods enumerated on the bill of lading than are proved actually to have been packed in the container.

7.06 **Carriage of containers on deck**

In the law of carriage by sea, as stated in 5.23, it may be a deviation to stow goods on the deck of a ship. However, this would not be so in the case where there is a custom of the trade to stow on deck, or if the shipper agrees to deck stowage, *e.g.* by means of a "liberty to carry on deck" clause in the bill of lading.[35] Modern container ships are designed to carry containers on deck, and containers are themselves designed to protect the goods from the elements. Thus the continued existence of this rule is a potential source of difficulty.

Two decisions of the courts of the United States are particularly relevant in this context. In the early case of *Encyclopaedia Britannica* v. *The Hong Kong Producer*[36] a container load of books were shipped on the weather deck of a conventional ship and were damaged by sea water. A "liberty to carry on deck" clause was held not to have been properly incorporated into the Bill of lading. In consequence the carrier was held to be in breach of contract and liable without limit for the damage.[37] However, in the later case of *Du Pont de Nemours* v. *The Mormacvega*[38] a ship had been refitted to enable it to carry containers

[33] See 5.47.

[34] This should also apply to where a container is "said to contain" a certain quantity. See also *The Red Jacket*, n. 29 above, where the plaintiff was held bound by an indication in the Bill of lading that the goods were packed in "bundles" in the container even though this was proved not to be the case.

[35] See also 5.29 as regards the exclusion of the Hague-Visby Rules when the Bill of lading states that the goods are being carried on deck.

[36] [1969] 2 Lloyd's Rep. 536 (U.S.A.).

[37] The carrier was not allowed to rely on the Hague Rules limit, see 7.04 above, which otherwise would have applied.

[38] [1974] 1 Lloyd's Rep. 296 (U.S.A.).

and the procedure of the carrier was such that it was impossible to determine prior to actual loading where a given container would be stowed. In this case the court accepted that carriage on the deck of a specially constructed ship was for most goods as safe as stowage below deck (even though the container was, in fact, lost overboard!). Since therefore the deck was a usual place to stow the container the carrier had not committed an unreasonable deviation by doing so.

The realities of container shipping have been accepted in the United States to such an extent that it has even been said that a request for under-deck stowage would be ignored.[39] However, it is quite clear that the courts in England will not allow a carrier to ignore an agreement that the goods be stowed below deck, whether such an agreement is made orally,[40] or arises because the bill of lading acknowledges that the goods have been stowed under deck.[41] This will be a breach of contract although the carrier may still be allowed to limit his liability in accordance with the Hague-Visby Rules.[42] Where there is no such agreement, but equally no "liberty" to carry on deck, it has not yet been decided in England whether the carriage of a container load of goods on the "deck" of a container ship would be a deviation.

Changes in responsibilities due to containerisation 7.07

Where a full container load of goods is carried from the consignor's premises for delivery to the consignee, the shipper or consignor will normally "pack" the goods himself into the container. Clearly he will then bear the legal responsibilty in respect of the performance of this task. This is not unusual in respect of some types of carriage, such as carriage by road, and the relevant international convention may well take this possibility into account.[43]

In carriage by sea Article III(2) of the Hague-Visby Rules imposes a duty on the carrier to "properly and carefully" load and stow the goods.[44] The Rules, however, do not prohibit the carrier from contracting out of the performance of all or part of such operations. The duty only applies to those operations that he actually contracts to perform.[45] Thus where the shipper packs the goods into the container the responsibility of the carrier is to properly load and stow the container into the ship. However, the carrier also has a duty to exercise due diligence to ensure that the ship and its equipment are seaworthy at the start of the voyage[46] and this duty in this context is an important issue.

[39] Motley D.J. at first instance in *The Red Jacket*, see n. 29 above, and reported in [1978] 1 Lloyd's Rep. 300 at p. 303, commenting on the practice of the carriers without apparent criticism.

[40] *Evans* v. *Merzario* [1976] 2 Lloyd's Rep. 165.

[41] *The Nea Tyhi* [1982] 1 Lloyd's Rep. 606.

[42] As he was permitted to do in *The Nea Tyhi*, see n. 41 above. Compare, however, *The Hong Kong Producer*, n. 36 above.

[43] As in C.M.R., see 3.51.

[44] See 5.40.

[45] *Pyrene* v. *Scindia Navigation* [1954] 2 Q.B. 402.

[46] Under Art. III(1), see 5.32-5.33.

Where the container is owned by the carrier he is responsible for the fitness of the container supplied to the customer. Arguably this is part of his duty under Article III(1)(b) of the Hague-Visby Rules to exercise due diligence to properly equip the ship. Alternatively it may be considered to be a duty at common law under the bailment which arises from the supply of the container to the consignor.[47] This difference in classifying the duty is relevant to the fact that some container bills of lading exclude the carrier's liability if a defect in the container should have been apparent on a reasonable examination whilst it was being packed by the shipper.[48] Such a clause may be void under Article III(8) of the Hague-Visby Rules[49] if the courts accept that the carrier is responsible under Article III(1)(b) for the supply of a fit container.[50]

Where the container is supplied by the customer or a third party, the carrier will not be liable for damage caused by its defective condition. Nor will he be responsible for damage resulting from the poor stowage of the goods into the container by the shipper.[51] However, the carrier's duty under Article III(1) of the Hague-Visby Rules, to exercise due diligence to make the ship seaworthy includes a duty to exercise care in ensuring that containers loaded on board his ship are fit to be carried. Thus he may be in breach of his duty wherever damage is caused by the fact that a defective container has been loaded on board.[52] This duty should apply regardless of whoever owns the container. Furthermore it has been said[53] that a carrier has a duty to inquire of a shipper as to both the contents of a container delivered to him for carriage and as to how the contents have been secured in it. This is so that the carrier has the means to satisfy himself that the container has been packed in such a way that it is safe to carry.

Note finally that the United Kingdom has ratified the International Convention on Safe Containers 1972.[54] The regulations made under it provide for a system for the approval of containers and impose responsibilities in respect of maintenance and periodic inspection. Responsibility for maintenance and inspection is imposed on the owner or lessee (under a formal leasing contract) of the container. These duties can however be transferred to a bailee of the container for the period of hire by an express term in the contract of bailment.

7.08 The period of responsibilty under the Hague-Visby Rules

The Hague-Visby Rules only govern the carrier's responsibility for the goods between loading and discharge.[55] Liability for loss or

[47] As to bailment see 1.03.
[48] See clause 19(1)(c) of "Combidoc" reproduced in Appendix 7.
[49] See 5.27.
[50] See *The Red Jacket* [1978] 1 Lloyd's Rep. 300 at p. 310 (U.S.A.).
[51] Under Article IV(2)(i) of the Hague-Visby Rules, see 5.42.
[52] As held in *The Red Jacket*, see n. 50 above.
[53] In *The Red Jacket*, see n. 50 above, at p. 309. See further Harrington, "Legal problems arising from containerisation and intermodal transport" (1982) XVII E.T.L. 3.
[54] Implemented by The Freight Containers (Safety Convention) Regulations 1984.
[55] See 5.29.

damage to the goods occurring outside those periods can be excluded subject perhaps to the operation of the Unfair Contract Terms Act.[56] The realities of container transport are such that the goods are normally in the possession of the carrier well before loading[57] and remain in his charge for some time after discharge. This extended period of possession of the goods is not necessarily matched by any extension of liability under the Hague-Visby Rules.[58] If however the Hamburg Rules[59] ever come into effect they will extend the period of responsibility of the carrier from the point that he takes the goods in charge at the port of loading to the point of delivery at the port of discharge.

CONTRACTS FOR COMBINED TRANSPORT

Introduction 7.09

The essence of any contract for combined transport is to provide a service by means of which the link between the different means of transport is provided by an operator such as a carrier or forwarder. This is so whether such operator owns or controls the different means of transport.

However, whilst an operator may be prepared to provide the service, the extent of the responsibility that he undertakes will vary depending on the contract he makes with his customer. As we have seen in both Chapters 1 and 2[60] this depends on whether the operator agrees to take responsibility for the whole of the carriage. Alternatively the operator may only agree to be responsible for such part of the carriage as he performs himself and to act merely as an agent so far as any other carriers involved are concerned.[61] The history of contracts for combined transport reflects the increasing readiness of operators to accept responsibility for the whole of the carriage.

This is reflected in the development of the types of documents used in combined transport. In the early days of container services, if the main carrier providing the service was a shipping company, it was common to adapt traditional shipping documents to the new type of service. Other operators such as forwarders would likewise adapt their usual documentation. However in recent years the tendency has been to adopt a new type of contract called a "combined transport document." These developments are explained more fully in 7.10-7.15.

[56] See 5.44.

[57] Thus container Bills of lading are normally "received for shipment" Bills, see 5.07. See, however, 7.14.

[58] Although the Bill of lading may by contract extend it to cover this period. In the U.S.A. the Harter Act 1893 applies to regulate the carrier's liability in the period prior to loading and subsequent to discharge.

[59] See 5.27.

[60] See 1.77 and 2.03-2.04.

[61] See 7.10-7.11 below.

7.10 **The use of "through Bills of lading"**

At first where a shipping company was involved in providing through container services, it was common to adapt the traditional "through" bill of lading[62] to cover both the period of carriage by sea and any periods of land carriage. Through bills of lading are used when the shipping line issuing it does not itself serve the port of dispatch or destination so that the goods have to be "transhipped" at some point from one ship to another. This is often indicated on the face of the bill of lading by noting where appropriate that a period of "pre-carriage" was involved, or by indicating a different place of delivery than the port of discharge. The bill of lading reproduced in Appendix 5.A contains spaces where these indications can be given.

The company issuing the through bill of lading, whether for carriage by sea or for combined transport, may accept responsibility for the entire carriage.[63] Where the first carrier accepts freight for the whole carriage there may be a presumption that he accepts such responsibility, unless the contract or other circumstances indicate that he accepts responsibility only for that part of the carriage which he actually performs.[64] For many years however, it has been usual for such bills of lading to restrict the liability of the companies involved to the portions of carriage they each perform and subject to their respective standard trading conditions.[65] Normally the company which issues the bill of lading acts as agent for the other companies involved so that each of them enters into a contract with the shipper in respect of their portion.[66] An alternative is for the first carrier to act as an agent for the shipper thus similarly creating a contract between the shipper and the through carriers.[67] Again each carrier would be responsible only for the carriage that he actually performs. The carrier issuing the bill of lading in effect acts as a forwarder[68] in respect of the

[62] For Bills of lading see 5.04.

[63] Although it may exclude liability in respect of the portions performed by its subcontractors, see further 2.06. In such a case the owner of the goods must endeavour to sue the appropriate subcontractor in tort rather than in contract, see 1.19 and 1.78-1.87. See also *The Danish Co-operative Society* v. *The Midland Railway Company* (1892) 8 T.L.R. 212, where a consignee under a through Bill of lading was held entitled to sue a subcontractor in tort for having caused delay to the goods.

[64] This was the case in early cases on carriage by railway, see *Bristol and Exeter Ry.* v. *Collins* (1859) 7 H.L.C. 194, and *Muschamp* v. *Lancaster and Preston Junction Railway Company* (1841) 8 M. & W. 421. Similar cases can be found in carriage by inland waterways, *Hyde* v. *Trent and Mersey Navigation Company* (1793) 5 T.R. 389. Also in cases involving through carriage by sea and rail, see *Greeves* v. *West India and Pacific S.S. Co.* (1870) 22 L.T. 615.

[65] Even where the first carrier remains responsible for the whole of the carriage it is common for the contract to provide that the trading conditions of his subcontractors govern his liability as regards those portions of the carriage performed by them. Where a sea leg is involved, the through Bill of lading is usually made subject to the regular ocean Bill of lading of the shipowner, see *E. Clemens Horst* v. *Norfolk and North American S.S. Co.* (1906) 11 Com.Cas. 141.

[66] See *Crawford and Law* v. *Allan Line* [1912] A.C. 130.

[67] This arrangement, however, produces the difficulty that the Bill of lading issued by the first carrier may not be binding on subsequent carriers, see *Holland Colombo Trading* v. *Alawdeen* [1954] 2 LL.L. Rep. 45.

[68] See generally Chap. 2.

additional stages of the carriage. Clause 6 of the bill of lading in Appendix 5.A is an example of a contractual term which provides for this possibility.

Other "forwarding" contracts: transhipment clauses and forwarders' contracts 7.11

It is common also to combine a forwarding arrangement as described in 7.10 with a "liberty to tranship" clause in an ordinary bill of lading. A carrier by sea has no automatic right to tranship at common law, although he may however be justified in doing so if this is necessitated by reason of damage to the ship.[69] However, most bills of lading give the carrier a liberty to tranship, (*i.e.* to transfer the goods to a ship belonging to a different carrier in order to complete the carriage) or to forward to the agreed destination by some other means of carriage. Usually the carrier is given a complete discretion to do so.[70] It is common also to provide in such clauses that if the carrier does tranship, then he is no longer responsible for the carriage performed by the transhipment carrier, but is acting merely as a forwarder for the shipper in respect of the remainder of the carriage.

Where forwarders provide container services such as groupage arrangements,[71] they may well contract solely on an agency basis without accepting responsibility as a principal for the carriage of the goods. In such cases they issue a "house bill of lading" to their customer and themselves obtain the usual documents from the carriers they engage to perform the various stages of the carriage.

Difficulties arising from use of through bills, etc. 7.12

The use of a through bill of lading which restricts the liability of each carrier to the portion of carriage they each perform creates many problems especially for the customer. First there is the sheer complexity of such contracts which have to identify the different stages of carriage and attach different contractual liabilities to each. It may indeed be a difficult matter to determine which terms relate to which stage of the transport.[72] The terms relevant to a particular stage may be difficult for the customer to find out since they may have been incorporated into the contract by reference[73] rather than being spelt out in the through bill of lading. Having worked out the terms appropriate to the relevant stage of transport the customer will still be faced with the task of deciding which carrier to sue and may possibly be faced with the hazards of pursuing a potential defendant in a foreign country.

Such decisions about who to sue will be especially difficult if it is unclear at the outset at what stage of the carriage loss or damage

[69] *Shipton* v. *Thornton* (1838) 9 Ad. & E. 314.

[70] See clause 6 of the Bill of lading in Appendix 5.A.

[71] See 2.02.

[72] See *Lufty Ltd.* v. *Canadian Pacific Railway Co.* [1974] 1 Lloyd's Rep. 106. Equally it may be difficult to reconcile terms in different documents, see *E. Clemens Horst* v. *Norfolk and North American S.S. Co.*, see n. 65 above.

[73] *e.g.* see clause 12(2) of the British Rail Conditions of Carriage in Appendix 1.B.

occurred. This is a major problem in container transport since the place where damage has occurred is often unknown. Where the carrier issuing the bill of lading acknowledges receipt of the goods in apparent good order and condition,[74] the onus is on him to prove that the loss or damage took place on a stage of the carriage for which he is not responsible.[75] However, if this statement is qualified as indicated in 7.03 it will be for the claimant to prove at which stage the loss or damage occurred. The practice of intermediate carriers is to issue "interchange receipts" when they take over the container. These testify to the condition of the container on receipt by them and can be of considerable importance in determining at which stage of the carriage loss or damage actually occurred.[76]

Even if the claimant can rely initially on the statement of apparent good order and condition in the through bill of lading, the issuing carrier may prove that the loss or damage did not in fact occur during the stage for which he was responsible. The claimant will be left to search for the carrier who was responsible, and the limitation period may well have expired by the time he finds him. Such difficulties are also relevant whenever traditional forwarding contracts are involved.[77]

7.13 Combined transport documents, the "T.C.M." solution

The difficulties indicated above in 7.12 produced a demand for more protection for customers under the contracts available for combined transport. Recognition of this and the fact that container operators were developing integrated services led such operators to introduce new documents under which they accepted responsibility for the entire carriage whether they performed it entirely themselves or through subcontractors. However there was little consistency between these documents in dealing with some of the important problems of container carriage, *e.g.* the problem of concealed damage.[78]

The Draft Convention on the Combined Transport of Goods (T.C.M.)[79] was produced in 1971 in an attempt to harmonise the different documents in use.[80] Unfortunately this draft was not converted into a formal international convention.[81] Nevertheless its provisions have been adopted by important commercial bodies and through their work T.C.M. provides the basis for most standard forms of contract used in container transport today. Thus the International Chamber of Commerce (I.C.C.) in 1973 produced Uniform

[74] See 5.10.

[75] *Crawford and Law* v. *Allan Line*, see n. 66 above.

[76] As in *Lufty*, see n. 72 above.

[77] See generally Chap. 2.

[78] See generally Gronfors, "Container Bills of Lading and Multimodal Transport Contracts" in *Ocean Transport Documentation and its Simplification* U.N.C.T.A.D. 1980.

[79] Transport Combines des Marchandises.

[80] See Massey, "Prospects for a New Intermodal Legal Regime: A Critical Look at the T.C.M." (1972) 3 J.M.L.C. 725.

[81] For reasons indicated in 7.16.

Rules for a Combined Transport Document which were revised in 1975.[82] These are based on T.C.M. and are intended as minimum standard rules for use in documents issued by operators. Today the I.C.C. Rules are the basis for the Combidoc standard form combined transport document issued by B.I.M.C.O.[83] which is reproduced in Appendix 7 and discussed in 7.14. They are also the basis for the F.I.A.T.A.[84] Combined Transport Bill of Lading (F.B.L.).[85]

Apart from the use made of these forms, many container operators issue their own standard conditions which are often based at least in part on the Rules. However, these conditions often vary substantially from the Rules and these variations must be watched for carefully.

The Combidoc combined transport document 7.14

The Combidoc document, reproduced in Appendix 7. can be used to illustrate how the I.C.C. Rules generally operate in practice. The document is signed by the Combined Transport Operator (C.T.O.) and evidences a contract for combined transport. Under this contract the Combined Transport Operator agrees to perform and/or in his own name to procure performance of the carriage, and is given the freedom to use any reasonable means, methods, or routes, etc. The document can still apply even if only one method of transport, contrary to the original intentions of the parties, is in fact used. The essence of the contract is really the provision of transport generally rather than of a particular type of transport. The document can be in either a non-negotiable or negotiable form. The latter is provided to enable the document to be used like a bill of lading in documentary credit arrangements.[86]

The document is evidence that the goods have been received for carriage. Thus it is like a "received for shipment" bill of lading.[87] Where in fact carriage by sea is contemplated and the document is issued by a shipowner or charterer it may well be a document of title.[88] Furthermore if a "shipped" bill of lading[89] is required by the customer, the document can be converted into one if the shipowner, charterer or the master of the ship indorses the date of shipment on it. Regardless of whether or not this is done the carrier accepts responsibilty for the whole of the carriage from the time of taking the goods in charge until they are delivered.[90]

[82] I.C.C. pub. no. 298.

[83] The Baltic and International Maritime Conference.

[84] The International Federation of Freight Forwarders Associations.

[85] Which may be used only by forwarders who are members of their national associations such as the Institute of Freight Forwarders in the U.K. See also clause 3(C) of the I.F.F. Standard Trading Conditions 1984 in Appendix 2.

[86] See 5.02.

[87] See 5.07.

[88] See 5.11.

[89] See 5.07.

[90] See clause 9 of Combidoc reproduced in Appendix 7. Acceptance by forwarders of such responsibility, *e.g.* by issuing an F.B.L. (see 7.13 above), enables them to be fully recognised as Combined Transport Operators. Note that it is common for C.T.O.s to protect their servants and subcontractors from actions in tort by means of circular indemnities as described in 1.86. See *The Chevalier Roze* [1983] 2 Lloyd's Rep. 438.

The liability of the carrier for loss or damage is determined, under Combidoc, by two sets of rules:
(a) When the stage of transport where the loss or damage occurred is not known, (*i.e.* concealed loss or damage) his liability is determined by clause 10.[91] Under this clause the carrier is liable unless he can prove that one of the excepted perils listed in it applies. In effect the carrier is liable unless he proves that the loss or damage was not caused by his failure to exercise reasonable diligence. It is thus a similar liability to that provided by the Hague-Visby Rules.[92] This clause also provides for a limit of liability of 30 francs per kilo which is the same as the limit per kilo in the Hague-Visby Rules.[93] Many operators who issue their own documents provide for a limit which is less favourable to the customer.
(b) When the stage of transport where loss or damage occurred is known clause 11[94] provides for what is often called a "network" principle. The liability of the carrier in this case is determined by any compulsory international or national rules which would have applied had the claimant made a contract with the carrier solely for the stage where loss or damage occurred. Thus, *e.g.* if the goods were damaged whilst being carried by road and the C.M.R. Convention[95] would have applied had the contract been solely for carriage by road then C.M.R. will govern the liability of the carrier. In the case of carriage by sea Combidoc applies the original Hague Rules of 1924 if no compulsory rules such as the Hague-Visby Rules are applicable.[96] Where carriage by inland waterways is involved, the carrier can ensure that his liability for that stage is covered by the terms of his contract, if any, with such inland waterways carrier.[97] If no compulsory rules or the other rules indicated in clause 11 apply, then Combidoc applies the rule provided in clause 10 to govern the liability of the carrier.[98]

Liability for delay is governed by clause 12[99] under which the carrier accepts liability for delay only when the stage of transport where a delay occurred is known. Compensation for delay is limited to the amount of freight for that stage of transport subject to any compulsory rules that might apply. The time limit for claims as indicated in clause 4[1] is nine months from the date of delivery, or from the date when the goods should have been delivered or the date that they can be presumed to be lost.[2] This is to give the carrier some time to sue any responsible subcontractor within the usual one-year limitation period.[3]

[91] Equivalent to Rules 11 and 12 of the I.C.C. Rules.
[92] See 5.40.
[93] As it was expressed before conversion to S.D.R.'s, see 5.27 and 5.46.
[94] The equivalent of Rule 13 of the I.C.C. Rules.
[95] See Chap. 3.
[96] As permitted by Rule 13(b) of the I.C.C. Rules. For when the Hague-Visby Rules apply see 5.29.
[97] See the face of Combidoc in Appendix 7. This possibility is envisaged by Rule 13(c) of the I.C.C. Rules.
[98] As does Rule 13(d) of the I.C.C. Rules. Some C.T.O.s, however, apply the terms of their subcontractors in this case.
[99] The equivalent of Rule 14 of the I.C.C. Rules.
[1] The equivalent of Rule 19 of the I.C.C. Rules.
[2] See clause 14(2).
[3] *e.g.* under the Hague-Visby Rules, see 5.50.

International carriage conventions and combined transport documents 7.15

The Combined Transport Document outlined above in 7.14 has provided a practical commercial solution to the problems posed by the development of intermodal container services. It does not, however, necessarily resolve all the legal problems which arise. Particular difficulties still exist in respect of the application of compulsory rules contained in international conventions governing carriage by single modes of transport. Whilst the "network" approach is designed to reduce such problems to a minimum, clashes between combined transport documents and such compulsory rules do occur.[4]

Even though contracts of combined transport are concerned with the provision of transport in general, the courts are still likely to construe them as contracts for the particular means of transport actually used by the carrier. This approach is necessary to prevent the compulsory rules of international conventions from being easily evaded. Until there is an international convention in force which deals with them as a distinctly new type of contract, there will be occasions when the terms of contracts for combined transport will clash with compulsory rules. This will happen when the means of transport actually used fall within the application of such rules. The prospects for the adoption of such an international convention are considered in 7.16.

Multimodal Transport

The Multimodal Transport Convention 1980 7.16

The growing importance of intermodal carriage of containers has been a cause of concern to developing countries because of its potential impact on their economies. The T.C.M. Draft Convention[5] was not drafted with these concerns in mind and in consequence it has not been formally adopted. Further study was felt to be necessary which was undertaken by the United Nations Conference on Trade and Development (U.N.C.T.A.D.). This led to the formal adoption in 1980 of The United Nations Convention on International Multimodal Transport of Goods. The term "multimodal transport" was used rather than "combined transport" in order to distinguish this Convention from T.C.M. The 1980 Convention is not yet in force and is unlikely to be so for some time. If, however, it does come into force it may well become the most important of all the carriage conventions. The main provisions of the Convention are considered in 7.17.[6]

The Multimodal Transport Convention 1980, principal provisions 7.17

To alleviate the fears of developing countries both the Preamble and Article 4 of the Convention recognise the right of states to

[4] See *Mayhew Foods* v. *Overseas Container Line* [1984] 1 Lloyd's Rep. 317. See also the Belgian case referred to in 3.15, n. 61, where the court held the nine-month time limit for claims in the combined transport Bill of lading to be inapplicable to a period of road carriage governed by C.M.R.

[5] See 7.13.

[6] See also *Multimodal Transport, The 1980 U.N. Convention*, a set of papers published by Southampton University in 1980.

regulate and control multimodal transport operations in their territory. Thus by adopting the Convention, states do not sign away their right to exercise such control.

Article 1(1) of the Convention defines "international multimodal transport" as the "carriage of goods by at least two different modes of transport on the basis of a multimodal transport contract from a place in one country at which the goods are taken in charge by the multimodal transport operator to a place designated for delivery situated in a different country." However the "operations of pick-up and delivery of goods carried out in the performance of a unimodal transport contract, as defined in such contract, shall not be considered as international multimodal transport." This exception was included to satisfy the demands of carriers by air to continue to have their liability during the period of carriage by air governed by the Warsaw Convention[7] when they provide a pick-up and delivery service at each end of the air carriage[8]

Article 2 provides that the Convention applies to contracts of multimodal transport between places in two states when either the place of taking the goods in charge or the place for delivery, as provided for in the contract, are located in a Contracting State, *i.e.* a country which has adopted the Convention once it is in force.[9]

The Convention provides, in Article 5, for the issue of a multimodal transport document[10] which can be in either negotiable or non-negotiable form.[11] It is to be issued by a multimodal transport operator (M.T.O.) who is defined, in Article 1(2), as a person who "concludes a multimodal transport contract and who acts as a principal, not as an agent or on behalf of the consignor or of the carriers participating in the multimodal transport operations, and who assumes responsibility for the performance of the contract."[12]

The M.T.O. is made responsible for the goods between the time that he takes them in charge until the time of delivery.[13] By Article 16 he is made liable for loss, damage or delay unless he proves that he[14] "took all measures that could reasonably be required to avoid the occurrence and its consequences."[15] This creates a simple "uniform" system of liability regardless of the mode of transport on which the loss, damage or delay occurred.

The provisions dealing with the limits of liability are more complicated:

(a) Where the carriage involves a period of carriage by sea or by inland waterways, the M.T.O.'s liability for loss or damage to the

[7] See Chap. 6.

[8] By virtue of Article 31 of the Hague Protocol, see 6.21.

[9] Similar to C.M.R., see 3.10, but compare the Warsaw Convention, see 6.16.

[10] The failure to issue such a document would not appear to affect the application of the Convention.

[11] The reason for this option is explained in 7.14.

[12] Compare the contracts described in 7.10-7.11.

[13] Both for his own acts and omissions and, under Art. 15, for those of his servants or agents, when they are acting within the scope of their employment, and for those whose services he makes use of for the performance of the contract.

[14] And his servants and agents, etc., see n. 13 above.

[15] Compare the Warsaw Convention, see 6.41.

goods is limited by Article 18(1) to 920 S.D.R.'s[16] (approx £700) per package[17] or other shipping unit or 2·75 S.D.R.'s (approx £2) per kilo, whichever is the higher.[18]
(b) Where, however, the multimodal transport does not, according to the contract, include carriage of goods by sea or by inland waterways, the limit is set, by Article 18(3) at 8·33 S.D.R.'s (approx. £7) per kilo.[19]
(c) Where, however, the loss or damage occurred during one particular stage of the multimodal transport, and an applicable international convention or mandatory law would provide a higher limit[20] than the limits above, then by Article 19 the higher limit will govern the liability of the M.T.O. Thus the Convention creates what can be termed a limited "network" system of compensation.

In the case of delay[21] the liability of the M.T.O. is, by Article 18(4), limited to an amount equivalent to two-and-a-half times the freight payable for the goods delayed, but not exceeding the total freight payable under the multimodal transport contract.[22] All of these limits are subject to the possibility of their being increased by agreement between the M.T.O. and the consignor.[23] The M.T.O. however is not entitled to the benefit of the limitation of liability provided for by the Convention if the loss, damage or delay resulted from what we term "intentional or reckless misconduct."[24]

Under Article 25(1) the time limit for actions under the Convention is set at two years. However, notice of a claim must be given within six months, otherwise it will be time-barred. This provision grants the M.T.O. sufficient time to sue any subcontractor who may have caused the loss or damage. The Convention also contains provisions on jurisdiction,[25] and arbitration.[26] It also contains important provisions which attempt to resolve potential conflicts with other international conventions which might be applicable to particular sections of the carriage, *e.g.* the Warsaw Regime applicable to a period of international air carriage.[27] Thus Article 30(4) provides that carriage within Article 2 of C.M.R.[28] is not to be considered as international multimodal transport. Article 38 is also relevant in this context.

[16] See 3.60.

[17] A "container clause" similar to that contained in the Hague-Visby Rules, see 5.47 and 7.05, is provided in Art. 18(2).

[18] This is about one-third higher than the Hague-Visby limit and slightly higher than the Hamburg Rules limit, see 5.46.

[19] The same as the C.M.R. limit, see 3.60.

[20] As does C.O.T.I.F., see 4.19.

[21] Defined in Art. 16(2) as a failure to deliver the goods within a time expressly agreed upon or the time it would be reasonable to require of a diligent M.T.O.

[22] The same as under the Hamburg Rules, see 5.27.

[23] Under Art. 18(6).

[24] Art. 21(1), as are servants and agents, etc., deprived of the right to avail themselves of such limits for their reckless acts by Art. 21(2). For the meaning of intentional or reckless misconduct see 6.50.

[25] Art. 26, similar to C.M.R., see 3.70.

[26] Art. 27.

[27] As by Art. 31 of the Hague Protocol, see 6.21.

[28] For Art. 2 of C.M.R. see 3.13. Art. 30(4) also refers to similar rules in C.I.M. but only in respect of the previous 1970 C.I.M. Convention.

Appendix 1A

Road Haulage Association Limited

CONDITIONS OF CARRIAGE 1982

(hereinafter referred to as "the Carrier") is not a common carrier and accepts goods for carriage only upon that condition and the Conditions set out below. No servant or agent of the Carrier is permitted to alter or vary these Conditions in any way unless expressly authorised to do so.

1. Definitions

In these Conditions:

"Trader" means the customer who contracts for the services of the Carrier.

"Contract" means the contract of carriage between the Trader and the Carrier.

"Consignment" means goods in bulk or contained in one parcel, package or container, as the case may be, or any number of separate parcels, packages or containers sent at one time in one load by or for the Trader from one address to one address.

"Dangerous Goods" means:

(a) goods which are specified in the special classification of dangerous goods issued by the British Railways Board or which, although not specified therein, are not acceptable to the British Railways Board for conveyance on the ground of their dangerous or hazardous nature, or

(b) goods which, although not included in *(a)* above, are of a similar kind.

2. Parties and Sub-Contracting

(1) The Trader warrants that he is either the owner of the goods in any Consignment or is authorised by such owner to accept these Conditions on such owner's behalf.

(2) The Carrier and any other carrier employed by the Carrier may employ the services of any other carrier for the purpose of fulfilling the Contract in whole or in part and the name of every such other carrier shall be provided to the Trader on request.

(3) The Carrier contracts for itself and as agent of and trustee for its servants and agents and all other carriers referred to in (2) above and such other carrier's servants and agents and every reference in Conditions 3-17 inclusive hereof to "The Carrier" shall be deemed to include every such other carrier, servant and agent with the intention that they shall have the benefit of the Contract and collectively and together with the Carrier be under no greater liability to the Trader or any other party than is the Carrier hereunder.

3. Dangerous Goods

If the Carrier agrees to accept Dangerous Goods for carriage such goods must be accompanied by a full declaration of their nature and contents and be properly and safely packed and labelled in accordance with any statutory regulations for the time being in force for carriage by road.

4. Loading and Unloading

(1) When collection or delivery takes place at the Trader's premises the Carrier shall not be under any obligation to provide any plant, power, or labour in addition to the Carrier's carmen, required for loading or unloading at such premises.

(2) The Carrier shall not be required to provide service beyond the usual place of collection or delivery but if any such service is given by the Carrier it shall be at the sole risk of the Trader who shall indemnify the Carrier against all claims and demands whatever which could not have been made if such service had not been given.

(3) *(a)* Goods requiring special appliances for unloading from the vehicle by which they are carried are accepted for carriage only on condition that such appliances are made available by the Trader at destination.

(b) When the Carrier is, without prior arrangement in writing with the Trader, called upon to load or unload goods requiring special appliances for loading or unloading, the Carrier shall be under no liability whatever to the Trader for any damage whatever, however caused, arising out of such loading or unloading and the Trader shall indemnify the Carrier against all claims and demands whatever which could not have been made if such assistance had not been given.

5. Consignment Notes

The Carrier shall, if so required, sign a document prepared by the sender acknowledging the receipt of the Consignment but no such document shall be evidence of the condition or of the correctness of the declared nature, quantity, or weight of the Consignment at the time it is received by the Carrier.

6. Transit

(1) Transit shall commence when the Carrier takes possession of the Consignment whether at the point of collection or at the Carrier's premises.

(2) Transit shall (unless otherwise previously determined) end when the Consignment is tendered at the usual place of delivery at the consignee's address within the customary cartage hours of the district. Provided that:

(a) if no safe and adequate access or no adequate unloading facilities there exist then transit shall be deemed to end at the expiry of one clear day after notice in writing (or by telephone if so previously agreed in writing) of the arrival of the Consignment at the Carrier's premises has been sent to the consignee; and

(b) when for any other reason whatever a Consignment cannot be delivered or when a Consignment is held by the Carrier 'to await order' or 'to be kept till called for' or upon any like instructions and such instructions are not given or the Consignment is not called for and removed, within a reasonable time, then transit shall be deemed to end.

7. Undelivered or Unclaimed Goods

Where the Carrier is unable for any reason to deliver a Consignment to the consignee or as he may order, or where by virtue of the proviso to Condition 6(2) hereof transit is deemed to be at an end, the Carrier may sell the goods and payment or tender of the proceeds after deduction of all proper charges and expenses in relation thereto and of all outstanding charges in relation to the carriage and storage of the goods shall (without prejudice to any claim or right which the Trader may have against the Carrier otherwise arising under these Conditions) discharge the Carrier from all liability in respect of such goods, their carriage and storage.

Provided that:

(a) the Carrier shall do what is reasonable to obtain the value of the Consignment and

(b) the power of sale shall not be exercised where the name and address of the sender or of the consignee is known unless the Carrier shall have done what is reasonable in the circumstances to give notice to the sender or, if the name and address of the sender is not known, to the consignee that the goods will be sold unless within the time specified in such notice, being a reasonable time in the circumstances from the giving of such notice, the goods are taken away or instructions are given for their disposal.

8. Carrier's Charges

(1) The Carrier's charges shall be payable by the Trader without prejudice to the Carrier's rights against the consignee or any other person. Provided that when goods are consigned 'carriage forward' the Trader shall not be required to pay such charges unless the consignee fails to pay after a reasonable demand has been made by the Carrier for payment thereof.

(2) Except where a quotation states otherwise all quotations based on a tonnage rate shall apply to the gross weight unless:

(a) the goods exceed 2.25 cubic metres in measurement per tonne, in which case the tonnage rate shall be computed upon and apply to each measurement of 2.25 cubic metres or any part thereof, or

(b) the size or shape of a Consignment necessitates the use of a vehicle of greater carrying capacity than the weight of the consignment would otherwise require, in which case the tonnage rate shall be computed upon and apply to the carrying capacity of such vehicle as is reasonably required.

(3) Charges shall be payable on the expiry of any time limit previously stipulated and the Carrier shall be entitled to interest at the average of the overdraft interest rates being charged at Lloyds Bank Limited and Barclays Bank Limited current at this time, calculated on a daily basis on all amounts overdue to the Carrier.

9. Liability for Loss and Damage

(1) The Trader shall be deemed to have elected to accept the terms set out in (2) of this Condition unless, before the transit commences, the Trader has agreed in writing that the Carrier shall not be liable for any loss or misdelivery of or damage to goods however or whenever caused and whether or not caused or contributed to directly or indirectly by any act, omission, neglect, default or other wrongdoing on the part of the Carrier.

Appendix 1A

(2) Subject to these Conditons the Carrier shall be liable for:

(i) loss or misdelivery of or damage to livestock, bullion, money, securities, stamps, precious metals or precious stones only if

(a) the Carrier has specifically agreed in writing to carry any such items and

(b) the Trader has agreed in writing to reimburse the Carrier in respect of all additional costs which result from the carrying of the said items and

(c) the loss, misdelivery or damage is occasioned during transit and results from negligent act or omission by the Carrier;

(ii) any loss or misdelivery of or damage to any other goods occasioned during transit unless the same has arisen from, and the Carrier has used reasonable care to minimise the effects of,

(a) act of God;

(b) any consequences of war, invasion, act of foreign enemy, hostilities (whether war or not), civil war, rebellion, insurrection, military or usurped power or confiscation, requisition, or destruction of or damage to property by or under the order of any government or public or local authority;

(c) seizure or forfeiture under legal process;

(d) error, act, omission, mis-statement or misrepresentation by the Trader or other owner of the goods or by servants or agents of either of them;

(e) inherent liability to wastage in bulk or weight, latent defect or inherent defect, vice or natural deterioration of the goods;

(f) insufficient or improper packing;

(g) insufficient or improper labelling or addressing;

(h) riot, civil commotion, strike, lockout, general or partial stoppage or restraint of labour from whatever cause;

(j) consignee not taking or accepting delivery within a reasonable time after the Consignment has been tendered.

(3) The Carrier shall not in any circumstances be liable for loss of or damage to goods after transit of such goods is deemed to have ended within the meaning of Condition 6(2) hereof, whether or not caused or contributed to directly or indirectly by any act, omission, neglect, default or other wrongdoing on the part of the Carrier.

10. Fraud

The Carrier shall not in any circumstances be liable in respect of a Consignment where there has been fraud on the part of the Trader or the owner of the goods or the servants or agents of either in respect of that Consignment, unless the fraud has been contributed by the complicity of the Carrier or of any servant of the Carrier acting in the course of his employment.

11. Limitation of Liability

(1) Except as otherwise provided in these Conditions the liability of the Carrier in respect of loss or mis-delivery of or damage to goods shall in all circumstances be limited as follows:

(a) where loss, misdelivery or damage, however sustained, is in respect of the whole of the Consignment, to a sum calculated at the rate of £800 per tonne on either the gross weight of the Consignment or, where applicable, the tonnage computed in accordance with Condition 8(2)*(a)* or *(b)* hereof;

(b) where loss, misdelivery or damage, however sustained, is in respect of part of the Consignment, to the proportion of the sum ascertained in accordance with (1)*(a)* of this Condition which the actual value of that part of the Consignment bears to the actual value of the whole of the Consignment.

Provided that:

(i) nothing in this Condition shall limit the liability of the Carrier to less than the sum of £10;

(ii) the Carrier shall be entitled to require proof of the value of the whole of the Consignment and of any part thereof lost, misdelivered or damaged;

(iii) the Trader shall be entitled at any time prior to commencement of transit to give seven days' written notice to the Carrier requiring that the aforementioned £800 per tonne limit be increased but not so as to exceed the value of the Consignment and in the event of such notice being given the Trader shall within the said seven days agree with the Carrier an increase in the carriage charges in consideration of the said increased limit.

(2) Notwithstanding condition 11(1), the liability of the Carrier in respect of the indirect or consequential loss or damage, however arising and including loss of market, shall not exceed the amount of the carriage charges in respect of the Consignment or the amount of the claimant's proved loss, whichever is the smaller, unless;

(a) at the time of entering into the Contract with the Carrier the Trader declares to the Carrier a special interest in delivery in the case of loss or damage or of an agreed time limit being exceeded and agrees to pay a surcharge calculated on the amount of that interest, and

(b) prior to the commencement of transit the Trader has delivered to the Carrier written confirmation of the special interest, agreed time limit and amount of the interest.

12. Indemnity to the Carrier

The Trader shall indemnify the Carrier against:

(1) all consequences suffered by the Carrier (including but not limited to claims, demands, proceedings, fines, penalties, damages, costs, expenses, and loss of or damage to the carrying vehicle and to other goods carried) of any error, omission, misstatement or misrepresentation by the Trader or other owner of the goods or by any servant or agent of either of them, insufficient or improper packing, labelling or addressing of the goods or fraud as in Condition 10;

(2) all claims and demands whatever by whoever made in excess of the liability of the Carrier under these Conditions;

(3) all losses suffered by and claims made against the Carrier in consequence of loss of or damage to property caused by or arising out of the carriage by the Carrier of Dangerous Goods whether or not declared by the Trader as such;

(4) all claims made upon the Carrier by H.M. Customs and Excise in respect of dutiable goods consigned in bond whether or not transit has ended or been suspended.

13. Time Limits for Claims

The Carrier shall not be liable for:

(1) loss from a parcel, package or container or from an unpacked Consignment or for damage to a Consignment or any part of a Consignment unless he is advised thereof in writing otherwise than upon a consignment note or delivery document within three days, and the claim is made in writing within seven days, after the termination of transit;

(2) loss, misdelivery or non-delivery of the whole of a Consignment or of any separate parcel, package or container forming part of a Consignment unless he is advised of the loss, misdelivery or non-delivery in writing otherwise than upon a consignment note or delivery document within twenty-eight days, and the claim is made in writing within forty-two days, after the commencement of transit.

Provided that if the Trader proves that:

(a) it was not reasonably possible for the Trader to advise the Carrier or make a claim in writing within the time limit applicable and

(b) such advice or claim was given or made within a reasonable time,

the Carrier shall not have the benefit of the exclusion of liability afforded by this Condition.

14. General Lien

The Carrier shall have a general lien against the owner of the goods for any monies whatever due from the Trader or such other owner to the Carrier. If any such lien is not satisfied within a reasonable time the Carrier may at his absolute discretion sell the goods, or part thereof, as agent for the owner and apply the proceeds towards the monies due and the expenses of the retention, insurance and sale of the goods and shall, upon accounting to the Trader for any balance remaining, be discharged from all liability whatever in respect of the goods.

15. Unreasonable Detention

The Trader shall be liable for the cost of unreasonable detention of any vehicle, trailer, container or sheet but the rights of the Carrier against any other person in respect thereof shall remain unaffected.

16. Computation of Time

In the computation of time where any period provided by these Conditions is seven days or less, Saturdays, Sundays and all statutory public holidays shall be excluded.

17. Impossibility of Performance

The Carrier shall be relieved of its obligation to perform the Contract to the extent that the performance thereof is prevented by failure of the Trader, fire, weather conditions, industrial dispute, labour disturbance or cause beyond the reasonable control of the Carrier.

Appendix 1B

BR 18793/1

BRITISH RAILWAYS BOARD

GENERAL CONDITIONS OF CARRIAGE OF GOODS

(OTHER THAN GOODS FOR WHICH CONDITIONS ARE SPECIALLY PROVIDED)

Definitions

1. "The Board" means the British Railways Board and includes unless the context otherwise requires their sub-contractors, agents and servants.

"Trader" means any person sending or receiving goods by the Board's services and includes unless the context otherwise requires his servants and agents.

"sender" and "consignee" include unless the context otherwise requires their respective servants and agents.

"consignment" means goods accepted by the Board at one time from one sender at one address for carriage to one consignee at one address.

"sub-contractor" means any carrier engaged by the Board to carry goods on their behalf.

"private siding" means a railway or siding not belonging to the Board or their sub-contractor.

"dangerous goods" means goods included in the list of dangerous goods published by the Board or goods which present a comparable hazard.

"CTT": means consigned through TOPS.

"TOPS": means the Board's Total Operations Processing System.

Parties and sub-contracting

2. (1) The Board may engage sub-contractors to perform the contract of carriage or any part thereof on their behalf.

(2) The Board enter into the contract of carriage for themselves and on behalf of their sub-contractors, agents and servants all of whom shall have the benefit of the contract and shall be under no liability to the Trader in respect of the goods greater than or in addition to that of the Board under the contract.

Addressing, labelling and consignment note

3. (1) Every consignment of goods shall be addressed and labelled in accordance with the Board's requirements and except when otherwise agreed be accompanied by a consignment note containing such particulars as the Board may reasonably require.

(2) The Board shall if so required sign a document prepared by the sender acknowledging receipt of the consignment but no such document shall be evidence of the condition or of the correctness of the declared nature, quantity and weight of the consignment at the time it is received by the Board.

(3) In the case of goods consigned by the Boards CTT procedures the Trader shall in particular communicate to the Board before the goods are accepted by the Board for conveyance the following:-

(a) the flow number relating to the consignment

(b) the number and/or numbers of the wagon(s) being consigned.

(c) any other particulars that the Board from time to time may reasonably require.

Warranties

4. (1) In the absence of written notice to the contrary given to the Board at the time of delivery to them, all goods are warranted by the sender to be fit to be carried or stored.

(2) The Trader shall save harmless and keep the Board indemnified against all claims demands costs or expenses whatsoever and by whomsoever made or howsoever arising as a result of the Trader making an under declaration as to the actual weight and/or an incorrect description of all or any part of a consignment.

(3) The sender also warrants that if the goods are not his own unencumbered property he has the authority of all persons owning or interested in the goods to enter into the contract, and contracts on their behalf.

Liability for loss, damage or delay

5. A. Where goods are accepted by the Board for carriage at Board's risk subject to these conditions the Board shall be liable for:-

(1) loss or misdelivery of or damage to the goods occurring during transit as defined by these conditions unless the Board shall prove that such loss, misdelivery or damage has arisen from:-

(a) Act of God;

(b) any consequence of war, invasion, act of foreign enemy, hostilities (whether war be declared or not), civil war, rebellion, insurrection, military or usurped power or confiscation, requisition, destruction of or damage to property by or under the order of any government or public or local authority;

(c) seizure under legal process;

(d) act or omission of the Trader;

Appendix 1B

(e) inherent liability to wastage in bulk or weight, latent defect or inherent defect, vice or natural deterioration of the goods;

(f) insufficient or improper packing;

(g) insufficient or improper labelling or addressing;

(h) riot, civil commotion, strikes, lockouts, stoppage or restraint of labour from whatever cause;

(j) consignee not taking or accepting delivery within a reasonable time.

Provided that:-

(i) where loss, misdelivery or damage arises and the Board have failed to prove that they used all reasonable foresight and care in the carriage of the goods the Board shall not be relieved from liability for such loss, misdelivery or damage;

(ii) the Board shall not incur liability of any kind in respect of goods where there has been fraud on the part of the Trader;

(2) loss proved by the Trader to have been caused by delay in the carriage of the goods unless the Board prove that such delay has arisen without negligence on the part of the Board.

B. Where goods are accepted by the Board for carriage at Owner's risk, the Board shall not be liable for any loss or misdelivery of or damage or delay to the goods except upon proof by the Trader that the same was caused by the wilful misconduct of the Board. Provided that the Board's liability for non-delivery of a consignment or of any separate package forming part of a consignment (not being attributable to fire or to an accident to a train or vehicle) shall be determined as if the goods had been accepted for carriage at Board's risk.

Limit of liability

6. (1) Subject to these conditions, the liability of the Board in respect of any one consignment shall in any case be limited:-

(a) where the monetary loss however sustained is in respect of the whole of the consignment to a sum calculated at the rate of £2,000 per metric tonne on the gross weight of the consignment;

(b) where the monetary loss however sustained is in respect of part of a consignment to the proportion of the sum ascertained in accordance with (a) of this condition which the value of that part of the consignment bears to the value of the whole of the consignment.

Provided that:-

(i) nothing in this sub-paragraph shall limit the Board's liability below the sum of £20 in respect of any one consignment, and

(ii) the Board shall be entitled to require proof of the value of the whole consignment.

(2) The Board shall not in any case be liable for indirect or consequential damages or for loss of a particular market whether held daily or at intervals.

Time limit for claims

7. Claims will not be entertained:-

(a) (i) for loss from a package or from an unpacked consignment, or

(ii) for damage, misdelivery or delay

unless they are advised thereof in writing (otherwise than upon any of the Board's documents) within three clear days and the claim is made in writing within seven clear days of the end of the transit of the consignment, or the part of the consignment in respect of which the claim arises;

(b) for non-delivery of the whole of the consignment or of any entire wagon load or any separate package forming part of the consignment unless they are advised of the non-delivery in writing (otherwise than upon any of the Board's documents) within twenty-eight days and the claim be made in writing within forty-two days after transit began.

Provided that if in any particular case the Trader proves that:-

(i) it was not reasonably possible for the Trader to advise the Board in writing within the aforesaid times; and

(ii) such advice or claim was given or made within a reasonable time

the Board shall not have the benefit of this condition.

Charges

8. (1) The Board's charges for carriage and services incidental thereto including the charges referred to in paragraph (3) hereof shall be payable by the sender without prejudice to the Board's rights against the consignee or any other person. Provided that where the Board have accepted goods "Carriage Forward" the sender shall only pay such charges if the consignee fails to pay on demand.

(2) A claim or counter-claim shall not be made the reason for deferring or withholding payment of moneys payable to the Board.

(3) The Trader shall pay the Board's charges for the detention of the Board's wagons and other vehicles, containers, coverings and other equipment, or the use or occupation of any siding or other accommodation, whether before or after transit, or whilst transit is suspended, unless the Trader proves that such detention use or occupation has arisen from default of the Board.

Appendix 1B

Undelivered or unclaimed goods

9. Where goods are held by the Board after transit or whilst transit is suspended:-

(a) the Board may sell the goods and payment or tender of the proceeds of such sale after deducting the expenses of the sale and all other charges due in respect of the goods shall (without prejudice to any outstanding claim which the Trader may have against the Board) discharge the Board from all liability in respect of the goods. Provided that:-

(i) the goods shall not be sold unless the Board have done what is reasonable in the circumstances to notify the sender or the consignee that the goods will be sold unless within a reasonable time of the giving of the notice the goods are removed or instructions are given for their disposal;

(ii) the Board shall do what is reasonable to obtain the value of the goods.

(b) In respect of dangerous goods, at the Trader's sole risk and expense, the Board may, if they are satisfied it is reasonable to do so, destroy the goods, return them to the sender (who shall receive them at once) or otherwise dispose of them.

Transit

10. (1) Transit begins when the goods are handed to or collected by the Board for carriage.

(2) Transit shall be suspended:-

(a) when goods are held by the Board at some place other than the destination at the request or for the convenience of the Trader or because the Trader refuses or is unable to take delivery at the destination; or

(b) when the goods are detained for customs purposes;

and shall be resumed when the Board resume the carriage of the goods.

(3) Transit shall (unless otherwise previously determined) end:-

(a) in the case of goods to be delivered by the Board, when they are tendered at the usual place of delivery within the customary cartage hours of the delivery district, or at such other times or places as may be agreed between the Board and the Trader;

(b) in the case of goods not to be delivered by the Board or to be retained by the Board awaiting order, at the expiration of one clear day after notice of arrival has been given either orally or in writing to the consignee or, where the address of the consignee is not known, to the sender or, where the addresses of both sender and consignee are not known, or in the case of goods to be kept till called for, at the expiration of one clear day after the arrival of the goods at the place to which they are consigned;

(c) in the case of goods consigned to a private siding, when they are delivered at that siding, or at the place where the Trader has agreed with the Board to take delivery of goods consigned to the siding. Provided that if the Board through no fault of theirs are unable to delivery goods at such siding or place, transit shall end at the expiration of one clear day after notice has been given, either orally or in writing, to the consignee that the Board are ready and willing to deliver.

Warehousing

11. (1) After termination or during suspension of transit as defined in Condition 10 hereof, unless otherwise agreed in writing the Board will hold goods other than dangerous goods as warehousemen subject to their usual charges and Conditions for Warehousing and to the condition that the Board will not be liable for any loss of or damage to goods which have arrived at the destination or depot and for which the Board give notice that they have no suitable accommodation, by whomsoever and howsoever such loss or damage may be caused and whether or not occasioned by the neglect or default of the Board.

Provided that this condition shall not relieve the Board from any liability the Board might otherwise incur under these conditions in the unloading of the goods.

(2) The Board's liability for any loss of or damage to goods held by them as warehousemen pursuant to this condition shall in any case be subject to the limits and exclusions in Condition 6.

(3) Dangerous goods held by the Board after termination or during suspension of transit will be subject to:-

(a) the condition that the Board will not be liable for any loss of or damage to the goods except upon proof by the Trader that such loss or damage arose from wilful misconduct of the Board;

(b) the provisions of Condition 20 (2) (e) hereof.

Means of transport

12. (1) Goods accepted by the Board for carriage may be carried by such means of transport and by such route as the Board think fit and these conditions shall apply by whatever means or route the goods are carried.

(2) Goods carried wholly or partly by water shall in respect of the carriage by water be carried subject to the applicable Conditions of Carriage of the water carrier who carries the goods and the Board are authorised as agents to contract with the water carrier for the carriage by water of the goods subject to such Conditions.

The Board shall incur no liability whatsoever and howsoever arising during the course or in respect of such carriage by water.

In the absence of proof to the contrary where goods are carried partly by land and partly by water, any loss, damage or delay shall be deemed to have occurred whilst the goods are being carried by land.

Appendix 1B

Loading and unloading

13. (1) On collection or delivery at a Trader's premises the Board shall be under no obligation to provide any plant, power or labour (other than assistance by the Board's carmen) for loading or unloading.

(2) The Board's servants have no authority to give assistance other than in loading and unloading at the usual place of collection or delivery and the Board shall not be liable for any loss or damage however caused by any such other assistance being given.

(3) Goods requiring special appliances for unloading from a road vehicle are accepted for carriage only on condition that the sender has duly ascertained from the consignee that such appliances are available at destination. Where the Board are, without prior arrangement in writing with the Trader, called upon to load or unload goods for which special appliances are required the Board shall be under no liability whatsoever to the Trader for any damage howsoever caused, whether or not by the negligence of the Board, and the Trader shall be responsible for and indemnify the Board against any damage or liability which the Board may suffer or incur.

Computation of time

14. In the computation of time where the period provided by these conditions is seven days or less, Saturdays, Sundays and public holidays shall not be included.

Lien

15. Goods delivered to the Board will be received and held by them subject:-

(a) to a lien for moneys due to them for the carriage of and other proper charges or expenses upon or in connection with such goods and

(b) to a general lien for any moneys or charges due to them from the owners of such goods for any services rendered or accommodation provided in relation to the carriage or custody of goods,

and in case any lien is not satisfied within a reasonable time from the date upon which the Board first gave notice of the exercise of their lien to the owners of the goods, the goods may be sold and the proceeds of sale applied in or towards the satisfaction of every such lien and all proper charges and expenses in relation thereto, and the Board shall account to the owners of the goods for any surplus.

The general lien conferred by this Condition shall not prejudice an unpaid vendor's right of stoppage in transitu.

Other published Regulations

16. Goods are carried subject also to any other applciable published byelaws conditions or regulations relating to the carriage of goods by the Board for the time being in force and in the event of conflict between such byelaws conditions or regulations and these conditions the said byelaws conditions or regulations shall prevail.

Advice by post

17. Service of a notice sent by post shall be deemed to have been made at the time when the notice would have been delivered in the ordinary course of post.

Goods consigned in bond

18. In respect of dutiable goods consigned in bond the Trader will indemnify the Boards against claims made upon them by the Commissioners of Customs and Excise whether or not transit has been ended or suspended.

Zero rated goods for export

19. The Trader will indemnify the Board against any liability arising under Section 12 (8) of the Finance Act 1972 or any statutory modification or re-enactment thereof in respect of a failure to export zero rated goods or to comply with any condition in relation to zero rated goods intended to be exported.

Dangerous goods

20. (1) Where the Board accept dangerous goods (in this condition called "the goods") for carriage the goods will be carried subject to all the foregoing conditions and subject also to the special conditions specified and referred to in this condition and in the event of conflict between the said special conditions and the foregoing the special conditions shall prevail.

(2) The special conditions relating to the carriage of the goods are:-

(a) previous arrangements shall be made with the Board for the conveyance of the goods;

(b) at the time of tendering the goods for carriage the sender shall supply to the Board a declaration in writing stating the nature of the goods;

(c) the goods shall be packed in accordance with any statutory regulations in force applicable to the carriage of the goods and unless otherwise agreed in writing with the regulations for the packing, labelling and loading of dangerous goods published by the Board;

(d) any additional conditions set out or referred to on the consignment note which, in the event of any inconsistency with these conditions, shall prevail;

(e) the Trader, will be responsible for and indemnify the Board (and the London Transport Executive where goods are carried over their lines) against loss or damage and claims made upon them for which they may be or become liable in respect of injury to persons or damage to property arising from non-compliance with any of the provisions of this condition unless the Trader proves that the loss damage or injury is due to the wilful misconduct of the Board.

(3) The Board shall not be liable for loss of, damage or delay to the goods unless the Trader proves that such loss damage or delay was not caused wholly or partly by failure on his part to comply with any of the special conditions in paragraph (2) hereof.

1st August 1986

Appendix 1C

SALE OF GOODS ACT

(1979 c. 54)

Property passes when intended to pass

17.—(1) Where there is a contract for the sale of specific or ascertained goods the property in them is transferred to the buyer at such time as the parties to the contract intend it to be transferred.

(2) For the purposes of ascertaining the intention of the parties regard shall be had to the terms of the contract, the conduct of the parties and the circumstances of the case.

Rules for ascertaining intention

18.—Unless a different intention appears, the following are rules for ascertaining the intention of the parties as to the time at which the property in the goods is to pass to the buyer.

> *Rule* 1.—Where there is an unconditional contract for the sale of specific goods in a deliverable state the property in the goods passes to the buyer when the contract is made, and it is immaterial whether the time of payment or the time of delivery, or both, be postponed.
>
> *Rule* 2.—Where there is a contract for the sale of specific goods and the seller is bound to do something to the goods for the purpose of putting them into a deliverable state, the property does not pass until the thing is done and the buyer has notice that it has been done.

. . . . . .

> *Rule* 4.—When goods are delivered to the buyer on approval or on sale or return or other similar terms the property in the goods passes to the buyer:
>
> (*a*) when he signifies his approval or acceptance to the seller or does any other act adopting the transaction;
>
> (*b*) if he does not signify his approval or acceptance to the seller but retains the goods without giving notice of rejection, then, if a time has been fixed for the return of the goods, on the expiration of that time, and, if no time has been fixed, on the expiration of a reasonable time.
>
> *Rule* 5.—(1) Where there is a contract for the sale of unascertained or future goods by description, and goods of that description and in a deliverable state are unconditionally appropriated to the contract, either by the seller with the assent of the buyer or by the buyer with the assent of the seller, the property in the goods then passes to the buyer; and the assent may be express or implied, and may be given either before or after the appropriation is made.
>
> (2) Where, in pursuance of the contract, the seller delivers the goods to the buyer or to a carrier or other bailee or custodier (whether named by the buyer or not) for the purpose of transmis-

sion to the buyer, and does not reserve the right of disposal, he is to be taken to have unconditionally appropriated the goods to the contract.

Reservation of right of disposal

19.—(1) Where there is a contract for the sale of specific goods or where goods are subsequently appropriated to the contract, the seller may, by the terms of the contract or appropriation, reserve the right of disposal of the goods until certain conditions are fulfilled; and in such a case, notwithstanding the delivery of the goods to the buyer, or to a carrier or other bailee or custodier for the purpose of transmission to the buyer, the property in the goods does not pass to the buyer until the conditions imposed by the seller are fulfilled.

(2) Where goods are shipped, and by the Bill of lading the goods are deliverable to the order of the seller or his agent, the seller is *prima facie* to be taken to reserve the right of disposal.

(3) Where the seller of goods draws on the buyer for the price, and transmits the Bill of exchange and Bill of lading to the buyer together to secure acceptance or payment of the Bill of exchange, the buyer is bound to return the Bill of lading if he does not honour the Bill of exchange, and if he wrongfully retains the Bill of lading the property in the goods does not pass to him.

Risk prima facie passes with property

20.—(1) Unless otherwise agreed, the goods remain at the seller's risk until the property in them is transferred to the buyer, but when the property in them is transferred to the buyer the goods are at the buyer's risk whether delivery has been made or not.

(2) But where delivery has been delayed through the fault of either buyer or seller the goods are at the risk of the party at fault as regards any loss which might not have occurred but for such fault.

(3) Nothing in this section affects the duties or liabilities of either seller or buyer as a bailee or custodier of the goods of the other party.

Delivery to carrier

32.—(1) Where, in pursuance of a contract of sale, the seller is authorised or required to send the goods to the buyer, delivery of the goods to a carrier (whether named by the buyer or not) for the purpose of transmission to the buyer is *prima facie* deemed to be a delivery of the goods to the buyer.

(2) Unless otherwise authorised by the buyer, the seller must make such contract with the carrier on behalf of the buyer as may be reasonable having regard to the nature of the goods and the other circumstances of the case; and if the seller omits to do so, and the goods are lost or damaged in course of transit, the buyer may decline to treat the delivery to the carrier as a delivery to himself or may hold the seller responsible in damages.

(3) Unless otherwise agreed, where goods are sent by the seller to the buyer by a route involving sea transit, under circumstances in which it is usual to insure, the seller must give such notice to the buyer as may enable him to insure them during their sea transit; and if the seller fails to do so, the goods are at his risk during such sea transit.

Risk where goods are delivered at distant place

33.—Where the seller of goods agrees to deliver them at his own risk at a place other than that where they are when sold, the buyer must nevertheless (unless otherwise agreed) take any risk of deterioration in the goods necessarily incident to the course of transit.

Buyer's right of examining the goods

34.—(1) Where goods are delivered to the buyer, and he has not previously examined them, he is not deemed to have accepted them until he has had a reasonable opportunity of examining them for the purpose of ascertaining whether they are in conformity with the contract.

(2) Unless otherwise agreed, when the seller tenders delivery of goods to the buyer, he is bound on request to afford the buyer a reasonable opportunity of examining the goods for the purpose of ascertaining whether they are in conformity with the contract.

Acceptance

35.—(1) The buyer is deemed to have accepted the goods when he intimates to the seller that he has accepted them, or (except where Section 34 above otherwise provides) when the goods have been delivered to him and he does any act in relation to them which is inconsistent with the ownership of the seller, or when after the lapse of a reasonable time he retains the goods without intimating to the seller that he has rejected them.

(2) Paragraph 10 of Schedule 1 below applies in relation to a contract made before 22 April 1967 or (in the application of this Act to Northern Ireland) 28 July 1967.

Termination of lien

43.—(1) The unpaid seller of goods loses his lien or right of retention in respect of them—

(*a*) when he delivers the goods to a carrier or other bailee or custodier for the purpose of transmission to the buyer without reserving the right of disposal of the goods;

(*b*) when the buyer or his agent lawfully obtains possession of the goods;

(*c*) by waiver of the lien or right of retention.

(2) An unpaid seller of goods who has a lien or right of retention in respect of them does not lose his lien or right of retention by reason only that he has obtained judgment or decree for the price of the goods.

Right of stoppage in transit

44.— Subject to this Act, when the buyer of goods becomes insolvent the unpaid seller who has parted with the possession of the goods has the right of stopping them in transit, that is to say, he may resume possession of the goods as long as they are in course of transit, and may retain them until payment or tender of the price.

Duration of transit

45.—(1) Goods are deemed to be in course of transit from the time when they are delivered to a carrier or other bailee or custodier for the purpose of transmission to the buyer, until the buyer or his agent in that behalf takes delivery of them from the carrier or other bailee or custodier.

(2) If the buyer or his agent in that behalf obtains delivery of the goods before their arrival at the appointed destination, the transit is at an end.

(3) If, after the arrival of the goods at the appointed destination, the carrier or other bailee or custodier acknowledges to the buyer or his agent that he holds the goods on his behalf and continues in possession of them as bailee or custodier for the buyer or his agent, the transit is at an end, and it is immaterial that a further destination for the goods may have been indicated by the buyer.

(4) If the goods are rejected by the buyer, and the carrier or other bailee or custodier continues in possession of them, the transit is not deemed to be at an end, even if the seller has refused to receive them back.

(5) When goods are delivered to a ship chartered by the buyer it is a question depending on the circumstances of the particular case whether they are in the possession of the master as a carrier or as agent to the buyer.

(6) Where the carrier or other bailee or custodier wrongfully refuses to deliver the goods to the buyer or his agent in that behalf, the transit is deemed to be at an end.

(7) Where part delivery of the goods has been made to the buyer or his agent in that behalf, the remainder of the goods may be stopped in transit, unless such part delivery has been made under such circumstances as to show an agreement to give up possession of the whole of the goods.

How stoppage in transit is effected

46.—(1) The unpaid seller may exercise his right of stoppage in transit either by taking actual possession of the goods or by giving notice of his claim to the carrier or other bailee or custodier in whose possession the goods are.

(2) The notice may be given either to the person in actual possession of the goods or to his principal.

(3) If given to the principal, the notice is ineffective unless given at such time and under such circumstances that the principal, by the exercise of reasonable diligence, may communicate it to his servant or agent in time to prevent a delivery to the buyer.

(4) When notice of stoppage in transit is given by the seller to the carrier or other bailee or custodier in possession of the goods, he must re-deliver the goods to, or according to the directions of, the seller; and the expenses of the re-delivery must be borne by the seller.

Effect of sub-sale etc. by buyer

47.—(1) Subject to this Act, the unpaid seller's right of lien or retention or stoppage in transit is not affected by any sale or other disposition of the goods which the buyer may have made, unless the seller has assented to it.

(2) Where a document of title to goods has been lawfully transferred to any person as buyer or owner of the goods, and that person transfers the document to a person who takes it in good faith and for valuable consideration, then—

- (*a*) if the last-mentioned transfer was by way of sale the unpaid seller's right of lien or retention or stoppage in transit is defeated; and
- (*b*) if the last-mentioned transfer was made by way of pledge or other disposition for value, the unpaid seller's right of lien or retention or stoppage in transit can only be exercised subject to the rights of the transferee.

Appendix 2

THE INSTITUTE OF FREIGHT FORWARDERS LTD.

STANDARD TRADING CONDITIONS (1984 Edition)

The Customer's attention is drawn to the Clauses hereof which exclude or limit the Company's liability and those which require the Customer to indemnify the Company in certain circumstances.

Definitions

1. In these Conditions:

"Company"	is the IFF member trading under these Conditions.
"Conditions"	means the entire undertakings, terms, conditions and clauses embodied herein.
"person"	includes persons or any Body or Bodies Corporate.
"the Owner"	means the owner of the goods (including any packaging, containers or equipment) to which any business concluded under these Conditions relates and any other person who is or may become interested in them.
"Customer"	means any person at whose request or on whose behalf the Company undertakes any business, or provides advice, information or services.
"instructions"	means a statement of the Customer's specific requirements.

Headings

2. Headings of Clauses or groups of Clauses are for indicative purposes only.

Application

3. (A) Subject to sub-paragraphs (B) and (C) below, all and any activities of the Company in the Course of Business whether gratuitous or not are undertaken subject to these Conditions.

(B) If any legislation is compulsorily applicable to any business undertaken, these Conditions shall, as regards such business, be read as subject to such legislation and nothing in these Conditions shall be construed as a surrender by the Company of any of its rights or immunities or as an increase of any of its responsibilities or liabilities under such legislation and if any part of these Conditions be repugnant to such legislation to any extent such part shall as regards such business be overridden to that extent and no further.

(C) Subject to sub-clause (B) above, the Company and the Customer may agree that in respect of all or any part or parts of any contract for the movement of goods, the Company shall issue a FIATA Combined Transport Bill of Lading (FBL) subject to the current Standard Conditions governing FIATA Combined Transport Bills of Lading, provided that such document is issued subject to current ICC uniform rules for a combined transport document and that this is printed on the face of the document. Where such a document is issued, the terms and conditions embodied in it shall be paramount in governing the relationship between the Customer and the Company insofar as those terms and conditions are inconsistent with or repugnant to these Conditions.

The Company's General Responsibilities

4. (A) The Company shall perform its duties with a reasonable degree of care, diligence, skill and judgement.

(B) Subject to Clause 18 hereof, the Company shall carry out its services within a reasonable time.

(C) Subject to these Conditions and in particular to the discretion reserved to the Company below the Company shall take all reasonable steps to perform any of the Customer's instructions accepted by the Company.

(D) If at any stage in any transaction the Company should reasonably consider that there is good reason in the Customer's interests to depart from any of the Customer's instructions, the Company shall be permitted to do so and shall not incur any additional liability in consequence of so doing.

(E) When using its discretion as permitted in these Conditions, the Company shall do so with due regard to the interests of the Customer.

5. If after a contract has been agreed events or circumstances come to the attention of the Company which in the opinion of the Company make it wholly or in part impossible for the Company to fulfil its duties it shall take reasonable steps to inform the Customer of such events or circumstances and seek further instructions.

The Customer's Undertakings

6. (A) The Customer shall be deemed to be competent and to have reasonable knowledge of matters affecting the conduct of his business, including terms of sale and purchase and all other matters relating thereto.

(B) The Customer shall give sufficient and executable instructions, and the Company shall, within the limits of its duty of care and diligence, inform the Customer if it considers that the Customer's instructions are insufficient or inexecutable.

7. The Customer warrants that he is either the Owner or the authorised agent of the Owner and also that he is accepting these Conditions not only for himself but also as agent for and on behalf of the Owner.

8. In authorising the Customer to enter into any contract with the Company and/or in accepting any document issued by the Company in connection with such contract, the Owner, sender and consignee accept these Conditions for themselves and their agents and for any parties on whose behalf they or their agents may act, and in particular, but without prejudice to the generality of this clause, they accept that the Company shall have the right to enforce against them jointly and severally any liability of the Customer under these Conditions or to recover from them any sums to be paid by the Customer which upon proper demand have not been paid.

9. (A) The Customer shall indemnify the Company against all liability loss damage costs and expenses whatsoever arising out of the Company acting in accordance with the Customer's instructions or arising from any breach by the Customer of any warranty contained in these Conditions or from the negligence of the Customer.

(B) Without derogation from sub-clause (A) above, the Customer shall indemnify the Company against any liability assumed or incurred by the Company when by reason of carrying out the Customer's instructions the Company has reasonably become liable or may become liable to any other party.

10. Except to the extent caused by any negligence on the part of the Company the Customer shall be liable for and shall indemnify the Company in respect of all duties taxes imposts levies deposits and outlays of whatsoever nature levied by any authority in relation to the goods and for all payments fines costs expenses loss or damage whatsoever incurred or sustained by the Company in connection therewith.

11. (A) The Customer undertakes that no claim shall be made against any Director, servant or employee of the Company which imposes or attempts to impose upon them any liability in connection with any services which are the subject of these Conditions and if any such claim should nevertheless be made, to indemnify the Company against all consequences thereof.

(B) The Customer shall save harmless and keep the Company indemnified from and against all claims, costs and demands whatsoever and by whomsoever made or preferred in excess of the liability of the Company under the terms of these Conditions and without prejudice to the generality of this Clause this indemnity shall cover all claims costs and demands arising from or in connection with the negligence or breach of duty of the Company its servants sub-contractors or agents.

(C) In this Clause "sub-contractor" includes direct and indirect sub-contractors and their respective servants and agents and "agents" includes sub-agents and their respective servants or agents.

12. The Customer warrants that the description and particulars of any goods furnished by or on behalf of the Customer are full and accurate.

13. (A) The Customer shall warn the Company if any goods which are the subject of any transaction to which these Conditions apply are liable to taint or affect other goods; and the Customer shall indemnify the Company against any liability, loss, damage, costs or expenses incurred by the Company as a consequence of the Customer's failure to do so or his failure to do so in good time.

(B) Except where the Company has accepted instructions in respect of the preparation packing stowage labelling or marking of the goods the Customer warrants that all goods have been properly and sufficiently prepared, packed, stowed, labelled and/or marked, and that the preparation packing stowage labelling and marking are appropriate to any operations or transactions affecting the goods and the characteristics of the goods.

(C) Where the goods are carried in or on containers, trailers, flats, tilts, railway wagons, tanks, igloos, or any other unit load device specifically constructed for the carriage of goods by land, sea or air, (each hereafter individually referred to as "transport unit") then, save where the Company has accepted instructions as principal to load the transport unit, the Customer warrants

(i) that the transport unit has been properly and competently loaded;

(ii) that the goods are suitable for carriage in or on the transport unit; and

(iii) that the transport unit is in a suitable condition to carry the goods loaded therein (save to such extent as the Company has approved the suitability of the transport unit).

14. The Customer shall indemnify the Company in respect of any claims of a general average nature which may be made on it and shall provide such security as may be required by the Company in this connection.

15. The Customer agrees to make any claim against the Company in writing and without delay: in the event of delay in presentation of a claim causing prejudice to the Customer or to the Company, the Company shall be relieved of all and any liability in respect of such claim.

The Company's role

16. (A) Subject to Clauses 21 and 23 below, in the absence of specific agreement between the Customer and the Company, the

Appendix 2

Company shall be entitled to procure the carriage, storage, packing or handling of the goods as an Agent subject to these Conditions or to provide any or all of its services as a principal contractor.

(B) The offer and acceptance of a fixed price for the accomplishment of any task shall not itself determine whether such task is to be arranged by the Company acting as Agent or to be provided by the Company acting as a contracting principal.

(C) When acting as an Agent, the Company does not make or purport to make any contract with the Customer for the carriage, storage, packing or handling of any goods nor for any other physical service in relation to them and acts solely on behalf of the Customer in securing services by establishing contracts with third parties so that direct contractual relationships are established between the Customer and such third parties.

(D) The Company shall on demand by the Customer provide evidence of any contract entered into as Agent for the Customer. Insofar as the Company may be in default of this obligation, it shall be deemed to have contracted with the Customer as a principal for the performance of the Customer's instructions.

Company's General Conditions

17. The Company shall be discharged of all liability whatsoever howsoever arising in respect of any service provided for the Customer or which the Company has undertaken to provide unless suit be brought and written notice thereof given to the Company within nine months from the date of any event or occurrence alleged to give rise to a cause of action against the Company.

18. Except under special arrangements previously made in writing the Company accepts no responsibility for departure or arrival dates of goods.

19. (A) If delivery of the goods or any part thereof is not taken by the Customer, Consignee or Owner, at the time and place when and where the Company is entitled to call upon such person to take delivery thereof, the Company shall be entitled to store the goods or any part thereof at the sole risk of the Customer, whereupon the liability of the Company in respect of the goods or that part thereof stored as aforesaid shall wholly cease and the cost of such storage if paid for or payable by the Company or any Agent or subcontractor of the Company shall forthwith upon demand be paid by the Customer to the Company.

(B) (i) The Company shall be entitled at the expense of the Customer to dispose of (by sale or otherwise as may be reasonable in all the circumstances)

(a) on 21 days notice in writing to the Customer, or where the Customer cannot be traced and reasonable efforts have been made to contact any parties who may reasonably be supposed by the Company to have any interest in the goods, any goods which have been held by the Company for 90 days and which cannot be delivered as instructed; and

(b) without prior notice, goods which have perished, deteriorated or altered or are in immediate prospect of doing so in a manner which has caused or may reasonably be expected to cause loss or damage to third parties or to contravene any applicable laws or regulations.

(ii) The Company shall give appropriate credit to the Customer for any balance arising out of the proceeds of sale of the goods after deduction of the Company's costs of sale.

20. Except insofar as may be required to comply with the Customer's instructions as regards documentation, or except under special arrangements previously made in writing the Company shall not be obliged to arrange for the goods to be carried, stored or handled separately from other goods.

21. (A) No insurance will be effected except upon express instructions given in writing by the Customer and all insurances effected by the Company are subject to the usual exceptions and conditions of the policies of the insurance company or underwriters taking the risk. Unless otherwise agreed in writing the Company shall not be under any obligation to effect a separate insurance on each consignment but may declare it on any open or general policy held by the Company.

(B) Insofar as the Company agrees to arrange insurance, the Company acts solely as Agent for the Customer using its best endeavours to arrange such insurance and does so subject to the limits of liability contained in Clause 37 hereof.

22. Except in accordance with express instructions in writing previously received and accepted by the Company the Company shall not be obliged to make any declaration for the purpose of any statute, convention or contract as to the nature or value of any goods or as to any special interest in delivery.

23. (A) Except under special arrangements previously made in writing or under the terms of a printed document signed by the Company, any instructions relating to the delivery or release of goods in specified circumstances only, such as (but without prejudice to the generality of this clause) against payment or against surrender of a particular document, are accepted by the Company only as Agents for the Customer where third parties are engaged to effect compliance with the instructions.

(B) The Company shall not be under any liability in respect of such arrangements as are referred to under sub-clause (A) hereof save where such arrangements are made in writing.

(C) In any event, the Company's liability in respect of the performance or arranging the performance of such instructions shall not exceed that provided for in these Conditions in respect of loss of or damage to goods.

24. Advice and information, in whatever form it may be given, is provided by the Company for the Customer only and the Customer shall indemnify the Company against any liability, claims, loss, damage, costs or expenses arising out of any other person relying upon such advice or information. Except under special arrangements previously made in writing, advice and information which is not related to specific instructions accepted by the Company is provided gratuitously and without liability.

25. The defences and limits of liability provided for in these Conditions shall apply in any action against the Company whatsoever, howsoever arising, whether the action be founded in contract tort or otherwise.

Company's Special Conditions relating to Particular Goods

26. Except following instructions previously received in writing and accepted by the Company, the Company will not accept or deal with goods of a dangerous or damaging nature, nor with goods likely to harbour or encourage vermin or other pests. If such goods are accepted pursuant to special arrangement and then in the opinion of the Company they constitute a risk to other goods, property, life or health, the Company shall where reasonably practicable contact the Customer but reserves the right at the expense of the Customer to remove or otherwise deal with the goods.

27. Should any Customer otherwise than under special arrangements previously made in writing as set out in Clause 26 above, deliver to the Company or cause the Company to deal with or handle goods of a dangerous or damaging nature, or goods likely to harbour or encourage vermin or other pests, he shall be liable for all loss or damage arising in connection with such goods and shall indemnify the Company against all penalties, claims, damages, costs and expenses whatsoever arising in connection therewith, and the goods may be dealt with in such manner as the Company or any other person in whose custody they may be at any relevant time shall think fit.

28. (A) Except under special arrangement previously made in writing the Company will not accept or deal with bullion, coin, precious stones, jewellery, valuables, antiques, pictures, human remains, livestock or plants. Should any Customer nevertheless deliver any such goods to the Company or cause the Company to handle or deal with any such goods otherwise than under special arrangements previously made in writing the Company shall be under no liability whatsoever for or in connection with such goods howsoever arising.

(B) The Company may at any time waive its rights and exemptions from liability under sub-clause (A) above in respect of any one or more of the categories of goods mentioned herein or of any part of any category. If such waiver is not in writing, the onus of proving such waiver shall be on the Customer.

Company as a Forwarding Agent

29. Clauses 30 to 32 below inclusive apply where and to the extent that the Company in accordance with these Conditions is acting as agent on behalf of the Customer:

30. The Company shall be entitled and the Customer hereby expressly authorises the Company, except in so far as has been otherwise specifically agreed between the Company and the Customer, to enter into contracts on behalf of the Customer

(a) for the carriage of goods by any route or means or person;

(b) for the storage, packing, trans-shipment, loading, unloading or handling of the goods by any person at any place whether on shore or afloat and for any length of time;

(c) for the carriage or storage of goods in or on transport units as defined in Clause 13 (C) or with other goods of whatever nature; and

(d) to do such acts as may in the opinion of the Company be reasonably necessary in the performance of its obligations in the interests of the Customer.

31. The Company shall be entitled to perform any of its obligations herein by itself or by its parent, subsidiary or associated Companies or by any other person, firm or Company. In the absence of agreement to the contrary any contract to which these Conditions apply is made by the Company on its own behalf and also as agent for and on behalf of any such parent, subsidiary or associated Company, and any such Company shall be entitled to the benefit of these Conditions.

32. Where there is a choice of rates according to the extent or degree of the liability assumed by carriers, warehousemen or others, no declaration of value where optional will be made except under special arrangements previously made in writing; nor shall the Company be under any liability to the Customer by reason of having entered into any contract on behalf of the Customer whereby the extent or degree of the liability assumed by a carrier,

Appendix 2

warehouseman or other party is in any respect excluded or limited save where such contract is entered into contrary to specific instructions given by the Customer and accepted by the Company.

Company Contracting as Principal

33. Clauses 34 to 35 inclusive apply where and to the extent that the Company in accordance with these Conditions is contracting as principal.

34. The Company is not a common carrier and deals on the basis of these Conditions alone. The Company reserves to itself a reasonable liberty as to the means, route and procedure to be followed in the handling, storage and transportation of goods.

35. (A) When and to the extent that the Company has contracted as principal for the performance of any services, it undertakes to perform and/or in its own name to procure the performance of those services, and subject always to the totality of these Conditions accepts liability for loss of or damage to goods taken into its charge occurring between the time when it takes the goods into its charge and the time when the Company is entitled to call upon the Customer, Consignee or Owner to take delivery of the goods.

(B) The Company shall be deemed to have taken the goods into its charge when they have been received by the Company or have been released or handed over by the Customer or any person acting on behalf of the Customer to any person acting on behalf of the Company in accordance with any directions of the Company for the performance of the Customer's instructions.

Limitations of Liabilities

36. Subject always to Clauses 3 above and 37 below the Company shall be relieved of liability for any loss or damage if and to the extent that such loss or damage was caused by:

(a) the act or omission of the Customer, or person other than the Company acting on behalf of the Customer, or of the person from whom the Company took the goods in charge;

(b) insufficiency of the packing and/or marks and/or labels and/or numbers save where the Company had undertaken to carry out the packing, application of marks or labelling or numbering of the goods;

(c) handling, loading, stowage or unloading of the goods by the Customer or any person acting on behalf of the Customer;

(d) inherent vice of the goods;

(e) strike, lock out, stoppage or restraint of labour, the consequences of which the Company was unable to avoid by the exercise of reasonable diligence;

(f) any cause or event which the Company was unable to avoid and the consequences whereof the Company was unable to prevent by the exercise of reasonable diligence.

The burden of proving that the loss or damage was due to one or more of the above causes or events shall rest upon the Company.

37. (A) Subject to Clause 3 above and sub-clauses (D) and (F) below the Company's liability howsoever arising and notwithstanding that the cause of loss or damage be unexplained shall not exceed

(i) in the case of claims for loss or damage to goods

(a) the value of any goods lost or damaged, or

(b) a sum at the rate of two Special Drawing Rights as defined by the International Monetary Fund, (hereinafter referred to as SDR's), per kilo of gross weight of any goods lost or damaged

whichever shall be the least

(ii) in the case of all other claims

(a) the value of the goods the subject of the relevant transaction between the Company and its Customer, or

(b) a sum at the rate of two SDR's per kilo of the gross weight of the goods the subject of the said transaction, or

(c) 75,000 SDR's in respect of any one transaction whichever shall be the least.

For the purposes of paras (i) and (ii) above the value of the goods shall be their value at the place and time they are delivered to the Consignee in accordance with the relevant transaction between the Company and the Customer or should have been so delivered. SDR's shall be calculated as at the date when the claim was first notified to the Company in writing.

(B) Subject to Clause 3 above, and sub-clauses (D) and (F) below, the Company's liability for loss or damage as a result of failure to deliver or arrange delivery of goods in a reasonable time or (where there is a special arrangement under Clause 18) to adhere to agreed departure or arrival dates shall not in any circumstances whatever exceed a sum equal to twice the amount of the Company's charges in respect of the relevant transaction.

(C) Save in respect of such loss or damage as is referred to at sub-clause (B) and subject to Clause 3 above and sub-clauses (D) and (F) below, the Company shall not in any circumstances whatsoever be liable for indirect or consequential loss such as (but not limited to) loss of profits, loss of market or the consequences of delay or deviation however caused.

(D) By special arrangement agreed in writing, the Company may accept liability in excess of the limits set out in sub-clauses (A) to (C) above upon the Customer agreeing to pay the Company's additional charges for accepting such increased liability. Details of the Company's additional charges will be provided upon request.

(E) If expressly instructed so to do in writing by the Customer, the Company will use its best endeavours in accordance with Clause 21 hereof to procure insurance (where available) to indemnify the Customer in respect of any loss which he may suffer in excess of the amounts recoverable in accordance with these Conditions.

(F) In any case where, in accordance with these Conditions, the Company is liable to pay compensation in respect of loss or damage to goods, and it is known where such loss or damage occurred, the extent and the amount of the liability in respect of such loss or damage shall be determined by the provisions contained in any applicable convention or law, which provisions

(i) cannot be departed from by private contract to the detriment of the Claimant; and

(ii) would have applied if the Claimant had made a separate and direct contract with the actual provider of the particular service in respect of that service or that part of any operation where the loss or damage occurred and had received as evidence thereof any particular document which must be issued in order to make such convention or law applicable.

The relevant provisions of the Hague Visby rules contained in the protocol of Brussels dated February 23rd 1968 as enacted in the United Kingdom shall be applied to all carriage of goods by sea and where no mandatory international or national law applies to the carriage of goods by inland waterways also and such provisions shall be applied to all goods whether carried on deck or under deck.

Warsaw Convention

38. If the Company acts as principal in respect of a carriage of goods by air, the following notice is hereby given:

If the carriage involves an ultimate destination or stop in a country other than the country of departure, the Warsaw Convention may be applicable and the Convention governs and in most cases limits the liability of carriers in respect of loss of or damage to cargo. Agreed stopping places are those places (other than the places of departure and destination) shown under requested routing and/or those places shown in carriers' timetables as scheduled stopping places for the route. The address of the first carrier is the airport of departure.

Miscellaneous

39. The Customer shall pay to the Company in cash or as otherwise agreed all sums immediately when due without reduction or deferment on account of any claim, counterclaim or set off.

40. Despite the acceptance by the Company of instructions to collect freight, duties, charges or other expenses from the Consignee or any other person the Customer shall remain responsible for such freight, duties, charges or expenses on receipt of evidence of proper demand and in the absence of evidence of payment (for whatever reason) by such Consignee or other person when due.

41. (A) Subject to sub-clause (B) hereof, the Company shall have a general lien on all goods and documents relating to goods in its possession, custody or control for all sums due at any time from the Customer or Owner, and shall be entitled to sell or dispose of such goods or documents as agent for and at the expense of the Customer and apply the proceeds in or towards the payment of such sums on 28 days notice in writing to the Customer. Upon accounting to the Customer for any balance remaining after payment of any sum due to the Company and the costs of sale or disposal the Company shall be discharged of any liability whatsoever in respect of the goods or documents.

(B) When the goods are liable to perish or deteriorate, the Company's right to sell or dispose of the goods shall arise immediately upon any sum becoming due to the Company subject only to the Company taking reasonable steps to bring to the Customer's attention its intention of selling or disposing of the goods before doing so.

42. The Company shall be entitled to retain and be paid all brokerages commissions allowances and other remunerations customarily retained by or paid to freight forwarders.

Jurisdiction and Law

43. The English Courts shall have exclusive jurisdiction to deal with any dispute which has arisen or may arise out of or in connnection with the business of the Company.

44. Subject to Clause 3 (B) hereof these Conditions and any act or contract to which they apply shall be governed by English Law.

Appendix 3A

CARRIAGE OF GOODS BY ROAD ACT 1965

(1965 c. 37)

An Act to give effect to the Convention on the Contract for the International Carriage of Goods by Road signed at Geneva on 19th May 1956; and for purposes connected therewith.

[5th August 1965]

Convention to have force of law

1. Subject to the following provisions of this Act, the provisions of the Convention on the Contract for the International Carriage of Goods by Road (in this Act referred to as "the Convention"), as set out in the Schedule to this Act, shall have the force of law in the United Kingdom so far as they relate to the rights and liabilities of persons concerned in the carriage of goods by road under a contract to which the Convention applies.

Designation of High Contracting Parties

2.—(1) Her Majesty may by Order in Council from time to time certify who are the High Contracting Parties to the Convention and in respect of what territories they are respectively parties.

(2) An Order in Council under this section shall, except so far as it has been superseded by a subsequent Order, be conclusive evidence of the matters so certified.

Power of court to take account of other proceedings

3.—(1) A court before which proceedings are brought to enforce a liability which is limited by Article 23 in the Schedule to this Act may at any stage of the proceedings make any such order as appears to the court to be just and equitable in view of the provisions of the said Article 23 and of any other proceedings which have been, or are likely to be, commenced in the United Kingdom or elsewhere to enforce the liability in whole or in part.

(2) Without prejudice to the preceding subsection, a court before which proceedings are brought to enforce a liability which is limited by the said Article 23 shall, where the liability is, or may be, partly enforceable in other proceedings in the United Kingdom or elsewhere, have jurisdiction to award an amount less than the court would have awarded if the limitation applied solely to the proceedings before the court, or to make any part of its award conditional on the result of any other proceedings.

Registration of foreign judgments

4.—(1) Subject to the next following subsection, Part I of the Foreign Judgments (Reciprocal Enforcement) Act 1933 (in this section referred to as "the Act of 1933"), shall apply, whether or not it would otherwise have so applied, to any judgment which—

(*a*) has been given in any such action as is referred to in paragraph 1 of Article 31 in the Schedule to this Act, and (*b*) has been so given by any court or tribunal of a territory in respect of which one of the High Contracting Parties, other than the United Kingdom, is a party to the Convention, and

(*c*) has become enforceable in that territory.

(2) In the application of Part I of the Act of 1933, in relation to any such judgment as is referred to in the preceding subsection, Section 4 of that Act shall have effect with the omission of subsections (2) and (3).

(3) The registration in accordance with Part I of the Act of 1933, of any such judgment as is referred to in subsection (1) of this section shall constitute, in relation to that judgment, compliance with the formalities for the purposes of paragraph 3 of Article 31 in the Schedule to this Act.

Contribution between carriers

5.—(1) Where a carrier under a contract to which the Convention applies is liable in respect of any loss or damage for which compensation is payable under the Convention, nothing in Section 1 of the Civil Liability (Contribution) Act 1978, or Section 3(2) of the Law Reform (Miscellaneous Provisions) (Scotland) Act 1940, shall confer on him any right to recover contribution in respect of that loss or damage from any other carrier who, in accordance with Article 34 in the Schedule to this Act, is a party to the contract of carriage.

(2) The preceding subsection shall be without prejudice to the operation of Article 37 in the Schedule to this Act.

Actions against High Contracting Parties

6.—Every High Contracting Party to the Convention shall, for the purposes of any proceedings brought in a court in the United Kingdom in accordance with the provisions of Article 31 in the Schedule to this Act to enforce a claim in respect of carriage undertaken by that Party, be deemed to have submitted to the jurisdiction of that court, and accordingly rules of court may provide for the manner in which any such action is to be commenced and carried on; but nothing in this section shall authorise the issue of execution, or in Scotland the execution of diligence, against the property of any High Contracting Party.

Arbitrations

7.—(1) Any reference in the preceding provisions of this Act to a court includes a reference to an arbitration tribunal acting by virtue of Article 33 in the Schedule to this Act.

(2) For the purposes of Article 32 in the Schedule to this Act, as it has effect (by virtue of the said Article 33) in relation to arbitrations,—

(*a*) as respects England and Wales, subsections (3) to (5) of Section 34 of the Limitation Act 1980 (which determine the time at which an arbitration is deemed to be commenced), shall apply;

(*b*) as respects Northern Ireland, subsections (2) to (4) of Section 72 of the Statute of Limitations (Northern Ireland) 1958 (which make similar provision), shall apply; and

(*c*) as respects Scotland, an arbitration shall be deemed to be commenced when one party to the arbitration serves on the other party or parties a notice requiring him or them to appoint an arbiter or to agree to the appointment of an arbiter or, where the arbitration agreement provides that the reference shall be to a person named or designated in the agreement, requiring him or them to submit the dispute to the person so named or designated.

Resolution of conflicts between Conventions on carriage of goods

8.—(1) If it appears to Her Majesty in Council that there is any conflict between the provisions of this Act (including the provisions of the Convention as set out in the Schedule to this Act) and any provisions relating to the carriage of goods for reward by land, sea or air contained in—

(*a*) any other Convention which has been signed or ratified by or on behalf of Her Majesty's Government in the United Kingdom before the passing of this Act, or

(*b*) any enactment of the Parliament of the United Kingdom giving effect to such a Convention,

Her Majesty may by Order in Council make such provision as may seem to Her to be appropriate for resolving that conflict by amending or modifying this Act or any such enactment.

(2) Any statutory instrument made by virtue of this section shall be subject to annulment in pursuance of a resolution of either House of Parliament.

Amendments consequential on revision of Convention

8A.—(1) If at any time it appears to Her Majesty in Council that Her Majesty's Government in the United Kingdom have agreed to any revision of the Convention, Her Majesty may by Order in Council make such amendment of—

(*a*) this Act; and

. . . . . .

(*c*) Section 5(1) of the Carriage by Air and Road Act 1979,

as appear to Her to be appropriate in consequence of the revision.

(2) In the preceding subsection "revision" means an omission from, addition to or alteration of the Convention and includes replacement of the Convention or part of it by another convention.

(3) An Order in Council under this section shall not be made unless a draft of the Order has been laid before Parliament and approved by a resolution of each House of Parliament.

(4) In Section 8 of the Carriage of Passengers by Road Act 1974 (of which subsection (1) enables amendments of the provisions of that Act mentioned in paragraphs (*a*) and (*b*) of that subsection to be made by Order in Council in consequence of any revision of the Convention mentioned in that subsection, whether the revision operates by way of amendment of the text of the Convention as then in force or takes the form of a new convention or part of a new convention having substantially the same effect as the provisions set out in the Schedule to that Act)—

(*a*) in subsection (1) the words from "whether" to "Act" where it first occurs shall be omitted;

(*b*) at the end of paragraph (*b*) of subsection (1) there shall be inserted the words "and

(*c*) of section 5(1) of the Carriage by Air and Road Act 1979"; and

(*c*) after subsection (1) there shall be inserted the following subsection—

(1A) In the preceding subsection "revision" means an omission from, addition to or alteration of the Convention and includes replacement of the Convention or part of it by another convention.

Application to British possessions, etc.

9.—Her Majesty may by Order in Council direct that this Act shall extend, subject to such exceptions, adaptations and modifications as may be specified in the Order, to—

(*a*) the Isle of Man;
(*b*) any of the Channel Islands;
(*c*) any colony;
(*d*) any state or territory which is for the time being a protectorate or protected state for the purposes of the British Nationality Act, 1948.

Application to Scotland

10.—In its application to Scotland, the Schedule to this Act shall have effect as if—

(*a*) any reference therein to a plaintiff included a reference to a pursuer;
(*b*) any reference therein to a defendant included a reference to a defender; and
(*c*) any reference to security for costs included a reference to caution for expenses.

Application to Northern Ireland

11.—(1) In the application of this Act to Northern Ireland, any reference to an enactment of the Parliament of Northern Ireland shall be construed as a reference to that enactment as amended by any Act of that Parliament, whether passed before or after this Act, and to any enactment of that Parliament passed after this Act and re-enacting the said enactment with or without modification.

(2) In the application of Section 4 of this Act to Northern Ireland, any reference to the Foreign Judgments (Reciprocal Enforcement) Act 1933, is a reference to that Act as it applies in Northern Ireland.

Orders in Council

12.—An Order in Council made under any of the preceding provisions of this Act may contain such transitional and supplementary provisions as appear to Her Majesty to be expedient and may be varied or revoked by a subsequent Order in Council made under that provision.

Application to Crown

13.—This Act shall bind the Crown.

Short title, interpretation and commencement

14.—(1) This Act may be cited as the Carriage of Goods by Road Act 1965.

(2) The persons who, for the purposes of this Act, are persons concerned in the carriage of goods by road under a contract to which the Convention applies are—

(*a*) the sender,
(*b*) the consignee,
(*c*) any carrier who, in accordance with Article 34 in the Schedule to this Act or otherwise, is a party to the contract of carriage,
(*d*) any person for whom such a carrier is responsible by virtue of Article 3 in the Schedule to this Act,
(*e*) any person to whom the rights and liabilities of any of the persons referred to in paragraphs (*a*) to (*d*) of this subsection have passed (whether by assignment or assignation or by operation of law).

(3) Except in so far as the context otherwise requires, any reference in this Act to an enactment shall be construed as a reference to that enactment as amended or extended by or under any other enactment.

(4) This Act shall come into operation on such day as Her Majesty may by Order in Council appoint; but nothing in this Act shall apply in relation to any contract for the carriage of goods by road made before the day so appointed.

Section 1 SCHEDULE

CONVENTION ON THE CONTRACT FOR THE INTERNATIONAL CARRIAGE OF GOODS BY ROAD

CHAPTER I

SCOPE OF APPLICATION

Article 1

1. This Convention shall apply to every contract for the carriage of goods by road in vehicles for reward, when the place of taking over of the goods and the place designated for delivery, as specified in the contract, are situated in two different countries, of which at least one is a Contracting country, irrespective of the place of residence and the nationality of the parties.

2. For the purposes of this Convention, "vehicles" means motor vehicles, articulated vehicles, trailers and semi-trailers as defined in Article 4 of the Convention on Road Traffic dated 19th September 1949.

3. This Convention shall apply also where carriage coming within its scope is carried out by States or by governmental institutions or organizations.

4. This Convention shall not apply:
   (*a*) to carriage performed under the terms of any international postal convention;
   (*b*) to funeral consignments;
   (*c*) to furniture removal.

5. The Contracting Parties agree not to vary any of the provisions of this Convention by special agreements between two or more of them, except to make it inapplicable to their frontier traffic or to authorise the use in transport operations entirely confined to their territory of consignment notes representing a title to the goods.

Article 2

1. Where the vehicle containing the goods is carried over part of the journey by sea, rail, inland waterways or air, and, except where the provisions of Article 14 are applicable, the goods are not unloaded from the vehicle, this Convention shall nevertheless apply to the whole of the carriage. Provided that to the extent that it is proved that any loss, damage or delay in delivery of the goods which occurs during the carriage by the other means of transport was not caused by an act or omission of the carrier by road, but by some event which could only have occurred in the course of and by reason of the carriage by that other means of transport, the liability of the carrier by road shall be determined not by this Convention but in the manner in which the liability of the carrier by the other means of transport would have been determined if a contract for the carriage of the goods alone had been made by the sender with the carrier by the other means of transport in accordance with the conditions prescribed by law for the carriage of goods by that means of transport. If, however, there are no such prescribed conditions, the liability of the carrier by road shall be determined by this Convention.

2. If the carrier by road is also himself the carrier by the other means of transport, his liability shall also be determined in accordance with the provisions of paragraph 1 of this article, but as if, in his capacities as carrier by road and as carrier by the other means of transport, he were two separate persons.

CHAPTER II

PERSONS FOR WHOM THE CARRIER IS RESPONSIBLE

Article 3

For the purposes of this Convention the carrier shall be responsible for the acts and omissions of his agents and servants and of any other persons of whose services he makes use for the performance of the carriage, when such agents, servants or other persons are acting within the scope of their employment, as if such acts or omissions were his own.

CHAPTER III

CONCLUSION AND PERFORMANCE OF THE CONTRACT OF CARRIAGE

Article 4

The contract of carriage shall be confirmed by the making out of a consignment note. The absence, irregularity or loss of the consignment note shall not affect the existence or the validity of the contract or carriage which shall remain subject to the provisions of this Convention.

Article 5

1. The consignment note shall be made out in three original copies signed by the sender and by the carrier. These signatures may be printed or replaced by the stamps of the sender and the carrier if the law of the country in which the consignment note has been made out so permits. The first copy shall be handed to the sender, the second shall accompany the goods and the third shall be retained by the carrier.

2. When the goods which are to be carried have to be loaded in different vehicles, or are of different kinds or are divided into different lots, the sender or the carrier shall have the right to require a separate consignment note to be made out for each vehicle used, or for each kind or lot of goods.

Article 6

1. The consignment note shall contain the following particulars:

(*a*) the date of the consignment note and the place at which it is made out;
(*b*) the name and address of the sender;
(*c*) the name and address of the carrier;
(*d*) the place and the date of taking over of the goods and the place designated for delivery;
(*e*) the name and address of the consignee;
(*f*) the description in common use of the nature of the goods and the method of packing, and, in the case of dangerous goods, their generally recognised description;
(*g*) the number of packages and their special marks and numbers;
(*h*) the gross weight of the goods or their quantity otherwise expressed;
(*i*) charges relating to the carriage (carriage charges, supplementary charges, customs duties and other charges incurred from the making of the contract to the time of delivery);

(*j*) the requisite instructions for Customs and other formalities;
(*k*) a statement that the carriage is subject, notwithstanding any clause to the contrary, to the provisions of this Convention.

Where applicable, the consignment note shall also contain the following particulars:

(*a*) a statement that transhipment is not allowed;
(*b*) the charges which the sender undertakes to pay;
(*c*) the amount of "cash on delivery" charges;
(*d*) a declaration of the value of the goods and the amount representing special interest in delivery;
(*e*) the sender's instructions to the carrier regarding insurance of the goods;
(*f*) the agreed time-limit within which the carriage is to be carried out;
(*g*) a list of the documents handed to the carrier.

3. The parties may enter in the consignment note any other particulars which they may deem useful.

Article 7

1. The sender shall be responsible for all expenses, loss and damage sustained by the carrier by reason of the inaccuracy or inadequacy of:

(*a*) the particulars specified in Article 6, paragraph 1, (*b*) (*d*), (*e*), (*f*), (*g*), (*h*) and (*j*);
(*b*) the particulars specified in Article 6, paragraph 2;
(*c*) any other particulars or instructions given by him to enable the consignment note to be made out or for the purpose of their being entered therein.

2. If, at the request of the sender, the carrier enters in the consignment note the particulars referred to in paragraph 1 of this article, he shall be deemed, unless the contrary is proved, to have done so on behalf of the sender.

3. If the consignment note does not contain the statement specified in article 6, paragraph 1(*k*), the carrier shall be liable for all expenses, loss and damage sustained through such omission by the person entitled to dispose of the goods.

Article 8

1. On taking over the goods, the carrier shall check:

(*a*) the accuracy of the statements in the consignment note as to the number of packages and their marks and numbers, and
(*b*) the apparent condition of the goods and their packaging.

2. Where the carrier has no reasonable means of checking the accuracy of the statements referred to in paragraph 1(*a*) of this article, he shall enter his reservations in the consignment note together with the grounds on which they are based. He shall likewise specify the grounds for any reservations which he makes with regard to the apparent condition of the goods and their packaging. Such reservations shall not bind the sender unless he has expressly agreed to be bound by them in the consignment note.

3. The sender shall be entitled to require the carrier to check the gross weight of the goods or their quantity otherwise expressed. He may also require the contents of the packages to be checked. The carrier shall be entitled to claim the cost of such checking. The result of the checks shall be entered in the consignment note.

Article 9

1. The consignment note shall be *prima facie* evidence of the making of the contract of carriage, the conditions of the contract and the receipt of the goods by the carrier.

2. If the consignment note contains no specific reservations by the carrier, it shall be presumed, unless the contrary is proved, that the goods and their packaging appeared to be in good condition when the carrier took them over and that the number of packages, their marks and numbers corresponded with the statements in the consignment note.

Article 10

The sender shall be liable to the carrier for damage to persons, equipment or other goods, and for any expenses due to defective packing of the goods, unless the defect was apparent or known to the carrier at the time when he took over the goods and he made no reservations concerning it.

Article 11

1. For the purposes of the Customs or other formalities which have to be completed before delivery of the goods, the sender shall attach the necessary documents to the consignment note or place them at the disposal of the carrier and shall furnish him with all the information which he requires.

2. The carrier shall not be under any duty to enquire into either the accuracy or the adequacy of such documents and information. The sender shall be liable to the carrier for any damage caused by the absence, inadequacy or irregularity of such documents and information, except in the case of some wrongful act or neglect on the part of the carrier.

3. The liability of the carrier for the consequences arising from the loss or incorrect use of the documents specified in and accompanying the consignment note or deposited with the carrier shall be that of an agent, provided that the compensation payable by the carrier shall not exceed that payable in the event of loss of the goods.

Article 12

1. The sender has the right to dispose of the goods, in particular by asking the carrier to stop the goods in transit, to change the place at which delivery is to take place or to deliver the goods to a consignee other than the consignee indicated in the consignment note.

2. This right shall cease to exist when the second copy of the consignment note is handed to the consignee or when the consignee exercises his right under Article 13, paragraph 1; from that time onwards the carrier shall obey the orders of the consignee.

3. The consignee shall, however, have the right of disposal from the time when the consignment note is drawn up, if the sender makes an entry to that effect in the consignment note.

4. If in exercising his right of disposal the consignee has ordered the delivery of the goods to another person, that other person shall not be entitled to name other consignees.

5. The exercise of the right of disposal shall be subject to the following conditions:

(*a*) that the sender or, in the case referred to in paragraph 3 of this article, the consignee who wishes to exercise the right produces the first copy of the consignment note on which the new instructions to the carrier have been entered and indemnifies the carrier against all expenses, loss and damage involved in carrying out such instructions;

(*b*) that the carrying out of such instructions is possible at the time when the instructions reach the person who is to carry them out and does not either interfere with the normal working of the carrier's undertaking or prejudice the senders or consignees of other consignments;

(*c*) that the instructions do not result in a division of the consignment.

6. When, by reason of the provisions of paragraph 5(*b*) of this article, the carrier cannot carry out the instructions which he receives, he shall immediately notify the person who gave him such instructions.

7. A carrier who has not carried out the instructions given under the conditions provided for in this article, or who has carried them out without requiring the first copy of the consignment note to be produced, shall be liable to the person entitled to make a claim for any loss or damage caused thereby.

Article 13

1. After arrival of the goods at the place designated for delivery, the consignee shall be entitled to require the carrier to deliver to him, against a receipt, the second copy of the consignment note and the goods. If the loss of the goods is established or if the goods have not arrived after the expiry of the period provided for in Article 19, the consignee shall be entitled to enforce in his own name against the carrier any rights arising from the contract of carriage.

2. The consignee who avails himself of the rights granted to him under paragraph 1 of this article shall pay the charges shown to be due on the consignment note, but in the event of dispute on this matter the carrier shall not be required to deliver the goods unless security has been furnished by the consignee.

Article 14

1. If for any reason it is or becomes impossible to carry out the contract in accordance with the terms laid down in the consignment note before the goods reach the place designated for delivery, the carrier shall ask for instructions from the person entitled to dispose of the goods in accordance with the provisions of article 12.

2. Nevertheless, if circumstances are such as to allow the carriage to be carried out under conditions differing from those laid down in the consignment note and if the carrier has been unable to obtain instructions in reasonable time from the person entitled to dispose of the goods in accordance with the provisions of Article 12, he shall take such steps as seem to him to be in the best interests of the person entitled to dispose of the goods.

Article 15

1. Where circumstances prevent delivery of the goods after their arrival at the place designated for delivery, the carrier shall ask the sender for his instructions. If the consignee refuses the goods the sender shall be entitled to dispose of them without being obliged to produce the first copy of the consignment note.

2. Even if he has refused the goods, the consignee may nevertheless require delivery so long as the carrier has not received instructions to the contrary from the sender.

3. When circumstances preventing delivery of the goods arise after the consignee, in exercise of his rights under Article 12, paragraph 3, has given an order for the goods to be delivered to another person, paragraphs 1 and 2 of this article shall apply as if the consignee were the sender and that other person were the consignee.

Article 16

1. The carrier shall be entitled to recover the cost of his request for instructions and any expenses entailed in carrying out such instructions,

unless such expenses were caused by the wrongful act or neglect of the carrier.

2. In the cases referred to in Article 14, paragraph 1, and in Article 15, the carrier may immediately unload the goods for account of the person entitled to dispose of them and thereupon the carriage shall be deemed to be at an end. The carrier shall then hold the goods on behalf of the person so entitled. He may however entrust them to a third party, and in that case he shall not be under any liability except for the exercise of reasonable care in the choice of such third party. The charges due under the consignment note and all other expenses shall remain chargeable against the goods.

3. The carrier may sell the goods, without awaiting instructions from the person entitled to dispose of them, if the goods are perishable or their condition warrants such a course, or when the storage expenses would be out of proportion to the value of the goods. He may also proceed to the sale of the goods in other cases if after the expiry of a reasonable period he has not received from the person entitled to dispose of the goods instructions to the contrary which he may reasonably be required to carry out.

4. If the goods have been sold pursuant to this article, the proceeds of sale, after deduction of the expenses chargeable against the goods, shall be placed at the disposal of the person entitled to dispose of the goods. If these charges exceed the proceeds of sale, the carrier shall be entitled to the difference.

5. The procedure in the case of sale shall be determined by the law or custom of the place where the goods are situated.

Chapter IV

Liability of the Carrier

Article 17

1. The carrier shall be liable for the total or partial loss of the goods and for damage thereto occurring between the time when he takes over the goods and the time of delivery, as well as for any delay in delivery.

2. The carrier shall however be relieved of liability if the loss, damage or delay was caused by the wrongful act or neglect of the claimant, by the instructions of the claimant given otherwise than as the result of a wrongful act or neglect on the part of the carrier, by inherent vice of the goods or through circumstances which the carrier could not avoid and the consequences of which he was unable to prevent.

3. The carrier shall not be relieved of liability by reason of the defective condition of the vehicle used by him in order to perform the carriage, or by reason of the wrongful act or neglect of the person from whom he may have hired the vehicle or of the agents or servants of the latter.

4. Subject to Article 18, paragraphs 2 to 5, the carrier shall be relieved of liability when the loss or damage arises from the special risks inherent in one or more of the following circumstances:

(*a*) Use of open unsheeted vehicles, when their use has been expressly agreed and specified in the consignment note;

(*b*) the lack of, or defective condition of packing in the case of goods which, by their nature, are liable to wastage or to be damaged when not packed or when not properly packed;

(*c*) handling, loading, stowage or unloading of the goods by the sender, the consignee or persons acting on behalf of the sender or the consignee;

(*d*) the nature of certain kinds of goods which particularly exposes them to total or partial loss or to damage, especially through breakage, rust, decay, desiccation, leakage, normal wastage, or the action of moth or vermin;

(*e*) insufficiency or inadequacy of marks or numbers on the packages;

(*f*) the carriage of livestock.

5. Where under this article the carrier is not under any liability in respect of some of the factors causing the loss, damage or delay, he shall only be liable to the extent that those factors for which he is liable under this article have contributed to the loss, damage or delay.

Article 18

1. The burden of proving that loss, damage or delay was due to one of the causes specified in Article 17, paragraph 2, shall rest upon the carrier.

2. When the carrier establishes that in the circumstances of the case, the loss or damage could be attributed to one or more of the special risks referred to in article 17, paragraph 4, it shall be presumed that it was so caused. The claimant shall however be entitled to prove that the loss or damage was not, in fact, attributable either wholly or partly to one of these risks.

3. This presumption shall not apply in the circumstances set out in article 17, paragraph 4(*a*), if there has been an abnormal shortage, or a loss of any package.

4. If the carriage is performed in vehicles specially equipped to protect the goods from the effects of heat, cold, variations in temperature or the humidity of the air, the carrier shall not be entitled to claim the benefit of article 17, paragraph 4(*d*), unless he proves that all steps incumbent on him in the circumstances with respect to the choice, maintenance and use of such equipment were taken and that he complied with any special instructions issued to him.

5. The carrier shall not be entitled to claim the benefit of article 17, paragraph 4(*f*), unless he proves that all steps normally incumbent on him in the circumstances were taken and that he complied with any special instructions issued to him.

Article 19

Delay in delivery shall be said to occur when the goods have not been delivered within the agreed time-limit or when, failing an agreed time-limit, the actual duration of the carriage having regard to the circumstances of the case, and in particular, in the case of partial loads, the time required for making up a complete load in the normal way, exceeds the time it would be reasonable to allow a diligent carrier.

Article 20

1. The fact that goods have not been delivered within thirty days following the expiry of the agreed time-limit, or, if there is no agreed time-limit, within sixty days from the time when the carrier took over the goods, shall be conclusive evidence of the loss of the goods, and the person entitled to make a claim may thereupon treat them as lost.

2. The person so entitled may, on receipt of compensation for the missing goods, request in writing that he shall be notified immediately should the goods be recovered in the course of the year following the payment of compensation. He shall be given a written acknowledgment of such request.

3. Within the thirty days following receipt of such notification, the person entitled as aforesaid may require the goods to be delivered to him against payment of the charges shown to be due on the consignment note and also against refund of the compensation he received less any charges included therein but without prejudice to any claims to compensation for delay in delivery under article 23 and, where applicable, article 26.

4. In the absence of the request mentioned in paragraph 2 or of any instructions given within the period of thirty days specified in paragraph 3, or if the goods are not recovered until more than one year after the payment of compensation, the carrier shall be entitled to deal with them in accordance with the law of the place where the goods are situated.

Article 21

Should the goods have been delivered to the consignee without collection of the "cash on delivery" charge which should have been collected by the carrier under the terms of the contract of carriage, the carrier shall be liable to the sender for compensation not exceeding the amount of such charge without prejudice to his right of action against the consignee.

Article 22

1. When the sender hands goods of a dangerous nature to the carrier, he shall inform the carrier of the exact nature of the danger and indicate, if necessary, the precautions to be taken. If this information has not been entered in the consignment note, the burden of proving, by some other means, that the carrier knew the exact nature of the danger constituted by the carriage of the said goods shall rest upon the sender or the consignee.

2. Goods of a dangerous nature which, in the circumstances referred to in paragraph 1 of this article, the carrier did not know were dangerous, may, at any time or place, be unloaded, destroyed or rendered harmless by the carrier without compensation; further, the sender shall be liable for all expenses, loss or damage arising out of their handing over for carriage or of their carriage.

Article 23

1. When, under the provisions of this Convention, a carrier is liable for compensation in respect of total or partial loss of goods, such compensation shall be calculated by reference to the value of the goods at the place and time at which they were accepted for carriage.

2. The value of the goods shall be fixed according to the commodity exchange price or, if there is no such price, according to the current market price or, if there is no commodity exchange price or current market price, by reference to the normal value of goods of the same kind and quality.

3. Compensation shall not, however, exceed 8.33 units of account per kilogram of gross weight short.

4. In addition, the carriage charges, Customs duties and other charges incurred in respect of the carriage of the goods shall be refunded in full in case of total loss and in proportion to the loss sustained in case of partial loss, but no further damages shall be payable.

5. In the case of delay, if the claimant proves that damage has resulted therefrom the carrier shall pay compensation for such damage not exceeding the carriage charges.

6. Higher compensation may only be claimed where the value of the goods or a special interest in delivery has been declared in accordance with articles 24 and 26.

7. The unit of account mentioned in this Convention is the Special Drawing Right as defined by the International Monetary Fund. The amount mentioned in paragraph 3 of this article shall be converted into the national currency of the state of the court seised of the case on the basis of the value of that currency on the date of that judgment or the date agreed upon by the parties.

Article 24

The sender may, against payment of a surcharge to be agreed upon, declare in the consignment note a value for the goods exceeding the limit laid down in article 23, paragraph 3, and in that case the amount of the declared value shall be substituted for that limit.

Article 25

1. In case of damage, the carrier shall be liable for the amount by which the goods have diminished in value, calculated by reference to the value of the goods fixed in accordance with article 23, paragraphs 1, 2 and 4.

2. The compensation may not, however, exceed:

(*a*) if the whole consignment has been damaged the amount payable in the case of total loss;

(*b*) if part only of the consignment has been damage, the amount payable in the case of loss of the part affected.

Article 26

1. The sender may, against payment of a surcharge to be agreed upon, fix the amount of a special interest in delivery in the case of loss or damage or of the agreed time-limit being exceeded, by entering such amount in the consignment note.

2. If a declaration of a special interest in delivery has been made, compensation for the additional loss or damage proved may be claimed, up to the total amount of the interest declared, independently of the compensation provided for in articles 23, 24 and 25.

Article 27

1. The claimant shall be entitled to claim interest on compensation payable. Such interest, calculated at five per centum per annum shall accrue from the date on which the claim was sent in writing to the carrier or, if no such claim has been made, from the date on which legal proceedings were instituted.

2. When the amounts on which the calculation of the compensation is based are not expressed in the currency of the country in which payment is claimed, conversion shall be at the rate of exchange applicable on the day and at the place of payment of compensation.

Article 28

1. In cases where, under the law applicable, loss, damage or delay arising out of carriage under this Convention gives rise to an extra-contractual claim, the carrier may avail himself of the provisions of this Convention which exclude his liability or which fix or limit the compensation due.

2. In cases where the extra-contractual liability for loss, damage or delay of one of the persons for whom the carrier is responsible under the terms of article 3 is in issue, such person may also avail himself of the provisions of this Convention which exclude the liability of the carrier or which fix or limit the compensation due.

Article 29

1. The carrier shall not be entitled to avail himself of the provisions of this chapter which exclude or limit his liability or which shift the burden of proof if the damage was caused by his wilful misconduct or by such default on his part as, in accordance with the law of the court or tribunal seised of the case, is considered as equivalent to wilful misconduct.

2. The same provision shall apply if the wilful misconduct or default is committed by the agents or servants of the carrier or by any other persons of whose services he makes use for the performance of the carriage, when such agents, servants or other persons are acting within the scope of their employment. Furthermore, in such a case such agents, servants or other

persons shall not be entitled to avail themselves, with regard to their personal liability, of the provisions of this chapter referred to in paragraph 1.

Chapter V

Claims and Actions

Article 30

1. If the consignee takes delivery of the goods without duly checking their condition with the carrier or without sending him reservations giving a general indication of the loss or damage, not later than the time of delivery in the case of apparent loss or damage and within seven days of delivery, Sundays and public holidays excepted, in the case of loss or damage which is not apparent, the fact of his taking delivery shall be *prima facie* evidence that he has received the goods in the condition described in the consignment note. In the case of loss or damage which is not apparent the reservations referred to shall be made in writing.

2. When the condition of the goods has been duly checked by the consignee and the carrier, evidence contradicting the result of this checking shall only be admissible in the case of loss or damage which is not apparent and provided that the consignee has duly sent reservations in writing to the carrier within seven days, Sundays and public holidays excepted, from the date of checking.

3. No compensation shall be payable for delay in delivery unless a reservation has been sent in writing to the carrier, within twenty-one days from the time that the goods were placed at the disposal of the consignee.

4. In calculating the time-limits provided for in this Article the date of delivery, or the date of checking, or the date when the goods were placed at the disposal of the consignee, as the case may be, shall not be included.

5. The carrier and the consignee shall give each other every reasonable facility for making the requisite investigations and checks.

Article 31

1. In legal proceedings arising out of carriage under this Convention, the plaintiff may bring an action in any court or tribunal of a contracting country designated by agreement between the parties and, in addition, in the courts or tribunals of a country within whose territory

(*a*) the defendant is ordinarily resident, or has his principal place of business, or the branch or agency through which the contract of carriage was made, or

(*b*) the place where the goods were taken over by the carrier or the place designated for delivery is situated,

and in no other courts or tribunals.

2. Where in respect of a claim referred to in paragraph 1 of this article an action is pending before a court or tribunal competent under that paragraph, or where in respect of such a claim a judgment has been entered by such a court or tribunal no new action shall be started between the same parties on the same grounds unless the judgment of the court or tribunal before which the first action was brought is not enforceable in the country in which the fresh proceedings are brought.

3. When a judgment entered by a court or tribunal of a contracting country in any such action as is referred to in paragraph 1 of this article has become enforceable in that country, it shall also become enforceable in each of the other contracting States, as soon as the formalities required in the country concerned have been complied with. The formalities shall not permit the merits of the case to be re-opened.

4. The provisions of paragraph 3 of this article shall apply to judgments after trial, judgments by default and settlements confirmed by an order of the court, but shall not apply to interim judgments or to awards of damages, in addition to costs against a plaintiff who wholly or partly fails in his action.

5. Security for costs shall not be required in proceedings arising out of carriage under this Convention from nationals of contracting countries resident or having their place of business in one of those countries.

Article 32

1. The period of limitation for an action arising out of carriage under this Convention shall be one year. Nevertheless, in the case of wilful misconduct, or such default as in accordance with the law of the court or tribunal seised of the case, is considered as equivalent to wilful misconduct, the period of limitation shall be three years. The period of limitation shall begin to run:

(*a*) in the case of partial loss, damage or delay in delivery, from the date of delivery;

(*b*) in the case of total loss, from the thirtieth day after the expiry of the agreed time-limit or where there is no agreed time-limit from the sixtieth day from the date on which the goods were taken over by the carrier;

(*c*) in all other cases, on the expiry of a period of three months after the making of the contract of carriage.

The day on which the period of limitation begins to run shall not be included in the period.

2. A written claim shall suspend the period of limitation until such date as the carrier rejects the claim by notification in writing and returns the documents attached thereto. If a part of the claim is admitted the period of limitation shall start to run again only in respect of that part of the claim still in dispute. The burden of proof of the receipt of the claim, or of the reply and of the return of the documents, shall rest with the party relying upon these facts. The running of the period of limitation shall not be suspended by further claims having the same object.

3. Subject to the provisions of paragraph 2 above, the extension of the period of limitation shall be governed by the law of the court or tribunal seised of the case. That law shall also govern the fresh accrual of rights of action.

4. A right of action which has become barred by lapse of time may not be exercised by way of counter-claim or set-off.

Article 33

The contract of carriage may contain a clause conferring competence on an arbitration tribunal if the clause conferring competence on the tribunal provides that the tribunal shall apply this Convention.

Chapter VI

Provisions Relating to Carriage Performed by Successive Carriers

Article 34

If carriage governed by a single contract is performed by successive road carriers, each of them shall be responsible for the performance of the whole operation, the second carrier and each succeeding carrier becoming a party to the contract of carriage, under the terms of the consignment note, by reason of his acceptance of the goods and the consignment note.

Article 35

1. A carrier accepting the goods from a previous carrier shall give the latter a dated and signed receipt. He shall enter his name and address on the second copy of the consignment note. Where applicable, he shall enter on the second copy of the consignment note and on the receipt reservations of the kind provided for in article 8, paragraph 2.

2. The provisions of article 9 shall apply to the relations between successive carriers.

Article 36

Except in the case of a counter-claim or a set-off raised in an action concerning a claim based on the same contract of carriage, legal proceedings in respect of liability for loss, damage or delay may only be brought against the first carrier, the last carrier or the carrier who was performing that portion of the carriage during which the event causing the loss, damage or delay occurred; an action may be brought at the same time against several of these carriers.

Article 37

A carrier who has paid compensation in compliance with the provisions of this Convention, shall be entitled to recover such compensation, together with interest thereon and all costs and expenses incurred by reason of the claim, from the other carriers who have taken part in the carriage, subject to the following provisions:

(*a*) the carrier responsible for the loss or damage shall be solely liable for the compensation whether paid by himself or by another carrier;

(*b*) when the loss or damage has been caused by the action of two or more carriers, each of them shall pay an amount proportionate to his share of liability; should it be impossible to apportion the liability, each carrier shall be liable in proportion to the share of the payment for the carriage which is due to him;

(*c*) if it cannot be ascertained to which carriers liability is attributable for the loss or damage, the amount of the compensation shall be apportioned between all the carriers as laid down in (*b*) above.

Article 38

If one of the carriers is insolvent, the share of the compensation due from him and unpaid by him shall be divided among the other carriers in proportion to the share of the payment for the carriage due to them.

Article 39

1. No carrier against whom a claim is made under articles 37 and 38 shall be entitled to dispute the validity of the payment made by the carrier making the claim if the amount of the compensation was determined by judicial authority after the first mentioned carrier had been given due notice of the proceedings and afforded an opportunity of entering an appearance.

2. A carrier wishing to take proceedings to enforce his right of recovery may make his claim before the competent court or tribunal of the country in which one of the carriers concerned is ordinarily resident, or has his principal place of business or the branch or agency through which the contract of carriage was made. All the carriers concerned may be made defendants in the same action.

3. The provisions of article 31, paragraphs 3 and 4, shall apply to judgments entered in the proceedings referred to in articles 37 and 38.

4. The provisions of article 32 shall apply to claims between carriers. The period of limitation shall, however, begin to run either on the date of the

final judicial decision fixing the amount of compensation payable under the provisions of this Convention, or, if there is no such judicial decision, from the actual date of payment.

Article 40

Carriers shall be free to agree among themselves on provisions other than those laid down in articles 37 and 38.

CHAPTER VII

NULLITY OF STIPULATIONS CONTRARY TO THE CONVENTION

Article 41

1. Subject to the provisions of Article 40, any stipulation which would directly or indirectly derogate from the provisions of this Convention shall be null and void. The nullity of such a stipulation shall not involve the nullity of the other provisions of the contract.

2. In particular, a benefit of insurance in favour of the carrier or any other similar clause, or any clause shifting the burden of proof shall be null and void.

[*Chapter VIII of the Convention is not reproduced. This deals with the coming into force of the Convention, the settlement of disputes between the High Contracting Parties and related matters.*]

PROTOCOL OF SIGNATURE

1. This Convention shall not apply to traffic between the United Kingdom of Great Britain and Northern Ireland and the Republic of Ireland.

Appendix 3B

LETTRE DE VOITURE INTERNATIONALE (CMR) **INTERNATIONAL CONSIGNMENT NOTE**

230197

COPY 1 SENDER
COPY 2 CONSIGNEE
COPY 3 CARRIER

Approved by FTA/RHA/SITPRO UK 1981

Sender (Name, Address, Country) Expéditeur (Nom, Addresse, Pays) 1	Customs Reference/Status Référence/désignation pour mise en douane 2
	Senders/Agents Reference Référence de l'expéditeur/de l'agent 3
Consignee (Name, Address, Country) Destinataire (Nom, Addresse, Pays) 4	Carrier (Name, Address, Country) Transporteur (Nom, Addresse, Pays) 5
Place & date of taking over the goods (place, country, date) Lieu et date de la prise en charge des marchandises (Lieu, pays, date) 6	Successive Carriers Transporteurs successifs 7
Place designated for delivery of goods (place, country) Lieu prévu pour la livraison des marchandises (lieu, pays) 8	This carriage is subject, notwithstanding any clause to the contrary, to the Convention on the Contract for the International Carriage of Goods by Road (CMR) Ce transport est soumis nonobstant toute clause contraire à la Convention Relative au Contrat de Transport International de Marchandises par Route (CMR)

*NB FOR DANGEROUS GOODS INDICATE 1. CORRECT TECHNICAL NAME (PROPER SHIPPING NAME) 2. HAZARD CLASS 3. UN NUMBER 4. FLASHPOINT (IF ANY) IN °C.

Marks & Nos; No & Kind of Packages; Description of Goods* Marques et Nos; No et nature des colis; Désignation des marchandises* 9	Gross weight (kg) Poids Brut (kg) 10	Volume (m³) Cubage (m³) 11

Carriage Charges Prix de transport 12	Sender's Instructions for Customs, etc ... Instructions de l'Expéditeur (optional) 13
Reservations Réserves 14	Documents attached Documents Annexés (optional) 15
	Special agreements Conventions particulières (optional) 16

Goods Received/Marchandises Reçues 17	Signature of Carrier/Signature du transporteur 18	Company completing this note Société émettrice 19
		Place and Date; Signature Lieu et date; Signature 20

730

Appendix 4

The sections to the left of the thick line must be completed by the Consignor and the other sections by the Railway
Les parties situées à gauche de la ligne grasse doivent être remplies par l'expéditeur, les autres par le chemin de fer
Die links der fettgedruckten Linie gelegenen Teile hat der Absender, die ubrigen die Eisenbahn auszufullen

X Indicate by a cross where appropriate-Désigner par une croix ce qui convient-Zutreffendes ankreuzen (Spaces-Cases-Felder 22, 27, 28, 76)

(9) **CIM**

Consignment Note
Lettre de voiture
Frachtbrief

(35) (36) (37) (38) (39) (40) (41) (42)

(43) Authorisation of Loading-Autorisation de chargement-Verladebewilligung

International Carriage by Rail
Transport international ferroviaire
Internationale Eisenbahnbeförderung

Consignment note- Petite Vitesse-Frachtgut

BR 20105/113

(10) Consignor (name, address)-Expéditeur (nom, adresse)-Absender (Name, Anschrift)

(11)

(12) Declarations-Déclarations-Erklärungen (CIM Art. 13, 19, 26, etc.)

(13) Consignor's reference-Référence expéditeur-Absender-Referenz

(14) Consignee (name, address, country)-Destinataire (nom, adresse, pays)-Empfänger (Name, Anschrift, Land)

(15)

Loading Tackle-Containers-Agrès-Conteneurs-Lademittel-Container

(16) Category (17) Mark and Number (16) Catégorie-Art (17) Marque et No.-Merkwal und Nr.

(18) Exchangeable Pallets / Palettes échangeables / Tauschpaletten — quantity / Nombre / Anzahl — EUR — EUR

(19) Wagons-Wagons-Wagen No

(20) Tare-Tare-Eigenmasse Kg — P

(44) Load Limit / Lim de charge / Lastgrenze

(45) Axles / Essieux / Achsen

(21) Information for consignee / Informations pour le destinataire / Vermerke für den Empfänger (CIM Art. 13 § 3)

(22) Prepayment instructions-Mention d'affranchissement-Frankaturvermerk (see-voir-siehe CIM Art. 15 § 2) including-y compris-einschliesslich

1. Carriage charges paid-Franco de port-Franko Fracht- up to-jusqu à-bis ▶

2. All charges paid / Franco de tous frais / Franko aller Kosten

3. Charges paid not exceeding / Franco pour / Franko (specified amount) (somme déterminée) ▶ (bestimmter Betrag)

(23) Tariffs and routes requested / Tarifs et itinéraires demandés / Verlangte Tarife und Wege

(46) 1 3

(47) To be cleared through Customs at-A dédouaner à-Zu verzollen in

(24) Destination station and place of delivery / Gare destinataire et lieu de livraison / Bestimmungsbahnhof und Ablieferungsstelle

(48)

(49) Route-Itinéraires-Leitungswege

(27) Wagon load / Wagon complet / Wagenladung 1 — Part load / Détail / Stückgut 2

(25) Marks (where required)/No. of packages/Nature of packing/Description of goods-Marques (le cas échéant)/Nombre/Nature de l'emballage/Désignation de la marchandise-Zeichen (gegebenenfalls)/Anzahl/Art der Verpackung/Bezeichnung des Gutes

(33) **RID** yes-oui-ja

(26) Mass-Masse Kg

(50) Goods-Marchandises-Waren

(28) Loaded by-Chargé par-Verladen durch: Consignor / Expéditeur / Absender 1 — Railway / Chemin de fer / Eisenbahn 2

(29) Interest in Delivery / Intérêt à la livraison / Interesse an der Lieferung — Currency / Monnaie / Währung (51)

ORIGINAL OF THE CONSIGNMENT NOTE- ORIGINAL DE LA LETTRE DE VOITURE- FRACHTBRIEFORIGINAL

Reserved for customs-Reservé à la douane-Fur zollamtliche Vermerke

(32) Documents attached to the Consignment Note / Annexes à la lettre de voiture-Beilagen zum Frachtbrief

(30) Disbursements-Débours-Barvorschuss — Currency / Monnaie / Währung (52)

(31) Cash on Delivery-Remboursement-Nachnahme — Currency / Monnaie / Währung (53)

(69) Ex. Rate (74) (69) Cours (74)

1 Carriage from the forwarding station / Port de la gare expéditrice / Fracht vom Versandbahnhof to-pour-bis (54) (55) Tariff applied (56) (57) (58) (59) Rate (60) Chargeable mass Kg (61) Paid-Franco-Franko (62) To pay-Dû-Überw

(63) Code (64) Km — Currency / Monnaie / Währung (70) — (65) Other charges / Frais / Gebühren = = = = — (66) Ex. rate (71) (67) (72) (68) (73) (69) Ex. Rate (74)

2 Carriage-Port-Fracht-from-de-von to-pour-bis (54) (55) Tarif appliqué (56) (57) (58) (59) Prix par unite (60) Masse taxée Kg (61) (62)

(63) Code (64) Km — Currency / Monnaie / Währung (70) — (65) Other charges / Frais / Gebühren = = = = — (66) Cours (71) (67) (72) (68) (73) (69) Cours (74)

3 Carriage-Port-Fracht-from-de-von to-pour-bis (54) (55) Angewandter Tarif (56) (57) (58) (59) Frachtsatz (60) Frachtpfl. Masse Kg (61) (62)

(63) Code (64) Km — Currency / Monnaie / Währung (70) — (65) Other charges / Frais / Gebühren = = = = — (66) Kurs (71) (67) (72) (68) (73) (69) Kurs (74)

(75) Advice of Collection / Avis d'encaissement / Nachnahmebegleitschein

See the reverse / Voir au verso / Rückseite beachten

(76) Charges Note / Bulletin d'affranchissement / Frankaturrechnung — yes-oui-ja

(77)

Total charges or To carry forward / Montant général ou A reporter / Gesamtbetrag oder Zu übertragen

(78)

(79) Forwarding station date stamp-Timbre à date de la gare expéditrice-Tagesstempel des Versandbahnhofes

(80) Destination station date stamp-Timbre à date de la gare destinataire-Tagesstempel des Bestimmungsbahnhofes

1

(81) Weighing stamp-Timbre de pesage-Wiegestempel

Mass ascertained-Masse constatée-Festgestellte Masse

(82) Country-Pays-Land / Station-Gare-Bahnhof

Control label / Etiquette de contrôle / Kontroll-Etikette

C'ment-Exp.-Vers.

(83) Date of forwarding (day-month) / Date d'expédition (jour-mois) / Versanddatum (Tag-Monat)

(84) Received-Arrivage-Empfang

Appendix 5A

LINER BILL OF LADING

Page 1

(Liner terms approved by The Baltic and International Maritime Conference)
Code Name: "CONLINEBILL"

Amended January 1st, 1950, August 1st, 1952, January 1st, 1973, July 1st, 1974, August 1st, 1976, January 1st, 1978

1. **Definition.**
Wherever the term "Merchant" is used in this Bill of Lading, it shall be deemed to include the Shipper, the Receiver, the Consignee, the Holder of the Bill of Lading and the Owner of the cargo.

2. **General Paramount Clause.**
The Hague Rules contained in the International Convention for the Unification of certain rules relating to Bills of Lading, dated Brussels the 25th August 1924 as enacted in the country of shipment shall apply to this contract. When no such enactment is in force in the country of shipment, the corresponding legislation of the country of destination shall apply, but in respect of shipments to which no such enactments are compulsorily applicable, the terms of the said Convention shall apply.
Trades where Hague-Visby Rules apply.
In trades where the International Brussels Convention 1924 as amended by the Protocol signed at Brussels on February 23rd 1968 – The Hague-Visby Rules – apply compulsorily, the provisions of the respective legislation shall be considered incorporated in this Bill of Lading. The Carrier takes all reservations possible under such applicable legislation, relating to the period before loading and after discharging and while the goods are in the charge of another Carrier, and to deck cargo and live animals.

3. **Jurisdiction.**
Any dispute arising under this Bill of Lading shall be decided in the country where the carrier has his principal place of business, and the law of such country shall apply except as provided elsewhere herein.

4. **Period of Responsibility.**
The Carrier or his Agent shall not be liable for loss of or damage to the goods during the period before loading and after discharge from the vessel, howsoever such loss or damage arises.

5. **The Scope of Voyage.**
As the vessel is engaged in liner service the intended voyage shall not be limited to the direct route but shall be deemed to include any proceeding or returning to or stopping or slowing down at or off any ports or places for any reasonable purpose connected with the service including maintenance of vessel and crew.

6. **Substitution of Vessel, Transhipment and Forwarding.**
Whether expressly arranged beforehand or otherwise, the Carrier shall be at liberty to carry the goods to their port of destination by the said or other vessel or vessels either belonging to the Carrier or others, or by other means of transport, proceeding either directly or indirectly to such port and to carry the goods or part of them beyond their port of destination, and to tranship, land and store the goods either on shore or afloat and reship and forward the same at Carrier's expense but at Merchant's risk. When the ultimate destination at which the Carrier may have engaged to deliver the goods is other than the vessel's port of discharge, the Carrier acts as Forwarding Agent only.
The responsibility of the Carrier shall be limited to the part of the transport performed by him on vessels under his management and no claim will be acknowledged by the Carrier for damage or loss arising during any other part of the transport even though the freight for the whole transport has been collected by him.

7. **Lighterage.**
Any lightering in or off ports of loading or ports of discharge to be for the account of the Merchant.

8. **Loading, Discharging and Delivery**
of the cargo shall be arranged by the Carrier's Agent unless otherwise agreed.
Landing, storing and delivery shall be for the Merchant's account.
Loading and discharging may commence without previous notice.
The Merchant or his Assign shall tender the goods when the vessel is ready to load and as fast as the vessel can receive and – but only if required by the Carrier – also outside ordinary working hours notwithstanding any custom of the port. Otherwise the Carrier shall be relieved of any obligation to load such cargo and the vessel may leave the port without further notice and deadfreight is to be paid.
The Merchant or his Assign shall take delivery of the goods and continue to receive the goods as fast as the vessel can deliver and – but only if required by the Carrier – also outside ordinary working hours notwithstanding any custom of the port. Otherwise the Carrier shall be at liberty to discharge the goods and any discharge to be deemed a true fulfilment of the contract, or alternatively to act under Clause 16.
The Merchant shall bear all overtime charges in connection with tendering and taking delivery of the goods as above.
If the goods are not applied for within a reasonable time, the Carrier may sell the same privately or by auction.
The Merchant shall accept his reasonable proportion of unidentified loose cargo.

9. **Live Animals and Deck Cargo**
shall be carried subject to the Hague Rules as referred to in Clause 2 hereof with the exception that notwithstanding anything contained in Clause 19 the Carrier shall not be liable for any loss or damage resulting from any act, neglect or default of his servants in the management of such animals and deck cargo.

10. **Options.**
The port of discharge for optional cargo must be declared to the vessel's Agents at the first of the optional ports not later than 48 hours before the vessel's arrival there. In the absence of such declaration the Carrier may elect to discharge at the first or any other optional port and the contract of carriage shall then be considered as having been fulfilled. Any option can be exercised for the total quantity under this Bill of Lading only.

11. **Freight and Charges.**
(a) Prepayable freight, whether actually paid or not, shall be considered as fully earned upon loading and non-returnable in any event. The Carrier's claim for any charges under this contract shall be considered definitely payable in like manner as soon as the charges have been incurred.
Interest at 5 per cent., shall run from the date when freight and charges are due.
(b) The Merchant shall be liable for expenses of fumigation and of gathering and sorting loose cargo and of weighing onboard and expenses incurred in repairing damage to and replacing of packing due to excepted causes and for all expenses caused by extra handling of the cargo for any of the aforementioned reasons.
(c) Any dues, duties, taxes and charges which under any denomination may be levied on any basis such as amount of freight, weight of cargo or tonnage of the vessel shall be paid by the Merchant.
(d) The Merchant shall be liable for all fines and/or losses which the Carrier, vessel or cargo may incur through non-observance of Custom House and/or import or export regulations.
(e) The Carrier is entitled in case of incorrect declaration of contents, weights, measurements or value of the goods to claim double the amount of freight which would have been due if such declaration had been correctly given. For the purpose of ascertaining the actual facts, the Carrier reserves the right to obtain from the Merchant the original invoice and to have the contents inspected and the weight, measurement or value verified.

12. **Lien.**
The Carrier shall have a lien for any amount due under this contract and costs of recovering same and shall be entitled to sell the goods privately or by auction to cover any claims.

13. **Delay.**
The Carrier shall not be responsible for any loss sustained by the Merchant through delay of the goods unless caused by the Carrier's personal gross negligence.

14. **General Average and Salvage.**
General Average to be adjusted at any port or place at Carrier's option and to be settled according to the York-Antwerp Rules 1974. In the event of accident, danger, damage or disaster before or after commencement of the voyage resulting from any cause whatsoever, whether due to negligence or not, for which or for the consequence of which the Carrier is not responsible by statute, contract or otherwise, the Merchant shall contribute with the Carrier in General Average to the payment of any sacrifice, losses or expenses of a General Average nature that may be made or incurred, and shall pay salvage and special charges incurred in respect of the goods. If a salving vessel is owned or operated by the Carrier, salvage shall be paid for as fully as if the salving vessel or vessels belonged to strangers.

15. **Both-to-Blame Collision Clause.** (This clause to remain in effect even if unenforcible in the Courts of the United States of America).
If the vessel comes into collision with another vessel as a result of the negligence of the other vessel and any act, negligence or default of the Master, Mariner, Pilot or the servants of the Carrier in the navigation or in the management of the vessel, the Merchant will indemnify the Carrier against all loss or liability to the other or non-carrying vessel or her Owner in so far as such loss or liability represents loss of or damage to or any claim whatsoever of the owner of the said goods paid or payable by the other or non-carrying vessel or her Owner to the owner of said cargo and set-off, or recouped or recovered by the other or non-carrying vessel or her Owner as part of his claim against the carrying vessel or Carrier. The foregoing provisions shall also apply where the Owner, operator or those in charge of any vessel or vessels or objects other than, or in addition to, the colliding vessels or objects are at fault in respect of a collision or contact.

16. **Government directions, War, Epidemics, Ice, Strikes, etc.**
(a) The Master and the Carrier shall have liberty to comply with any order or directions or recommendations in connection with the transport under this contract given by any Government or Authority, or anybody acting or purporting to act on behalf of such Government or Authority, or having under the terms of the insurance on the vessel the right to give such orders or directions or recommendations.
(b) Should it appear that the performance of the transport would expose the vessel or any goods onboard to risk of seizure or damage or delay, resulting from war, warlike operations, blockade, riots, civil commotions or piracy, or any person onboard to the risk of loss of life or freedom, or that any such risk has increased, the Master may discharge the cargo at port of loading or any other safe and convenient port.
(c) Should it appear that epidemics, quarantine, ice – labour troubles, labour obstructions, strikes, lockouts, any of which onboard or on shore – difficulties in loading or discharging would prevent the vessel from leaving the port of loading or reaching or entering the port of discharge or there discharging in the usual manner and leaving again, all of which safely and without delay, the Master may discharge the cargo at port of loading or any other safe and convenient port.
(d) The discharge under the provisions of this clause of any cargo for which a Bill of Lading has been issued shall be deemed due fulfilment of the contract. If in connection with the exercise of any liberty under this clause any extra expenses are incurred, they shall be paid by the Merchant in addition to the freight, together with return freight if any and a reasonable compensation for any extra services rendered to the goods.
(e) If any situation referred to in this clause may be anticipated, or if for any such reason the vessel cannot safely and without delay reach or enter the loading port or must undergo repairs, the Carrier may cancel the contract before the Bill of Lading is issued.
(f) The Merchant shall be informed if possible.

17. **Identity of Carrier.**
The Contract evidenced by this Bill of Lading is between the Merchant and the Owner of the vessel named herein (or substitute) and it is therefore agreed that said Shipowner only shall be liable for any damage or loss due to any breach or non-performance of any obligation arising out of the contract of carriage, whether or not relating to the vessel's seaworthiness. If, despite the foregoing, it is adjudged that any other is the Carrier and/or bailee of the goods shipped hereunder, all limitations of, and exonerations from, liability provided for by law or by this Bill of Lading shall be available to such other.
It is further understood and agreed that as the Line, Company or Agents who has executed this Bill of Lading for and on behalf of the Master is not a principal in the transaction, said Line, Company or Agents shall not be under any liability arising out of the contract of carriage, nor as Carrier nor bailee of the goods.

18. **Exemptions and Immunities of all servants and agents of the Carrier.**
It is hereby expressly agreed that no servant or agent of the Carrier (including every independent contractor from time to time employed by the Carrier) shall in any circumstances whatsoever be under any liability whatsoever to the Merchant for any loss, damage or delay arising or resulting directly or indirectly from any act, neglect or default on his part while acting in the course of or in connection with his employment and, but without prejudice to the generality of the foregoing provisions in this clause, every exemption, limitation, condition and liberty herein contained and every right, exemption from liability, defence and immunity of whatsoever nature applicable to the Carrier or to which the Carrier is entitled hereunder shall also be available and shall extend to protect every such servant or agent of the Carrier acting as aforesaid and for the purpose of all the foregoing provisions of this clause the Carrier is or shall be deemed to be acting as agent or trustee on behalf of and for the benefit of all persons who are or might be his servants or agents from time to time (including independent contractors as aforesaid) and all such persons shall to this extent be or be deemed to be parties to the contract evidenced by this Bill of Lading.
The Carrier shall be entitled to be paid by the Merchant on demand any sum recovered or recoverable by the Merchant or any other from such servant or agent of the Carrier for any such loss, damage or delay or otherwise.

19. **Optional Stowage. Unitization.**
(a) Goods may be stowed by the Carrier as received, or, at Carrier's option, by means of containers, or similar articles of transport used to consolidate goods.
(b) Containers, trailers and transportable tanks, whether stowed by the Carrier or received by him in a stowed condition from the Merchant, may be carried on or under deck without notice to the Merchant.
(c) The Carrier's liability for cargo stowed as aforesaid shall be governed by the Hague Rules as defined above notwithstanding the fact that the goods are being carried on deck and the goods shall contribute to general average and shall receive compensation in general average.

ADDITIONAL CLAUSES

(To be added if required in the contemplated trade).

A. Demurrage.
The Carrier shall be paid demurrage at the daily rate per ton of the vessel's gross register tonnage as indicated on Page 2 if the vessel is not loaded or discharged with the dispatch set out in Clause 8, any delay in waiting for berth at or off port to count. Provided that if the delay is due to causes beyond the control of the Merchant, 24 hours shall be deducted from the time on demurrage.
Each Merchant shall be liable towards the Carrier for a proportionate part of the total demurrage due, based upon the total freight on the goods to be loaded or discharged at the port in question.
No Merchant shall be liable in demurrage for any delay arisen only in connection with goods belonging to other Merchants.
The demurrage in respect of each parcel shall not exceed its freight.
(This Clause shall only apply if the Demurrage Box on Page 2 is filled in).

B. U.S. Trade. Period of Responsibility.
In case the Contract evidenced by this Bill of Lading is subject to the U.S. Carriage of Goods by Sea Act, then the provisions stated in said Act shall govern before loading and after discharge and throughout the entire time the goods are in the Carrier's custody.

Appendix 5A

Page 2

LINER BILL OF LADING

B L No.

Reference No.

Shipper

Consignee

Notify address

Pre-carriage by* | Place of receipt by pre-carrier*

Vessel | Port of loading

Port of discharge | Place of delivery by on-carrier*

Marks and Nos.	Number and kind of packages; description of goods	Gross weight	Measurement

Particulars furnished by the Merchant

Freight details, charges etc.

Daily demurrage rate (additional Clause A)

SHIPPED on board in apparent good order and condition, weight, measure, marks, numbers, quality, contents and value unknown, for carriage to the Port of Discharge or so near thereunto as the Vessel may safely get and lie always afloat, to be delivered in the like good order and condition at the aforesaid Port unto Consignees or their Assigns, they paying freight as indicated to the left plus other charges incurred in accordance with the provisions contained in this Bill of Lading. In accepting this Bill of Lading the Merchant expressly accepts and agrees to all its stipulations on both pages, whether written, printed, stamped or otherwise incorporated, as fully as if they were all signed by the Merchant.
One original Bill of Lading must be surrendered duly endorsed in exchange for the goods or delivery order.
IN WITNESS whereof the Master of the said Vessel has signed the number of original Bills of Lading stated below, all of this tenor and date, one of which being accomplished, the others to stand void.

Freight payable at	Place and date of issue
Number of original Bs/L	Signature

* Applicable only when document used as a Through Bill of Lading

Appendix 5B

Adopted by
the Documentary Committee of the General
Council of British Shipping, London
and the Documentary Committee of The Japan
Shipping Exchange, Inc., Tokyo

1. Shipbroker

RECOMMENDED
THE BALTIC AND INTERNATIONAL MARITIME CONFERENCE
UNIFORM GENERAL CHARTER (AS REVISED 1922 and 1976)
INCLUDING "F.I.O." ALTERNATIVE, ETC.
(To be used for trades for which no approved form is in force)
CODE NAME: "GENCON"

Part I

2. Place and date

3. Owners/Place of business (Cl. 1)

4. Charterers/Place of business (Cl. 1)

5. Vessel's name (Cl. 1)

6. GRT/NRT (Cl. 1)

7. Deadweight cargo carrying capacity in tons (abt.) (Cl. 1)

8. Present position (Cl. 1)

9. Expected ready to load (abt.) (Cl. 1)

10. Loading port or place (Cl. 1)

11. Discharging port or place (Cl. 1)

12. Cargo (also state quantity and margin in Owners' option, if agreed; if full and complete cargo not agreed state "part cargo") (Cl. 1)

13. Freight rate (also state if payable on delivered or intaken quantity) (Cl. 1)

14. Freight payment (state currency and method of payment; also beneficiary and bank account) (Cl. 4)

15. Loading and discharging costs (state alternative (a) or (b) of Cl. 5; also indicate if vessel is gearless)

16. Laytime (if separate laytime for load. and disch. is agreed, fill in a) and b). If total laytime for load. and disch., fill in c) only) (Cl. 6)

a) Laytime for loading

b) Laytime for discharging

c) Total laytime for loading and discharging

17. Shippers (state name and address) (Cl. 6)

18. Demurrage rate (loading and discharging) (Cl. 7)

19. Cancelling date (Cl. 10)

20. Brokerage commission and to whom payable (Cl. 14)

21. Additional clauses covering special provisions, if agreed.

It is mutually agreed that this Contract shall be performed subject to the conditions contained in this Charter which shall include Part I as well as Part II. In the event of a conflict of conditions, the provisions of Part I shall prevail over those of Part II to the extent of such conflict.

Signature (Owners)

Signature (Charterers)

19-0

Printed and sold by Fr. G. Knudtzon Ltd., 55, Toldbodgade, Copenhagen, by authority of The Baltic and International Maritime Conference (BIMCO), Copenhagen.

Appendix 5B

PART II

"Gencon" Charter (As Revised 1922 and 1976)

Including "F.I.O." Alternative, etc.

1. It is agreed between the party mentioned in Box 3 as Owners of the steamer or motor-vessel named in Box 5, of the gross/nett Register tons indicated in Box 6 and carrying about the number of tons of deadweight cargo stated in Box 7, now in position as stated in Box 8 and expected ready to load under this Charter about the date indicated in Box 9, and the party mentioned as Charterers in Box 4 that:
The said vessel shall proceed to the loading port or place stated in Box 10 or so near thereto as she may safely get and lie always afloat, and there load a full and complete cargo (if shipment of deck cargo agreed same to be at Charterers' risk) as stated in Box 12 (Charterers to provide all mats and/or wood for dunnage and any separations required, the Owners allowing the use of any dunnage wood on board if required) which the Charterers bind themselves to ship, and being so loaded the vessel shall proceed to the discharging port or place stated in Box 11 as ordered on signing Bills of Lading or so near thereto as she may safely get and lie always afloat and there deliver the cargo on being paid freight on delivered or intaken quantity as indicated in Box 13 at the rate stated in Box 13.

2. Owners' Responsibility Clause
Owners are to be responsible for loss of or damage to the goods or for delay in delivery of the goods only in case the loss, damage or delay has been caused by the improper or negligent stowage of the goods (unless stowage performed by shippers/Charterers or their stevedores or servants) or by personal want of due diligence on the part of the Owners or their Manager to make the vessel in all respects seaworthy and to secure that she is properly manned, equipped and supplied or by the personal act or default of the Owners or their Manager.
And the Owners are responsible for no loss or damage or delay arising from any other cause whatsoever, even from the neglect or default of the Captain or crew or some other person employed by the Owners on board or ashore for whose acts they would, but for this clause, be responsible, or from unseaworthiness of the vessel on loading or commencement of the voyage or at any time whatsoever. Damage caused by contact with or leakage, smell or evaporation from other goods or by the inflammable or explosive nature or insufficient package of other goods not to be considered as caused by improper or negligent stowage, even if in fact so caused.

3. Deviation Clause
The vessel has liberty to call at any port or ports in any order, for any purpose, to sail without pilots, to tow and/or assist vessels in all situations, and also to deviate for the purpose of saving life and/or property.

4. Payment of Freight
The freight to be paid in the manner prescribed in Box 14 in cash without discount on delivery of the cargo at mean rate of exchange ruling on day or days of payment, the receivers of the cargo being bound to pay freight on account during delivery, if required by Captain or Owners.
Cash for vessel's ordinary disbursements at port of loading to be advanced by Charterers if required at highest current rate of exchange, subject to two per cent. to cover insurance and other expenses.

5. Loading/Discharging Costs

* *(a) Gross Terms*
The cargo to be brought alongside in such a manner as to enable vessel to take the goods with her own tackle. Charterers to procure and pay the necessary men on shore or on board the lighters to do the work there, vessel only heaving the cargo on board.
If the loading takes place by elevator, cargo to be put free in vessel's holds, Owners only paying trimming expenses.
Any pieces and/or packages of cargo over two tons weight, shall be loaded, stowed and discharged by Charterers at their risk and expense.
The cargo to be received by Merchants at their risk and expense alongside the vessel not beyond the reach of her tackle.

* *(b) F.i.o. and free stowed/trimmed*
The cargo shall be brought into the holds, loaded, stowed and/or trimmed and taken from the holds and discharged by the Charterers or their Agents, free of any risk, liability and expense whatsoever to the Owners.
The Owners shall provide winches, motive power and winchmen from the Crew if requested and permitted; if not, the Charterers shall provide and pay for winchmen from shore and/or cranes, if any. (This provision shall not apply if vessel is gearless and stated as such in Box 15).

* *indicate alternative (a) or (b), as agreed, in Box 15.*

6. Laytime

* *(a) Separate laytime for loading and discharging*
The cargo shall be loaded within the number of running hours as indicated in Box 16, weather permitting, Sundays and holidays excepted, unless used, in which event time actually used shall count.
The cargo shall be discharged within the number of running hours as indicated in Box 16, weather permitting, Sundays and holidays excepted, unless used, in which event time actually used shall count.

* *(b) Total laytime for loading and discharging*
The cargo shall be loaded and discharged within the number of total running hours as indicated in Box 16, weather permitting, Sundays and holidays excepted, unless used, in which event time actually used shall count.

(c) Commencement of laytime (loading and discharging)
Laytime for loading and discharging shall commence at 1 p.m. if notice of readiness is given before noon, and at 6 a.m. next working day if notice given during office hours after noon. Notice at loading port to be given to the Shippers named in Box 17.
Time actually used before commencement of laytime shall count.
Time lost in waiting for berth to count as loading or discharging time, as the case may be.

* *indicate alternative (a) or (b) as agreed, in Box 16.*

7. Demurrage
Ten running days on demurrage at the rate stated in Box 18 per day or pro rata for any part of a day, payable day by day, to be allowed Merchants altogether at ports of loading and discharging.

8. Lien Clause
Owners shall have a lien on the cargo for freight, dead-freight, demurrage and damages for detention. Charterers shall remain responsible for dead-freight and demurrage (including damages for detention), incurred at port of loading. Charterers shall also remain responsible for freight and demurrage (including damages for detention) incurred at port of discharge, but only to such extent as the Owners have been unable to obtain payment thereof by exercising the lien on the cargo.

9. Bills of Lading
The Captain to sign Bills of Lading at such rate of freight as presented without prejudice to this Charterparty, but should the freight by Bills of Lading amount to less than the total chartered freight the difference to be paid to the Captain in cash on signing Bills of Lading.

10. Cancelling Clause
Should the vessel not be ready to load (whether in berth or not) on or before the date indicated in Box 19, Charterers have the option of cancelling this contract, such option to be declared, if demanded, at least 48 hours before vessel's expected arrival at port of loading. Should the vessel be delayed on account of average or otherwise, Charterers to be informed as soon as possible, and if the vessel is delayed for more than 10 days after the day she is stated to be expected ready to load, Charterers have the option of cancelling this contract, unless a cancelling date has been agreed upon.

11. General Average
General average to be settled according to York-Antwerp Rules, 1974. Proprietors of cargo to pay the cargo's share in the general expenses even if same have been necessitated through neglect or default of the Owners' servants (see clause 2).

12. Indemnity
Indemnity for non-performance of this Charterparty, proved damages, not exceeding estimated amount of freight.

13. Agency
In every case the Owners shall appoint his own Broker or Agent both at the port of loading and the port of discharge.

14. Brokerage
A brokerage commission at the rate stated in Box 20 on the freight earned is due to the party mentioned in Box 20.
In case of non-execution at least $1/3$ of the brokerage on the estimated amount of freight and dead-freight to be paid by the Owners to the Brokers as indemnity for the latter's expenses and work. In case of more voyages the amount of indemnity to be mutually agreed.

15. GENERAL STRIKE CLAUSE
Neither Charterers nor Owners shall be responsible for the consequences of any strikes or lock-outs preventing or delaying the fulfilment of any obligations under this contract.
If there is a strike or lock-out affecting the loading of the cargo, or any part of it, when vessel is ready to proceed from her last port or at any time during the voyage to the port or ports of loading or after her arrival there, Captain or Owners may ask Charterers to declare, that they agree to reckon the laydays as if there were no strike or lock-out. Unless Charterers have given such declaration in writing (by telegram, if necessary) within 24 hours, Owners shall have the option of cancelling this contract. If part cargo has already been loaded, Owners must proceed with same, (freight payable on loaded quantity only) having liberty to complete with other cargo on the way for their own account.
If there is a strike or lock-out affecting the discharge of the cargo on or after vessel's arrival at or off port of discharge and same has not been settled within 48 hours, Receivers shall have the option of keeping vessel waiting until such strike or lock-out is at an end against paying half demurrage after expiration of the time provided for discharging, or of ordering the vessel to a safe port where she can safely discharge without risk of being detained by strike or lock-out. Such orders to be given within 48 hours after Captain or Owners have given notice to Charterers of the strike or lock-out affecting the discharge. On delivery of the cargo at such port, all conditions of this Charterparty and of the Bill of Lading shall apply and vessel shall receive the same freight as if she had discharged at the original port of destination, except that if the distance of the substituted port exceeds 100 nautical miles, the freight on the cargo delivered at the substituted port to be increased in proportion.

16. War Risks ("Voywar 1950")
(1) In these clauses "War Risks" shall include any blockade or any action which is announced as a blockade by any Government or by any belligerent or by any organized body, sabotage, piracy, and any actual or threatened war, hostilities, warlike operations, civil war, civil commotion, or revolution.

(2) If at any time before the Vessel commences loading, it appears that performance of the contract will subject the Vessel or her Master and crew or her cargo to war risks at any stage of the adventure, the Owners shall be entitled by letter or telegram despatched to the Charterers, to cancel this Charter.

(3) The Master shall not be required to load cargo or to continue loading or to proceed on or to sign Bill(s) of Lading for any adventure on which or any port at which it appears that the Vessel, her Master and crew or her cargo will be subjected to war risks. In the event of the exercise by the Master of his right under this Clause after part or full cargo has been loaded, the Master shall be at liberty either to discharge such cargo at the loading port or to proceed therewith. In the latter case the Vessel shall have liberty to carry other cargo for Owners' benefit and accordingly to proceed to and load or discharge such other cargo at any other port or ports whatsoever, backwards or forwards, although in a contrary direction to or out of or beyond the ordinary route. In the event of the Master electing to proceed with part cargo under this Clause freight shall in any case be payable on the quantity delivered.

(4) If at the time the Master elects to proceed with part or full cargo under Clause 3, or after the Vessel has left the loading port, or the

Appendix 5B

PART II

"Gencon" Charter (As Revised 1922 and 1976)

Including "F.I.O." Alternative, etc.

last of the loading ports, if more than one, it appears that further performance of the contract will subject the Vessel, her Master and crew or her cargo, to war risks, the cargo shall be discharged, or if the discharge has been commenced shall be completed, at any safe port in vicinity of the port of discharge as may be ordered by the Charterers. If no such orders shall be received from the Charterers within 48 hours after the Owners have despatched a request by telegram to the Charterers for the nomination of a substitute discharging port, the Owners shall be at liberty to discharge the cargo at any safe port which they may, in their discretion, decide on and such discharge shall be deemed to be due fulfilment of the contract of affreightment. In the event of cargo being discharged at any such other port, the Owners shall be entitled to freight as if the discharge had been effected at the port or ports named in the Bill(s) of Lading or to which the Vessel may have been ordered pursuant thereto.

(5) (a) The Vessel shall have liberty to comply with any directions or recommendations as to loading, departure, arrival, routes, ports of call, stoppages, destination, zones, waters, discharge, delivery or in any other wise whatsoever (including any direction or recommendation not to go to the port of destination or to delay proceeding thereto or to proceed to some other port) given by any Government or by any belligerent or by any organized body engaged in civil war, hostilities or warlike operations or by any person or body acting or purporting to act as or with the authority of any Government or belligerent or of any such organized body or by any committee or person having under the terms of the war risks insurance on the Vessel, the right to give any such directions or recommendations. If, by reason of or in compliance with any such direction or recommendation, anything is done or is not done, such shall not be deemed a deviation.

(b) If, by reason of or in compliance with any such directions or recommendations, the Vessel does not proceed to the port or ports named in the Bill(s) of Lading or to which she may have been ordered pursuant thereto, the Vessel may proceed to any port as directed or recommended or to any safe port which the Owners in their discretion may decide on and there discharge the cargo. Such discharge shall be deemed to be due fulfilment of the contract of affreightment and the Owners shall be entitled to freight as if discharge had been effected at the port or ports named in the Bill(s) of Lading or to which the Vessel may have been ordered pursuant thereto.

(6) All extra expenses (including insurance costs) involved in discharging cargo at the loading port or in reaching or discharging the cargo at any port as provided in Clauses 4 and 5 (b) hereof shall be paid by the Charterers and or cargo owners, and the Owners shall have a lien on the cargo for all moneys due under these Clauses.

17. GENERAL ICE CLAUSE

Port of loading

(a) In the event of the loading port being inaccessible by reason of ice when vessel is ready to proceed from her last port or at any time during the voyage or on vessel's arrival or in case frost sets in after vessel's arrival, the Captain for fear of being frozen in is at liberty to leave without cargo, and this Charter shall be null and void.

(b) If during loading the Captain, for fear of vessel being frozen in, deems it advisable to leave, he has liberty to do so with what cargo he has on board and to proceed to any other port or ports with option of completing cargo for Owners' benefit for any port or ports including port of discharge. Any part cargo thus loaded under this Charter to be forwarded to destination at vessel's expense but against payment of freight, provided that no extra expenses be thereby caused to the Receivers, freight being paid on quantity delivered (in proportion if lumpsum), all other conditions as per Charter.

(c) In case of more than one loading port, and if one or more of the ports are closed by ice, the Captain or Owners to be at liberty either to load the part cargo at the open port and fillup elsewhere for their own account as under section (b) or to declare the Charter null and void unless Charterers agree to load full cargo at the open port.

(d) This Ice Clause not to apply in the Spring.

Port of discharge

(a) Should ice (except in the Spring) prevent vessel from reaching port of discharge Receivers shall have the option of keeping vessel waiting until the re-opening of navigation and paying demurrage, or of ordering the vessel to a safe and immediately accessible port where she can safely discharge without risk of detention by ice. Such orders to be given within 48 hours after Captain or Owners have given notice to Charterers of the impossibility of reaching port of destination.

(b) If during discharging the Captain for fear of vessel being frozen in deems it advisable to leave, he has liberty to do so with what cargo he has on board and to proceed to the nearest accessible port where she can safely discharge.

(c) On delivery of the cargo at such port, all conditions of the Bill of Lading shall apply and vessel shall receive the same freight as if she had discharged at the original port of destination, except that if the distance of the substituted port exceeds 100 nautical miles, the freight on the cargo delivered at the substituted port to be increased in proportion.

Appendix 5C

Adopted by the Documentary Committee of the Chamber of Shipping of the United Kingdom and the Documentary Committee of The Japan Shipping Exchange, Inc.

Issued 6/2/1909
Amended 10/3/1911
Amended 6/3/1912
Amended 10/4/1920
Amended 1/3/1939
Amended 1/1/1950
Amended 1/7/1974

1. Shipbroker	**THE BALTIC AND INTERNATIONAL MARITIME CONFERENCE** **UNIFORM TIME-CHARTER (Box Layout 1974)** **CODE NAME: "BALTIME 1939"** PART I
	2. Place and date
3. Owners/Place of business	4. Charterers/Place of business
5. Vessel's name	6. GRT/NRT
7. Class	8. Indicated horse power
9. Total tons d.w. (abt.) on Board of Trade summer freeboard	10. Cubic feet grain/bale capacity
11. Permanent bunkers (abt.)	
12. Speed capability in knots (abt.) on a consumption in tons (abt.) of	
13. Present position	
14. Period of hire (Cl. 1)	15. Port of delivery (Cl. 1)
	16. Time of delivery (Cl. 1)
17. (a) Trade limits (Cl. 2)	
(b) Cargo exclusions specially agreed	
18. Bunkers on re-delivery (state min. and max. quantity) (Cl. 5)	
19. Charter hire (Cl. 6)	20. Hire payment (state currency, method and place of payment; also beneficiary and bank account) (Cl. 6)
21. Place or range of re-delivery (Cl. 7)	22. War (only to be filled in if Section (C) agreed) (Cl. 21)
23. Cancelling date (Cl. 22)	24. Place of arbitration (only to be filled in if place other than London agreed) (Cl. 23)
25. Brokerage commission and to whom payable (Cl. 25)	
	26. Numbers of additional clauses covering special provisions, if agreed

It is mutually agreed that this Contract shall be performed subject to the conditions contained in this Charter which shall include Part I as well as Part II. In the event of a conflict of conditions, the provisions of Part I shall prevail over those of Part II to the extent of such conflict.

Signature (Owners)	Signature (Charterers)

Printed and sold by Fr. G. Knudtzon Ltd., 55, Toldbodgade, Copenhagen,
by authority of The Baltic and International Maritime Conference, Copenhagen.

40-0

Appendix 5C

PART II
"BALTIME 1939" Uniform Time-Charter (Box Layout 1974)

It is agreed between the party mentioned in Box 3 as Owners of the Vessel named in Box 5 of the gross/net Register tonnage indicated in Box 6, classed as stated in Box 7 and of indicated horse power as stated in Box 8, carrying about the number of tons deadweight indicated in Box 9 on Board of Trade summer freeboard inclusive of bunkers, stores, provisions and boiler water, having as per builder's plan a cubic-feet grain bale capacity as stated in Box 10, exclusive of permanent bunkers, which contain about the number of tons stated in Box 11, and fully loaded capable of steaming about the number of knots indicated in Box 12 in good weather and smooth water on a consumption of about the number of tons best Welsh coal or oil-fuel stated in Box 12, now in position as stated in Box 13 and the party mentioned as Charterers in Box 4, as follows:

1. Period Port of Delivery Time of Delivery
The Owners let and the Charterers hire the Vessel for a period of the number of calendar months indicated in Box 14 from the time (not a Sunday or a legal Holiday unless taken over) the Vessel is delivered and placed at the disposal of the Charterers between 9 a.m. and 6 p.m., or between 9 a.m. and 2 p.m. if on Saturday at the port stated in Box 15 in such available berth where she can safely lie always afloat, as the Charterers may direct, she being in every way fitted for ordinary cargo service.
The Vessel to be delivered at the time indicated in Box 16.

2. Trade
The Vessel to be employed in lawful trades for the carriage of lawful merchandise only between good and safe ports or places where she can safely lie always afloat within the limits stated in Box 17.
No live stock nor injurious, inflammable or dangerous goods (such as acids, explosives, calcium carbide, ferro silicon, naphtha, motor spirit, tar, or any of their products) to be shipped.

3. Owners to Provide
The Owners to provide and pay for all provisions and wages, for insurance of the Vessel, for all deck and engine-room stores and maintain her in a thoroughly efficient state in hull and machinery during service.
The Owners to provide one winchman per hatch. If further winchmen are required, or if the stevedores refuse or are not permitted to work with the Crew, the Charterers to provide and pay qualified shore-winchmen.

4. Charterers to Provide
The Charterers to provide and pay for all coals, including galley coal, oil-fuel, water for boilers, port charges, pilotages (whether compulsory or not), canal steersmen, boatage, lights, tug-assistance, consular charges (except those pertaining to the Master, Officers and Crew), canal, dock and other dues and charges, including any foreign general municipality or state taxes, also all dock, harbour and tonnage dues at the ports of delivery and re-delivery (unless incurred through cargo carried before delivery or after re-delivery), agencies, commissions, also to arrange and pay for loading, trimming, stowing (including dunnage and shifting boards, excepting any already on board), unloading, weighing, tallying and delivery of cargoes, surveys on hatches, meals supplied to officials and men in their service and all other charges and expenses whatsoever including detention and expenses through quarantine (including cost of fumigation and disinfection).
All ropes, slings and special runners actually used for loading and discharging and any special gear, including special ropes, hawsers and chains required by the custom of the port for mooring to be for the Charterers' account. The Vessel to be fitted with winches, derricks, wheels and ordinary runners capable of handling lifts up to 2 tons.

5. Bunkers
The Charterers at port of delivery and the Owners at port of re-delivery to take over and pay for all coal or oil-fuel remaining in the Vessel's bunkers at current price at the respective ports.
The Vessel to be re-delivered with not less than the number of tons and not exceeding the number of tons of coal or oil-fuel in the Vessel's bunkers stated in Box 18

6. Hire
The Charterers to pay as hire the rate stated in Box 19 per 30 days, commencing in accordance with Clause 1 until her re-delivery to the Owners.

Payment
Payment of hire to be made in cash, in the currency stated in Box 20, without discount, every 30 days, in advance, and in the manner prescribed in Box 20.
In default of payment the Owners to have the right of withdrawing the Vessel from the service of the Charterers, without noting any protest and without interference by any court or any other formality whatsoever and without prejudice to any claim the Owners may otherwise have on the Charterers under the Charter.

7. Re-delivery
The Vessel to be re-delivered on the expiration of the Charter in the same good order as when delivered to the Charterers (fair wear and tear excepted) at an ice-free port in the Charterers' option at the place or within the range stated in Box 21, between 9 a.m. and 6 p.m., and 9 a.m. and 2 p.m. on Saturday, but the day of re-delivery shall not be a Sunday or legal Holiday.

Notice
The Charterers to give the Owners not less than ten days' notice at which port and on about which day the Vessel will be re-delivered.
Should the Vessel be ordered on a voyage by which the Charter period will be exceeded the Charterers to have the use of the Vessel to enable them to complete the voyage, provided it could be reasonably calculated that the voyage would allow re-delivery about the time fixed for the termination of the Charter, but for any time exceeding the termination date the Charterers to pay the market rate if higher than the rate stipulated herein.

8. Cargo Space
The whole reach and burthen of the Vessel, including lawful deck-capacity to be at the Charterers' disposal, reserving proper and sufficient space for the Vessel's Master, Officers, Crew, tackle, apparel, furniture, provisions and stores.

9. Master
The Master to prosecute all voyages with the utmost despatch and to render customary assistance with the Vessel's Crew. The Master to be under the orders of the Charterers as regards employment, agency, or other arrangements. The Charterers to indemnify the Owners against all consequences or liabilities arising from the Master, Officers or Agents signing Bills of Lading or other documents or otherwise complying with such orders as well as from any irregularity in the Vessel's papers or for overcarrying goods. The Owners not to be responsible for shortage, mixture, marks, nor for number of pieces or packages, nor for damage to or claims on cargo caused by bad stowage or otherwise.
If the Charterers have reason to be dissatisfied with the conduct of the Master, Officers, or Engineers, the Owners, on receiving particulars of the complaint, promptly to investigate the matter, and, if necessary and practicable, to make a change in the appointments.

10. Directions and Logs
The Charterers to furnish the Master with all instructions and sailing directions and the Master and Engineer to keep full and correct logs accessible to the Charterers or their Agents.

11. Suspension of Hire etc.
(A) in the event of drydocking or other necessary measures to maintain the efficiency of the Vessel, deficiency of men or Owners' stores, breakdown of machinery, damage to hull or other accident, either hindering or preventing the working of the Vessel and continuing for more than twentyfour consecutive hours, no hire to be paid in respect of any time lost thereby during the period in which the Vessel is unable to perform the service immediately required. Any hire paid in advance to be adjusted accordingly.
(B) In the event of the Vessel being driven into port or to anchorage through stress of weather, trading to shallow harbours or to rivers or ports with bars or suffering an accident to her cargo, any detention of the Vessel and/or expenses resulting from such detention to be for the Charterers' account even if such detention and/or expenses, or the cause by reason of which either is incurred, be due to, or be contributed to by, the negligence of the Owners' servants.

12. Cleaning Boilers
Cleaning of boilers whenever possible to be done during service, but if impossible the Charterers to give the Owners necessary time for cleaning. Should the Vessel be detained beyond 48 hours hire to cease until again ready.

13. Responsibility and Exemption
The Owners only to be responsible for delay in delivery of the Vessel or for delay during the currency of the Charter and for loss or damage to goods onboard, if such delay or loss has been caused by want of due diligence on the part of the Owners or their Manager in making the Vessel seaworthy and fitted for the voyage or any other personal act or omission or default of the Owners or their Manager. The Owners not to be responsible in any other case nor for damage or delay whatsoever and howsoever caused even if caused by the neglect or default of their servants. The Owners not to be liable for loss or damage arising or resulting from strikes, lockouts or stoppage or restraint of labour (including the Master, Officers or Crew) whether partial or general.
The Charterers to be responsible for loss or damage caused to the Vessel or to the Owners by goods being loaded contrary to the terms of the Charter or by improper or careless bunkering or loading, stowing or discharging of goods or any other improper or negligent act on their part or that of their servants.

14. Advances
The Charterers or their Agents to advance to the Master, if required, necessary funds for ordinary disbursements for the Vessel's account at any port charging only interest at 6 per cent. p.a., such advances to be deducted from hire.

15. Excluded Ports
The Vessel not to be ordered to nor bound to enter: a) any place where fever or epidemics are prevalent or to which the Master, Officers and Crew by law are not bound to follow the Vessel

Ice
b) any ice-bound place or any place where lights, lightships, marks and buoys are or are likely to be withdrawn by reason of ice on the Vessel's arrival or where there is risk that ordinarily the Vessel will not be able on account of ice to reach the place or to get out after having completed loading or discharging. The Vessel not to be obliged to force ice. If on account of ice the Master considers it dangerous to remain at the loading or discharging place for fear of the Vessel being frozen in and/or damaged, he has liberty to sail to a convenient open place and await the Charterers' fresh instructions.
Unforeseen detention through any of above causes to be for the Charterers' account.

16. Loss of Vessel
Should the Vessel be lost or missing, hire to cease from the date when she was lost. If the date of loss cannot be ascertained half hire to be paid from the date the Vessel was last reported until the calculated date of arrival at the destination. Any hire paid in advance to be adjusted accordingly.

17. Overtime
The Vessel to work day and night if required. The Charterers to refund the Owners their outlays for all overtime paid to Officers and Crew according to the hours and rates stated in the Vessel's articles.

18. Lien
The Owners to have a lien upon all cargoes and sub-freights belonging to the Time-Charterers and any Bill of Lading freight for all claims under this Charter, and the Charterers to have a lien on the Vessel for all moneys paid in advance and not earned.

19. Salvage
All salvage and assistance to other vessels to be for the Owners' and the Charterers' equal benefit after deducting the Master's and Crew's proportion and all legal and other expenses including hire paid under the charter for time lost in the salvage, also repairs of damage and coal or oil-fuel consumed. The Charterers to be bound by all measures taken by the Owners in order to secure payment of salvage and to fix its amount.

20 Sublet
The Charterers to have the option of subletting the Vessel, giving due notice to the Owners, but the original Charterers always to remain responsible to the Owners for due performance of the Charter.

21. War
(A) The Vessel unless the consent of the Owners be first obtained not to be ordered nor continue to any place or on any voyage nor be used on any service which will bring her within a zone which is dangerous as the result of any actual or threatened act of war, war hostilities, warlike operations, acts of piracy or of hostility or malicious damage against this or any other vessel or its cargo by any person, body or State whatsoever, revolution, civil war, civil commotion or the operation of international law, nor be exposed in any way to any risks or penalties whatsoever consequent upon the imposition of Sanctions, nor carry any goods that may in any way expose her to any risks of seizure, capture, penalties or any other interference of any kind whatsoever by the belligerent or fighting powers or parties or by any Government or Ruler.

(B) Should the Vessel approach or be brought or ordered within such zone, or be exposed in any way to the said risks, (1) the Owners to be entitled from time to time to insure their interests in the Vessel and/or hire against any of the risks likely to be involved thereby on such terms as they shall think fit, the Charterers to make a refund to the Owners of the premium on demand; and (2) notwithstanding the terms of Clause 11 hire to be paid for all time lost including any lost owing to loss of or injury to the Master, Officers, or Crew or to the action of the Crew in refusing to proceed to such zone or to be exposed to such risks.

(C) In the event of the wages of the Master, Officers and/or Crew or the cost of provisions and/or stores for deck and/or engine room and/or insurance premiums being increased by reason of or during the existence of any of the matters mentioned in section (A) the amount of any increase to be added to the hire and paid by the Charterers on production of the Owners' account therefor, such account being rendered monthly.

(D) The Vessel to have liberty to comply with any orders or directions as to departure, arrival, routes, ports of call, stoppages, destination, delivery or in any other wise whatsoever given by the Government of the nation under whose flag the Vessel sails or any other Government or any person (or body) acting or purporting to act with the authority of such Government or by any committee or person having under the terms of the war risks insurance on the Vessel the right to give any such orders or directions.

(E) In the event of the nation under whose flag the Vessel sails becoming involved in war, hostilities, warlike operations, revolution, or civil commotion, both the Owners and the Charterers may cancel the Charter and, unless otherwise agreed, the Vessel to be re-delivered to the Owners at the port of destination or, if prevented through the provisions of section (A) from reaching or entering it, then at a near open and safe port at the Owners' option, after discharge of any cargo on board.

(F) If in compliance with the provisions of this clause anything is done or is not done, such not to be deemed a deviation.
Section (C) is optional and should be considered deleted unless agreed according to Box 22.

22. Cancelling
Should the Vessel not be delivered by the date indicated in Box 23, the Charterers to have the option of cancelling.
If the Vessel cannot be delivered by the cancelling date, the Charterers, if required, to declare within 48 hours after receiving notice thereof whether they cancel or will take delivery of the Vessel.

23. Arbitration
Any dispute arising under the Charter to be referred to arbitration in London (or such other place as may be agreed according to Box 24) one Arbitrator to be nominated by the Owners and the other by the Charterers, and in case the Arbitrators shall not agree then to the decision of an Umpire to be appointed by them, the award of the Arbitrators or the Umpire to be final and binding upon both parties.

24. General Average
General Average to be settled according to York/Antwerp Rules, 1974. Hire not to contribute to General Average.

25. Commission
The Owners to pay a commission at the rate stated in Box 25 to the party mentioned in Box 25 on any hire paid under the Charter, but in no case less than is necessary to cover the actual expenses of the Brokers and a reasonable fee for their work. If the full hire is not paid owing to breach of Charter by either of the parties the party liable therefor to indemnify the Brokers against their loss of commission.
Should the parties agree to cancel the Charter, the Owners to indemnify the Brokers against any loss of commission but in such case the commission not to exceed the brokerage on one year's hire.

Appendix 5D

BILLS OF LADING ACT 1855

(1855 c. 111 ss.1-3)

An Act to amend the Law relating to Bills of Lading.

[14th August 1855]

1.—Every consignee of goods named in a Bill of lading, and every endorsee of a Bill of lading, to whom the property in the goods therein mentioned shall pass upon or by reason of such consignment or endorsement, shall have transferred to and vested in him all rights of suit, and be subject to the same liabilities in respect of such goods as if the contract contained in the Bill of lading had been made with himself.

Rights under Bills of lading to vest in Consignee or Endorsee.

2.—Nothing herein contained shall prejudice or affect any right of stoppage in transitu, or any right to claim freight against the original shipper or owner, or any liability of the consignee or endorsee by reason or in consequence of his being such consignee or endorsee, or of his receipt of the goods or in consequence of such consignment or endorsement.

Not to affect Right of Stoppage in transitu or Claims for Freight.

3.—Every Bill of lading in the hands of a consignee or endorsee for valuable consideration, representing goods to have been shipped on board a vessel, shall be conclusive evidence of such shipment as against the master or other person signing the same, notwithstanding that such goods or some part thereof may not have been so shipped, unless such holder of the Bill of lading shall have had actual notice at the time of receiving the same that the goods had not been in fact laden on board: Provided, that the master or other person so signing may exonerate himself in respect of such misrepresentation by showing that it was caused without any default on his part, and wholly by the fraud of the shipper, or of the holder, or some person under whom the holder claims.

Bill of lading in Hands of Consignee, &c. conclusive Evidence of Shipment as against Master, &c. Proviso.

Appendix 5E

CARRIAGE OF GOODS BY SEA ACT 1971

(1971 c. 19)

Application of Hague Rules as amended

1.—(1) In this Act, "the Rules" means the International Convention for the unification of certain rules of law relating to bills of lading signed at Brussels on 25th August 1924, as amended by the Protocol signed at Brussels on 23rd February 1968 and by the Protocol signed at Brussels on 21st December 1979.

(2) The provisions of the Rules, as set out in the Schedule to this Act, shall have the force of law.

(3) Without prejudice to subsection (2) above, the said provisions shall have effect (and have the force of law) in relation to and in connection with the carriage of goods by sea in ships where the port of shipment is a port in the United Kingdom, whether or not the carriage is between ports in two different States within the meaning of Article X of the Rules.

(4) Subject to subsection (6) below, nothing in this section shall be taken as applying anything in the Rules to any contract for the carriage of goods by sea, unless the contract expressly or by implication provides for the issue of a bill of lading or any similar document of title.

(5) The Secretary of State may from time to time by order made by statutory instrument specify the respective amounts which for the purposes of paragraph 5 of Article IV of the Rules and of Article IV bis of the Rules are to be taken as equivalent to the sums expressed in francs which are mentioned in sub-paragraph (*a*) of that paragraph.

(6) Without prejudice to Article X(*c*) of the Rules, the Rules shall have the force of law in relation to—

(*a*) any bill of lading if the contract contained in or evidenced by it expressly provides that the Rules shall govern the contract, and

(*b*) any receipt which is a non-negotiable document marked as such if the contract contained in or evidenced by it is a contract for the carriage of goods by sea which expressly provides that the Rules are to govern the contract as if the receipt were a bill of lading,

but subject, where paragraph (*b*) applies, to any necessary modifications and in particular with the omission in Article III of the Rules of the second sentence of paragraph 4 and of paragraph 7.

(7) If and so far as the contract contained in or evidenced by a bill of lading or receipt within paragraph (*a*) or (*b*) of subsection (6) above applies to deck cargo or live animals, the Rules as given the force of law by that subsection shall have effect as if Article I(*c*) did not exclude deck cargo and live animals.

In this subsection "deck cargo" means cargo which by the contract of carriage is stated as being carried on deck and is so carried.

SCHEDULE

THE HAGUE RULES AS AMENDED BY THE BRUSSELS PROTOCOL 1968

Article I

In these Rules the following words are employed, with the meanings set out below:—

(*a*) "Carrier" includes the owner or the charterer who enters into a contract of carriage with a shipper.
(*b*) "Contract of carriage" applies only to contracts of carriage covered by a bill of lading or any similar document of title, in so far as such document relates to the carriage of goods by sea, including any bill of lading or any similar document as aforesaid issued under or pursuant to a charter party from the moment at which such bill of lading or similar document of title regulates the relations between a carrier and a holder of the same.
(*c*) "Goods" includes goods, wares, merchandise, and articles of every kind whatsoever except live animals and cargo which by the contract of carriage is stated as being carried on deck and is so carried.
(*d*) "Ship" means any vessel used for the carriage of goods by sea.
(*e*) "Carriage of goods" covers the period from the time when the goods are loaded on to the time they are discharged from the ship.

Article II

Subject to the provisions of Article VI, under every contract of carriage of goods by sea the carrier, in relation to the loading, handling, stowage, carriage, custody, care and discharge of such goods, shall be subject to the responsibilities and liabilities, and entitled to the rights and immunities hereinafter set forth.

Article III

1. The carrier shall be bound before and at the beginning of the voyage to exercise due diligence to—
(*a*) Make the ship seaworthy.
(*b*) Properly man, equip and supply the ship.
(*c*) Make the holds, refrigerating and cool chambers, and all other parts of the ship in which goods are carried, fit and safe for this reception, carriage and preservation.

2. Subject to the provisions of Article IV, the carrier shall properly and carefully load, handle, stow, carry, keep, care for, and discharge the goods carried.

3. After receiving the goods into his charge the carrier or the master or agent of the carrier shall, on demand of the shipper, issue to the shipper a Bill of lading showing among other things—
(*a*) The leading marks necessary for identification of the goods as the same are furnished in writing by the shipper before the loading of such goods starts, provided such marks are stamped or otherwise shown clearly upon the goods if uncovered, or on the cases or coverings in which such goods are contained, in such a manner as should ordinarily remain legible until the end of the voyage.
(*b*) Either the number of packages or pieces, or the quantity, or weight, as the case may be, as furnished in writing by the shipper.
(*c*) The apparent order and condition of the goods.

Provided that no carrier, master or agent of the carrier shall be bound to state or show in the Bill of lading any marks, number, quantity, or weight which he has reasonable ground for suspecting not accurately to represent the goods actually received, or which he has had no reasonable means of checking.

4. Such a Bill of lading shall be *prima facie* evidence of the receipt by the carrier of the goods as therein described in accordance with paragraph 3(*a*), (*b*) and (*c*). However, proof to the contrary shall not be admissible when the bill of lading has been transferred to a third party acting in good faith.

5. The shipper shall be deemed to have guaranteed to the carrier the accuracy at the time of shipment of the marks, number, quantity and

weight, as furnished by him, and the shipper shall indemnify the carrier against all loss, damages and expenses arising or resulting from inaccuracies in such particulars. The right of the carrier to such indemnity shall in no way limit his responsibility and liability under the contract of carriage to any person other than the shipper.

6. Unless notice of loss or damage and the general nature of such loss or damage be given in writing to the carrier or his agent at the port of discharge before or at the time of the removal of the goods into the custody of the person entitled to delivery thereof under the contract of carriage, or, if the loss or damage be not apparent, within three days, such removal shall be *prima facie* evidence of the delivery by the carrier of the goods as described in the bill of lading.

The notice in writing need not be given if the state of the goods has, at the time of their receipt, been the subject of joint survey or inspection.

Subject to paragraph 6 *bis* the carrier and the ship shall in any event be discharged from all liability whatsoever in respect of the goods, unless suit is brought within one year of their delivery or of the date when they should have been delivered. This period may, however, be extended if the parties so agree after the cause of action has arisen.

In the case of any actual apprehended loss or damage the carrier and the receiver shall give all reasonable facilities to each other for inspecting and tallying the goods.

6 *bis*. An action for indemnity against a third person may be brought even after the expiration of the year provided for in the preceding paragraph if brought within the time allowed by the law of the Court seized of the case. However, the time allowed shall be not less than three months, commencing from the day when the person bringing such action for indemnity has settled the claim or has been served with process in the action against himself.

7. After the goods are loaded the Bill of lading to be issued by the carrier, master, or agent of the carrier, to the shipper shall, if the shipper so demands, be a "shipped" Bill of lading, provided that if the shipper shall have previously taken up any document of title to such goods, he shall surrender the same as against the issue of the "shipped" Bill of lading, but at the option of the carrier such document of title may be noted at the port of shipment by the carrier, master, or agent with the name or names of the ship or ships upon which the goods have been shipped and the date or dates of shipment, and when so noted, if it shows the particulars mentioned in paragraph 3 of Article III, shall for the purpose of this article be deemed to constitute a "shipped" Bill of lading.

8. Any clause, covenant, or agreement in a contract of carriage relieving the carrier or the ship from liability for loss or damage to, or in connection with, goods arising from negligence, fault, or failure in the duties and obligations provided in this article or lessening such liability otherwise than as provided in these Rules, shall be null and void and of no effect. A benefit of insurance in favour of the carrier or similar clause shall be deemed to be a clause relieving the carrier from liability.

Article IV

1. Neither the carrier nor the ship shall be liable for loss or damage arising or resulting from unseaworthiness unless caused by want of due diligence on the part of the carrier to make the ship seaworthy, and to secure that the ship is properly manned, equipped and supplied, and to make the holds, refrigerating and cool chambers and all other parts of the ship in which goods are carried fit and safe for their reception, carriage and preservation in accordance with the provisions of paragraph 1 of Article III. Whenever

loss or damage has resulted from unseaworthiness the burden of proving the exercise of due diligence shall be on the carrier or other person claiming exemption under this article.

2. Neither the carrier nor the ship shall be responsible for loss or damage arising or resulting from—

(*a*) Act, neglect, or default of the master, mariner, pilot, or the servants of the carrier in the navigation or in the management of the ship.
(*b*) Fire, unless caused by the actual fault or privity of the carrier.
(*c*) Perils, dangers and accidents of the sea or other navigable waters.
(*d*) Act of God.
(*e*) Act of war.
(*f*) Act of public enemies.
(*g*) Arrest or restraint of princes, rulers or people, or seizure under legal process.
(*h*) Quarantine restrictions.
(*i*) Act or omission of the shipper or owner of the goods, his agent or representative.
(*j*) Strikes or lockouts or stoppage of restraint of labour from whatever cause, whether partial or general.
(*k*) Riots and civil commotions.
(*l*) Saving or attempting to save life or property at sea.
(*m*) Wastage in bulk or weight or any other loss or damage arising from inherent defect, quality or vice of the goods.
(*n*) Insufficiency of packing.
(*o*) Insufficiency or inadequacy of marks.
(*p*) Latent defects not discoverable by due diligence.
(*q*) Any other cause arising without the actual fault or privity of the carrier, or without the fault or neglect of the agents or servants of the carrier, but the burden of proof shall be on the person claiming the benefit of this exception to show that neither the actual fault or privity of the carrier nor the fault or neglect of the agents or servants of the carrier contributed to the loss or damage.

3. The shipper shall not be responsible for loss or damage sustained by the carrier or the ship arising or resulting from any cause without the act, fault or neglect of the shipper, his agents or his servants.

4. Any deviation in saving or attempting to save life or property at sea or any reasonable deviation shall not be deemed to be an infringement or breach of these Rules or of the contract of carriage, and the carrier shall not be liable for any loss or damage resulting therefrom.

5. (*a*) Unless the nature and value of such goods have been declared by the shipper before shipment and inserted in the bill of lading, neither the carrier nor the ship shall in any event be or become liable for any loss or damage to or in connection with the goods in an amount exceeding 666·67 per package or unit or 2 units of account per kilogramme of gross weight of the goods lost or damaged, whichever is the higher.

(*b*) The total amount recoverable shall be calculated by reference to the value of such goods at the place and time at which the goods are discharged from the ship in accordance with the contract or should have been so discharged.

The value of the goods shall be fixed according to the commodity exchange price, or, if there be no such price, according to the current market price, or, if there be no commodity exchange price or current market price, by reference to the normal value of goods of the same kind and quality.

(*c*) Where a container, pallet or similar article of transport is used to consolidate goods, the number of packages or units enumerated in the Bill of lading as packed in such article of transport shall be deemed the number of packages or units for the purpose of this paragraph as far as these packages or units are concerned. Except as aforesaid such article of transport shall be considered the package or unit.

(*d*) A franc means a unit consisting of 65·5 milligrammes of gold of millesimal fineness 900. The date of conversion of the sum awarded into national currencies shall be governed by the law of the Court seized of the case.

(*e*) Neither the carrier nor the ship shall be entitled to the benefit of the limitation of liability provided for in this paragraph if it is proved that the damage resulted from an act or omission of the carrier done with intent to cause damage, or recklessly and with knowledge that damage would probably result.

(*f*) The declaration mentioned in sub-paragraph (*a*) of this paragraph, if embodied in the Bill of lading, shall be *prima facie* evidence, but shall not be binding or conclusive on the carrier.

(*g*) By agreement between the carrier, master or agent of the carrier and the shipper other maximum amounts than those mentioned in sub-paragraph (*a*) of this paragraph may be fixed, provided that no maximum amount so fixed shall be less than the appropriate maximum mentioned in that sub-paragraph.

(*h*) Neither the carrier nor the ship shall be responsible in any event for loss or damage to, or in connection with, goods if the nature or value thereof has been knowingly mis-stated by the shipper in the Bill of lading.

6. Goods of an inflammable, explosive or dangerous nature to the shipment whereof the carrier, master or agent of the carrier has not consented with knowledge of their nature and character, may at any time before discharge be landed at any place, or destroyed or rendered innocuous by the carrier without compensation and the shipper of such goods shall be liable for all damages and expenses directly or indirectly arising out of or resulting from such shipment. If any such goods shipped with such knowledge and consent shall become a danger to the ship or cargo, they may in like manner be landed at any place, or destroyed or rendered innocuous by the carrier without liability on the part of the carrier except to general average, if any.

Article IV bis

1. The defences and limits of liability provided for in these Rules shall apply in any action against the carrier in respect of loss or damage to goods covered by a contract of carriage whether the action be founded in contract or in tort.

2. If such an action is brought against a servant or agent of the carrier (such servant or agent not being an independent contractor), such servant or agent shall be entitled to avail himself of the defences and limits of liability which the carrier is entitled to invoke under these Rules.

3. The aggregate of the amounts recoverable from the carrier, and such servants and agents, shall in no case exceed the limit provided for in these Rules.

4. Nevertheless, a servant or agent of the carrier shall not be entitled to avail himself of the provisions of this article, if it is proved that the damage resulted from an act or omission of the servant or agent done with intent to cause damage or recklessly and with knowledge that damage would probably result.

Article V

A carrier shall be at liberty to surrender in whole or in part all or any of his rights and immunities or to increase any of his responsibilities and obligations under these Rules, provided such surrender or increase shall be embodied in the bill of lading issued to the shipper. The provisions of these Rules shall not be applicable to charter parties, but if Bills of lading are issued in the case of a ship under a charter party they shall comply with the terms of these Rules. Nothing in these Rules shall be held to prevent the insertion in a Bill of lading of any lawful provision regarding general average.

Article VI

Notwithstanding the provisions of the preceding articles, a carrier, master or agent of the carrier and a shipper shall in regard to any particular goods be at liberty to enter into any agreement in any terms as to the responsibility and liability of the carrier for such goods, and as to the rights and immunities of the carrier in respect of such goods, or his obligation as to seaworthiness, so far as this stipulation is not contrary to public policy, or the care or diligence of his servants or agents in regard to the loading, handling, stowage, carriage, custody, care and discharge of the goods carried by sea, provided that in this case no bill of lading has been or shall be issued and that the terms agreed shall be embodied in a receipt which shall be a non-negotiable document and shall be marked as such.

Any agreement so entered into shall have full legal effect.

Provided that this article shall not apply to ordinary commercial shipments made in the ordinary course of trade, but only to other shipments where the character or condition of the property to be carried or the circumstances, terms and conditions under which the carriage is to be performed are such as reasonably to justify a special agreement.

Article VII

Nothing herein contained shall prevent a carrier or a shipper from entering into any agreement, stipulation, condition, reservation or exemption as to the responsibility and liability of the carrier or the ship for the loss or damage to, or in connection with, the custody and care and handling of goods prior to the loading on, and subsequent to the discharge from, the ship on which the goods are carried by sea.

Article VIII

The provisions of these Rules shall not affect the rights and obligations of the carrier under any statute for the time being in force relating to the limitation of the liability of owners of sea-going vessels.

Article IX

These Rules shall not affect the provisions of any international Convention or national law governing liability for nuclear damage.

Article X

The provisions of these Rules shall apply to every bill of lading relating to the carriage of goods between ports in two different States if:

(*a*) the bill of lading is issued in a contracting State,
or

(*b*) the carriage is from a port in a contracting State,
or

(*c*) the contract contained in or evidenced by the bill of lading provides that these Rules or legislation of any State giving effect to them are to govern the contract,

whatever may be the nationality of the ship, the carrier, the shipper, the consignee, or any other interested person.

. . . . . .

Appendix 6A

CARRIAGE BY AIR ACT 1961

(1961 c. 27)

FIRST SCHEDULE

THE WARSAW CONVENTION WITH THE AMENDMENTS

MADE IN IT BY THE HAGUE PROTOCOL

PART I

THE ENGLISH TEXT

CONVENTION

FOR THE UNIFICATION OF CERTAIN RULES RELATING TO

INTERNATIONAL CARRIAGE BY AIR

CHAPTER 1

SCOPE—DEFINITIONS

Article 1

(1) This Convention applies to all international carriage of persons, baggage or cargo performed by aircraft for reward. It applies equally to gratuitous carriage by aircraft performed by an air transport undertaking.

(2) For the purposes of this Convention, the expression *international carriage* means any carriage in which, according to the agreement between the parties, the place of departure and the place of destination, whether or not there be a break in the carriage or a transhipment, are situated either within the territories or two High Contracting Parties or within the territory of a single High Contracting Party if there is an agreed stopping place within the territory of another State, even if that State is not a High Contracting Party. Carriage between two points within the territory of a single High Contracting Party without an agreed stopping place within the territory of another State is not international carriage for the purposes of this Convention.

(3) Carriage to be performed by several successive air carriers is deemed, for the purposes of this Convention, to be one undivided carriage if it has been regarded by the parties as a single operation, whether it had been agreed upon under the form of a single contract or of a series of contracts, and it does not lose its international character merely because one contract or a series of contracts is to be performed entirely within the territory of the same State.

Article 2

(1) This Convention applies to carriage performed by the State or by legally constituted public bodies provided it falls within the conditions laid down in Article 1.

(2) This Convention shall not apply to carriage of mail and postal packages.

CHAPTER II

DOCUMENTS OF CARRIAGE

SECTION 1.—PASSENGER TICKET

Article 3

(1) In respect of the carriage of passengers a ticket shall be delivered containing:

(*a*) an indication of the places of departure and destination;

(*b*) if the places of departure and destination are within the territory of a single High Contracting Party, one or more agreed stopping places being within the territory of another State, and indication of at least one such stopping place;

(*c*) a notice to the effect that, if the passenger's journey involves an ultimate destination or stop in a country other than the country of departure, the Warsaw Convention may be applicable and that the Convention governs and in most cases limits the liability of carriers for death or personal injury and in respect of loss of or damage to baggage.

(2) The passenger ticket shall constitute *prima facie* evidence of the conclusion and conditions of the contract of carriage. The absence, irregularity or loss of the passenger ticket does not affect the existence or the validity of the contract of carriage which shall, none the less, be subject to the rules of this Convention. Nevertheless, if, with the consent of the carrier, the passenger embarks without a passenger ticket having been delivered, or if the ticket does not include the notice required by paragraph (1)(*c*) of this Article, the carrier shall not be entitled to avail himself of the provisions of Article 22.

SECTION 2.—BAGGAGE CHECK

Article 4

(1) In respect of the carriage of registered baggage, a baggage check shall be delivered, which, unless combined with or incorporated in a passenger ticket which complies with the provisions of Article 3, paragraph (1), shall contain:

(*a*) an indication of the places of departure and destination;

(*b*) if the places of departure and destination are within the territory of a single High Contracting Party, one or more agreed stopping places being within the territory of another State, an indication of at least one such stopping place;

(*c*) a notice to the effect that, if the carriage involves an ultimate destination or stop in a country other than the country of departure, the Warsaw Convention may be applicable and that the Convention governs and in most cases limits the liability of carriers in respect of loss of or damage to baggage.

(2) The baggage check shall constitute *prima facie* evidence of the registration of the baggage and of the conditions of the contract of carriage. The absence, irregularity or loss of the baggage check does not affect the existence or the validity of the contract of carriage which shall, none the less, be subject to the rules of this Convention. Nevertheless, if the carrier takes charge of the baggage without a baggage check having been delivered

or if the baggage check (unless combined with or incorporated in the passenger ticket which complies with the provisions of Article 3, Paragraph (1)(*c*)) does not include the notice required by paragraph (1)(*c*) of this Article, he shall not be entitled to avail himself of the provisions of Article 22, paragraph (2).

Section 3.—Air Waybill

Article 5

(1) Every carrier of cargo has the right to require the consignor to make out and hand over to him a document called an "air waybill"; every consignor has the right to require the carrier to accept this document.

(2) The absence, irregularity or loss of this document does not affect the existence or the validity of the contract of carriage which shall, subject to the provisions of Article 9, be none the less governed by the rules of this Convention.

Article 6

(1) The air waybill shall be made out by the consignor in three original parts and be handed over with the cargo.

(2) The first part shall be marked "for the carrier," and shall be signed by the consignor. The second part shall be marked "for the consignee"; it shall be signed by the consignor and by the carrier and shall accompany the cargo. The third part shall be signed by the carrier and handed by him to the consignor after the cargo has been accepted.

(3) The carrier shall sign prior to the loading of the cargo on board the aircraft.

(4) The signature of the carrier may be stamped; that of the consignor may be printed or stamped.

(5) If, at the request of the consignor, the carrier makes out the air waybill, he shall be deemed, subject to proof to the contrary, to have done so on behalf of the consignor.

Article 7

The carrier of cargo has the right to require the consignor to make out separate waybills when there is more than one package.

Article 8

The air waybill shall contain:

(*a*) an indication of the places of departure and destination;

(*b*) if the places of departure and destination are within the territory of a single High Contracting Party, one or more agreed stopping places being within the territory of another State, an indication of at least one such stopping place;

(*c*) a notice to the consignor to the effect that, if the carriage involves an ultimate destination or stop in a country other than the country of departure, the Warsaw Convention may be applicable and that the Convention governs and in most cases limits the liability of carriers in respect of loss of or damage to cargo.

Article 9

If, with the consent of the carrier, cargo is loaded on board the aircraft without an air waybill having been made out, or if the air waybill does not include the notice required by Article 8, paragraph (*c*), the carrier shall not be entitled to avail himself of the provisions of Article 22, paragraph (2).

Article 10

(1) The consignor is responsible for the correctness of the particulars and statements relating to the cargo which he inserts in the air waybill.

(2) The consignor shall indemnify the carrier against all damage suffered by him, or by any other person to whom the carrier is liable, by reason of the irregularity, incorrectness or incompleteness of the particulars and statements furnished by the consignor.

Article 11

(1) The air waybill is *prima facie* evidence of the conclusion of the contract, of the receipt of the cargo and of the conditions of carriage.

(2) The statements in the air waybill relating to the weight, dimensions and packing of the cargo, as well as those relating to the number of packages, are *prima facie* evidence of the facts stated; those relating to the quantity, volume and condition of the cargo do not constitute evidence against the carrier except so far as they both have been, and are stated in the air waybill to have been, checked by him in the presence of the consignor, or relate to the apparent condition of the cargo.

Article 12

(1) Subject to his liability to carry out all his obligations under the contract of carriage, the consignor has the right to dispose of the cargo by withdrawing it at the aerodrome of departure or destination, or by stopping it in the course of the journey on any landing, or by calling for it to be delivered at the place of destination or in the course of the journey to a person other than the consignee named in the air waybill, or by requiring it to be returned to the aerodrome of departure. He must not exercise this right of disposition in such a way as to prejudice the carrier or other consignors and he must repay any expenses occasioned by the exercise of this right.

(2) If it is impossible to carry out the orders of the consignor the carrier must so inform him forthwith.

(3) If the carrier obeys the orders of the consignor for the disposition of the cargo without requiring the production of the part of the air waybill delivered to the latter, he will be liable, without prejudice to his right of recovery from the consignor, for any damage which may be caused thereby to any person who is lawfully in possession of that part of the air waybill.

(4) The right conferred on the consignor ceases at the moment when that of the consignee begins in accordance with Article 13. Nevertheless, if the consignee declines to accept the waybill or the cargo, of if he cannot be communicated with, the consignor resumes his right of disposition.

Article 13

(1) Except in the circumstances set out in the preceding Article, the consignee is entitled, on arrival of the cargo at the place of destination, to require the carrier to hand over to him the air waybill and to deliver the cargo to him, on payment of the charges due and on complying with the conditions of carriage set out in the air waybill.

(2) Unless it is otherwise agreed, it is the duty of the carrier to give notice to the consignee as soon as the cargo arrives.

(3) If the carrier admits the loss of the cargo, or if the cargo has not arrived at the expiration of seven days after the date on which it ought to have arrived, the consignee is entitled to put into force against the carrier the rights which flow from the contract of carriage.

Article 14

The consignor and the consignee can respectively enforce all the rights given them by Articles 12 and 13, each in his own name, whether he is acting in his own interest or in the interest of another, provided that he carries out the obligations imposed by the contract.

Article 15

(1) Articles 12, 13 and 14 do not effect either the relations of the consignor or the consignee with each other or the mutual relations of third parties whose rights are derived either from the consignor or from the consignee.

(2) The provisions of Articles 12, 13 and 14 can only be varied by express provision in the air waybill.

(3) Nothing in this Convention prevents the issue of a negotiable air waybill.

Article 16

(1) The consignor must furnish such information and attach to the air waybill such documents as are necessary to meet the formalities of customs, octroi or police before the cargo can be delivered to the consignee. The consignor is liable to the carrier for any damage occasioned by the absence, insufficiency or irregularity of any such information or documents, unless the damage is due to the fault of the carrier or his servants or agents.

(2) The carrier is under no obligation to enquire into the correctness or sufficiency of such information or documents.

CHAPTER III

LIABILITY OF THE CARRIER

Article 17

The carrier is liable for damage sustained in the event of the death or wounding of a passenger or any other bodily injury suffered by a passenger, if the accident which caused the damage so sustained took place on board the aircraft or in the course of any of the operations of embarking or disembarking.

Article 18

(1) The carrier is liable for damage sustained in the event of the destruction or loss of, or of damage to, any registered baggage or any cargo, if the occurrence which caused the damage so sustained took place during the carriage by air.

(2) The carriage by air within the meaning of the preceding paragraph comprises the period during which the baggage or cargo is in charge of the carrier, whether in an aerodrome or on board an aircraft, or, in the case of a landing outside an aerodrome, in any place whatsoever.

(3) The period of the carriage by air does not extend to any carriage by land, by sea or by river performed outside an aerodrome. If, however, such a carriage takes place in the performance of a contract for carriage by air, for the purpose of loading, delivery or transshipment, any damage is presumed, subject to proof to the contrary, to have been the result of an event which took place during the carriage by air.

Article 19

The carrier is liable for damage occasioned by delay in the carriage by air of passengers, baggage or cargo.

Article 20

The carrier is not liable if he proves that he and his servants or agents have taken all necessary measures to avoid the damage or that it was impossible for him or them to take such measures.

Article 21

If the carrier proves that the damage was caused by or contributed to by the negligence of the injured person the court may, accordance with the provisions of its own law, exonerate the carrier wholly or partly from his liability.

Article 22

(1) In the carriage of persons the liability of the carrier for each passenger is limited to the sum of two hundred and fifty thousand francs. Where, in accordance with the law of the court seised of the case, damages may be awarded in the form of periodical payments the equivalent capital value of the said payments shall not exceed two hundred and fifty thousand francs. Nevertheless, by special contract, the carrier and the passenger may agree to a higher limit of liability.

(2)—(*a*) In the carriage of registered baggage and of cargo, the liability of the carrier is limited to a sum of two hundred and fifty francs per kilogramme, unless the passenger or consignor has made, at the time when the package was handed over to the carrier, a special declaration of interest in delivery at destination and has paid a supplementary sum if the case so requires. In that case the carrier will be liable to pay a sum not exceeding the declared sum, unless he proves that that sum is greater than the passenger's or consignor's actual interest in delivery at destination.

(*b*) In the case of loss, damage or delay of part of registered baggage or cargo, or of any object contained therein, the weight to be taken into consideration in determining the amount to which the carrier's liability is limited shall be only the total weight of the package or packages concerned. Nevertheless, when the loss, damage or delay of a part of the registered baggage or cargo, or of an object contained therein, affects the value of other packages covered by the same baggage check or the same air waybill, the total weight of such package or packages shall also be taken into consideration in determining the limit of liability.

(3) As regards objects of which the passenger takes charge himself the liability of the carrier is limited to five thousand francs per passenger.

(4) The limits prescribed in this Article shall not prevent the court from awarding, in accordance with its own law, in addition, the whole or part of the court costs and of the other expenses of the litigation incurred by the plaintiff. The foregoing provision shall not apply if the amount of the damages awarded, excluding court costs and other expenses of the litigation, does not exceed the sum which the carrier has offered in writing to the plaintiff within a period of six months from the date of the occurrence causing the damage, or before the commencement of the action, if that is later.

(5) The sums mentioned in francs in this Article shall be deemed to refer to a currency unit consisting of sixty-five and a half milligrammes of gold of millesimal fineness nine hundred. These sums may be converted into national currencies in round figures. Conversion of the sums into national currencies other than gold shall, in case of judicial proceedings, be made according to the gold value of such currencies at the date of the judgment.

Article 23

(1) Any provision tending to relieve the carrier of liability or to fix a lower limit than that which is laid down in this Convention shall be null and void, but the nullity of any such provision does not involve the nullity of the whole contract, which shall remain subject to the provisions of this Convention.

(2) Paragraph (1) of this Article shall not apply to provisions governing loss or damage resulting from the inherent defect, quality or vice of the cargo carried.

Article 24

(1) In the cases covered by Articles 18 and 19 any action for damages, however founded, can only be brought subject to the conditions and limits set out in this Convention.

(2) In the cases covered by Article 17 the provisions of the preceding paragraph also apply, without prejudice to the questions as to who are the persons who have the right to bring suit and what are their respective rights.

Article 25

The limits of liability specified in Article 22 shall not apply if it is proved that the damage resulted from an act or omission of the carrier, his servants or agents, done with intent to cause damage or recklessly and with knowledge that damage would probably result; provided that, in the case of such act or omission of a servant or agent, it is also proved that he was acting within the scope of his employment.

Article 25A

(1) If an action is brought against a servant or agent of the carrier arising out of damage to which this Convention relates, such servant or agent, if he proves that he acted within the scope of his employment, shall be entitled to avail himself of the limits of liability which that carrier himself is entitled to invoke under Article 22.

(2) The aggregate of the amounts recoverable from the carrier, his servants and agents, in that case, shall not exceed the said limits.

(3) The provision of paragraphs (1) and (2) of this Article shall not apply if it is proved that the damage resulted from an act or omission of the servant or agent done with intent to cause damage or recklessly and with knowledge that damage would probably result.

Article 26

(1) Receipt by the person entitled to delivery of baggage or cargo without complaint is *prima facie* evidence that the same has been delivered in good condition and in accordance with the document of carriage.

(2) In the case of damage, the person entitled to delivery must complain to the carrier forthwith after the discovery of the damage, and, at the latest, within seven days from the date of receipt in the case of baggage and fourteen days from the date of receipt in the case of cargo. In the case of delay the complaint must be made at the latest within twenty-one days from the date on which the baggage or cargo have been placed at his disposal.

(3) Every complaint must be made in writing upon the document of carriage or by separate notice in writing despatched within the times aforesaid.

(4) Failing complaint within the times aforesaid, no action shall lie against the carrier, save in the case of fraud on his part.

Article 27

In the case of the death of the person liable, an action for damages lies in accordance with the terms of this Convention against those legally representing his estate.

Article 28

(1) An action for damages must be brought, at the option of the plaintiff, in the territory of one of the High Contracting Parties, either before the court having jurisdiction where the carrier is ordinarily resident, or has his principal place of business, or has an establishment by which the contract

has been made or before the court having jurisdiction at the place of destination.

(2) Questions of procedure shall be governed by the law of the court seised of the case.

Article 29

Article 29 extended (S.) by Prescription and Limitation (Scotland) Act 1973 (c. 52), s.20(3)

(1) The right to damages shall be extinguished if an action is not brought within two years, reckoned from the date of arrival at the destination, or from the date on which the aircraft ought to have arrived, or from the date on which the carriage stopped.

(2) The method of calculating the period of limitation shall be determined by the law of the court seised of the case.

Article 30

(1) In the case of carriage to be performed by various successive carriers and falling within the definition set out in the third paragraph of Article 1, each carrier who accepts passengers, baggage or cargo is subjected to the rules set out in this Convention, and is deemed to be one of the contracting parties to the contract of carriage in so far as the contract deals with that part of the carriage which is performed under his supervision.

(2) In the case of carriage of this nature, the passenger or his representative can take action only against the carrier who performed the carriage during which the accident or the delay occurred, save in the case where, by express agreement, the first carrier has assumed liability for the whole journey.

(3) As regards baggage or cargo, the passenger or consignor will have a right of action against the first carrier, and the passenger or consignee who is entitled to delivery will have a right of action against the last carrier, and further, each may take action against the carrier who performed the carriage during which the destruction, loss, damage or delay took place. These carriers will be jointly and severally liable to the passenger or to the consignor or consignee.

Chapter IV

Provisions Relating to Combined Carriage

Article 31

(1) In the case of combined carriage performed partly by air and partly by any other mode of carriage, the provisions of this Convention apply only to the carriage by air, provided that the carriage by air falls within the terms of Article 1.

(2) Nothing in this Convention shall prevent the parties in the case of combined carriage from inserting in the document of air carriage conditions relating to other modes of carriage, provided that the provisions of this Convention are observed as regards the carriage by air.

Chapter V

General and Final Provisions

Article 32

Any clause contained in the contract and all special agreements entered into before the damage occurred by which the parties purport to infringe the rules laid down by this Convention, whether by deciding the law to be applied, or by altering the rules as to jurisdiction, shall be null and void. Nevertheless for the carriage of cargo arbitration clauses are allowed, subject to this Convention, if the arbitration is to take place within one of the jurisdictions referred to in the first paragraph of Article 28.

Article 33

Nothing contained in this Convention shall prevent the carrier either from refusing to enter into any contract of carriage, or from making regulations which do not conflict with the provisions of this Convention.

Article 34

The provisions of Articles 3 to 9 inclusive relating to documents of carriage shall not apply in the case of carriage performed in extraordinary circumstances outside the normal scope of an air carrier's business.

Article 35

The expression "days" when used in this Convention means current days not working days.

Article 36

The Convention is drawn up in French in a single copy which shall remain deposited in the archives of the Ministry for Foreign Affairs of Poland and of which one duly certified copy shall be sent by the Polish Government to the Government of each of the High Contracting Parties.

Article 40A

(1) [*This paragraph is not reproduced. It defines "High Contracting Party."*]

(2) For the purposes of the Convention the word *territory* means not only the metropolitan territory of a State but also all other territories for the foreign relations of which that State is responsible.

[*Articles 37, 38, 39, 40 and 41 and the concluding words of the Convention are not reproduced. They deal with the coming into force of the Convention.*]

Additional Protocol

(With reference to Article 2)

The High Contracting Parties reserve to themselves the right to declare at the time of ratification or of accession that the first paragraph of Article 2 of this Convention shall not apply to international carriage by air performed directly by the State, its colonies, protectorates or mandated territories or by any other territory under its sovereignty, suzerainty or authority.

Appendix 6B

THE CARRIAGE BY AIR ACTS (APPLICATION OF PROVISIONS) ORDER 1967

(1967 NO. 480)

SCHEDULE 2

INTERNATIONAL CARRIAGE UNDER THE UNAMENDED WARSAW CONVENTION

PART B

Article 3

(1) For the carriage of passengers the carrier must deliver a passenger ticket which shall contain the following particulars:—

(*a*) the place and date of issue;
(*b*) the place of departure and of destination;
(*c*) the agreed stopping places, provided that the carrier may reserve the right to alter the stopping places in case of necessity, and that if he exercises that right, the alteration shall not have the effect of depriving the carriage of its international character;
(*d*) the name and address of the carrier or carriers;
(*e*) a statement that the carriage is subject to the rules relating to liability established by the Warsaw Convention.

(2) The absence, irregularity or loss of the passenger ticket does not affect the existence or the validity of the contract of carriage, which shall none the less be subject to the rules of this Schedule. Nevertheless, if the carrier accepts a passenger without a passenger ticket having been delivered he shall not be entitled to avail himself of those provisions of this Schedule which exclude or limit his liability.

Article 4

(1) For the carriage of baggage, other than small personal objects of which the passenger takes charge himself, the carrier must deliver a baggage check.

(2) The baggage check shall be made out in duplicate, one part for the passenger and the other part for the carrier.

(3) The baggage check shall contain the following particulars:—

(*a*) the place and date of issue;
(*b*) the place of departure and of destination;
(*c*) the name and address of the carrier or carriers;
(*d*) the number of the passenger ticket;
(*e*) a statement that delivery of the baggage will be made to the bearer of the baggage check;
(*f*) the number and weight of the packages;
(*g*) the amount of the value declared in accordance with Article 22(2);
(*h*) a statement that the carriage is subject to the rules relating to liability established by the Warsaw Convention.

(4) The absence, irregularity or loss of the baggage check does not affect the existence or the validity of the contract of carriage, which shall none the less be subject to the rules of this Schedule. Nevertheless, if the carrier

accepts baggage without a baggage check having been delivered, or if the baggage check does not contain the particulars set out at (*d*) (*f*), and (*h*) above, the carrier shall not be entitled to avail himself of those provisions of this Schedule which exclude or limit his liability.

Article 8

The air waybill shall contain the following particulars:—

(*a*) the place and date of its execution;
(*b*) the place of departure and of destination;
(*c*) the agreed stopping places, provided that the carrier may reserve the right to alter the stopping places in case of necessity, and that if he exercises that right the alteration shall not have the effect of depriving the carriage of its international character;
(*d*) the name and address of the consignor;
(*e*) the name and address of the first carrier;
(*f*) the name and address of the consignee, if the case so requires;
(*g*) the nature of the cargo;
(*h*) the number of the packages, the method of packing and the particular marks or numbers upon them;
(*i*) the weight, the quantity and the volume or dimensions of the cargo;
(*j*) the apparent condition of the cargo and of the packing;
(*k*) the freight, if it has been agreed upon, the date and place of payment, and the person who is to pay it;
(*l*) if the cargo is sent for payment on delivery, the price of the cargo, and, if the case so requires, the amount of the expenses incurred;
(*m*) the amount of the value declared in accordance with Article 22(2);
(*n*) the number of parts of the air waybill;
(*o*) the documents handed to the carrier to accompany the air waybill;
(*p*) the time fixed for the completion of the carriage and a brief note of the route to be followed, if these matters have been agreed upon;
(*q*) a statement that the carriage is subject to the rules relating to liability established by the Warsaw Convention.

Article 9

If the carrier accepts cargo without an air waybill having been made out, or if the air waybill does not contain all the particulars set out in Article 8(*a*) to (*i*) inclusive and (*q*), the carrier shall not be entitled to avail himself of the provisions of this Schedule which exclude or limit his liability.

Article 20

. . . . . .

(2) In the carriage of cargo and baggage the carrier is not liable if he proves that the damage was occasioned by negligent pilotage or negligence in the handling of the aircraft or in navigation and that, in all other respects, he and his servants or agents have taken all necessary measures to avoid the damage.

Article 22

(1) In the carriage of passengers the liability of the carrier for each passenger is limited to the sum of 125,000 francs. Where, in accordance with the law of the Court seised of the case, damages may be awarded in the

form of periodical payments, the equivalent capital value of the said payments shall not exceed 125,000 francs. Nevertheless, by special contract, the carrier and the passenger may agree to a higher limitof liability.

(2) In the carriage of registered baggage and of cargo, the liability of the carrier is limited to a sum of 250 francs per kilogramme, unless the consignor has made, at the time when the package was handed over to the carrier, a special declaration of the value at delivery and has paid a supplementary sum if the case so requires. In that case the carrier will be liable to pay a sum not exceeding the declared sum, unless he proves that that sum is greater than the actual value to the consignor at delivery.

(3) As regards objects of which the passenger takes charge himself the liability of the carrier is limited to 5,000 francs per passenger.

(4) The sums mentioned above shall be deemed to refer to the French franc consisting of $65\frac{1}{2}$ milligrammes gold of millesimal fineness 900. These sums may be converted into any national currency in round figures.

Article 23

Any provision tending to relieve the carrier of liability or to fix a lower limit than that which is laid down in this Schedule shall be null and void, but the nullity of any such provision does not involve the nullity of the whole contract, which shall remain subject to the provisions of this Schedule.

Article 25

(1) The carrier shall not be entitled to avail himself of the provisions of this Schedule which exclude or limit his liability, if the damage is caused by his wilful misconduct or by such default on his part as, in accordance with the law of the Court seised of the case, is considered to be equivalent to wilful misconduct.

(2) Similarly the carrier shall not be entitled to avail himself of the said provisions, if the damage is caused as aforesaid by any servant or agent of the carrier acting within the scope of his employment.

Appendix 7

Code Name: "COMBIDOC"

Consignor

CT Doc. No.

Reference No.

Negotiable

COMBINED TRANSPORT DOCUMENT

Issued by The Baltic and International Maritime Conference (BIMCO) and the International Shipowners' Association (INSA), subject to International Chamber of Commerce Uniform Rules for a Combined Transport Document (ICC Publication No. 298).

July 1st, 1977

Consigned to order of

Notify address

Place of receipt

Ocean vessel | Port of loading | Name of sub-contractors for carriage by inland waterways *

Port of discharge | Place of delivery | Date of sub-contract for carriage by inland waterways *

Marks and Nos. | Quantity and description of goods | Gross weight, kg, Measurement, m³

Particulars above declared by Consignor

Freight and charges

RECEIVED the goods in apparent good order and condition and, as far as ascertained by reasonable means of checking, as specified above unless otherwise stated.

The CTO, in accordance with and to the extent of the provisions contained in this CT Document, and with liberty to sub-contract, undertakes to perform and/or in his own name to procure performance of the combined transport and the delivery of the goods, including all services which are necessary to such transport from the place and time of taking the goods in charge to the place and time of delivery and accepts responsibility for such transport and such services.

One of the CT Documents must be surrendered duly endorsed in exchange for the goods or delivery order.

IN WITNESS whereof CT Document(s) has/have been signed in the number indicated below, one of which being accomplished the other(s) to be void.

Freight payable at	Place and date of issue
Number of original CT Documents	Signed for the Combined Transport Operator (CTO)

Note:

The Merchant's attention is called to the fact that according to Clauses 10 to 12 of this CT Document, the liability of the CTO is, in most cases, limited in respect of loss of or damage to the goods and delay. The liability of the CTO in respect of loss or damage occurring during carriage by inland waterways shall be covered by the provisions of his contract with the sub-contractors mentioned above (*) and dated as likewise indicated (*).

As agent(s) to the CTO

p.t.o.

Appendix 7

COMBINED TRANSPORT DOCUMENT

CODE NAME: "C O M B I D O C"

Issued July 1st. 1977

I. GENERAL PROVISIONS

1. Applicability. Notwithstanding the heading "Combined Transport Document", the provisions set out and referred to in this CT Document shall also apply, if the transport as described on the face of the Document contrary to the original intentions of the parties is performed by one mode of transport only.

2. Definitions. "CTO" means the party on whose behalf this CT Document has been signed "Merchant" includes the Shipper, the Receiver, the Consignor, the Consignee, the Holder of this CT Document and the Owner of the Goods.
"Delivery" means delivering the goods to or placing the goods at the disposal of the party entitled to receive them.
"Goods" means the cargo accepted from the Consignor and includes any container, transportable tank, not supplied by or on behalf of the CTO.
"Franc" means a unit consisting of 65.5 milligrammes of gold of millesimal fineness 900.

3. CTO's Tariff. The terms of the CTO's applicable Tariff at the date of shipment are incorporated herein. Copies of the relevant provisions of the applicable Tariff are available from the CTO upon request. In the case of inconsistency between this CT Document and the applicable Tariff, this CT Document shall prevail.

4. Time Bar. The CTO shall be discharged of all liability under this CT Document unless suit is brought within nine months after,
i) the delivery of the goods, or,
ii) the date when the goods should have been delivered, or
iii) the date, when in accordance with Clause 14, failure to deliver the goods would, in the absence of evidence to the contrary, give to the party entitled to receive delivery the right to treat the goods as lost.

5. Law and Jurisdiction. Disputes arising under this CT Document shall be determined at the option of the Claimant by the courts and subject to Clause 11 of this CT Document in accordance with the law at
(a) the place where the CTO has his principal place of business, or
(b) the place where the goods were taken in charge by the CTO or the place designated for delivery.
No proceedings may be brought before other courts unless the parties expressly agree on both the choice of another court or arbitration tribunal and the law to be then applicable.

II. PERFORMANCE OF THE CONTRACT

6. Methods and Routes of Transportation.
(1) The CTO is entitled to perform the transport in any reasonable manner and by any reasonable means, methods and routes.
(2) In accordance herewith, for instance, in the event of carriage by sea, vessels may sail with or without pilots, undergo repairs, adjust equipment, drydock and tow vessels in all situations.

7. Optional Stowage.
(1) Goods may be stowed by the CTO by means of containers, trailers, transportable tanks, flats, pallets, or similar articles of transport used to consolidate goods.
(2) Containers, trailers and transportable tanks, whether stowed by the CTO or received by him in a stowed condition from the Merchant, may be carried on or under deck without notice to the Merchant.

8. Hindrances, etc. Affecting Performance.
(1) The CTO shall use reasonable endeavours to complete the transport and to deliver the goods at the place designated for delivery.
(2) If at any time the performance of the contract as evidenced by this CT Document is or will be affected by any hindrance, risk, delay, difficulty or disadvantage of whatsoever kind, and if by virtue of sub-clause (1) the CTO has no duty to complete the performance of the contract, the CTO (whether or not the transport is commenced) may elect to
(a) treat the performance of this contract as terminated and place the goods at the Merchant's disposal at any place which the CTO shall deem safe and convenient; or
(b) deliver the goods at the place designated for delivery.
In any event the CTO shall be entitled to full freight for goods received for transportation and additional compensation for extra costs resulting from the circumstances referred to above.

III. CTO's LIABILITY

9. (1) The CTO assumes liability and undertakes to pay compensation for loss of or damage to the goods occurring within the time of taking them into his charge and the time of delivery, to the extent set out in this CT Document.
(2) The CTO accepts responsibility for the acts and omissions of his agents or servants, when such agents or servants are acting within the scope of their employment, as if such acts and omissions were his own; further, he accepts responsibility for the acts and omissions of any other persons whose services he uses for the performance of the contract evidenced by this CT Document.

10. When the Stage of Transport Where the Loss or Damage Occurred is Not Known.
(1) Compensation as per Clause 9 (1) shall be calculated by reference to the value of such goods at the place and time they are or, in accordance with the contract of combined transport, they should have been delivered to the Consignee.
(2) The value of the goods shall be determined according to the current commodity exchange price or, if there is no such price, according to the current market price, or, if there is no commodity exchange price or current market price, by reference to the normal value of goods of the same kind and quality.
(3) Compensation shall not exceed 30 francs per kilo of gross weight of the goods lost or damaged, unless, with the consent of the CTO, the Consignor has declared a higher value for the goods and such higher value has been stated in this CT Document, in which case such higher value shall be the limit.
(4) The CTO shall not, in any case, be liable for an amount greater than the actual loss to the person entitled to make the claim.
(5) The CTO shall not be liable to pay compensation if the loss or damage was caused by:
(a) an act or omission of the Merchant, or person other than the CTO acting on behalf of the Merchant, or from whom the CTO took the goods in charge;
(b) insufficient or defective condition of the packing or marks;
(c) handling, loading, stowage or unloading of the goods by the Merchant or any person acting on his behalf;
(d) inherent vice of the goods;
(e) strike, lockout, stoppage or restraint of labour, the consequences of which the CTO could not avoid by the exercise of reasonable diligence;
(f) any cause or event which the CTO could not avoid and the consequences of which he could not prevent by the exercise of reasonable diligence;
(g) a nuclear incident if the operator of a nuclear installation or a person acting for him is liable for this damage under an applicable international Convention or national law governing liability in respect of nuclear energy.
(6) The burden of proving that the loss or damage was due to one or more of the causes or events mentioned in sub-clause (5) shall rest upon the CTO.
When the CTO establishes that, in the circumstances of the case, the loss or damage could be attributed to one or more of the causes or events specified in (b) to (d) of sub-clause (5), it shall be presumed that it was so caused. The claimant shall, however, be entitled to prove that the loss or damage was not, in fact, caused wholely or partly by one or more of these causes or events.

11. When the Stage of Transport Where the Loss or Damage Occurred is Known.
(1) The liability of the CTO in respect of such loss or damage shall be determined:
(a) by the provisions contained in any international Convention or national law, which provisions:
i) cannot be departed from by private contract, to the detriment of the claimant, and
ii) would have applied if the claimant had made a separate and direct contract with the CTO in respect of the particular stage of transport where the loss or damage occurred and received as evidence thereof any particular document which must be issued in order to make such international Convention or national law applicable; or
(b) in respect of any carriage by sea, by the Hague Rules contained in the International Convention for the Unification of Certain Rules relating to Bills of Lading, dated 25th August, 1924, even if these Rules do not apply to the carriage by sea by virtue of sub-paragraph (a) of this Clause. Furthermore, the Hague Rules shall apply to all goods, whether carried on deck or under deck, or
(c) by the provisions of Clause 10 in cases where the provisions of sub-paragraphs (a) and (b) of this Clause do not apply.
(2) Without prejudice to the provisions of Clause 15, when, under the provisions of sub-clause (1), the liability of the CTO shall be determined by the provisions of any international Convention or national law, this liability shall be determined as though the CTO were the carrier referred to in any such Convention or national law. However, the CTO shall not be exonerated from liability where the loss or damage is caused or contributed to by the acts or omissions of the CTO in his capacity as such, or his servants or agents when acting in such capacity and not in the performance of the carriage.

12. Delay. The CTO is liable to pay compensation for delay only when the stage of transport where a delay occurred is known, and to the extent that there is liability according to the provisions in Clause 11, sub-clause (1), paragraph (a). However, the amount of such compensation shall not exceed the amount of the freight for that stage of transport, provided that this limitation is not contrary to the applicable international Convention or national law.

13. Notice of Loss. Except in respect of goods treated as lost in accordance with Clause 14 of this CT Document the CTO shall be deemed prima facie to have delivered the goods as described in this CT Document unless notice of loss of, or damage to, the goods, indicating the general nature of such loss or damage, shall have been given in writing to the CTO or to his representative at the place of delivery before or at the time of removal of the goods into the custody of the person entitled to delivery thereof under this CT Document, or, if the loss or damage is not apparent, within seven consecutive days thereafter.

14. Delivery/Non-Delivery of Goods.
(1) If the goods are not taken delivery of by the Merchant within a reasonable time after the CTO has called upon him to take delivery, the CTO shall be at liberty to put the goods in safe custody on behalf of the Merchant at the Merchant's risk and expense.
(2) Failure to effect delivery within 90 days after the time it would be reasonable to allow for diligent completion of the combined transport operation shall, in the absence of evidence to the contrary, give to the party entitled to receive delivery the right to treat the goods as lost.

15. Defences and Limits for the CTO, Servants, etc.
(1) The defences and limits of liability provided for in this CT Document shall apply in any action against the CTO for loss of, damage or delay to the goods, whether the action be founded in contract or in tort.
(2) If an action for loss or damage to the goods is brought against a servant, agent or independent contractor, such person shall be entitled to avail himself of the defences and limits of liability which the CTO is entitled to invoke under this CT Document.
(3) The aggregate of the amounts recoverable from the CTO and his servants, agents or independent contractors shall in no case exceed the limits provided for in this CT Document.
(4) The CTO shall not be entitled to the benefit of the limitation of liability provided for in Clause 10 if it is proved that the loss or damage resulted from an act or omission of the CTO done with intent to cause damage or recklessly and with knowledge that damage would probably result.

IV. DESCRIPTION OF GOODS

16. CTO's Responsibility. This CT Document shall be prima facie evidence of the taking in charge by the CTO of the goods as therein described in respect of the particulars which he had reasonable means of checking. Proof to the contrary shall not be admissible when this CT Document is issued in negotiable form and has been transferred to a third party acting in good faith.

17. Consignor's Responsibility. The Consignor shall be deemed to have guaranteed to the CTO the accuracy at the time the goods were taken in charge by the CTO, of the description of the goods, marks, numbers, measurements, quantity and weight, as furnished by him, and the Consignor shall indemnify the CTO against all loss, damage and expenses arising or resulting from inaccuracies in or inadequacy of such particulars. The right of the CTO to such indemnity shall in no way limit his responsibility and liability under this CT Document to any person other than the Consignor.

18. Dangerous Goods.
(1) The Consignor shall comply with rules which are mandatory according to the national law or by reason of international Convention, relating to the carriage of goods of a dangerous nature, and shall in any case inform the CTO in writing of the exact nature of the danger before goods of a dangerous nature are taken in charge by the CTO and indicate to him, if need be, the precautions to be taken.
(2) If the Consignor fails to provide such information and the CTO is unaware of the dangerous nature of the goods and the necessary precautions to be taken and if, at any time, they are deemed to be a hazard to life or property, they may at any place be unloaded, destroyed or rendered harmless, as circumstances may require, without compensation, and the Consignor shall be liable for all loss, damage, delay or expenses arising out of their being taken in charge, or their carriage, or of any service incidental thereto.
The burden of proving the CTO knew the exact nature of the danger constituted by the carriage of the said goods shall rest upon the person entitled to the goods.
(3) If any goods shipped with the knowledge of the CTO as to their dangerous nature shall become a danger to the ship or cargo, they may in like manner be landed at any place or destroyed or rendered innocuous by the CTO without liability on the part of the CTO except to General Average, if any.

19. Consignor-packed Containers, etc.
(1) If a container has not been filled, packed or stowed by the CTO, the CTO shall not be liable for any loss of or damage to its contents and the Merchant shall cover any loss or expense incurred by the CTO, if such loss, damage or expense has been caused by
(a) negligent filling, packing or stowing of the container;
(b) the contents being unsuitable for carriage in container; or
(c) the unsuitability or defective condition of the container unless the container has been supplied by the CTO and the unsuitability or defective condition would not have been apparent upon reasonable inspection at or prior to the time when the container was filled, packed or stowed.
(2) The provisions of sub-clause (1) of this Clause also apply with respect to trailers, transportable tanks, flats and pallets which have not been filled, packed or stowed by the CTO.
(3) The CTO does not accept liability for the functioning of reefer equipment or trailers supplied by the Merchant.

V. FREIGHT AND LIEN

20. Freight.
(1) Freight shall be deemed earned on receipt of the goods by the CTO and shall be paid in any event.
(2) The Merchant's attention is drawn to the stipulations concerning currency in which the freight and charges are to be paid, rate of exchange, devaluation and other contingencies relative to freight and charges in the relevant tariff conditions. If no such stipulation as to devaluation exists or is applicable the following clause to apply:
If the currency in which freight and charges are quoted is devalued or revalued between the date of the freight agreement and the date when the freight and charges are paid, then all freight and charges shall be automatically and immediately changed in proportion to the extent of the devaluation or revaluation of the said currency. When the CTO has consented to payment in other currency than the above mentioned currency, then all freight and charges shall – subject to the preceding paragraph – be paid at the highest selling rate of exchange for banker's sight draft current on the day when such freight and charges are paid. If the banks are closed on the day when the freight is paid the rate to be used will be the one in force on the last day the banks were open.
(3) For the purpose of verifying the freight basis, the CTO reserves the right to have the contents of containers, trailers or similar articles of transport inspected in order to ascertain the weight, measurement, value, or nature of the goods. If on such inspection it is found that the declaration is not correct, it is agreed that a sum equal either to five times the difference between the correct freight and the freight charged or to double the correct freight less the freight charged, whichever sum is the smaller, shall be payable as liquidated damages to the CTO notwithstanding any other sum having been stated on this CT Document as the freight payable.
(4) All dues, taxes and charges levied on the goods and other expenses in connection therewith shall be paid by the Merchant.

21. Lien. The CTO shall have a lien on the goods for any amount due under this contract and for the costs of recovering the same, and may enforce such lien in any reasonable manner.

VI. MISCELLANEOUS PROVISIONS

22. General Average.
(1) General Average to be adjusted at any port or place at the CTO's option, and to be settled according to the York-Antwerp Rules 1974, this covering all goods, whether carried on or under deck. The New Jason Clause as approved by BIMCO to be considered as incorporated herein.
(2) Such security including a cash deposit as the CTO may deem sufficient to cover the estimated contribution of the goods and any salvage and special charges thereon, shall, if required, be submitted to the CTO prior to delivery of the goods.

23. Both-to-Blame Collision Clause. The Both-to-Blame Collision Clause as adopted by BIMCO to be considered incorporated herein.

INDEX